JET
JOCKEYS

JET JOCKEYS

FLYING THE RAF'S
FIRST JET FIGHTERS

PETER CAYGILL

Airlife
England

Copyright © 2002 by Peter Caygill

First published in the UK in 2002
by Airlife Publishing Ltd

British Library Cataloguing-in-Publication Data
  A catalogue record for this book
  is available from the British Library

ISBN 1 84037 313 X

Typeset by Phoenix Typesetting, Ilkley, West Yorkshire
Printed in England by Biddles Ltd., Guildford and King's Lynn

Airlife Publishing Ltd
101 Longden Road, Shrewsbury, SY3 9EB, England
E-mail: airlife@airlifebooks.com
Website: www.airlifebooks.com

CONTENTS

ACKNOWLEDGEMENTS

In compiling this book I would like to thank the many individuals who have helped with personal accounts of their experiences with the RAF. In alphabetical order they are as follows:

Wg Cdr Geoff Amor MBE, Sqn Ldr Dennis Barry CDG, Tom Broomhead, Brian Burdett, Sqn Ldr Mike Butt, Alex Carder, Wg Cdr Brian Carroll, Sqn Ldr Alan Colman, Noel 'Snowy' Davies, Malcolm de Garis, Wg Cdr Peter Desmond MBE, Sqn Ldr Iain Dick, Sqn Ldr Neville Duke DSO DFC AFC OBE, Sqn Ldr Sam Easy, Colin Edwards, Howard Fitzer, Jack Fuller, Trevor Egginton, Graham Elliott, Ian Forrester, Chris Golds AFC, Clive Gosling, AVM Paddy Harbison CB CBE AFC, Sqn Ldr Peter Hay, John Harrison, Don Headley, Wg Cdr Peter Hicks, Bob Hillard, Paul Hodgson, Sqn Ldr John Holdway, Wg Cdr Barry Holmes MBE, Ted Hooton, Roger Hymans, Fred Insole, Grp Capt John Jennings DFC, Murray Jones, D. Kenyon, Dennis Keys, Eric Knighton, AVM John Lawrence, Wg Cdr Sid Little OBE, Sqn Ldr Ivan Logan, Roger Mansfield, Air Cdre Mike 'Dusty' Miller CBE AFC, Ray Morrell, Derek 'Mort' Morter, Sqn Ldr Hugh Murland, Wg Cdr Edwin Nieass MBE, J.R. Pintches, O.C. Potter, Hank Prosser, Peter Sawyer, Air Cdre David Simmons CBE AFC, Geoff Steggall, Bruce Spurr, Grp Capt Peter Vangucci AFC, Tony Warner, Eric Watson, Sqn Ldr Ian Wilson, John Worley, Guy Woods.

Thanks are also due to the staff at the Public Record Office and the many people who have helped with contacts and other information, in particular Bob Cossey of the 74 Squadron Association, the late Wg Cdr Eric King of the 616 Squadron Association and Les Green of the 89 Squadron Reunion Club.

INTRODUCTION

As an air-minded youngster, the late 1950s had to be the best period to be growing up. At the time I lived less than a mile from RAF Leeming in North Yorkshire, home to 228 OCU whose long-nosed Meteors and Javelins proved to be an irresistible distraction during lessons at the local Junior school. Nearby Middleton St George provided a constant supply of Hunters and all the RAF's other jet fighters appeared on a regular basis in Leeming's circuit. Once a year the Battle of Britain Open Day allowed the opportunity to get within touching distance of these amazing machines (no barriers in those days) and stare in awe at the God-like men who flung them all over the sky. Sadly I was destined not to follow in their footsteps (the nearest I got to 'high-performance flight' came via the controls of a Piper Warrior) but memories of the early jets linger on and in particular the thought – what were they like to fly?

To attempt to answer that question extensive research was carried out at the Public Record Office where I read numerous flight trials reports issued by the Central Fighter Establishment at West Raynham, Squadron Operations Record Books, and selected Courts of Inquiry into aircraft accidents. My enquiries also led me to contact over sixty pilots and navigators whose accounts provide a unique insight of the aircraft under review and of life in the RAF after the Second World War. Their stories put the reader very much 'in the cockpit' and in so doing highlight not only each machine's individual characteristics, but some of the difficulties that had to be faced on a day-to-day basis. Rather than being superhuman they have all shown themselves to be ordinary individuals who show little of the image that was foisted upon them by an adoring public. Having said that, yesterday's pilots rose to extraordinary heights and were part of an age that saw flight develop more quickly than any other period in history.

The book is split into two sections comprising day fighters and night/all-weather fighters, in each case commencing with the ubiquitous Meteor and ending with the Hunter and Javelin respectively. Today, some of these aircraft can only be seen gathering dust in museums but others still take to the air as representatives of one of the most exciting eras in aviation history. Turned out in better-than-new condition, they are permanent reminders of a particular golden age, one in which the British aircraft industry alone (given official sanction and backing) was capable of producing state of the art fighters and every schoolboy's dream was to become a 'Jet Jockey'.

Part One

Day Fighters

CHAPTER ONE

GLOSTER METEOR

The Gloster Meteor, more than any other type of aircraft, produced the first generation of RAF 'jet jockeys' and was to continue as a first-line fighter until the mid-1950s. Although early aircraft were relatively under-powered, their performance being little better than contemporary piston-engined fighters, subsequent Marks were fitted with more powerful Rolls-Royce jet engines which provided almost a surfeit of power. Generally referred to as the 'Meatbox', the Meteor was rugged and dependable, and many former pilots still regard it with great affection.

The design of what would become the Meteor began in 1940 when George Carter, chief designer of the Gloster Aircraft Company, produced preliminary brochures of a jet-powered fighter to which Specification F.9/40 was issued by the Ministry of Aircraft Production (MAP). Carter had already schemed the E.28/39 research aircraft, powered by a single Whittle jet engine, but due to the relatively low levels of thrust that the current jet engines produced, he was well aware that a fighter aircraft for the RAF would need two engines to provide an acceptable level of performance. His design therefore allowed for two jet engines to be carried in mid-wing nacelles. The structure was purely conven-tional with straight-set wings, the only concessions to modernity being the use of a tricycle undercarriage and high-set tailplane to remove it from the jet efflux.

On 7 February 1941, Gloster received an order from the MAP for twelve F.9/40s, an order that was subsequently reduced to six before being increased to eight. The first prototype, DG202, began taxi trials in the summer of 1942 but Rover who were producing the Whittle W.2B motor, consistently failed to provide engines with sufficient thrust for flight, as a result of which the whole jet fighter programme was put in jeopardy. Fortunately there were others in the field of jet propulsion, notably Metropolitan Vickers and Major Frank Halford of de Havillands. It was to be the latter's H.1 (later to be developed into the Goblin) that powered the first F.9/40 to take to the air when Gloster test pilot Michael Daunt flew DG206 from Cranwell on 5 March 1943. Problems with the Whittle engines were eventually solved following the transfer of production from Rover to Rolls-Royce, and during the rest of 1943 the other F.9/40s, which had been gathering dust awaiting flight-cleared engines, were able to join the development programme powered by the W.2B/23.

The first Meteor I, EE210, flew on 12 January 1944 and was little different to the F.9/40, except that it had a clear vision canopy to the rear and also a bullet fairing at the junction of fin and tailplane in an attempt to reduce directional instability, which had been apparent on the prototypes. By 4 May sixteen Meteor Is had been delivered to Farnborough for evaluation, but it would appear that a number of aircraft in this batch, if not all, flew without the standard armament of four 20mm Hispano cannon. Few major snags were found and in the next few weeks these aircraft were flown by pilots of 616 Squadron, which had been designated as the first unit to fly the Meteor. The first pilots to convert were Squadron Leader L.W. Watts DFC and Flight Lieutenant Mike Cooper who described his introduction to the new jet fighter in a wartime memoir, *Meteor Age*:

'Early in May 1944 the squadron moved to Culmhead, near Exeter, still equipped with the Spitfire HF.VII. About mid-May a twin-engined Oxford was delivered to us and dual instruction given to some pilots. I had previously flown Oxfords on a night-fighter course . . . and after only two short flights I was declared competent on twin-engined planes. Then, on 26 May 1944, our squadron commander and I were sent to Farnborough and it was here that I learnt that our new aircraft was to be the twin-engined jet-propelled Meteor. Security was extremely tight and we were forbidden to talk openly about the aircraft, even on the station. On the following day we were led out to the middle of the airfield where we could see two strange looking aircraft parked close to a number of caravans. They were painted yellow, with "P" for prototype clearly marked on the fuselage and were still the property of the Ministry of Supply.

Wing Commander "Willie" Wilson was in charge of the flight and we were taken to his caravan and introduced; he was most pleasant and easy going. He handed each of us a sheet of paper on which was typed the "pilot's notes" on how to start up and fly the Meteors. We were then led to a separate plane, climbed into the cockpit and studied the notes. After a short while we reported back to the Wing Co who asked "Any problems?" We replied in the negative and he just said "then fly the bloody things!" This we did and experienced very little trouble. I flew EE213 and the C.O. EE214. We each had two flights that day and two more on the twenty-ninth. After the first three flights we both felt completely confident with the aircraft, so much so that on our fourth flight we flew around in formation, possibly the first ever Meteor formation flying.'

After carrying out several more flights, Watts and Cooper returned to their squadron to take part in operations over the D-Day period flying the unit's Spitfire HF.VIIs. Once the beachheads had been established, small groups of pilots were sent to Farnborough to be checked out on the Meteor while the rest of the squadron carried on with operations over France. Despite its radical nature, briefings on the Meteor were presented in elementary fashion, as Flight Sergeant Sam Easy recalls :

'Our briefing and cockpit checks were presented superbly by the Wing Commander who appreciated the considerable differences between flying Spitfires and the jet-propelled Meteors. Simplicity was his watchword. When describing the start-up procedure, the engines were described as

4

Bunsen burners, the paraffin as gas, igniters were matches and high-pressure cocks, gas taps. Continuing his briefing he would say: "After lighting the Bunsen burners you can taxi out to the runway. Now you Spitfire jockeys are used to a large engine blocking your forward view; there is nothing there with the Meteor. So, before commencing your take off, picture the attitude of the aircraft and its relationship to the runway, particularly the forward view, and try to assume the same attitude just prior to touch down".'

Squadron Leader Dennis Barry converted onto the Meteor I at the same time and describes his first flight:

'We were briefed for our first flight by clustering around the Meteor, peering into the cockpit while the Wing Co went through the cockpit drill, explaining the instruments and the aircraft's flying characteristics . . . we felt confident, if a little over-awed. Next we were told we could take off on our first familiarisation flight. As I taxied out to the end of the Farnborough runway I ran through the cockpit drill and then positioned the aircraft ready for take off. Throttles forward to maximum revs while holding on the brakes; then brakes released and slowly accelerate down the runway. No swing, no drag. Hold the stick level until 80 mph indicated, then ease the stick back and lift off the runway at 120 mph. Wheels up and climb away, retracting the flaps. The rate of climb is originally poor, 500 feet a minute, but as the power builds up the rate increases.

Local flying now, the aircraft is quiet with no noise from the engines, only a "whooshing" sound from the air passing the cockpit, like a glider. The visibility is good with only a short nose in front and is similar to being in an airship's observation car. The Meteor feels heavy on the controls when compared to the Spitfire, especially when full of fuel, and aerobatics are forbidden in the Mark I due to it being underpowered. After a forty-five minute flight, down for landing, remembering that one has to land straight off with no overshooting as the power drops off when the airspeed is reduced. On landing the Meteor decelerates slowly, being heavy. Landing successfully completed, I return to my colleagues satisfied with the aircraft except for the lack of power.'

Although the flying characteristics of the Meteor were entirely straightforward, some initial difficulties were experienced as recalled by Flight Lieutenant Mike Cooper:

'All pilots experienced two particular problems. The first, that of judging the correct speed at which to approach the aerodrome when preparing to land. We all found that at first we had to make one or two extra circuits, with the throttles fully closed, before the airspeed had reduced sufficiently to allow lowering of the wheels and flaps. This slow reduction of speed was due to the very smooth streamlines of the Meteor and the absence of a propeller. The second problem was the slow response from the engines.

We had to learn to judge, much earlier than with a Spitfire, when more or less power was needed. This applied equally to the approach to landing, when needing to abort a landing, and when taxiing.'

With an all-up weight of 13,795 lb, the Meteor I was over twice as heavy as a Spitfire V and after landing it could take some stopping, as Flying Officer Ian Wilson soon discovered.

'The excellent forward view was a bit disconcerting on landing compared to the almost complete lack of vision from a Spitfire cockpit, particularly when the nosewheel oleo was a bit soft and the aircraft was in a nose-down attitude on the runway after landing. This happened on my first Meteor flight causing me to temporarily release the brakes. This, together with ineffective brakes, caused me to run onto the grass at the end of the runway, fortunately being brought to a halt by sinking into very soft ground. Brakes were poor on early aircraft and it was common for them to fail due to serious overheating. Members of the ground crew were positioned to stop the aircraft on reaching the dispersal area, since by then the brakes were virtually useless. We did learn to increase drag by holding the nose up after touch down for as long as possible.'

The first two Meteors, EE213/G and EE214/G, were delivered to 616 Squadron on 20 July, and the day after the unit moved to Manston to commence 'anti-Diver' patrols on the lookout for V-1 flying bombs, which had begun the assault on London. With the squadron now led by Wing Commander Andrew McDowall DFM, the first operational sorties were carried out on 27 July as recorded in the squadron ORB.

'Today the Meteors go into operation. History is made! The first British jet-propelled aircraft flies in defence of Britain against the flying bomb. At 1430 hrs F/O MacKenzie took off to patrol a line between Ashford and Robertsbridge, this line covering the main "in-roads" of the flying bomb. Uneventful patrols were made by W/C McDowall, W/C Wilson, F/O Rodger, W/O Wilkes. S/L Watts was unfortunate in having trouble with his guns as he was about to open the squadron's "Diver" score near Ashford. F/O Dean sighted one "Diver" and followed in line-astern at 405mph. He closed in to 1,000yds on "bomb" estimated flying at 390mph when he was turned back by Control owing to the proximity of balloons. Pilots are convinced that given favourable weather and good "plots" nothing can prevent the Meteor knocking down the latest Axis gamble.'

Despite the large amount of testing that had been carried out on the Meteor before it entered service, problems were soon encountered with the 20mm Hispano cannons which frequently refused to work or jammed after a few rounds had been fired. By 4 August a remedy had still to be found, although Flying Officer T.D. 'Dixie' Dean had success without them as his combat report testifies.

'At 1545hrs I was scrambled (under Kinsley 11 Control) for anti-Diver patrol between Ashford and Robertsbridge. Flying at 4,500ft, 340mph IAS, I saw one Diver four to five miles south-east of Tenterden flying at 1,000ft on a course of 330 degrees, estimated speed of 365mph (1616hrs).

From two and a half miles behind the Diver I dived down from 4,500ft at 470mph. Closing in to attack I found my 4x20mm guns would not fire owing to technical trouble now being investigated. I then flew my Meteor alongside the Diver for approx 20–30 seconds. Gradually I manoeuvred my wingtip a few inches under the wing of the Diver, then pulling my aircraft upwards sharply, I turned the Diver over on its back and sent it diving to earth approx four miles south of Tonbridge. On return to Manston I was informed that R.O.C. had confirmed one Diver had crashed at position given by me. This is the first pilotless aircraft to be destroyed by a jet-propelled aircraft.'

Date	4.8.44
Squadron	616
Aircraft	Meteor Mark 1 (EE216)
Pilot	F/O Dean
Call sign	Hugo 24

Time up : 1545hrs   Time down : 1635hrs

Weather 3/10 cloud at 5,000ft, visibility good

Shortly afterwards, 616 Squadron achieved a second 'kill' when Flying Officer J.K. Rodger shot down a V-1 which crashed five miles north-west of Tenterden.

Difficulties with the 20mm Hispano cannon installation in the Meteor were eventually overcome, but in helping to eradicate the faults, pilots encountered further difficulties in attaining accurate speed control as Mike Cooper recalls:

'The problem with the guns was caused by updraught in the under-fuselage ejector slots preventing the empty shell cases from being ejected. Modifications were made and the guns fired perfectly. However, during the gun failure investigations pilots were called upon to carry out many airborne gun firing tests. A favourite area in which to test the guns was the mud flats in the Thames estuary. We found that if we dived down to fire the guns at the same steep angle that we were used to with the Spitfire, the Meteor's speed became too great for comfort near the ground. The Meteor Is were not fitted with airbrakes thus we had to fly in at a much more shallow angle, almost parallel with the ground. Now unfortunately, the projectiles flung a shower of mud upwards and our speed took us right through it. Several Meteors returned with the metal of the engine nacelle, wings and fuselage dented or torn.'

Not surprisingly, the arrival of the first Meteors in the battle zone caused considerable curiosity from neighbouring units and many aircraft popped into Manston to see what all the fuss was about. Among these was the Tempest of

EE249 of No. 616 Squadron.

Wing Commander Roland Beamont DSO DFC, leader of the Newchurch Wing, whose first impressions of the Meteor as a weapon of war were not at all favourable as he later recounted in his book *Testing Years* (Ian Allan – 1980).

'It ought to have been an impressive experience but somehow it was not. The low, thin-fuselaged, blunt-nosed profile was not enhanced by an awkward looking high tail, with two bulges at mid-wing on either side which were distinctly more reminiscent of beer barrels than of aero-dynamically refined engine nacelles. McDowall's briefing was simple and casual. The Meteor, it appeared, was a straightforward aeroplane in most respects but had some limitations as a fighter. It was slow to accelerate and decelerate and it was very fast – but by the time it had reached its maximum IAS of about 480mph it was fuel-limited and needed to land! I was warned to expect a long take off and flat climb and to give myself plenty of room on the approach to get the speed off.

The cockpit with its deep hole effect and upright sitting position was surrounded by the heaviest iron-to-glass ratio windscreen and canopy structure I had seen on a fighter since the early Typhoon. All this coupled with control runs creaking with static friction did little to improve the first impression. But the engines were a different matter. The starting cycle began with a mild whine followed by a dull boom of light-up and then only a subdued, smooth hum as idling rpm stabilised. It was difficult for a hardened piston-engine pilot to believe that an engine was running at all with none of the usual heavy propeller and engine vibration or acrid exhaust gases, and only steady figures on the engine instruments, and a smell of paraffin to prove it.

With the second engine lit, taxiing was a dual experience of new sensations. The tricycle undercarriage eliminated any difficulties and tendency to swing and provided vision completely uninhibited by the nose, but getting going at all required a large proportion of the available power and a comparatively long wait while the Wellands wound themselves up. By the time we had reached Manston's long runway I had come to several conclusions about this aircraft, most of them uncomplimentary. Take off was completely undramatic with a quiet hum from the turbines and the tricycle undercarriage running true until the nosewheel lift speed – in later years to be jargonised as "rotation" – was eventually reached. A strong pull was needed here and as the Meteor whistled into the air it was immediately apparent that its control forces on all axes were heavy, even at low speed while the undercarriage was retracting.

With power set at max continuous, we lumbered quietly round the circuit gaining speed and height slowly – this was no Tempest or Spitfire in climb performance. I levelled out to gain speed while checking gunsight and safety catch as this flight over Kent would be well into "Flying Bomb Alley" which Sector Control radio advised was currently active. With the nose slightly down, speed increased steadily with no fierce acceleration to about 480 mph IAS, faster than I had been in level flight, and still increasing. The engine noise level was imperceptible beneath the rising airflow noise and the stiffening controls confirmed that we were not only going fast, but that we had no operational manoeuvrability worth mentioning at that point. Throughout this acceleration a small-amplitude short-period directional oscillation had been apparent, and this was a case of classic "snaking" which would clearly affect gun aiming.

The fuel gauges were already below half and so it was necessary to haul this projectile round and aim it back at Manston, slowing down on the way to check at low speed the basic stability and control responses which proved to be conventional. A long, flat approach to Manston with the turbines humming quietly was the only pleasurable part of the sortie, except for the landing. This was simple with a pleasantly responsive elevator flaring to a gentle touchdown on the soft-action main undercarriage, followed by the still unfamiliar pitching on to the nosewheel for a nose-down, full-vision landing roll with no swing at all. It had been an interesting experience and I was readily convinced that gas turbines would become the power for the future when more thrust was available. In the meantime it seemed that the Meteor could be regarded as a useful test bed for its jet engines but not by any measure as suitable for fighter operations as they were at that stage of the war. Furthermore I felt that the cumbersome twin engine, high-tail configuration was unlikely to be capable of development into a truly effective fighter aeroplane, although with greatly increased power/weight ratio it might make a useful interceptor/bomber destroyer.'

Although there was much interest in the RAF's new jet fighters, operations were carried out from Manston amid strict security. Flight Sergeant Geoff Amor recalls having to sign the Official Secrets Act and during the funeral of Flight

Sergeant Donald Gregg, who became the RAF's first jet casualty in a crash-landing at Great Chart airfield on 15 August, he and Flight Lieutenant Clive Gosling were told to say that Gregg had been flying a Spitfire, should anyone ask. Each aircraft carried a 'G' suffix to the serial number, which meant that they had to be provided with an armed guard (complete with alsatian dog), and when the Engineering Officers (of which there were two instead of the usual one) needed to refer to a manual, it had to be collected from a safe. With such an air of secrecy there were many who were unaware of the Meteors' presence and Flying Officer Ian Wilson met one such individual over Kent.

'I was leading a section of three aircraft briefed to carry out practice low level attacks on Ack Ack gun positions on the coast south of Ramsgate. After several such attacks I split the formation up and carried out a climbing turn to head west at around 5–6,000ft. I recognised a Spitfire ahead of and below me heading east. There was no risk of collision so I ignored him until he raised his nose and his guns flashed. I felt one shell strike my aircraft, and soon realised I had lost elevator control. My immediate reaction was to bale out, but the hood would not wind back at cruising speed. After reducing speed I realised the aircraft was still

Squadron Leader Dennis Barry.

10

trundling along in straight and level flight. Opening up the throttle caused the nose to rise and closing it caused it to lower. I botched my first landing attempt by lowering full flap on final approach which caused the nose to rise quite dramatically. Fortunately raising the flaps and opening the throttle saved the day and my second attempt was successful.'

By the end of August 1944 most of the V-1 launching sites in the Pas de Calais had been overrun by Allied ground forces, by which time 616 Squadron's tally stood at thirteen. For the rest of the year the Meteors were kept well away from the front line and in October some aircraft were detached to Debden for fighter affiliation duties with the USAAF 8th Air Force, as Dennis Barry recalls:

'The Americans wanted to practise anti-jet combat tactics, having met Me 262s over Germany. In the time we were there our small formation had to contend with virtual armadas of up to 140 B-17 or B-24 bombers plus escorts. Wing Commander Wilson commented in his report on these trials, that the results must have proved very depressing to the Americans as it would appear that the Meteors could sail in as and when they pleased, each "destroying" two or three Fortresses or Liberators, and pull away without the escort fighters (even Mustangs) being able to do very much about it.'

Towards the end of the year the first Meteor IIIs were delivered to 616 Squadron, although the first examples retained the original Welland engines as used in the Mark I. Flight Lieutenant Clive Gosling (a former production test pilot with Supermarine) recalls his impressions.

'After having flown the Spitfire VIIIG with the first Griffon 61 engines which gave some 2,035hp, I had been used to a lot of power, together with considerable torque. There were no such problems with the Meteor III. It was an easy aircraft to fly, but it was underpowered. The take off was sedate to say the least, there was no swing, the acceleration was smooth and the nose wheel lifted easily with moderate back pressure on the stick. Once in the air you had to allow for the slow throttle response which was very noticeable after the instant response of the Spitfire.

The controls were reasonably well harmonised and the overall stability at high speed was good apart from its tendency to "snake" which could not be held by the pilot. The rate of climb was good but not outstanding compared with the Spitfire XIV. It gained speed rapidly in the dive and during aerobatics you had to give yourself plenty of room to recover. The view was good, the cockpit was well laid out and the most important instrument to keep a check on was the jet pipe temperature gauge. The usual approach speed was about 160mph with full flap, crossing the boundary at 120mph. You had to make sure that you were going to get in as in the event of an overshoot, the aircraft took some time to accelerate. On landing the nosewheel was held off the ground to provide aerodynamic drag. The brakes were good but they had to be used with discretion as there was no air compressor. A compressed air system stored in cylinders was all you had.

We never really flew high enough or fast enough at height to get into the area of limiting Mach number. I believe it was about 0.74, this compared with the fact that I often reached 0.85–0.86 flying experimentally with the Spitfire and 0.84 was no trouble. We usually allowed ourselves forty-five minutes per sortie at about 350–400mph. This short endurance meant that we were limited in operational radius which prevented us getting at the opposing fighters. I had the impression that we were only operational for symbolic reasons.'

Asked to sum up his time on Meteors with 616 Squadron, Gosling replied with just one word – 'Frustration!'

On 4 February 1945 a detachment of four aircraft, led by Wing Commander McDowall, flew to Melsbroek in Belgium to join 2nd Tactical Air Force, the rest of the squadron remaining at Colerne where they had taken up residence on 17 January. Initially they were not cleared to fly over enemy territory, a restriction that was imposed following concern that the secrets of the aircraft and its engines might become known to the Germans should one be shot down. Painted in an all-white colour scheme to aid identification, early sorties were carried out over Allied lines to familiarise ground forces with the new aircraft and the limitation on operational use was only rescinded in April, by which time the original detachment had been joined by the rest of the squadron.

Although Meteors had been in service now for nine months, pilots still had to contend with the possibility of engine failure, a hazard that had been apparent almost from the very beginning as Mike Cooper explains:

'Serviceability of the Meteor Is and IIIs posed quite a problem. Besides the gun failures on the Is, a frequent occurrence on both marks was over-heating of the main thrust bearing in the engines. Pilots were told to watch carefully the jet pipe temperature and if the readings rose above a certain level, the engine had to be shut down. Many pilots experienced this problem and returning to base on one engine was common. The bearings were made of plain white metal – only by substituting roller bearings for the white metal ones was the problem eventually solved.

Wing Commander McDowall was the first victim of engine failure when we were still in the U.K. Running short of fuel and unable to reach base he force-landed in a field. Following normal Spitfire forced landing procedure, he came in with wheels up but because of the smooth, clean lines of the Meteor's belly, the plane careered across the field and through hedges before coming to rest. It was a complete write-off, though the Wing Commander himself was uninjured. This incident was the reason for an order that all future forced landings in Meteors were to be carried out with wheels down.'

In the early Meteors engine relights required considerable dexterity on the part of the pilot as Flight Sergeant Geoff Amor recalls:

'The original positioning of the relight buttons was on the right hand side of the instrument panel and I well recall the contortions one had to go

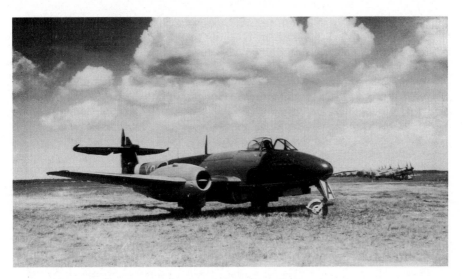

Meteor III of No. 616 Squadron at Luneberg – May 1945.

through to attempt a relight. One hand had to be on the button, the other on the high pressure cock and the stick held between the knees. Later the relight buttons were wired onto the high pressure cocks leaving one hand free to fly the aircraft.

I was posted to Melsbroek on 21 February 1945 as part of the reinforcement for the original detachment of four white Meteors. Whilst there I did have a couple of mishaps. I dented a wingtip on a fuel bowser and the next afternoon I was the only pilot on duty in the ops caravan when the Station Commander rang having received my F.765C. He asked if my air compressor had been u/s and I had to explain, to his surprise, that we did not have a compressor but just an air bottle which was filled to 420psi before take off and this had to last out for the whole trip. On that same day I had an engine catch fire on take off due to failure of the magnesium alloy. My logbook comments afterwards were: "Landed safely, put out fire!"'

The detachment was joined by the rest of the squadron on 1 April, the others having moved from Colerne to Andrews Field on 28 February. 616 then began a series of moves to keep pace with the Allied advance and over the next five weeks flew from Gilze-Rijen and Kluis in Holland, Quackenbruck, Fassberg and Luneberg in Germany. Operations consisted mostly of armed reconnaissance sorties on the lookout for trucks, armoured vehicles and tanks. Although 616 had been widely engaged in demonstrating the Meteor, there were many who had not encountered jet aircraft before and for some it could be a terrifying experience. Ian Wilson recalls an amusing incident which occurred on 3 April:

'On returning to Gilze-Rijen, I was diverted to Eindhoven because of a thunderstorm over the airfield. After a forty minute flight I didn't have much fuel left and aviation kerosene was not available. When the weather cleared I decided to return to Gilze-Rijen since I had just enough fuel remaining to return to Eindhoven if necessary. I briefed a member of the ground crew on start-up procedures, removal of the starter trolley etc., and then climbed in and started the engines. When I looked around for this airman he wasn't there any more. Not being used to the deafening scream of jet engines at close quarters he had run off! I had no choice but to unstrap, climb down (avoiding the air intake) unplug the lead from the starter socket, secure the cover and remove the wheel chocks. Otherwise the return flight was uneventful.'

Concern over engine reliability was occasionally compounded by the hazards of operating over enemy territory. Ian Wilson again:

'For 24 April 1945 my flying logbook records "Meteor III YQ-C, recce Nordholz airfield, 55 minutes", and my comments at the time, "Port engine hit by debris, hole in port wing, starboard engine u/s, fired at two fuel tankers, flak accurate". On the return flight I switched off the starboard engine because the rear engine-bearing temperature was off the clock. Sometime later the port engine started to overheat and sounded rough so I switched it off and restarted the starboard engine. Fortunately it kept going for the rest of the flight. After landing it was discovered that the oil tank for the port engine was holed and empty.'

On 29 April two long-serving and highly experienced pilots were lost when Squadron Leader Watts and his No. 2, Flight Sergeant B. Cartmel, collided in cloud during a tactical reconnaissance. The two Meteors exploded in the air, killing both pilots instantly. A few days later Watts was replaced as 'A' Flight commander by Squadron Leader Tony Gaze DFC, and at the same time Wing Commander W.E. 'Smokey' Schrader DFC took over from Wing Commander McDowall.

By this stage of the war the *Luftwaffe* had virtually ceased to exist and the nearest 616 Squadron came to an aerial victory occurred on 3 May when Flight Lieutenant Tony Jennings forced a Fieseler Fi 156 Storch to land before destroying it with cannon fire. Several other machines were also shot up on the ground including two Ju 87s, two He 111s and one Me 109. 616 moved to Lubeck on 7 May where it remained until 31 August when it was disbanded and renumbered as 263 Squadron. During this period several items of German military equipment were 'liberated' including a twin-engined Siebel 204, an Fw 190 and two Me 262s. The 262s were flown back to Lubeck by Wing Commander Schrader and Flight Lieutenant Clive Gosling who recalls his impressions of the German aircraft:

'Compared to the Meteor III, the 262 was a much better fighter, it had better, lighter controls, more fire power and a very good view. However it was not an aircraft for the inexperienced – it had to be flown. The engines had a very short life and unless a failure in flight was caught immediately,

No. 616 Squadron pilots at Lubeck, June 1945. Back Row (LtoR) Woodacre, Stoddard, ?, ?, Winder (groundcrew), Howell (Adj), Epps, Moon, Hobson, Gosling, Miller, Mason (Doctor), Watts. Middle Row (LtoR) Ridley Clegg, Wilson, Rogers, Barry, Schrader, Gaze, George, Ellis (Eng), Mullenders. Front Row (LtoR) Amor, Easy, Kistrop, Cooper, Dean, Jennings, Packer, Wilkes.

it would go into a spiral dive from which there was no recovery. In both aircraft it was inadvisable to dogfight with conventional fighters. In the Meteor as speed decreased, so did power and acceleration and you were easily outfought. If you played with piston-engined fighters you kept your speed up and dived and zoomed. With a wing loading of about 60 lb/sq.ft, the 262 touched down at about 125mph and took some stopping. It also had a longer take-off run. With reliable engines, I would sooner have gone to war in a 262 than a Meteor.'

With development of the Whittle centrifugal jet now under the control of Rolls-Royce, rapid progress had been made in the quest for more power resulting in the W.2B/37 (Derwent I) rated at 2,000lb.s.t. which increased top speed of the Meteor III to 458mph at sea level and 493mph at 30,000ft. By now mass production was well under way at Gloster's Hucclecote factory and the Meteor was set to become the RAF's premier day fighter. Squadron Leader Hugh Murland first encountered it with 74 Squadron at Colerne:

'My first thoughts on the Meteor were of its enormity and clumsiness, which disappeared once airborne when its speed recompensed its relative lack of manoeuvrability. The first Meteors we flew could be identified by the trail of smoke that they always left in the air and the cockpit canopies which were of the gull-wing type. One of the advantages with the Meteor was greatly improved forward vision – after the huge nose of the Spitfire you could suddenly see everything! Almost too much in fact. In the Spit, when airborne, you could tell you were flying straight and level by the nose in relation to the horizon. Now suddenly there was no nose and flying it for the first time you were confronted with the problem of how you were flying level without constant reference to the instruments. We overcame the problem by switching on the gunsight – and bingo! There was a ready made horizon.

It had a bigger cockpit in which you could turn your head comfortably and there was far less noise. With no engine in front there was no oil being sprayed back onto the windscreen. Other memorable differences included the easier engine control and, not least, the ability to climb like a home-sick angel! Initial acceleration with the Meteor was slower than the Spitfire by virtue of the characteristics of the early jet engines. In those early marks of Meteor duration was very limited with the maximum permitted sortie length being twenty minutes and a maximum of fifty miles from base. After fifteen minutes Flying Control routinely called up to remind us it was time we were back in the circuit. For some it was a good opportunity to get lost. When one of my colleagues flew a Meteor for just the second time he eventually landed some 105 miles from Colerne. We practised dog-fighting with anything encountered, but fast in and out was the effective way for us, we couldn't mix it successfully in close-quarter, steep turns etc. I recall having a mock fight with a Corsair which was alternately flicking over from tight left-hand to tight right-hand turns much faster than I could. Overall, compared with the Spitfire, the size and lack of agility of the Meteor came as a shock, together with its trundling acceleration on take off.'

No. 74 Squadron pilots with EE341 – Hugh Murland in cockpit.

According to a story that did the rounds at the time, an American pilot declined the chance of a flight in a Meteor as he was concerned over the aircraft's endurance. In his words, 'With twenty minutes fuel I aim to be landing not taking off!'

By the beginning of 1946, Warrant Officer Charlie Potter had over two years operational flying experience with 234 Squadron. For him the Meteor challenged all his senses which had become accustomed to the sensations produced by Spitfires and Mustangs.

'In early February 1946 we moved to Molesworth to convert onto Meteor IIIs. The course consisted of two hours dual instruction in an Oxford followed by a ten minute solo then a forty minute familiarisation on the Meteor, all on the same day. At the end of March the squadron flew to Boxted where we remained until I was demobbed in June [234 Squadron was disbanded on 1 September 1946]. During my three and a half months on Meteors I clocked up only eighteen hours as flying was severely restricted. Of this total, ten hours was spent on formation flying and flypasts.

The conversion from Spitfires and Mustangs was not difficult in spite of the change from single to twin engines, traditional to tricycle undercarriage and piston to jet engine. However, all the senses recognised great differences. Both Spitfire and Mustang had their own distinctive smell and so had the Meteor, which was reinforced because of the paraffin fuel used instead of high octane petrol. Secondly, vision – the forward, sideways and downwards view from the Meteor was tremendous compared with the others because the cockpit was set forward of the wing and engines instead of sitting on top of the wing and having an enormous Merlin in front of it. Thirdly, sound – the smooth whirl of the jets was so much quieter it was almost like flying in silence. Finally, the feel – the lack of vibration was most noticeable giving a roller ride as opposed to one like a very hard-sprung sports car. The handling was heavier than the Spitfire (and even the Mustang) and reaction slower, but the silence and smoothness is the overall memory.'

In early 1946 the Central Fighter Establishment (CFE) at West Raynham carried out a series of tests on the Meteor III which also included a comparative assessment with a Tempest V. The aircraft used were EE281, EE428 and EE446, all standard production machines, and flight limitations included a maximum permissible speed of 500mph IAS/0.74 IMN imposed for structural considerations. Take off was found to be entirely straightforward and using one-third flap (in conditions of no wind) the Meteor was airborne in about 650 yards at approximately 105mph. Once in the air all controls were effective although ailerons and rudder were classed as heavy, the former in particular coming in for adverse comment. The elevators, in contrast, were light and there was very little change of trim during flight, only a slight sink when the flaps were raised which was easily corrected.

In a general handling test the Meteor was described as being pleasant to fly and at no time did it show any tendency to 'tighten' in a turn. Comment was again passed on the lack of trim changes on a typical fighter sortie, although this was offset by the Meteor's propensity to 'snake' in turbulence and at the upper end of its speed range. The only cure for this was to throttle back, use of rudder only aggravating the situation. The view forwards and to the sides was excellent but was greatly restricted to the rear by the metal armourplate. In addition there was considerable distortion in the glazing. It was also considered that the upright seating position, and the low setting of the rudder pedals, was not ideal for combating the effects of 'g'.

The Meteor's behaviour in compressibility was assessed as follows:

IAS (mph)	Altitude	Mach No.	Remarks
500	4–5,000ft	0.68	Severe snaking combined with lateral oscillation, controls still effective
510	5,500–6,000ft	0.72	Violent snaking and lateral oscillation. Stick nearly solid but still effective. Nose up tendency
528	6,000ft	0.73	Violent juddering (vibration up and down), stick also vibrating badly, entirely ineffective and solid. On throttling back, controls become effective after a short pause

The Meteor's limiting speed was reached in only a fifteen degree dive, but there was ample warning of compressibility and the forward stick load that was necessary to maintain the dive quickly became very uncomfortable. The aircraft was easily recovered by throttling back and gently easing out of the dive. If the pilot pulled too hard, this only served to induce excessive 'g' which aggravated the effects and introduced juddering at lower Mach numbers. A marked difference was also noted in the characteristics of individual aircraft, as much as 30mph, caused by dented panels and dirty aerofoil sections.

Landing proved to be easy, although even with full flap the angle of glide was rather shallow and speed decreased slowly. Crosswinds of up to 30mph at ninety degrees to the runway were encountered and no difficulty was experienced. The overall assessment however was that the Meteor III, as tested, was unsuitable for operations as a result of its tendency to snake at high speed. This effect was also noted during simulated ground attack sorties when speed built up quickly in the dive.

When flown against a Tempest V, the Meteor, not surprisingly, was found to be faster at all heights, the greatest speed difference occurring at 1,000ft where the Meteor attained 465mph and the Tempest 381mph. During accelerations from 190mph IAS, the Tempest had a slight initial advantage but after approximately thirty seconds, as the Meteor approached 300mph IAS, it drew rapidly away and was out of range (i.e. 600yd ahead) within 1½ miles. In deceleration from straight and level flight, the Meteor only fell behind the Tempest when its

airbrakes were deployed, these then had to be quickly retracted to avoid dropping completely out of range.

During zoom climbs the two aircraft were initially evenly matched, but as
soon as the nose of the Meteor came up to the level flight attitude it started to
pull away rapidly and by the time its best climb speed had been reached
(225mph), it was approximately 750 feet above and 600 yards ahead of the
Tempest. As regards turning circles, the Meteor with its lower wing loading had
a clear advantage under all conditions and could get on to the tail of the Tempest
in four turns, but the Tempest had a better rate of roll which meant that the
Meteor was at a distinct disadvantage during initial combat manoeuvres. In the
dive, if the throttles were not opened, there was little to choose between the two,
but when they were fully open the Meteor was 500 yards ahead by the time it
reached its limiting speed. In conclusion, the Meteor was superior in nearly all
departments but was handicapped by its heavy ailerons and poor manoeuvrability in the rolling plane.

A further negative aspect of the Meteor's performance was the problem of
engine surge which was particularly bad above 20,000ft and could occur at any
time, even during steady flight. It was found that surge was dependent very much
on air temperature and it could only be avoided by opening the throttles very
gradually which diminished the aircraft's value as a weapon of war. The CFE
report concluded with the following statement: 'The occurrence (of surge), and
the reduction of power caused by partially closing the throttle to stop it, prevents
existing jet aircraft giving their calculated performance or any useful combat
performance at high altitude.'

The Meteor F.3's limiting Mach number was eventually raised to 0.79 by
extending the engine nacelles fore and aft to increase fineness ratio, but only the
last fifteen of the 210 F.3s produced were so configured. Yet more power was
just around the corner as Rolls-Royce had developed the Derwent 5 which
was, in effect, a scaled down Nene. This new engine produced 3,500lb.s.t. and
together with the long-chord nacelles developed for the F.3, led to the F.4 which
was to be flown by thirty-one RAF and Auxiliary squadrons. The new mark also
featured a strengthened airframe, pressurised cockpit and a reduction in
wingspan to 37ft 2in., a modification which was introduced retrospectively
following concerns over the strength factors of the original long-span wing. This
increased the Meteor's rate of roll, but adversely affected its climb performance
and increased take-off and landing speeds.

Although investigation into the problems of transonic flight was still in its
infancy, it was decided to make an attempt on the World Air Speed Record
which was still that set in April 1939 by Fritz Wendel in a Messerschmitt Me
109R at 469mph. Preparations began in the late summer of 1945 and two F.3s,
EE454 and EE455, were taken from the production line and brought up to F.4
standard. Armament and radios were removed, cannon ports faired over and a
high gloss paint finish applied. The two pilots selected for the record attempt
were Group Captain H.J. Wilson AFC and Gloster's Eric Greenwood, and the
three-kilometre course was to be over Herne Bay, off the north Kent coast, with
runs to be made on an easterly heading towards Reculver. Numerous delays

Meteor F.4 VW268 of No. 205 AFS Middleton St George.

were caused by bad weather, and it was not until 7 November that the record was finally broken, Wilson achieving a speed of 606mph, with Greenwood just behind at 603mph.

It was felt that the Meteor could go faster still and although a further attempt would probably only raise the record by a small amount, this might be enough to put it beyond the reach of the first successful American jet fighter, the Lockheed P-80 Shooting Star. Consequently, on 14 June 1946, the RAF's High Speed Flight was officially reformed at Tangmere with a total of six Meteor F.4s, to fly over a course laid out over the Channel near Littlehampton. Initially the aircraft allotted to the Flight had standard Derwent 5s, but the two aircraft scheduled to make the record attempt, EE549 and EE550, had these replaced by up-rated Derwents of 4,200lb.s.t.

Stability problems caused by compressibility were never far away and several pilots experienced heart-stopping moments during low-level runs when the nose began to drop at speeds approaching 600mph IAS. Pilots selected were Group Captain E.M. 'Teddy' Donaldson DSO AFC, Gloster Chief Test Pilot Bill Waterton and Squadron Leader Neville Duke DSO DFC. Weather conditions proved to be far from ideal – temperatures during the time that the High Speed Flight was at Tangmere were the lowest for nearly sixty years, ranging between 10 and 15 degrees C on most days, and there was often a gusting wind with moderate turbulence. Despite this, the record was eventually raised to 616mph by Donaldson on 7 September. Further attempts were made to raise the record later in the month without success, although better weather would probably have produced a figure of at least 621mph, which equates to 1,000 kph. The following is an extract from one of Neville Duke's reports detailing a flight in EE550 on 24 September:

'Never having flown this aircraft before (previous experience with EE549) I had planned to make one run over the course to get the feel of the aircraft at speeds around 600mph+. After take off all was well until turning onto the course at Bognor pier when the engines were opened up from cruising (13,800 rpm) to 15,200 rpm. The acceleration on opening up was rapid and speed jumped from 500 to 580mph very quickly. As this speed was gained, the nose tended to rise strongly – it was of sufficient strength to require trimming out.

As speed further increased to the 600mph mark, the nose tended to go down steadily and strongly, again re-trimming being necessary. At the same time the port wing started to go down and although rudder trim was quickly applied, it was necessary to use both hands on the stick to keep the nose and the wing up. The wing low became so heavy that it was necessary to prop my elbow against the side of the cockpit to brace the control column. At the same time a very heavy and maximum foot load on the starboard rudder pedal was used to help the wing.

By the time the aircraft was at its maximum speed indicating around 603–605mph IAS below 300ft (Mach No. approx 0.81+) a terrific amount of vibration and buffeting was occurring over the whole airframe emanating from the tail – all controls were vibrating and pressure was increasing on these controls. Heat in the cockpit rose rapidly due to skin friction and on occasions a fore and aft pitching took place. Although the air was calm the accelerometer registered from +7g to –3g due to the buffeting of compressibility.

On the first run I was unable to keep the aircraft in a straight line on the course as the left wing was slightly down. On a third run the aircraft veered uncontrollably off to the left and I had to pull up to avoid the balloons marking the course. At the end of each measured 3km stretch the aircraft was pulled up slightly and the throttles pulled back a little by a quick snatch – it being necessary to regain a hold on the stick with both hands quickly. The aircraft soon became decompressed – the speed when compressibility comes on being about 595mph IAS (0.78 MN) and with this the nose tends to rise rapidly.

After landing from this abandoned attempt, the aileron trim was altered to make the aircraft right wing low. Experience on the second attempt was as before but right wing low up to 550mph IAS, in trim 550 to 570mph. Above this speed the trim was ineffective and the port wing went down as hard as before. A little more time was available however to get properly lined up on the course and maintained by having the right wing down slightly. Six runs were made, the official speed averaged 613mph (one run at 625mph).'

Bill Waterton also experienced severe wing drop in EE550 and despite rectification work being carried out by the manufacturers, the problem persisted. In contrast the lateral stability characteristics of EE549 were much better and Neville Duke recalls that variations in the behaviour of individual aircraft at high speed was a common problem with production Meteors (and Vampires) of the period.

The Meteor F.4 was tested at CFE in December 1947, although the flight envelope was not explored fully due to temporary limitations of Mach 0.76 and 25,000ft. The following extracts cover aerobatics and single-engined handling:

'Rolling – the Meteor IV rolls well either way up to speeds of 400kt IAS but above this the ailerons become progressively heavier with increase of speed, until at 510kt IAS they are practically immovable.

Looping – elevators are light throughout the speed range and care must be exercised in the first and final quarters of the loop or excessive "g" will result. Use of the elevator trim tab is advisable throughout the complete loop as changes of speed are great. Commencing the loop at 5,000ft, 380kt IAS, approximately 7,000ft will be gained and the speed at the top will be in the region of 180kt IAS. The height lost in the pull out will be slightly greater than that gained in the climb and the speed at the bottom of the loop, with throttles closed and no dive brakes, will be around 420kt IAS. For operational purposes the full loop in the Meteor IV is of very little value, and strain can easily be placed on the aircraft in the final quarter through pilots attempting to pull out of the loop too rapidly. The roll off the top, however, is a useful method of utilizing the exceptionally good zoom qualities of the aircraft and is simple in execution.

Inverted flight – the aircraft is pleasant to handle in the inverted flight position and although at low speeds (280–300kt IAS) forward movement of the control column is necessary to maintain level flight, there is no difficulty in climbing inverted.

Stalling – ample warning is given when the aircraft is approaching the stall. The aircraft tends to drop a wing but this can be counteracted by coarse use of aileron which causes the aircraft to stall straight with heavy buffeting. Normal recovery procedure is immediately effective (i.e. easing the control column forward and allowing speed to build up).

The Meteor IV has an excellent single-engine performance and the majority of aerobatic manoeuvres can be executed with little difficulty. As speed decreases more opposite rudder is required to keep the aircraft straight until at approximately 180kt IAS, full opposite rudder and trim are insufficient to maintain a straight course at full power. When this occurs the good engine should be slowly throttled back. With one engine the final approach should be made at a slightly higher speed, 110–115kt IAS, and the live engine should not be cut until it is certain that there is no risk of undershooting.

Overshooting on one engine is straightforward provided the decision to go around is made before speed has been reduced below 145kt IAS. An overshoot below this speed is more difficult but can be carried out from 110kt IAS without danger, provided the live engine is opened up carefully and the yaw counteracted by powerful use of rudder. The pilot must always bear in mind that if the starboard engine has failed he most likely will have to operate the undercarriage and flaps by hand pump. The minimum fuel required for one overshoot on one engine is 25 gallons.'

Despite CFE's rather optimistic findings, flight under asymmetric conditions would be one of the major killers during Meteor operations, the irony being that most of these fatalities occurred during training when student pilots were being taught the correct procedures should an engine fail.

Although the short-span Meteor F.4 could reach heights in excess of 40,000ft, its degree of manoeuvre at such heights was extremely limited and pilots found themselves effectively balanced on a knife edge, in flight conditions where stall speed was only marginally lower than indicated airspeed. At altitude even the most basic of turns increased loading sufficiently to bring on buffet and without extreme care on the part of the pilot, combat manoeuvring could easily lead to a stall, the subsequent downwards pitch often resulting in loss of control due to compressibility. The only course of action was to deploy airbrakes as soon possible to slow down, but this still led to the loss of several thousands of feet after which all hope of a successful interception had gone.

Much research was carried out to discover the Meteor's characteristics at high altitude, notably by A&AEE Boscombe Down. Squadron Leader Neville Duke was one of those who took part in the test programme:

'We did quite a lot of high altitude test work at Boscombe Down in 1947 and 1948 with the Meteor Mk.4. The highest altitude attained was 50,200ft in February 1948 with RA417. From my log book, most of the tests were between 45,000ft and 48,000ft with RA397 and RA438. These aircraft had no pressure cabin. Using pure oxygen one could survive indefinitely at 40,000ft but above that height survival time is limited. At 43,000ft about one hour, at 45,000ft ten minutes and at 46,000ft about ten seconds. For these very good reasons we had a pressure waistcoat arrangement which forced oxygen into the bloodstream and lungs and this, together with a very tight fitting oxygen mask allowed operations up to 47,000ft. At these heights we were approaching "coffin corner" where there was only a small margin between indicated climbing speed and the Mach number when the onset of compressibility and associated handling problems occurred with the Meteor. The margin for manoeuvre was also small since the indicated speed was not much above stalling speed . . . all in all not a very happy situation to be in!'

From November 1947 to May 1948 CFE carried out a number of trials with the Meteor F.4 which highlighted some of the difficulties of flight at high altitude. During practice interceptions at 40,000ft it was discovered that in a 2g turn at Mach 0.75 the Meteor's turn radius was 1.75 miles. It was calculated that with a normal ninety degree collision course approach, the turn to get behind a target had to be commenced at 3.6 times the turn radius, a distance of 6.25 miles which caused pilots great difficulty in assessing accurate range. Trials showed that the 'crossing contact' (non collision course) reduced this distance by 2–3 miles and it was recommended that this procedure should be used at heights of 35–40,000ft, despite the fact that GCI stations found this type of interception far more difficult to control.

Further problems were encountered with regard to aiming. At 40,000ft, and with a range of 1,000 yards, attacks could not be made at more than twenty degrees angle off because the Meteor's rate of turn was so limited that the pilot could not track the bomber with his sight. Difficulty was also experienced during attacks from astern due to target slipstream which induced compressibility effects to the extent that the Meteor lost so much height that the attack was completely nullified. This applied to attacks carried out above Mach 0.77 with an overtake speed of 35kts. It was also found that there was a greater tendency for snags to develop during operations at altitude, mainly concerning pressurisation, hydraulics and instruments.

With Meteors now in squadron service in large numbers, there was increasing concern over the chances of pilots baling out successfully. In case of emergency, the hood could be jettisoned by pulling a handle on the top right-hand side of the front panel but Pilot's Notes did not offer any advice on how best to avoid the high-set tail on vacating the aircraft. As far as is known, the only successful bale-out from a Meteor F.3 involved Squadron Leader Dennis Barry of 616 Squadron.

'On the morning of 8 January 1950, I was leader of a Vic section climbing through solid cloud which extended from 1,000ft up to 25,000ft. On completion of the exercise we descended back towards base but within a short space of time I realised that my engines had cut and also that my cockpit canopy had iced up due to lack of pressure supplied by pumps on the engines. I jettisoned the canopy, but owing to the circumstances, coupled with the thick cloud, I was unable to attempt a landing and proceeded to open country. I was now in a dilemma as nobody had successfully baled out of a Meteor I/III at that date. I consequently decided to stall the aircraft, finding that the port wing dropped sufficiently to enable me to heave myself out of the cockpit into the centre of the spin, thus avoiding the tail. My parachute opened and I saw the plane [EE472] crash in a field.'

By late 1947 it was clear that the performance of the F.3/4 was about to be eclipsed by newer jet fighters under development in the U.S.A. and Russia, and so Gloster began looking at ways of improving the Meteor to maintain its credibility for U.K. defence and retain the chance of export to foreign air forces. As already related, early Meteors suffered from directional 'snaking' and it was not until the development of the two-seat T.7 with a lengthened fuselage that this problem was largely overcome. The new fuselage was also used on the last day-fighter variant of the Meteor, the F.8, which also featured a revised tailplane, additional internal fuel (ninety-five gallons), Martin-Baker ejector seat, improved canopy and Rolls-Royce Derwent 8s of 3,500lb.s.t.

Early examples of the Meteor F.8 were tested at CFE in September 1950. Take off and climb performance were similar to the F.4, the aircraft becoming airborne in a little over 700 yards in conditions of zero wind using thirty degrees of flap, although due to the new tail, an improvement in rudder control quickly became apparent with lighter pedal forces and better directional control. In terms of speed the F.8's limiting Mach number was 0.02 higher than the corresponding figure for the F.4 which allowed an increase of about 12kt TAS. As no extra power was available this increase could not be exploited below 35,000ft,

Meteor F.8s of No. 74 Squadron's aerobatic team circa 1951 – F/L 'Bertie' Beard
leading.

except in a dive. Above this height the F.8 was capable of flying faster than the
F.4 as the latter was limited by Mach number and not power available. At
40,000ft the clean F.8 stalled at 125kt IAS, a figure which was increased by about
5kt IAS when a ventral fuel tank was carried. As the stalling speed of the F.8 was
approximately 5kt higher than the F.4 at all altitudes, the absolute speed range
(stall to limiting Mach) of the two marks was virtually identical. At high IMN the
F.8 was more pleasant to fly and unlike the F.4, showed no tendency to pitch as
compressibility was approached.

Although acceleration was similar to the F.4, the installation of larger
hydraulic jacks to operate the dive brakes fully up to 490kt IAS gave the F.8 a
considerable advantage in deceleration. This was found to be particularly useful
at low level as it allowed a quick turn of comparatively small radius to be made
when taking evasive action or after sighting a target in poor visibility.
Decelerations from 490–350kt IAS took nine seconds and were accompanied
by buffeting and yawing, and a marked nosedown change of trim. Turn rates
and radii at all heights were similar and there was no improvement in aileron
control (this would have to wait until the introduction of spring tab ailerons).

As regards overall flying characteristics the F.8 was rated an improvement
over the F.4 with lighter rudder forces and more pleasant elevators, although its
slightly higher wing loading led to it being a little less manoeuvrable at all
altitudes. From the pilot's point of view one of the F.8's biggest advantages was
its increased fuel capacity of 595 gallons which allowed patrol times to be
increased by 20–30 minutes. Range could also be increased by stopping one
engine although the improvement decreased with height, 23% at sea level to no
gain at all at 25,000ft.

The Meteor F.8 became the RAF's standard day fighter in the early 1950s and went on to serve with nineteen regular squadrons as well as ten squadrons in the Royal Auxiliary Air Force. Squadron Leader Sid Little flew the F.8 with 616 Squadron and remembers it with affection.

'The F.8's cockpit was comfortable and well laid out and the canopy gave excellent all-round vision. It was a pleasure to fly. It was fast, the controls were light, trimming was effective and rate of roll was about ninety degrees per second at 300 knots. Rate of climb was also considered good at the time – about 4,500 feet per minute, and it took just over six minutes to reach 30,000ft. Most of our sorties were between 20–40,000 feet but the Meteor struggled as it reached its ceiling. I remember intercepting a Canberra and not being able to stay with him as he climbed away when he saw me. The Meteor had a good heating/pressurisation system and VHF reception was normally "loud and clear". We did many exercises practising quarter attacks on towed banners, head-on attacks and enjoyed "tail chases". Towing the banner itself was less popular! Fuel consumption was high at low level but much better higher up, the use of ventral and under-wing tanks allowed longer trips, and on one summer camp to Malta we staged through Istres in the south of France with fuel to spare. Overall the Meteor was generally well liked and I would place it above the Vampire as an air-to-air fighter.'

Owing to the Meteor's excellent handling qualities at low to medium speeds, aerobatic teams proliferated like never before, many of them coming from

Meteor F.8s of No. 1 Squadron at Tangmere.

Flying Training Command where the T.7 was the standard jet trainer. Flight Lieutenant Alan Colman flew Meteors for seven years and recalls his impressions of the aircraft as an aerobatic machine, together with two incidents where things did not go according to plan:

'For me the Meteor was the most marvellous, breathtaking and simple-to-fly aeroplane. Compared to piston-engined machines it was quiet, smooth and incredibly stable, lacking most of the directional and pitch trim changes associated with speed and, particularly, power changes. Perhaps because I had not been flying for long enough to have developed ingrained "piston" habits, the engine response characteristics were easily mastered – more anticipation was needed initially, not just in making power changes, but also because of the weight and sheer aerodynamic "slipperiness" of the aeroplane, but you soon got used to it. The aeroplane accelerated forever and slowed down equally slowly so there was no desperate need for rapid throttle response. The reserve of power, overall stability and the precision of the flying control response made formation flying an absolute delight.

As a newly arrived flying instructor at Worksop I was selected to fly as No. 3 in a formation aerobatic four-ship to be led by our even-newer squadron boss. After a few gentle wing-overs to warm up, the leader announced that we were to execute a roll. He began the roll very slowly, and without raising the nose perceptibly. By the time we were halfway round we were already diving almost vertically at which point he realised that he had made a mistake and shouted "Break! Break!" Sensing imminent contact with terra firma, we all pulled frantically and tried to roll away from the rest of the formation. I saw huge trees rushing towards me and then blacked out. On coming round, shaking, I was climbing vertically through 5,000ft. There was no sign of the rest of the formation and I gingerly found my way back to base and landed, convinced that the other three must have died. In fact all of us were OK. The boss apologised, excusing his incompetence on the fact that he hadn't done any formation aerobatics before, except on Bulldogs!

On another occasion, during an aerobatic demonstration in a Mark 7 my seat harness broke during an inverted fly-by, depositing me helpless in the canopy and unable to reach the controls. Luckily another instructor was in the rear seat. He was able to recover the aircraft while I wriggled back into my seat. He seemed to think that it was all rather funny!'

Although its behaviour at the stall was fairly benign, the Meteor's characteristics in the spin could be disconcerting, especially if entered from unusual attitudes as Alan Colman recalls:

'The normal level stall was innocuous, with heavy pre-stall warning buffet, the nose eventually fell away relatively slowly and, occasionally, a wing would drop. The stall in a turn was also preceded by serious buffeting but nothing nasty would happen unless you kept hauling, when it would roll either under or over the top losing height rapidly. Recovery in both cases was easy with a firm reduction in angle of attack and the wings levelled while power was progressively applied.

For the training spin the standard procedure was to climb to around 30,000ft, and then reduce speed in a slight climb with the throttles closed. As soon as aerodynamic buffet was well established (at about 125kt at that height) full rudder was applied and the control column was hauled fully back. Most Meteors were reluctant to spin when asked and it was always amusing to see the various protesting manoeuvres that individual airframes would perform initially, as if trying to talk you out of it! Vigorous yaw and roll was inevitable with the controls held in that position and the airframe buffet was quite violent, but it frequently completed two horizontal (shuddering) rolls before the nose dropped towards the vertical and there was a sudden increase in the rate of rotation. At that stage the student was taught to apply full opposite rudder and to push the stick forward, ensuring that the ailerons were kept central. As soon as the rotation ceased the Meteor, pointing vertically, accelerated rapidly earthwards and airbrakes would sometimes be required to limit the airspeed while the aircraft was eased out of the dive.

Other aspects of the Meteor's spinning habits usually only became apparent to those of us who took dog-fighting and/or aerobatics seriously. One eventually discovered that, pointing vertically upwards with no airspeed at all, particularly at high altitude, could provoke the Meteor to enter a spin of extreme rapidity which could require an alarming number of turns before recovery action became effective. Further, occasionally, such a spin would turn out to be inverted which, because of the extreme rate of rotation, was almost impossible to spot. In such a case normal recovery action just made things worse, but the aeroplane would recover abruptly if the controls were centralised. I once rode a Mark 8 down from 45,000ft to 15,000ft discovering the above!'

Natural metal and camouflage schemes as displayed by two No. 74 Squadron Meteor F.8s.

Reference has already been made to single-engined flying in Meteors which could be dangerous if the controls were mishandled or a pilot exhibited poor speed control. Flying Officer Edwin Nieass of 74 Squadron remembers some of the problems:

'We practised single-engine flying, and landings with one engine throttled back, and over the years a good many pilots came to grief in such exercises. The engines on the Meteor were sufficiently wide of the fuselage to impart a very strong turning moment. The minimum safe speed on one engine was 150kt and at that speed full opposite rudder had to be maintained to keep straight, which was a mighty strain on the leg muscles, even with full trim applied. Turning against the live engine was tricky and turning away from it needed concentration to avoid overdoing the turn. Consequently, a badly judged landing approach, which necessitated increasing power on the live engine, was liable to result in loss of directional control, frequently with a fatal conclusion. Trying to open up the idling engine to help recovery was rarely helpful because of the lag in response before power was developed. From my experience, the reliability of the Derwent engines did not justify the amount of single-engine practice landings undertaken, with all the risks they entailed for pilots inexperienced on type.'

Fred Insole flew Meteor F.4s and F.8s with 500 Squadron from West Malling and also has clear memories of flying with asymmetric power:

'The engines were so reliable that failure, or an emergency shut-down, was a rare thing indeed. The deliberate shutting down of an engine to conserve fuel at low levels was very common – any pilot would do so without concern and re-light for landing. Although asymmetric was usually no problem, the RAF training policy meant that no pupil ever forgot their asymmetric flying on Meteors. The detail was a single-engine approach to about 300ft with an overshoot at normal approach speed. This was a lethal practice. With full power on the live engine, the aircraft would just manage to climb at minimum speed – with rudder leg quivering with fatigue, it was agony. One mistake and it was all over without any chance of recovery. So many died in practising for this remote possibility.'

The Rolls-Royce Derwent was probably the most flexible and rugged engine of its day and exhibited excellent reliability despite the abuse it suffered, especially during pilot training. Despite the fact that engine failures were extremely rare, single-engined practice was set to continue, leading to questions being asked in the House of Commons as concern mounted over high accident rates. Alan Colman recalls some of the asymmetric procedures that he taught as a QFI at 211 FTS, Worksop, and an amazing escape he witnessed at CFS:

'The most important thing to bear in mind was speed. To control a Meteor with full power on one engine you had to have strong legs (and the seat

29

position adjusted perfectly) and at least 150kt IAS. You never reduced speed below that magic number unless you had plenty of height in hand to convert to speed if you lost an engine. On take off that was the speed you aimed to achieve as quickly as possible. In addition to demonstrating (at a safe height) the consequences of an engine failure at full throttle and take-off speed (about 120kt), we used to teach students basic aerobatics on one engine as a means of giving them confidence and making them familiar with the rule that, as speed was reduced, power on the "good" engine could only be used with great care and with the resulting yaw perfectly balanced with rudder. In the simulated take-off case, if coarse corrective rudder was not applied at once, the aeroplane would yaw and flick inverted in less than a second. Going over the top of an asymmetric loop, for instance, you could demonstrate that it was necessary to almost close the throttle on the live engine momentarily, or you would lose control!

One major trap that the Meteor could spring on the unwary was the effect on asymmetric performance of inadvertently leaving the airbrakes out. I had a very lucky escape at Middleton St George where, on about my third solo in a Meteor 4, I tried to execute a go-around on one engine having forgotten to retract the airbrakes. As I struggled to clear the top of station headquarters I realised what had gone wrong and whipped them in. A second longer and I would have been at the bottom of a smoking hole.

On the CFS course for new instructors we had to practice all the procedures that we would be using when we started to teach our own students. One of the things we used to practise was night circuits with "roller" landings. One of our number was a well built, slightly portly individual, called Pete Stonham. Pete touched down in his Mk.7 on one of the night "rollers" and, as was the procedure, he applied full power to go-around without raising the flaps, which were always left fully down until safely airborne and the undercarriage was up. The second he became airborne, with a huge bang, the complete turbine assembly fell off one engine, carved its way through the nacelle and struck the runway in a spectacular cloud of sparks, leaving a groove cut into the concrete. Turbine blades flew everywhere, some penetrating the fuel tanks. Being experienced on type, and quick, Pete snatched enough power off the good engine to maintain directional control but he would still have died if Little Rissington had not been on top of a hill. To the consternation of those in the control tower, the Meteor was seen to disappear over the boundary and then sink out of sight into the darkness. However, he managed to use that height to clean-up his aeroplane and get enough power on to make a safe circuit and landing a few minutes later. A classic demonstration of the asymmetric handling qualities of the Meteor, aided by brilliant piloting and incredible luck.'

A story, possibly apocryphal, tells of a Meteor pilot who got into trouble during a single-engined approach, put on full power on the good engine, only to perform a complete barrel roll at very low altitude before smashing through the approach lights and ending up on his belly in the undershoot area at the end of the runway. Despite his unorthodox arrival, he walked away unscathed.

In addition to the perils of flying on one engine, Meteor pilots had to be wary of another related trap known as the 'Phantom Dive'. This mainly occurred in the circuit and was usually fatal. Flight Lieutenant Bruce Spurr was an instructor at CFS:

'When the undercarriage was selected "down", a resistor caused the left leg to lower first, causing a yaw which the pilot had to correct until the right-hand mainwheel lowered. With excessive yaw, the fuselage and engine nacelles presented at an angle to the airflow caused turbulence and sudden loss of lift, which was aggravated if the airbrakes were left out in the circuit. In addition, the long nose of the Meteor required an adequate area of fin and rudder and its effectiveness was affected by the turbulent wake from the forward parts of the fuselage. Thus the aircraft could suddenly be heading earthwards in a sideways dive needing more height than was available for recovery. Even before this phenomenon became well known I had discovered that at virtually all cruising speeds the application of an excessive amount of rudder would cause a sudden nose-down pitch, sometimes causing negative "g". I always made my students do this once, and the violence of it caused them never to forget to keep the slip needle central.'

Although the 'Phantom Dive' is usually associated with the T.7, Alan Colman had a similar experience in a Meteor F.8:

'I was returning to Worksop from a formation aerobatic sortie as No. 2 and, as usual, we ran in towards the airfield at low level at 300kt in echelon starboard. Over the runway threshold "breaking, breaking, GO" was called and we peeled off at half second intervals into a very steeply banked climbing turn onto the downwind leg. As one snapped into the "break", the throttles were closed and airbrakes extended. Then, as speed decayed through 200kt, one notch of flap was selected (giving a nose-down trim change) followed by undercarriage down at 165kt and airbrakes in. All this, with lots of practice, would place the aeroplane at 1,000ft downwind, about 200 yards behind the aircraft in front, with just time to start increasing the power and adjusting the trim as the turn continued onto the final approach. On this occasion things went badly wrong.

When you dumped the gear down in a Meteor the left leg always came down first and caused the aircraft to yaw, momentarily, until the other leg appeared. At this juncture my Meteor, still with around thirty degrees of left bank applied, suddenly headed earthwards. I had time to get the airbrakes in, level the wings and start applying power but I was down among the treetops before I checked the descent and regained full control. Was that the purists definition of the "Phantom Dive"? I honestly don't know, but thereafter, as far as my students were concerned, that was it, I had discovered just how easily you got into it. In the end that spectacular type of low-level formation break was banned and, as far as I know, still is.'

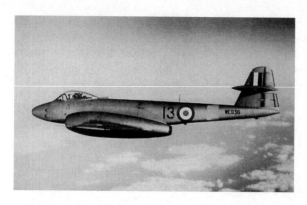

Meteor F.8 WE936 of No. 211 FTS Worksop.

The Meteor F.8 may have been an able performer at low to medium levels, but by the early 1950s it had been outclassed by more advanced designs. Flying Officer Edwin Nieass flew the F.8 with 74 Squadron, and later as a flight commander with 245 Squadron:

'We regularly operated the Meteor 8 at 30,000ft and on occasions up to 40,000ft. Above 30,000ft the controls became sloppy and it was not easy to manoeuvre freely or maintain height in steep turns. Practice interceptions in up to wing strength in battle formation were frequently carried out at heights of up to 30,000ft, and I also recall our USAF exchange squadron commander on 74 Squadron taking twelve aircraft on an aerobatic tailchase as an exercise in control to maintain position and avoid whiplash at the tail end. The Meteor 7, being unpressurised, was rarely flown above 20,000ft, although on occasions I recall operating up to 40,000ft, its limiting height. When flying unpressurised at that height for more than a few minutes it was not unusual to experience the bends, with pain in wrist and elbow joints. We always flew on oxygen at all heights.

Fuel consumption, and consequently endurance, was a problem. We always flew with a ventral tank attached, this degraded performance to some extent, but it was essential to provide a reasonable operating time. At heights over 20,000ft, we could achieve an average sortie time of one hour, with a maximum of one hour fifteen minutes. We also flew a lot of low level interceptions and cross countries at heights down to 250ft at 300kt but could only manage about 40–45 minutes. Underwing tanks were usually only used for ferry flights because handling and performance was degraded.

We frequently met other Meteor squadrons on exercise, including Dutch and Belgian squadrons. Meteor v. Meteor was interesting and success in dogfights depended on the skill of the pilot. When we mixed it with RCAF Sabres, however, it was a different matter. We could not match them for speed, although we could out-turn them at heights below 20,000ft. We also intercepted Lincolns and USAF B-29s, when the practice was to make steep diving attacks from a ninety degree overhead approach to try to nullify their armament. Latterly the Canberra came into service and we were hard pressed to reach it at height, or to catch it. The most humiliating experience was trying to intercept John Cunningham in the Comet when he was doing the flight trials. We couldn't get near it!

On instruments in bad weather, the Meteor was comfortable to fly although sometimes when descending from height there was a tendency for the canopy and windscreen to mist over and in cold conditions, to frost over. The customary method of effecting a squadron or wing descent through cloud was for aircraft to be streamed in pairs at ten-second intervals behind the leader who called turns and headings in the descent, succeeding pairs turning at ten, twenty and so on seconds after each call. The same procedure was used in what was called a snake climb through cloud and both systems worked well. There was an almost complete lack of navigation aids in the Meteor apart from a Mk.4 gyro-magnetic compass and from late 1952 the fitting of DME (Distance Measuring Equipment), although the number of beacons was extremely limited. Homings to base in bad weather were made with the aid of bearings taken by air traffic control on transmissions from the aircraft. Descents through cloud to base were done similarly by QGH, homing bearings being given from ATC using CRD/F equipment, which gave a visual indication of aircraft transmission bearings on a cathode ray tube. The aircraft was homed overhead the airfield, sent outbound on a heading thirty degrees off the runway reciprocal and at half height turned inbound onto the runway heading. For a short period in the early fifties we had the benefit of a GCA unit on the airfield which enabled operations in much reduced cloud bases.'

Alan Colman also completed a full tour with 74 Squadron and recalls operations with the Meteor F.8:

'Our normal operational maximum was 35,000ft. At that height the aeroplane was at the limit of its performance envelope and there was a very small reserve of power and speed left for station-keeping adjustments in formation or to engage a target. The highest I ever flew a Meteor (a Mk 8) was 48,000ft. I was in a formation of four which had been scrambled to try to intercept Meteors of the Day Fighter Leaders School from West Raynham who were returning from a sortie over Holland. The GCI reported that DFLS were at 45,000ft so we set out to try and get above them to give us an element of surprise. It was a total farce because, although we did achieve complete surprise, our aeroplanes became totally uncontrollable in compressibility as soon as we began our "attack" and we passed vertically right through their formation, all of us either upside down or rolling helplessly. In all honesty, the Meteor was virtually useless as an interceptor above 30,000ft.

During my time on 74 Sqn we regularly exercised against Venoms and F-84 Thunderjets at very low level (300ft) on so-called *Rat and Terrier* exercises, also against Sea Furies when on convoy patrol. At higher level we exercised against Canberras, B-47 Stratojets, Lincolns, B-29s and B-50s. Apart from its heavy aileron controls the Meteor was a superior aeroplane at low level, being strong, fast and having a good field of view. Because of its acceleration and ability to hold speed in manoeuvres it could catch virtually anything (eventually) and could out-climb and out-turn it. At high level it was a different story. The Canberra and B-47 were just as fast as the Meteor, but able to operate at heights above 35,000ft where the Meteor was hopeless. At that sort of height the Canberra could out-turn a Meteor and hold its speed in the process.

We had more fun in the "unofficial" engagements which were usually against the early model F-86 Sabre. Once again, above 25,000ft the Sabre was totally superior because all it had to do was take advantage of its greater speed range and dive away. If the Sabres were above you to start with your only defence was to execute hard turns towards the attack. Each time you executed such a defensive manoeuvre at height you lost energy and became progressively slower and more vulnerable while the Sabres (if they knew what they were about) zoom-climbed back above you for another attack. On the other hand, if you managed to find F-86s below you and they were tempted to try and "mix it", the Meteor could give them a very nasty fright. At 20,000ft or below the Meteor could out-turn, out-accelerate and out-climb a Sabre. It also had much more effective airbrakes which, used at the right time, could cause a high speed attacker to overshoot his target and become a sitting duck. This was particularly so against the F-86A which was relatively underpowered and had automatic wing leading-edge slats. In a very hard turn the slats often operated asymmetrically which caused the Sabre to flick out of the turn. At such a moment spectacular camera gun footage was possible, especially if you had your nose almost up his jet-pipe!

The Meteor F.8 I was allocated as my personal mount was a real old dog. In fact it carried the identification letter "D" and was therefore always referred to as "D-Dog". It was an early production model, serial VZ512, and lacked improvements coming through on the newer aircraft such as the larger engine intakes (always called "deep breathers"), all-clear canopy and spring-tab ailerons. In fact, the geared-tab ailerons on this aircraft were desperately heavy and much physical effort was required to manoeuvre it. Above 250kt it became progressively right-wing heavy such that both hands and a knee were required to hold the wing up at 350kt. It was this aircraft that gave me one of my biggest frights in a lifetime of flying.

When in the middle of a cross-over turn in battle formation at 27,000ft, the canopy disintegrated with a huge bang. I was blinded by dust disturbed by this "explosive decompression" and had to scratch the ice off the ASI, compass and altimeter in order to find my way back to base. Luckily the weather was good. Apart from the inconveniences above, wearing only a light-weight flying suit I was frozen with cold but soon realised that a bigger worry was the ejector seat firing blind, which was flapping wildly, having partially deployed out of its housing on top of the seat. If it really caught the slipstream the seat would fire and the Meteor and I would part company! Needless to say I flew back to Horsham very slowly and it was a blue-with-cold but much relieved pilot who brought his aircraft to a stop on the runway while an airman climbed up and inserted the ejector seat safety pin. Eventually "D-Dog" was routinely subjected to a "Major" inspection during which it was found that the mainspar was cracked. That almost certainly explained its weird handling characteristics. It didn't reappear on the squadron order of battle and I believe that it was unceremoniously scrapped.

Having won the Dacre Trophy in 1952, 74 Squadron had something of an obsession with air firing proficiency and the highlight of the year was the APC detachment to Acklington. We had a chance to fire on our usual "flag" targets and also on glider targets towed by Tempests. The big difference was that the targets were towed at 20,000ft instead of the 7,000ft or so which was the upper limit on our home firing range off the Norfolk coast near Yarmouth. The extra altitude made a huge difference to the handling of the Meteor during the standard close-in and abbreviated "high quarter" type of attack we used. I well remember one occasion when my aircraft suddenly flick-rolled out of control due to compressibility effects just as I had started to fire. I watched in terror as I hurtled inverted over the top of the "flag" missing it by about six feet!

On another occasion I carefully emptied every round of 20mm ammunition into a glider target only to see it fly on serenely and, apparently, undamaged. Determined to see if I had hit it at all I approached the glider intending to formate on it to have a look. Just as I was easing into position the glider fell apart before my eyes, leaving nothing behind the Tempest but the tow rope. However, my biggest air-firing drama had nothing to do with gunnery skill or handling qualities. Having completed my initial turn-in during a quarter attack on another glider target, I was tracking the glider through my gunsight when, without any warning from the tug pilot or the GCI radar that was supposed to be watching us, a giant American ten-engined B-36 bomber suddenly filled my windscreen, passing straight through my line of fire. Half a second later and I would have either collided with the bomber or shot it down!'

VZ512 'D-Dog' of No. 74 Squadron.

Canopy disintegration was not an uncommon experience with the Meteor and with flailing of the blind, as fitted to early type ejector seats, pilots initially were in some danger of leaving their aircraft involuntarily. Pilot Officer Ray Morrell also had a canopy blow out when flying with 226 OCU at Stradishall, the first of three incidents on consecutive Tuesdays.

'On 22 June 1954 I was flying Meteor F.8 WF751 on a low level *Rat and Terrier* exercise. I was flying in excess of 450kt almost paralleling the A11 between Thetford and Newmarket when the hood went, presumably from a bird strike although there was no evidence of one on inspection after landing. I knew at once what had happened but still felt compelled to turn my head to look and confirm the fact. I immediately closed the throttles and pulled the stick back and climbed vertically, taking my feet off the rudder bar in case I was ejected out as there seemed to be some damage around the ejector seat blind. I spent the return flight flying pretty slowly and trying to make sure that the blind did not come out any further.

The following Tuesday I had an engine go on take off immediately after rotation but managed to put it straight back on the ground. Although I came partially off the runway I was able to bring it back on and taxy off the end. I remember doing this as I had been told off the week before by the Wing Commander (Tech) for not clearing and blocking his runway. This "flight" was not logged as, in my opinion at the time, I had not actually flown. The third incident was in WA816 and occurred exactly a week later. I did not really want to fly that day as I believe that things happen in threes. However, it was late afternoon and everyone had completed three trips and I was wanted to make up a four. No-one else was available. The exercise was practice high-quarter attacks. The whole trip went well and we were returning to the field and I remember thinking to myself, "Well that's over". I was landing number four but got too close to the number three on finals. I was tipped slowly over nearly onto my back and I still have a vivid memory of the person in the runway caravan vacating his position quite rapidly. I managed to straighten up at very low level and overshot for a go around and another landing.'

While the two-seat Meteor had a somewhat dubious reputation in the circuit, there were times when it could be extremely forgiving. Sergeant Bob Hillard flew Vampire FB.5s with 249 Squadron at Deversoir in Egypt but managed to get in plenty of Meteor time in the unit's two T.7s.

'The Meteors were mostly used for instrument training and this gave me the opportunity to do a lot of safety pilot work in the front seat. It was during such an exercise that I had reason to be grateful for the stability of the Meteor, and the skill of the ground staff in setting the trim. Sergeant Derek Evans was in the back and we set off to do our usual I/F practice which did not take long to complete. As there was some time left, we let down for some low flying which, as a ground attack unit was second nature to us, so I had no qualms about letting Derek do this from the back seat.

36

T.7 WG945 of the MEAF Instrument Training Flight – 1951.

Down went the nose, up went the speed, and as we approached the ground the nose of the aircraft gently rose, eventually settling down to what was probably a good 350kt, at what seemed like only a few feet above the desert.

There seemed to be some nice smooth flying from Derek as well, but I had an eye on the fuel and suggested to him that it was time to go home. There was a pause, then Derek asked why I was asking HIM to go home. It seemed logical, I told him, as HE was flying it. Another pause, "but I'm not", he said, "I haven't touched a thing for ages." I gave the pole a little tweak and he was right, there wasn't anyone at the other end. We were both certain that we had done the "you/I have control" bit, but not a lot was said on the way back!'

There was at least one occasion when a Meteor T.7 landed itself due to a similar mix-up in communications, the aircraft's rugged construction allowing the crew to walk away from the wreckage to contemplate the valuable lesson in airmanship that had just been learned. Flying Officer Derek 'Mort' Morter of 74 Squadron was another who owed his life to the Meteor's ability to withstand considerable punishment. The following incident took place on 26 August 1953 and involved F.8 VZ557:

'I was leading four aircraft on an early morning ground attack sortie in the Thetford Battle Training area; the enemy was a Welsh Infantry Brigade, Territorial Army. On one pass several gesticulating Brown Jobs sheltering under a tree caught my attention. Their gestures did not seem complimentary to the Royal Air Force so I decided that they would be my next target. Suffice to say that I was so determined to teach them some manners that I left my pull-up a little late . . . well that's my story! As a result I, and the Meteor also, passed noisily through the upper half of several trees. I returned to base noting that the wing leading edges were very badly dented, the ventral tank had obviously been damaged because of its position, but both engines were running fine. After orbiting base and watching senior officers' cars rushing to ATC as I burnt off fuel, I carried out a slow speed check and operated all the services, at the same time contemplating my now definitely uncertain RAF career. A successful landing was made after crossing the hedge 15 knots faster than normal.

The damage was severe, more extensive than I thought, and assessed as Category 4 (Cat 5 was a write off). The engines had swallowed so many leaves it looked as if someone had thrown gallons of green paint into the intakes. An inquiry was convened. In the meantime the Welsh invited me and the other three pilots to a dining-in night in order to "court martial" me. The prosecution presented as evidence several relieved "live" officers, many tree branches and soiled underwear; I hadn't a leg to stand on. From the RAF I earned myself an AOC's reproof, and a lesson that I never forgot, but with untold gratitude and admiration for the strength of the "Meatbox" and its Rolls-Royce engines.'

Sadly, many pilots were not so lucky. Flying Officer Murray Jones also flew Meteors with 74 Squadron and 226 OCU:

'There were a number of fatalities from a wide variety of causes. One pilot flew into the ground while night flying, another disappeared over the North Sea in adverse weather conditions, one got lost and was killed attempting a belly landing in a field, one lost control during a tail chase and spun in, one had engine failure while inverted at low altitude, one became disorientated during live air-to-air firing in poor visibility and crashed into the sea, one trimmed his aircraft into a curve of pursuit during a high quarter attack and on completion tried to execute a slow roll, the nose dropped and he attempted to pull through, but had insufficient height and hit the ground. Two of my friends died in unrelated incidents because their Meteors disintegrated around them.

One particularly unfortunate incident involved a student at Stradishall returning at high speed from an air firing exercise over the North Sea. A USAF Sabre happened to be formating on him at the time and the pilot witnessed the disintegration of the Meteor's canopy. Part of it hit the RAF pilot on the head and knocked him out. His aircraft dived under power vertically into the ground. The Sabre pilot landed at Stradishall straight away and made a full report of what he had seen. From this it was established that during re-arming the rear of the canopy had been lifted and propped to give access to the ammunition storage boxes. In this particular case, on lowering the canopy, the prop was not correctly stored and the canopy was placed under an arching stress, which led to failure. Practices were revised as a consequence.

On another occasion one of our flight commanders at Stradishall had his tail chopped off by an F-84 and he was obliged to eject. The seat spun so violently that his arms and legs were extended from his body by the gravitational force and he found great difficulty in bringing his arms into

FTU Staff Display Team, Benson September 1957. F/L George Hill, F/L Alan Colman, F/O 'Butch' Hamer, F/L Ray Hoggarth.

his body in order to release himself from his seat. Improvements were made to the seat design as a result of this incident. On a lighter note, I remember one exercise when the Horsham Wing were simulating a high altitude bombing attack on the North Midlands, approaching from the North Sea. We were successfully intercepted from above by the Linton-on-Ouse Wing but as they dived on us they ran into compressibility problems and the entire wing plunged past us in a near vertical dive – a spectacular sight! We watched all this with a certain amount of amusement and completed our simulated attack without further interference.'

Because of the problems that were being experienced with the introduction of the Swift and Hunter, the Meteor F.8's retirement from first-line squadron service was delayed until April 1957 when 245 Squadron finally converted onto the Hunter F.4. For many pilots the Meteor's passing was like saying goodbye to an old friend, it had proved to be a solid, trusty ally, one which had taught them much about jet-powered flight and had seen them through to fly more advanced types of aircraft. This attitude is, perhaps, a little surprising considering the Meteor's poor safety record, but the high accident rate was brought about to a large extent by decisions taken with regard to the training syllabus and attempts to meet an operational commitment that was beyond the aircraft's capability, rather than any deficiencies in the basic design. As a former QFI with 1,500 hours on type, Alan Colman knew the Meteor better than most:

'As a wartime design forced to carry on in service well beyond its "sell-by date", it was kept going by steady improvements to the engines, coupled with the fitment of modern equipment in the cockpit. However, from the beginning of the 1950s it was outclassed, particularly at high level. When it was designed it was a brilliant and elegant concept, and through all the changes and modifications it remained an absolute delight to fly – strong, stable and reliable with superb acceleration. As a trainer it provided probably the most effective and comprehensive single-type introduction to both pure-jet flying and asymmetric handling yet devised. Many thousands of fast jet and transport jet pilots learned their basic skills on this classic aeroplane. It served us well.'

CHAPTER TWO

DE HAVILLAND VAMPIRE

In early 1942, despite gearing up for full-scale production of the high-performance twin-engined Mosquito, de Havilland at Hatfield were looking to the future by becoming involved in the new world of jet-powered flight. Their engine division, under Major Frank Halford, was already working on a centrifugal jet which was first tested on 13 April 1942, just 248 days after the first drawings had been issued. Progress with the new engine was relatively trouble free and by 26 September nearly 200 hours of bench running had already been carried out. Reaping the benefits of a unified organisation, (which was in marked contrast to the situation at Gloster), the airframe section produced a highly compact design which was tailor made for a single Halford H.1 (Goblin) jet engine.

Although produced to Specification E.6/41, the resultant DH.100 (initially named Spider Crab) was designed from the outset to be equipped with four 20mm Hispano cannon and was a thoroughly practical fighter. Its layout was reminiscent of the American P-38 Lightning and it featured a small pod-like fuselage with the tail surfaces mounted on slender twin booms. This maximised the efficiency of the turbine by keeping jet-pipe length to a minimum, the engine being fed by air intakes mounted in the wing roots either side of the fuselage. The wings were straight, but highly tapered, and had a thickness/chord ratio of 14%. All but the cockpit area was of conventional stressed skin construction, the front part of the nacelle being a plywood honeycomb as on the Mosquito.

The first DH.100, LZ548, was flown for the first time on 20 September 1943 by Geoffrey de Havilland Jr and was followed by two more prototypes, LZ551 and MP838, the latter being delivered to Boscombe Down for handling trials in April 1944. The subsequent report commended its high speed (in excess of 500mph) and excellent aileron control, but also noted directional instability and slow acceleration in level flight. Due to de Havilland's preoccupation with the Mosquito, initial production of the Vampire was passed to English Electric Co. Ltd, the first example, TG274, flying for the first time from Samlesbury on 20 April 1945. The Vampire replaced the Halifax on production lines and modifications were progressively introduced throughout the initial batch. All aircraft after TG314 featured an uprated Goblin 2 of 3,100lb.s.t. and could also be fitted with Mosquito-type auxiliary fuel tanks to increase range. Later, TG336 introduced the use of pressurised cockpits, and one-piece canopies were fitted from TG386.

Only six Vampires were delivered to the RAF before the end of World War Two and the first operational unit to be re-equipped, 247 Squadron at Chilbolton, received its first aircraft on 14 March 1946, an event described in somewhat effusive style in the Squadron ORB:

'The day broke with low ominous clouds rolling across the sky. Towards midday, as the ceiling was lifting slightly, a whistling noise was heard quite unlike that of the Tempest everyone had long been accustomed to. On rushing out of dispersal, there, streaking across the sky, a Vampire was seen. At last our long awaited jets were arriving. By teatime, seven of them had arrived and curious crowds were soon gathered around getting what gen they could from the ferry pilots.'

Over the next few days 247 Squadron's pilots had their first taste of jet-powered flight although when it came to trying out the new machine there was a definite 'pecking order' which commenced with the Wing Leader, Wing Commander Dyson MBE DFC. On 21 March Geoffrey de Havilland Jr flew in to Chilbolton to give a demonstration of the Vampire's capabilities that left most of his audience open mouthed in awe. Flying within the airfield boundaries, his

Vampire F.1 TG278.

display was carried out at high speed at very low altitude, with ninety degree banked turns just above the ground and aerobatic manoeuvres including an upwards 'figure of eight' to show off the Vampire's excellent vertical penetration. The whole routine was finished off with an exemplary landing.

Throughout the coming weeks Chilbolton saw frequent visits from high-ranking RAF officers, eager to try out the Vampire for themselves, including the C.-in-C. of Fighter Command, Air Marshal Sir James Robb KBE CB DSO DFC AFC, who expressed his delight at its performance. More high profile activity occurred on 23 May when a specially equipped photographic Lancaster arrived to take publicity photos for British Movietone News and daily newspapers. During 247 Squadron's work-up period on the Vampire much emphasis was placed on formation flying as the unit was due to take part in the Victory Day flypast scheduled to take place on 8 June. Twelve aircraft, led by Squadron Leader C. S. Stuart Vos DFC, departed for West Malling on 1 June to prepare for the big day and despite poor weather conditions on 8 June, nine Vampires flew in formation over London as part of the celebrations. Following a brief return to Chilbolton, 247 Squadron moved to Odiham at the end of June where they were soon joined by 54 and 130 Squadrons to form the first, and only, Vampire Wing in Fighter Command.

Pilot Officer (later Group Captain) John Jennings joined 247 Squadron in 1947 having already completed a full tour on Mustangs and Tempests.

'My first flight in the Vampire I was on 19 May 1947. Of course there were no dual seaters in the early days of jet fighters – I still recall being handed the pilot's notes and after a somewhat cursory verbal test on its contents, being told to go fly the aircraft. Feelings of real pleasure whilst taxiing and at take off, with the wonderful visibility that one got with the nose wheel as opposed to lack of same with piston-engined fighters, were mixed with feelings of trepidation on landing at the proximity of the ground. The Vampire was so small you could stand with feet firmly on the ground and look into the cockpit. I had been a great fan of the Mustang, but I quickly got to love the Vampire. I loved everything about it apart from its very limited endurance and the lack of a re-light system if the fire went out. This latter item was to cause me serious embarrassment on two later occasions.

We were limited to flights of about thirty-five minutes and the absolute ceiling was 35,000ft. The three squadrons at Odiham were reduced to a cadre basis – eight aircraft and ten pilots – and flying was severely restricted. In the eight months from May to December 1947, I flew a total of sixty-five hours. Although the aircraft handled superbly and was a wonderful vehicle for aerobatics, it was short on power and could misbehave in certain circumstances. Whilst firing on an air-to-ground target at APC (RAF Acklington), one of the squadron pilots pulled out of his dive too sharply, the aircraft flicked one way then the other before hitting the sea.

Towards the end of 1947 the F.1 was replaced by the F.3 with an increase in fuel capacity from 202 to 326 gallons. The F.3 was also provided with two underwing 100-gallon drop tanks, although bigger tanks could be used for ferry flights. Much of our flying was taken up with individual handling, QGH approaches, cine attacks, formation flying, interspersed with major exercises involving bomber forces including Superfortresses of the USAF. It was on one of these (Exercise Foil) that 247 lost its then C.O., Squadron Leader Beddow. I was leading a pair behind him at the time. Whilst taking off from Bentwaters, where we had landed after a previous sortie, some Hornets (the enemy) attacked the airfield and in pursuing them, he entered a high-speed stall and crashed onto a house in Ipswich. Fortunately no-one on the ground was killed, but two children were injured. This incident was another example of how the Vampire could be unforgiving.'

During 1946 four Vampire Is passed through CFE at West Raynham for service trials, a process that was not without mishap. The first aircraft to arrive, TG305 on 7 March, was soon damaged when the wheels were retracted on the ground due to the pilot operating the undercarriage lever instead of the flap lever. A replacement was flown in on 28 March in the form of TG295 but, two weeks later, an engine change was required when its Goblin ingested an airman's hat during run-up and suffered a 'seizure'. Following another engine change due to a cracked impeller blade, a more serious failure occurred which resulted in the impeller breaking up completely and damaging the air intake ducts. TG295 was replaced by TG346 on 18 October but this aircraft lost its hood on its very first trip and was soon heading back to 33 MU at Lyneham for modification work. TG332 was also flown by CFE from 21 July, it also underwent two engine changes, one caused by loose flame-tube attachments in the expansion chambers, the other being the result of another cracked impeller blade.

The CFE findings with regard to general handling, aerobatics and high-speed flight are included in the following extracts from their report on the Vampire I.

'The Vampire is delightfully simple and pleasant to fly but it is slightly unstable in the yawing plane and has a tendency to snake at high speed in bumpy weather. The rudders are very sensitive, especially at high speed, when any slight movement of the rudder pedals causes considerable yaw and introduces momentary high frequency snaking. The elevators are extremely effective and light throughout the speed range above 130mph IAS. If the aircraft is trimmed for straight and level flight, only the normal amount of change of trim is required when entering a dive or a climb. At speeds lower than 130mph elevator control becomes less effective and large stick movements are necessary to effect even a slight change in the attitude of the aircraft. This is particularly noticeable when approaching to land.

Ailerons are light throughout the speed range, though not as positive or effective as desired for a fighter aircraft. In the rolling plane, initial response is immediate, but on further movement of the control column, response is lacking and a good rate of roll cannot be obtained. This is particularly noticeable at low speeds (200–250mph IAS). The best speed for rolls seems to be between 300–350mph IAS and as the speed reaches 400mph IAS the rolling deteriorates and the controls become heavier. During the trials it became apparent that the Vampire suffered from overbalanced ailerons at speeds over 460mph IAS with a tendency for the ailerons to "snatch" at higher speeds. The harmonisation of all three controls is satisfactory, but further development of aileron control is necessary.

The Vampire is a delightful aircraft for aerobatics and all conventional aerobatic manoeuvres are simple to perform, though rather delicate handling of both elevator and rudders are necessary. Rolls should be carried out with the nose well above the horizon, as when the aircraft is inverted there appears to be a definite blanking-off of the slipstream over the elevator, which necessitates a large forward movement of the control column to keep the nose from dropping. Increased pressure on the rudder must not be used to hasten the latter part of the roll, as this may bring on a high-speed stall.

When carrying out tight turning manoeuvres at high speed, particularly near the ground, the pilot must be prepared for the effects of high acceleration. In this aircraft high "g" is apparently easy to reach owing to high speed and manoeuvrability and is felt by the pilot more than in any previous operational aircraft. It is considered that a general issue of "g" suits to Vampire squadrons would help to delay the effects and may avoid some accidents. When the dive brakes are used, considerable buffeting and momentary change of the aircraft's attitude occurs. The reduction in speed when the dive brakes are applied is very slight and it is considered that their effectiveness could be improved.

The stalling speeds (IAS) for the Vampire are

	Goblin I	Goblin II
U/c and flaps Up	95mph	102mph
U/c and flaps Down	78–80mph	85mph

There is adequate warning in the form of buffeting when the aircraft approaches the stall. If the control column is held back at the stall the starboard wing will drop quite sharply, but can easily be picked up with opposite rudder. Recovery is normal and extremely simple. The high-speed stall is quite vicious and the aircraft tends to flick, but here again ample warning is given by control buffeting and juddering.

No compressibility effects are noticeable until a Mach meter reading of 0.73 is reached when there is a very mild nose-down trim change which is easily countered by a slight backward pressure on the control column. At Mach 0.75 general irregular vibration and snaking may be felt throughout the aircraft and also possibly slight lateral rocking. Between Mach 0.75–0.77 a quick irregular pitching oscillation or "porpoising" occurs, the "g" varying between zero and +3.5. This motion cannot be checked by use of the elevator but is not dangerous because, once porpoising sets in, the aircraft automatically tends to pull out and will only continue porpoising if held in the dive. Stick forces at high Mach number are light. The behaviour varied somewhat from one aircraft to another, there might be vibration without porpoising and vice versa, but compressibility effects nearly always occurred between Mach 0.75–0.77. The limiting Mach number is 0.75 but should this limit be inadvertently exceeded, the aeroplane will tend to recover of its own accord.'

In addition to discussing handling characteristics, the report also commented on various other aspects of Vampire operations and was particularly critical of the cockpit layout when it came to instrument and bad-weather flying. When sitting in the normal position it was found that the directional gyro was obscured by the control column and, although this became visible in turns, the altimeter or turn and slip then disappeared from view depending on which way the stick was moved. The fuel gauges were also found to be partially concealed by the stick and the thickness of the windscreen frames badly reduced visibility, a situation which was made even worse when flying in rain.

During testing of the Vampire I, the opportunity was taken to compare it with the Meteor III. The Vampire was found to be faster at all heights, the advantage ranging from 25mph at sea level, to 50mph at 30,000ft. During acceleration tests, the aircraft were flow in line abreast at a speed of 170mph IAS and then subjected to full throttle. ASI readings were taken after two minutes with the following results:

Height	Vampire I	Meteor III
Sea level	460mph IAS	418mph IAS
10,000ft	395mph IAS	346mph IAS
20,000ft	325mph IAS	220mph IAS

The figures shown above are those for the Goblin I-powered Vampire.

During decelerations, the Vampire gradually fell behind the Meteor when both aircraft were operated in the clean configuration, but when airbrakes were opened, the Meteor immediately decelerated much more quickly, so that after thirty seconds it was approximately 200 yards behind the Vampire. To evaluate dive performance, both aircraft were flown at 8,000ft at 250mph IAS and dived at thirty degrees with throttles fully open. There was no noticeable gain with the Vampire powered by the Goblin I, but that fitted with the Goblin II gradually drew ahead. At 2,500ft the Meteor had to be throttled back as it had reached its limiting speed of 500mph IAS (35mph lower than the corresponding figure for the Vampire). For assessment of zoom climbs, the aircraft were dived to 4,000ft (420mph IAS) and were then opened up to full throttle and put into a forty-degree climb. The climb was then stopped as speed fell through 210mph IAS by which time height was approximately 10,000ft. At this point the positioning of both aircraft was the same, although tests with the Goblin II Vampire showed it to have gained about 500ft.

When it came to turning circles the Vampire was superior at all speeds, despite the wingloading of the two aircraft being practically equal. With the Meteor positioned on the Vampire's tail, it was found that the latter could reverse

Vampire F.1 TG442 of No. 203 AFS Driffield.

the situation in only one and a half turns. In terms of rate of roll, the pair were evenly matched, the Vampire being slightly superior at all speeds when rolling to the right, but slightly inferior when rolling to the left. Although rates of roll were much the same, this was achieved despite the aircraft having very different characteristics in terms of lateral control. The Meteor's ailerons were heavy to operate, but positive, whereas the Vampire's were much lighter but there was a tendency for its ailerons to become less effective as the roll was continued.

Overall, the Vampire I (Goblin I) matched the Meteor III in dives up to 500mph IAS, zoom climbs at maximum power and rates of roll, and had shown itself to be markedly better in level speed at all altitudes, accelerations and rates of turn. The Goblin II powered Vampire proved superior in all tactical manoeuvres and it was concluded that it should have no difficulty in obtaining a decisive position.

In total, 136 Vampire Is were built and in addition to equipping the Odiham Wing, they were also used by Nos. 3, 5 and 20 Squadrons. The Vampire's simplicity meant that it was an ideal means of bringing the Royal Auxiliary Air Force into the jet age and it entered service with 605 (County of Warwick) Squadron on 3 July 1948 to be followed by 501, 600, 608 and 613 Squadrons. The first attempt to improve the basic Vampire design resulted in the F.3 which was developed to Specification F.3/47 and featured increased internal tankage (plus the ability to carry 100- or 200-gallon drop tanks), a redesigned rear end with lowered tailplane, and a return to the traditional de Havilland practice of using curved vertical surfaces. Vampire F.3 production for the RAF ran to 117, all manufactured by English Electric at Preston, and it was to remain in service until late 1952.

In 1948 the opportunity arose for Vampires to take part in the annual RAF goodwill mission to the USA and in July pilots from the Odiham Wing (54, 72 and 247 Squadrons) became the first to fly the Atlantic in jet-powered aircraft.

47

The formation was led by Squadron Leader Bobby Oxspring DFC and had navigation back-up from two Mosquitos, with a third, flown by Wing Commander Harold 'Micky' Martin DSO DFC of Dambusters fame, relaying meteorological information. The route was via Stornoway, Keflavik (Iceland), Bluie West One (Greenland) and Goose Bay. Despite the Vampire F.3's increased tankage, fuel margins were critical and there was the ever-present hazard of canopy icing to contend with during the long, slow descents from 30,000ft. In the event the RAF made it into the record books by the smallest of margins as the USAF were simultaneously attempting the same feat from the opposite direction with Lockheed F-80s. The Vampires eventually beat the Americans (led by Colonel Schilling) by a single leg.

With the clearance to use larger overload fuel tanks on the F.3, it was, perhaps, inevitable that consideration would be given to the carriage of bombs and rockets to give the Vampire a ground-attack capability. Trials were carried out with a Vampire I (TG444) which had square cut wingtips of reduced span and this led to the FB.5 with thicker wing-skinning and strong-points capable of uplifting 2,000lb of stores. To cater for increased all-up weight the undercarriage was modified to allow a longer stroke.

In June 1948 a series of tactical trials were carried out by CFE to assess the Vampire's suitability to the ground-attack role but as no FB.5s had flown at that time, simulated close-support sorties were conducted with four F.3s. The Vampire was found to be well suited to the task with good cockpit visibility (except in rain), and excellent manoeuvrability. Refuelling and rearming was straightforward and could be completed in twenty minutes and it was also considered that the aircraft would be easy to operate from narrow forward strips. With a ten knot headwind the Vampire was airborne in about 600 yards at an all-up weight of 10,000lb (without external stores) and the average landing run was 900 yards at an a.u.w of 8,000lb. However, it was noted that during operations from non-paved surfaces the ground deteriorated rapidly with ruts forming behind the jet orifice. Grass quickly became burnt during taxiing, these marks being easily visible from the air.

Dives were carried out to simulate rocket and bomb attacks during which the Vampire was steady and stable and showed no tendency to 'snake' as speed built up. This situation was not affected by operating the dive brakes which were used between 310–400kt. There was very little 'mush' in the pull out, and stick forces were light. When dive brakes were closed upon reaching weapon release height, the acceleration at 9,700rpm was good. Targets were approached either at 5–8,000ft or low level, and the following assessment was made:

'The best method for a simulated RP attack (from 5–8,000ft) is to approach in finger four formation and, when the target is sighted, to change formation to echelon port or starboard so that the leader is nearest to the target. The leader should pass over the area with the target under his port or starboard wingtip, the target then being at his eight o'clock or four o'clock. This gives a turn-in angle of about 120 degrees and a dive of between 25–30 degrees. For a dive-bombing attack the target should pass under the wing level with the boom giving an angle of dive of 40–50 degrees. Dive brakes should be extended as the turn is commenced. Breakaway should be carried out either at low level or by a zoom climbing turn, both of which seem to be effective. Using the above method the time that the formation appears to be vulnerable to AA fire from the target area is 30–40 seconds with a low breakaway and 50–60 seconds with a zoom climb.

A low-level approach and breakaway appeared to be very effective in achieving tactical surprise. The method used was to pick up an easily identified landmark between 1,000–3,000 yards from the target area and aim to commence the climb to attack height at that point. One minute before the ETA at the landmark, speed was increased from 320kt to 400kt in order to obtain a steep angle of climb. At the top of the climb (3–4,000ft) the formation turned into the target, carried out the attack and broke away at low level on the reciprocal of the approach track. It was not necessary to use dive brakes with this attack as the IAS at the commencement of the dive was about 260kt. The aircraft were seldom sighted from the target area until they were climbing to attack height. The time that the formation appeared to be vulnerable from the target area was 15–25 seconds. It was found that experienced pilots could navigate at low level at the cruising speed of the Vampire 3 (320kt) provided that meticulous pre-flight planning and briefing was carried out. However, pilots without previous low-level navigational experience had difficulty in locating targets.'

Although the Vampire FB.5 was to be used primarily as a ground-attack aircraft, it was also tasked with carrying out interceptions at all heights up to 40,000ft and further trials were carried out at CFE to ascertain its suitability in this role. Climbs were carried out to 40,000ft at the recommended power setting of 9,700rpm but the time taken (thirty minutes) was deemed to be wholly unacceptable. Only when full power was used (10,200rpm) was the time improved to seventeen minutes. With long-range tanks fitted it took twenty-three minutes to reach 30,000ft at 9,700rpm by which time the rate of climb had fallen to 500ft/min. By using maximum power 35,000ft could be attained in twenty minutes, the recommended climbing speeds being 280kt IAS reducing to 190kt.

The method of descent depended on whether time or range was the critical factor. If a pilot wanted to lose height as quickly as possible, the recommended technique was to throttle fully back, open dive brakes and descend initially at Mach 0.65 (200kt IAS) reducing to Mach 0.50 (295kt IAS) at 10,000ft and 4,000ft/min thereafter. By this method the descent from 40,000ft could be accomplished in seven minutes (with its superior dive brakes, a Meteor could be on the ground in five minutes). When maximum range was required the best method was to close the throttle and glide at 190kt which resulted in an average descent rate of 1,300ft/min and a ground distance covered of 160 miles. In a glide from high altitude, pilots experienced considerable discomfort through cold.

The ailerons on the FB.5 were found to be somewhat lighter than on the Vampire 3, a factor which was particularly noticeable at high altitude. As a result of clipping the wings the rate of roll was also much improved and it was considered that the Vampire was now superior to any contemporary fighter in this respect. Rate of turn was excellent and at 5,000ft radius of turn was three-eighths of a mile and at 35,000ft, one mile. Comparative figures for the Meteor were one mile and 1.7 mile respectively.

During comparative tests with a Meteor 4, the Vampire 5 was noted to be slower at all heights, the deficit ranging from 27mph at sea level to 13mph at 40,000ft. Acceleration was also not as good and the Vampire took from 30–60 seconds longer to accelerate to maximum speed. On the plus side, the Vampire handled much more pleasantly at high altitude, was more stable fore and aft, and was considerably less tiring to fly. As with the Meteor, the Vampire suffered considerably from internal cockpit misting and icing at altitude. The severity of the icing varied with the time that the aircraft had been flown at high altitude and the rapidity of the descent. Under the worst conditions all the windscreen panels became entirely covered with a hard, persistent coat of ice and the perspex canopy misted over as quickly as it could be wiped away. Ice, which formed inside the canopy, persisted for at least five minutes after reaching low altitude, a worrying situation when fuel reserves were likely to be getting low.

The CFE report concluded with an assessment of the Vampire 5 and Meteor 4 as regards air combat:

'In combats between the Meteor and Vampire, the better manoeuvrability and lighter controls of the latter were most evident and resulted in gaining the initiative in a short time at all heights. Combat commenced at 40,000ft had to be of a very gentle character and even under these conditions the aircraft very soon lost height to medium levels. During combat at 25,000ft from a head-on approach, the Vampire very soon got on the tail of the Meteor and found no difficulty in staying there regardless of the Meteor turning at maximum rate and lowering flaps and air brakes. The combat was joined at 300kt IAS and was eventually broken off at 180kt IAS. When the Meteor was allowed to position itself in firing range astern of the Vampire, the latter was able to shake it off and be astern of the Meteor in about two turns. There was no doubt also that the Vampire pilot was not called upon to exert himself to such an extent as was the Meteor pilot.

The Vampire 5 provides a very steady gun platform when flying straight through the whole of the speed range up to 0.76 Indicated Mach with no noticeable signs of aim wander. In accurate turns up to rate 2 at those speeds, the sight platform is still steady and tracking and ranging are straightforward, but the slightest inaccuracies or "ham-footedness" induces considerable "snaking" which is similar to, but less pronounced, than that experienced on the Meteor. Although difficult to damp out, it is easier than on the Meteor. If care is not taken this "snaking" occurs in straight flight immediately following a quick recovery from turns and may occur to a progressively lesser extent down to Mach 0.65. Even at high speeds the elevators remain very sensitive and precision flying is necessary in order to keep an accurate sight.

As altitude is increased the maximum turning rate deteriorates in direct relation to the maximum loading that can be imposed in a turn and around

30,000ft this figure is 3g compared with the Meteor's 2.6g. The Vampire's manoeuvrability at altitude allows it to attack at greater angles off than the Meteor and follow a smaller curve of pursuit. Between 25–30,000ft at angles greater than thirty degrees, the Meteor was unable to continue a steady curve of pursuit and a "fly through" resulted. The Vampire 5 however, can achieve good results up to angles of about fifty degrees and the breakaway can be a good deal more rapid particularly at lower altitudes.

With its better manoeuvrability and better handling at slower speeds, the Vampire has several advantages over the Meteor on the head-on attack. The initial turn is of less radius and need not be carried out so far ahead of the bombers, as the better manoeuvrability facilitates the positioning for a true head-on shot, and the closing speed is not as great. The stick forces are considerably less on the Vampire and the breakaway can be carried out safely at a closer range. However, if a repeat attack is to be made, the Vampire is naturally at a disadvantage when overtaking the bombers due to its slower speed and acceleration, but this is partly compensated for by the ability to carry out a high rate turn immediately after passing over the bomber at the conclusion of a head-on attack.'

One of the many problems that had to be faced by the first generation of jet jockeys was the fact that their aircraft suffered a basic lack of endurance which, allied with inadequate navigational facilities, meant that flight into worsening weather conditions could be an extremely hazardous operation. Since its introduction into RAF service, the Vampire had attracted interest from a number of foreign air forces including Italy's *Aeronautica Militare.* Eventually a total of eighty-two FB.52As were produced under licence by Fiat in Turin and Macchi in Varese, but while the deal was still being finalised it was thought that a visit by a formation of RAF Vampires would help negotiations by showing the Italians just what the aircraft was capable of. Consequently 73 Squadron, based at Takali in Malta, were tasked with sending five FB.5s to Rome's Ciampino airport.

On the morning of the 23 September 1949 the five Vampires took off from Ciampino to fly to Milan (Malpensa), a distance of approximately 275nm. Problems began when the lead aircraft suffered R/T failure en route and as Milan was approached weather conditions deteriorated considerably with cloud base down to 1,500ft and a visibility of around 1nm. Having flown an orbit of the city, the aircraft set course for Malpensa but were unable to locate the airfield due to haze. A second attempt was made but despite circling for twenty minutes, the airfield could still not be found. By now fuel reserves were insufficient to make for the alternate at Linate and all five Vampires crash-landed out of fuel to the south of Brescia. Happily no one was injured, but four of the aircraft (VT809, VT813, VT855 and VV204) were complete write-offs. The sole survivor (VF345) was repaired and taken to Bergamo airfield for an air test on 17 October. Perhaps sensing something, a large crowd of Italians gathered to watch. They were not to be disappointed. At the conclusion of the air test the Vampire careered off the end of the runway and was damaged beyond repair! (73

Vampire FB.5s of No. 226 OCU in the hangar at Stradishall.

Squadron went one better on 23 December 1954 when six Venom FB.1s were either crash-landed or abandoned due to bad weather encountered in Iraq.)

Notwithstanding flight in bad weather, with only one engine and no re-light system, any in-flight failure had to be the Vampire pilot's major concern. Pilot Officer John Jennings, who began flying the FB.5 with 247 Squadron in late 1949, suffered two flame outs in the space of a few months.

'The first Vampire 5 was received in November 1949 and I flew an acceptance air test on the 8th. On 16 December I was part of a formation of six aircraft tasked to fly in "snake" formation – pairs separated by a number of seconds who then climb through cloud and (hopefully!) come out above cloud in line-astern still separated by the initial interval. The cloud base was approximately 1,800ft at Odiham with tops forecast at 30,000ft. Unfortunately the tops proved to be nearer 35,000ft and we had almost joined up as a six in formation when my engine decided to quit. I decided to bail out and released my straps whilst at the same time calling my C.O. who was leading. I informed him of my intention. "Don't do that", he quickly rejoined, "nobody has bailed out of a Vampire successfully".

Subsiding back into my seat, and trying to maintain attitude and correct gliding speed (175kt), whilst at the same time trying to re-secure my harness, I considered the prospect of maintaining attitude (with failing instruments) through 33,000ft of cloud. Fortunately the cloud type at this altitude was of the kind that permitted two of my companions to formate on me and while I concentrated on keeping the correct speed, they made radio contact and, by signals, helped me to keep my attitude and turn onto headings as directed. I broke cloud at about 1,800ft in the vicinity of Tangmere by which time I was completely iced up – almost ¾–1in. all over the screens. However, I opened the hood and made a wheels-down landing on the Tangmere runway. Apart from some minor damage to the tyres, the aircraft was in one piece and after the engine was repaired, I flew the same aircraft back to Odiham four days later.

In March 1950 I started a new tour with 72 Squadron at North Weald and was chosen as No. 2 in the aerobatic team being formed by the C.O., Squadron Leader Don Kingaby DFM. This team subsequently did a number of demonstrations including a tour of Luxembourg/Belgium and was the first team to roll five aircraft in Vic. The team eventually flew seven in formation. On 27 April whilst returning to North Weald at low level after a pairs cine exercise, I again had engine failure. Surrendering speed for height, I cast around and spotted Chipping Ongar, a WW II airfield, in reasonable proximity. Once again I made a wheels down forced landing, the only real difficulty being the avoidance of a three-ton lorry on the beginning of the runway which, I subsequently discovered, had just turned up to paint white crosses on the runway to show that the airfield was disused!'

By now the Vampire was in service with a number of Advanced Flying Schools to provide realistic training for first-line fighter squadrons and this was where P2 Bob Hillard had his first taste of jet-powered flight:

'I first got close to a jet aircraft at 203 AFS at Driffield when, making my way to Flying Wing to report, I passed my first Vampire which I know now had had a wet-start and the fuel had been more or less drained from the jet-pipe. I did not expect the sheet of flame that appeared during the re-start. This, I thought, must be normal so what was I letting myself in for? At 203 one first had to convert to the Meteor 7, solo on it, and then go on to either the Meteor 4, or the Vampire I. There was something delightfully solid about the Meteor and I quite enjoyed the early part of the course. The Vampire was a complete anti-climax and I found it hard to believe that this could be a fighter, particularly during the take off where it seemed to trundle gently down the runway taking ages to get up to speed.

On one of the early Vampire sorties it seemed about time to find out about this compressibility I had been hearing about, so I set off luftwards to a reasonable height. Leaving the throttle wide open, I started a dive and watched the Mach number increase. The trim changed, becoming quite tail heavy. As Pilot's Notes suggested that different machines reacted in different ways it was a case of waiting to see what happened. Even so, I was startled by the sudden oscillations, quite violent I thought, sufficiently so as to make it hard to grab throttle and airbrakes, which were eventually used and normal flying was resumed. I don't think I had been authorised for that particular exercise and, having done it once, I could not see any value in repeating it.

On 21 November 1949 I was authorised to take Vampire F.I VF309/F for an aerobatic session but as I headed into the wild blue, I realised that I had not looked up the speeds for rolls and loops. Working on the principle that all was possible with plenty of speed, I did a few rolls and found the Vampire to be quite pleasant. As you can never have too much airspeed to do a loop, I stuffed the nose down, put on full chat, and when

Bob Hillard in cockpit of Vampire F.1 with F/L 'Nobby' Clarke.

the airspeed approached 400 hauled back on the pole and was gratified to find the ground above my head. I would guess that my upwards path may have been quite a leisurely one, as the speed at the top appeared to be rather low so a gentle tweak back should have put the ground back where it ought to be, under the aircraft. The gentle tweak, however, was not gentle enough and I was into my first Vampire spin. With recovery in mind, and as the good book recommended, it was a case of opposite rudder and stick forward at which point there was a judder and away it went in the opposite direction. This time I relaxed somewhat and took it easy on the controls with subsequent recovery. The Vampire could certainly be a feisty little beast if not handled absolutely correctly!'

The Vampire FB.5 served in limited numbers with regular units in the U.K., and became standard equipment for many R.Aux.A.F. squadrons. It was also a common sight in Germany and began to replace ageing Mosquitos in the fighter-bomber role in 2nd Tactical Air Force from early 1949, eventually equipping a total of fifteen squadrons including Number 4 Squadron which converted in July 1950 at Wunstorf. Pilot Officer Iain Dick recalls his introduction to the Vampire and some of the flying he carried out in the early 1950s:

'Remembering that we were an operational squadron "in the field", our conversion from our precious Mosquito FB.6s was really a hoot. Two instructors, Flt Lt Joe Crawshaw and a Canadian Flt Lt came over from CFS, Little Rissington. We borrowed a Meteor 7, had a few lectures on jet engine handling, had three dual trips in the Meteor and a solo trip, were handed Pilot's Notes for the Vamp and told to go off and sort it out. That was it. We flew the FB.5 which were modified to carry 8 x 60lb rockets fitted on zero-length rails under the engine intakes. Unfortunately, when firing the upper pair (they were tiered), the fins tended to cut a neat groove along the skin so a bar was fitted between the front and rear launchers. This became known as the "Trenchard Boom".

I found the Vampire an easy and exciting kite to fly at any speed. The first flight in a newly delivered aircraft was a slow, staged climb with a level flight of a few minutes every 3,000ft or so to "cook" the hood to get it used to the cold, otherwise it was liable to crack. For low-level practice attacks we flew a spaced-back finger four, ten or fifteen feet laterally, but some fifty yards longitudinally. The attack itself would go something like this – approach the target at 180 degrees to one side, just pass about half a mile, leader pulls up HARD, a few seconds later No. 2 pulls up HARD, wing-over 180 degrees, bead on target (lead aircraft still in the sights!), No. 1 fires and pulls away FAST, once clear, adjust aim, fire and get out fast, formate on No. 1 and circle for 3 and 4 to catch up. It was quite effective with the possibility of sixteen rockets per four aircraft attack being delivered in some sixty seconds. We used to fire at derelict tanks and I recall one occasion when a rocket hit the gun barrel and bent it. Another hit the turret ring and flipped the turret off the hull, and that with concrete heads!

Two particular trips stand out in my memory. On one occasion our boss (Sqn Ldr C.P.N. Newman DFC) had had a "thing" with an opposite number at Gütersloh so one dark night when Gütersloh had a dining-in night, we took off in a formation of (I think) twelve aircraft (not easy at night) and flew very low over Gütersloh mess releasing masses of toilet roll sheets that had been clamped in our flaps. The Groupie at Güt was not amused by the snow storm of bog sheets all over his field!

The other concerned our Flight Commander, Flt Lt Reggie Benwell who thought he would try a snake-climb in pairs, thirty seconds between pairs, of eight aircraft. I was his No. 2. Cloud was solid from 2,000ft to 25,000ft. At the top we would orbit while the other three pairs joined up, do some formation then peel off in pairs for a snake descent to base. Just as Reg was about to give the order to start the descent, a gap in the cloud appeared so he called to cancel the snake and go down as an eight-ship formation, airbrakes out and straight down. Unfortunately he was heading north and as we broke out of the bottom of the cloud there ahead was what appeared to be a disused grass airfield. "Where are we, No. 2?" he called. "No idea, leader, but suggest we steer 265 degrees to base" I replied. Some time later base appeared on the nose. On landing he asked "If you didn't know where we were, how did you know it was 265 degrees to base?" "Instincts of a homing pigeon" I said – which I really did have – "I wasn't going to tell you where we really were over the air as we were only a few miles west of Berlin!" Despite our incursion deep into the Soviet zone, the Russians never complained or retaliated.'

Iain Dick also experienced engine failure in a Vampire, although in his particular case it came at the worst possible time:

'The boss had arranged for a squadron "strike" on a friendly Army convoy but we were not sure as to its exact location. Flt Lt Roger Collins and I were detailed to find the convoy, pinpoint it while the others were at lunch, return to base, brief the rest, then go for our lunch. The area was northwest of base and it was very wide so Roger and I split it in two for quicker checking. My own aircraft WA119 (UP-M) was undergoing maintenance so I was allocated a recycled machine just delivered from a U.K. MU, WA145, lettered "J", which Reg Benwell had decided would be his. The Vamp was liable to "wet-start" where the plugs were flooded with fuel

WA119 of No. 4 Squadron being refuelled.

before they could light up, and "J" wet-started so Roger went off alone. I followed a few minutes later.

Most of the trees in Germany are coniferous, and from above, you can't see a thing below, so to spot hidden trucks I decided to have a look underneath. I was bombing across this field about 10–15 feet up and some 250kt when the engine wound down. I shot up but only made about 300ft (the minimum height for a free-fall parachute drop was given as 400ft). No bang seats then of course – or bone dome. From that height there was not much choice for a field, the largest one had the River Weser at the far end. I called "Mayday" and set about putting the kite down but made two mistakes, I forgot to ditch the hood and missed the hydraulics. I skimmed across the field but a couple of feet up at the far end was a banking which I hit. The impact broke the two bottom engine bolts which flipped the engine over my right shoulder, luckily as the fibre-board seat collapsed under me. With the harness now slack I was thrown into the gunsight which impacted with my head, and my teeth with the stick. At this point I lost all interest in the proceedings.

With the C.G. now well forward, the kite skated across the river, up the other banking shedding parts and coming to rest a few hundred yards from a German shepherd who had spent the war in the *Luftwaffe* Medical Corps fishing crews out of pranged aircraft! He and his mates got me out (the canopy was so distorted that it just pushed off), wrapped me in my parachute, poured coffee down my throat and waited. The ambulance with police motor-bike escort raced through the middle of Hannover in the rush hour to the Army hospital there. The docs, not used to flying casualties, gave me ten minutes to live! I came to a fortnight later – so ended my operational career. The Court of Inquiry decided "pilot error" but the

Engineering Officer at base thought otherwise and spent a weekend dismantling the engine. He found the cause – a badly fitted split-pin that held the fuel pump in contact with the engine drive had sheared and wrecked the fuel pump. No pump – no fuel – no power – no more flight. And the kite had just come out of major maintenance. Reg was lucky.'

Another 2 TAF unit, 14 Squadron, converted from Mosquitos at Celle in early 1951 and shortly afterwards moved to Fassberg, which was to be its home for the next four years. It was commanded by Squadron Leader R.A. 'Maxie' Sutherland, a former Typhoon pilot who had a reputation for being somewhat uncompromising, both in the air and on the ground. Although operating a completely new type of aircraft, the monthly target of 195 flying hours was soon exceeded with pilots being given plenty of practice in snake climbs, battle formation, section attacks and cine gun work, together with QGH approaches. One of the advantages of operating from Fassberg was its proximity to the nearby weapons range which allowed pilots to be over the target within five minutes of taking off. This, however, was to be the location for the squadron's first fatal accident with the Vampire when Flight Lieutenant P.F. Wingate crashed in VV538 during live rocketing on 8 June. It was thought that the crash may have been caused by the port ammunition door springing open in flight and shattering the cockpit, as the door and pieces of canopy were found some distance from the main wreckage.

For the rest of the year practice was interspersed with a number of exercises including *Spica* in August which saw the unit's Vampires fly to Oslo via Sylt. In the same month Exercise *Stopgap* required a minimum of twenty sorties to be flown each day in liaison with the Army, a figure that was easily achieved. Other highlights included a formation flypast over Le Bourget and Paris, high level exercises to attack targets in Holland and Belgium, and two detachments to the U.K., operations being flown from Aston Down and Wattisham. The only other major incident in the year occurred on 26 November when two aircraft collided during practice interceptions, WA109 landing safely at Wunstorf with WA169 being written off in a bellylanding at Fassberg. Both pilots escaped without injury.

In January 1952 a three-week detachment to Sylt was undertaken for air-to-air and air-to-ground firing. The average score was 6.2% on a 180kt tow, and 5.3% when the tow speed was raised to 220kt. Despite the fact that all aircraft were parked outside, the gun stoppage rate was 1 in 1,872 rounds, an all time record. Sadly, Pilot Officer E.S. Harbison, who had only been with the squadron for five days, was killed on 21 January when he spun into the sea in VV443 while making a practice attack. Although the flying target remained unchanged, 310 hours were flown in March mainly due to participation in Exercise *Skandia II* which involved operating from Schleswig, together with one flight from 2 Squadron (Meteor FR.9), 274 Squadron RDAF (Meteor F.8) and half of 16 Squadron (Vampire FB.5). Towards the end of the month "battle flight" was also carried out, entailing army co-op sorties with the 7th Armoured Division at Munster and the interception of USAF B-50s and RAF Lincolns.

Long-range high-level navigation sorties were flown in April (day and night) using either Hawkinge and Lille or Tangmere and Wahn as turning points and on 24 April the squadron simulated a raid on London during Exercise *Terrier*. The month also saw the first use of napalm when Wing Commander W.A. Smith, Squadron Leader Sutherland and Flight Lieutenants S.A. Barrett and J. Timilty carried out trials on the Fassberg range. Further tests and a demonstration took place the following month. In June, 14 Squadron detached to Duxford for two weeks, together with 98 Squadron, the Fassberg Wing intercepting large formations of bombers and taking part in a fighter sweep attacking south-east England from France. Towards the end of the month the squadron flew to Gilze-Rijen for Exercise *June Primer*, the Vampires being used mainly in the intruder role with dusk attacks on Wunstorf and Celle, and the escort of USAF F-84s attacking Jever.

Prior to these detachments aircraft strength was increased from eight to sixteen and throughout the month a number of new pilots arrived including nineteen-year-old Pilot Officer Don Headley who joined direct from 202 AFS at Valley.

'The OCUs were full at the time so they took four of us off the jet conversion course at Valley and sent us to see if we could be taught on the squadrons. Of the four, I went to 14, two went to Wunstorf and one went to Celle. The squadrons were not particularly pleased to get us without training, so we had to learn the hard way.

One day, shortly after I arrived "Maxie" Sutherland said "You, I've forgotten what your name is, get your flying kit on, I'm going to teach you low-level battle formation". We went out, got into our aeroplanes and I was still strapping in as he taxied out, so I had to finish off my straps as I followed him to the end of the runway. He had never given me a particular briefing on what we were going to do, so after we got airborne I dropped back a little and out to one side. We were very low and I'll swear that it was one of the few times I've seen a hedge between me and the leader! Then the next thing I knew there was a Vampire, plan view, right in front of me and I had to haul back on the stick to go over the top of him. He straightened up having done his turn and after I had got back down again he came onto the radio to say "That'll teach you when you're too close!" I then dropped back a bit, but he turned away from me which meant that I lagged behind. He called on the radio again and said "You're not guarding my tail". Eventually we went back and landed with me in a high sweat. When we got back to dispersal he put his cap on, lit a Gauloise which he always smoked, and stormed in with me running alongside carrying our parachutes. His final comment to me was "Right then, now you know what low-level battle formation is all about, don't you!" '

In the 1950s, pilots in Germany had virtual freedom of the skies and were not subject to the rules and regulations concerning low flying and noise that restrict their modern day counterparts. This lack of restraint was put to good use by 'Maxie' Sutherland who advocated 'attacking' anything that moved. His

Vampire FB.5s of No. 11 Squadron in echelon starboard.

favourite targets were trains, just as they had been during the latter stages of the Second World War, indeed some took the view that Sutherland had great difficulty in accepting that the war was actually over. The policy of attacking anything seen also resulted in numerous unrehearsed dogfights taking place as rival formations strove to get on each other's tail. On one occasion Flight Lieutenant 'Tim' Timilty was leading four Vampires back to Fassberg at 20,000ft when four Meteors were seen coming in from behind. Waiting until they were almost within range, Timilty announced, 'Conventional looping break, Go,' which sent all four Vampires up into a loop. This particular manoeuvre was news to everyone except the leader and, not surprisingly, all four stalled off the top into a semi-spin. The Meteors were not seen again, presumably because they were taking evasive action to avoid four out-of-control Vampires. Such improvisation was typical of the day and is in marked contrast to the more formal, fully briefed, dogfights of today.

Another facet of operations that had changed little since the war was the requirement to have large numbers of aircraft take off and land again in the shortest time possible. With the increased weight and speed of jet fighters, problems were encountered as Pilot Officer Don Headley recalls:

'When it was our turn to be on duty we used to sit in a Nissen hut at the end of the runway alongside the ORP. If a scramble came the duty bod would fire a Very cartridge in the air and everyone then dashed to their aeroplane which had been left with the straps all ready so that we could leap in and start the engine. It really was a case of every man for himself, there was no calculated 5–10 second gap as there is today, and on take off you missed the slipstream as best you could. We often flew in eights and for landing it was our squadron's aim to have all eight aeroplanes on the runway at once. We would approach the airfield in echelon port for a right-hand circuit and would break at two-second intervals to end up downwind in line astern. Coming round onto finals, inevitably, you hit slipstream and got wing drop. If you tried to pick it up with aileron, this caused the wing to go down even more because of the increase in incidence, so we used to come in kicking on coarse rudder like mad to keep the wings level.'

By July the squadron's monthly task had risen to 272 hours but this was exceeded by a large margin with 400 hours actually being flown. Very little navigation work was carried out as another detachment to Sylt was commenced on 14 July. During the month there were three minor incidents all affecting the same pilot, one case of damage due to debris being thrown up during air-to-ground firing and two bird strikes. In the autumn, 14 Squadron took part in two major exercises, *Holdfast* in September which involved operating under mobile conditions at Wunstorf, and *Ardent* in October when it simulated fast high-altitude bombers during attacks on targets in the U.K. October also saw the departure of 'Maxie' Sutherland, his replacement as C.O. being Squadron Leader Reggie Benwell. For the rest of the year flying was severely curtailed by bad weather with only 115 hours being possible in November and 172 hours in December.

In January 1953 a number of sorties were flown against the 5th Royal Tank Corps who were 'dismounted' and were carrying out infantry exercises south of the Hone range. Unfortunately for them, their ability to blend into the countryside was compromised by the lighting of camp fires which produced large amounts of smoke that quickly revealed the position of their RHQ. Rocketing trials were also carried out on the range at Fassberg to assess the effectiveness of

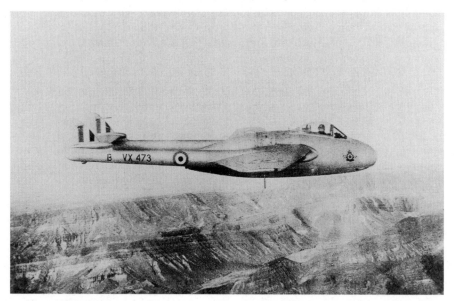

VX473 of No. 249 Squadron.

shallow and steep angles of dive, some sorties being flown with live heads. During the month one aircraft had its canopy disintegrate causing minor damage to the tailplane but there was another fatality when Pilot Officer K.D. Howe died after a crash-landing in WA206 on 23 February following engine failure.

Most training sorties were flown with 100-gallon drop tanks on the under-wing hard-points but, due to one of the Vampire's own particular quirks, the undercarriage had to be raised as soon as possible after take off when operating in this configuration. Pilot Officer Don Headley explains why:

'When we flew with wing tanks on we occasionally had problems getting the undercarriage "D" door to retract and getting the red warning light to go out. The problem was that there was a venturi formed between the "D" door and the wing tank because they were fairly close together so there was quite a bit of suction between the two. The idea was that as soon as you were airborne you would retract the undercarriage as quickly as you could before the speed built up, and you would also lean down and grab hold of the hydraulic pump and would manually pump that to add a bit more power to the hydraulic pressure to get the "D" door up. The unfortunate thing was that next door to the hydraulic pump handle was the jettison lever for the wing tanks and there was more than one case during take off of a pilot leaning down to grab the pump, grabbing the wrong one and jettisoning the wing tanks. On the plus side, at least the "D" door then locked up!'

On one training sortie Don Headley had a lucky escape after suffering from anoxia (now referred to as hypoxia). He was saved by the quick thinking of his section leader, Pilot Officer 'Pat' Bolger.

'Pat and I went up to 25–30,000ft to practise pairs in formation and I remember thinking, "Why is he turning so steeply?" I was having trouble keeping in formation, and then I saw another aeroplane join us. Eventually Pat called me up and said, "Are you feeling alright?" to which I replied, "Yes, fine," and it was then that he realised that something was wrong. He let down rapidly to low level having realised I was suffering from anoxia. The effects are rather like drunkeness, you gradually become over-confident and lose your coordination. You can also get double vision, and even now I can still remember seeing that other aeroplane in formation which was actually just double vision. In my case I came back to normal without realising it and it was only when we debriefed on the ground that I discovered what had happened. They checked the aeroplane throughout, couldn't find anything wrong with it so I got a hell of a rocket for not doing my oxygen tube up properly. They couldn't actually prove anything, but then again I couldn't positively remember having checked it.'

A return was made to Sylt in March but the four week detachment was disrupted by barostat problems, one failure occurring in the air and two shortly before take off. As a result all aircraft were grounded, flying only recommencing after the Easter break and several air tests. Following a two-week deployment to

Filton, 14 Squadron returned to Fassberg on 5 May and later in the month welcomed Squadron Leader J.T. Lawrence as its new C.O.

By now the days of the Vampire FB.5 were nearly over as the squadron began to receive the first examples of the Venom FB.1. Total Vampire hours for June still amounted to 327 however, Pilot Officer P.J. Fitzgerald successfully force-landing WA193 on 18 June after engine failure. Two other incidents were recorded, WG845 suffering brake failure on the runway which caused it to over-shoot (Cat 5), and VV628 hit a flock of birds during low flying (Cat 3). In July the squadron took part in Exercise *Coronet* from Gütersloh but the amount of flying was limited and consisted mainly of intercepting F-84s and performing area patrols. This proved to be the Vampire's swan song and during August most were ferried to other squadrons and MUs.

Within the next six months the Vampire virtually disappeared from the skies over Germany to be replaced by the Venom FB.1 and Sabre F.4. Its manoeu-vrability and light stick forces had made it a delight to fly and, with the attitudes of the time, pilots had been able to utilise its low-level performance to the full. Flying Officer J.R. Pintches, who flew with 234 Squadron at Oldenburg, recalls some of the pranks that were inflicted on the long-suffering German public and fellow RAF personnel:

'In Germany in 1953 there were very few rules and regulations which meant that you could fly very low indeed. One of the tricks played by some of our pilots was to fly down canal tow paths and surprise the odd cyclist, then pull up to see if he had fallen into the canal. Another popular game was to fly low and fast over the lake where the RAF Germany yacht club was situated. If you were lucky, you could blow a yacht over and leave the crew stranded in the water!'

The Vampire FB.5/9 was to continue in service with the R.Aux.A.F., but the disbandment of the Auxiliaries in 1957 also saw the retirement of single-seat

VZ304 of No. 249 Squadron at Deversoir.

Vampires from first-line duties. The familiar whistle of the Goblin engine was, however, to be heard for another decade thanks to the T.11 advanced trainer. Development of the two-seat DH.115 Vampire was carried out by de Havilland as a private venture and was based on the DH.113 Vampire NF.10 (*see* Chapter 8). The prototype (G-5-7) was built at Christchurch and was displayed in the static park at the 1950 Farnborough Air Show before its first flight which took place on 15 November. Carrying the serial number WW456, the aircraft was evaluated by pilots of 204 AFS at Swinderby and also by the staff of the Central Gunnery School at Leconfield, and in early 1952 it was announced that the Vampire T.11 was to be ordered as the RAF's standard advanced trainer.

The introduction of the Vampire into Training Command represented a radical departure from what had gone before as trainee pilots were to be introduced to jet-powered flight at a much earlier stage in their tuition. Previously, pilots had gained their wings on the Prentice and Harvard (later Balliol) piston-engined trainers, before moving onto Meteor T.7s at Advanced Flying Schools. The new sequence allowed for 120 hours on the Percival Provost T.1 to be followed by 110 hours on the Vampire T.11, after which a successful student would be awarded his wings. As a result of the revised training programme, Advanced Flying Schools were disbanded and pilots went directly to OCUs which formed the link between Flying Training Schools and first-line squadrons. Number 5 FTS at Oakington was chosen to introduce the new system and the first course to use the Vampire T.11 for its advanced flying commenced in May 1954.

The first aircraft to be delivered to Oakington featured a number of modifications to the original design, including a one-piece clear view canopy in place of the original heavily framed, top-hinged hood as copied from the DH.113, a centrally mounted blind-flying panel instead of individual panels as fitted previously, and long curving dorsal fillets to improve directional stability. Apart from the first few aircraft, all Vampire T.11s were fitted with ejector seats, an achievement that de Havilland were unable to match with the Vampire NF.10 and Venom NF.2/3 night fighters. Total production of the Vampire T.11 amounted to 804, of which 535 went to the RAF.

The Vampire trainer proved to be popular with instructors and students alike, its side-by-side seating mirrored that of the Provost (and later Jet Provost) so that initial conversion was carried out more efficiently, and performance and handling were the equivalent of the single-seat fighter. Flight Lieutenant Bruce Spurr flew the T.11 with CFS at Little Rissington and recalls its behaviour in the spin and a unique aerobatic manoeuvre he discovered quite by chance:

'There was very little difference between the T.11 and the FB.5. The ailerons were slightly heavier on the T.11 but it was only noticeable if one looked for it. The single-seat aircraft were certainly more comfortable because of the greater room and also because they didn't have ejector seats.

Intentional spinning was initially prohibited on all Marks, but around 1954 the T.11 was cleared for spinning and was part of the syllabus when I was instructing on the staff at CFS. The spin was accompanied by buffeting and the rate of rotation would fluctuate, as would the pitch of the aircraft. Usually as the nose of the aircraft came up the rate of rotation would slow, and increase as the nose dropped. The reason for this is analogous to a skater doing a spin on ice, bringing the arms in to the body to use inertia to speed up the rotation. Normal spin recovery action was usually effective.

On one occasion after completing an air test on a T.11 which had required a climb to 42,000ft to check pressurisation, I attempted to loop the aircraft from 40,000ft. Naturally I ran completely out of airspeed before I was completely inverted at the top of the loop (48,000ft showing on the altimeter). Keeping the power on caused the high-revving engine to act as a gyroscope with, initially, torque reaction starting the aircraft to roll around the engine. The roll started very slowly, and only because at near zero airspeed there was little resistance to what bit of torque came from the engine, which had to be at near max rpm. Suspended as it were with zero gravity near the zenith of the attempted loop, a push from a finger would be enough to displace the aircraft. This was followed by precessional forces causing other gyrations which can best be described as "tumbling" as the aircraft tried to stabilise itself as its downward vertical speed began to increase. On further attempts the same thing happened if power was kept on, but if the throttle was closed the aircraft just fell backwards into a straight dive.'

Flight Lieutenant Brian Carroll flew Vampire FB.5/9s and T.11s as a QFI with 7 FTS at Valley.

'Our training exercises covered the whole flight envelope of the aircraft from basic handling, circuit work, navigation, formation flying, night flying, aerobatics, instrument flying and spinning. Amongst that we would simulate emergencies, anything from hydraulic failures, instrument failures to engine failures. This required the student to carry out the correct procedures, particularly important when a simulated engine failure was given just after take off. Training profiles would vary depending on the actual exercise to be flown, but one would generally operate at around 25–35,000ft for general handling, with navigation, either high or low, at 35,000ft and 500ft respectively.

The Vampire was a delight throughout the speed range, though by modern standards the speeds were not so dramatic. What was impressive was the fact that one could carry out a loop, topping out above 40,000ft. I think the highest I ever saw was around 41,300ft. We would often ask a student how high he could do a loop, generally they would guess at 30,000ft, so a demo at 40,000ft always surprised them.

It was virtually vice-less, though like most aircraft one would treat it with respect. The "g" limit was six, and not having the luxury of "g" suits it placed quite a strain on the pilots, especially if one flew three or more sorties in a day of aerobatics and maximum steep turns. The max rate turn was performed in a spiral dive to maintain the speed. The first one would be demonstrated by the instructor, taking it to the limit of 6g – although nine times out of ten the student would black out and never see the latter

Vampire T.11 XD526 gets airborne from Little Rissington.

part of the turn. The aircraft would then be climbed back to 20,000ft and the student would have a go, usually only managing 4–5g with quite a struggle. At that stage the instructor would inform him that a bit more effort was required and would apply just enough back-pressure to increase loading, and once again the student would black out. The aero medical experts maintained that one could not "train" to accept high "g" loads but that was disproved time and time again, since all the instructors could cope with 6g without a suit. By the end of the course the students too would manage to pull 6g and stay with it.

As regards aerobatics, the Vampire was excellent in every respect, it was predictable in most manoeuvres, the exception being a stall-turn when some aircraft had a tendency to refuse to go in one direction. This was partly due to the gyroscopic effect of the engine, but was also assisted by small distortions in the airframe. It was particularly good for "glide" aeros, losing very little height since it had such good glide characteristics. This could be ably demonstrated by joining the upwind end of the circuit at normal height with the engine throttled right back to idle and at a nominal speed of 160kt. By delaying lowering the undercarriage and flaps, virtually no height was lost by the time one reached the downwind end of the runway. A standard turn around finals would be flown, the undercarriage being lowered about half way round the turn, flaps being delayed until certain of making the runway. Students flying this for the first time were always crossing the threshold too high and fast, much to their surprise.

The Vampire's characteristics in the spin were predictable, although some aircraft did have a tendency to prefer spinning in one direction rather than the other. Basically it was oscillatory and recovery was nearly always immediate. The T.11 could prove the exception and on just a few occasions

65

Vampire T.11s from RAF Valley over Snowdonia.

it would refuse to recover using normal anti-spin controls. This never happened to me, but a couple of other instructors did meet up with this problem, the only way then to make it recover was to jettison the hood. This caused such a change in the airflow that the controls had more bite and the aircraft would recover normally, though it would have lost considerably more height in the process.

My only complaint about the Vampire was that the cockpit heating was poor. This was most noticeable when operating at altitude for a long sortie. The inside of the canopy and the side screens would ice over, requiring the application of a glycol-soaked rag to clear the ice. Supervising high-level close formation was difficult since the only view for the instructor, and indeed the student, was through a very small hole in the side panel and even this was distorted by the glycol. Despite this we never had a serious incident, though I do recall one student who had great difficulty in rejoining formation at height. He would approach at frightening speeds, usually necessitating the rest of the formation to take avoiding action as he flashed past underneath only to make a further attempt with similar results. He eventually did sort it out, but on more than one occasion I thought our end was about to arrive!'

Although the Vampire was a relatively sedate performer by modern standards, the effects of 'g' could still be debilitating for those not accustomed to it, indeed Brian Carroll recalls an occasion when he inadvertently 'nobbled' Valley's corporal PTI (Physical Training Instructor) who was about to take part in the station sports day. This was an event of great importance, one that had been won for several years by the Admin Wing, the PTI being one of their star performers. Unfortunately the corporal chose the wrong moment to take a ride in a T.11 and put himself in the sick bay for a week following an aerobatic sortie. Admin Wing lost their title, much to their disgust, Carroll receiving some free beer courtesy of the Wing Commander (Flying) whose team won!

The T.11 continued in the training role until 29 November 1967 when it was retired at Leeming in a special ceremony to mark its last flight. Four Vampires led by Air Vice-Marshal Mike Lyne AFC, A.O.C. 23 Group, flew over the airfield and the event also included a display of formation flying by instructors from the Vampire Advanced Training Flight. It was fitting that Mike Lyne be part of the aircraft's departure as twenty years before, as a Squadron Leader, he had formed the very first Vampire aerobatic team when he was O.C. 54 Squadron at Odiham. During its career as a trainer the Vampire had been the means by which over 3,000 pilots had attained their wings.

Although the Vampire is, perhaps, not regarded with quite as much affection as the Meteor, its fine handling qualities still linger in the memory of those lucky enough to have flown it. Perhaps the last word on the aircraft should go to an American Colonel who was invited to fly one during a visit to this country. After a forty-minute flight he stepped out of the aircraft with a huge grin that spread from ear to ear. When asked if he had enjoyed his flight he replied, 'Sir, that is the nicest little toy I ever strapped to my aaass!'

CHAPTER THREE

DE HAVILLAND VENOM

With the Goblin jet engine in quantity production for the Vampire fighter, the engine division at de Havilland were soon looking for ways to derive more power from the basic centrifugal layout. By increasing the diameter of the impeller by 5in., it was discovered that mass flow could be increased from 60lb/sec to 88lb/sec which meant that thrust levels of up to 5,000lb could be attained. A new engine was quickly designed and test run for the first time at Hatfield on 2 September 1945. Named Ghost, it achieved fame on 8 May 1947 when it powered a specially modified Vampire (TG278) to a new world altitude record of 59,446ft.

It was quickly realised that the Vampire's thick wing and relatively low limiting Mach number would prevent it from taking full advantage of the increased power offered by the Ghost engine, and so a full redesign was carried out. The resultant aircraft, although similar in layout, had very little in common with its progenitor and the initial designation of Vampire Mark 8 was quickly dropped in favour of an entirely new type number and name, the de Havilland DH.112 Venom.

At 10% thickness/chord ratio, the wing on the Venom was much thinner and it also featured 17 degrees 6 minutes sweep back on the leading edge which moved the wing's centre of pressure rearwards in response to the new engine's increased weight. In order to prevent tip stalling, particularly on the approach to land, fences were installed at mid-span, and the wings were also stressed to allow stores of up to 1,000lb to be carried on each of two underwing pylons. A novel feature on British combat aircraft of the time was the fitment of wing-tip fuel tanks, each of seventy-five gallon capacity. Despite numerous other modifications to controls, wheels and brakes, fuel system etc., the Venom, with the exception of its all-new wing, looked virtually identical to the Vampires then rolling off the production line. Surprisingly, considering the level of re-engineering that had been undertaken, the first Venoms to be delivered to the RAF were not fitted with ejection seats.

Powered by a 4,850lb.s.t. Ghost 103, the prototype Venom FB.1, VV612, flew for the first time on 2 September 1949, and was exhibited at the SBAC Farnborough Air Show a few days later. It was sent to A&AEE at Boscombe Down in May 1950 where it was found to be considerably faster than the Vampire, its critical Mach number being around 0.84 which was a slight improvement on the later Meteors. The Venom was also a better performer at altitude and could attain heights of 50,000ft+ (thereby out-performing the much-vaunted F-86 Sabre which struggled to get to 47,000ft) although its degree of manoeuvre at such heights was extremely limited. Venoms were first delivered to CFE at West Raynham in April 1952, the service evaluation which followed leading to the detection of a worrying defect. A structural weakness was discovered in the wing and the first aircraft delivered for operational use had to be painted with red chord-wise bands on the wings as a reminder to pilots that a 6g limit had been imposed pending modifications.

Intentional spinning was prohibited, although if a pilot inadvertently got into a spin normal recovery action was usually effective. The Venom's behaviour was generally classical, with one or two minor quirks, as the following extract from Pilots' Notes indicates:

'The characteristics of the spin are rapid rolling about the longitudinal axis with the nose up for the first 1–1½ turns and then the nose dropping until the spin stabilises with the nose well down. When applying normal recovery action care should be taken to ensure that the ailerons are neutral and that the control column is moved slowly and progressively forward only until rotation ceases. Vigorous recovery action is to be avoided. If the undercarriage and flaps are down they should be raised. The recovery from a spin to port will normally take about ½–¾ of a turn, but in a spin to starboard the rate of rotation is faster and recovery will take longer (about 1–1½ turns). Since the principal rotation in the spin is in roll, recovery may be completed in an inverted attitude, and it is for this reason that the forward movement of the control column should not be continued after rotation has ceased, otherwise the aircraft may enter an inverted spin. On recovery, if in an inverted attitude it may be advantageous to half roll and ease the aircraft out of the ensuing dive. If the spin occurs at high altitude, once recovery has been effected the airbrakes should be used to prevent a high Mach number being reached. If an inverted spin occurs the standard recovery should be used, but again vigorous action should be avoided.'

Not long after the Venom entered service it began to develop a bad reputation when it came to terminal velocity dives. Although the noise and vibration could be unnerving on a first attempt, it was a relatively safe manoeuvre and there was little that pilots could do but wait until the aircraft's Mach number decreased on descending to lower levels, thereby allowing control to be regained. During high speed flight beyond its critical Mach number the Venom FB.1 was subject to varying trim changes as described in Pilots' Notes:

'Above 25,000ft a nose-up trim change will occur at approximately 0.88M above 35,000ft and approximately 0.86 below 35,000ft. The typical behaviour up to 0.88M is described below:

0.81-0.83M	Nose-down change of trim.
0.84M	Slight right wing heaviness, requiring only a small aileron movement to hold. Nose-down change of trim marked.
0.87M	Nose-down change of trim ceases. Slight airframe buffet commences. Slow nose-up change of trim. A push force on the control column has little effect and the Mach number drops fractionally when the nose-up trim disappears.

Above 35,000ft, if the angle of dive is steepened sufficiently to overcome the nose-up change of trim which occurs at about 0.88M, a progressive nose-down trim change occurs which is difficult to overcome due to the poor elevator effectiveness which becomes apparent above 0.89M. With the control column held fully back, with a heavy pull force, recovery is slow. Should this condition be reached, care must be taken to ease the stick forward when the nose-up trim change with decreasing Mach number (at about 0.88M) is reached, otherwise an excessive pitch-up will result.'

Similar characteristics were likely to occur below 25,000ft, but at lower Mach numbers, however, if the angle of dive was sufficient to take the aircraft to the extreme condition noted above (i.e. beyond the point where the nose-up trim change occurred) it was quite possible for the IAS limitation to be exceeded because of delayed recovery due to lack of elevator effectiveness.

Although the Venom had the best altitude performance of any RAF fighter of the time, it was equally at home at low level and during service with 2nd Tactical Air Force its major task was to be ground attack in which role it could be equipped with up to eight 60lb rocket projectiles or two bombs of either 500lb or 1,000lb. Trials were carried out at CFE in mid-1953 to ascertain the aircraft's behaviour when carrying external stores and to consider its tactical handling.

On take off the Venom accelerated adequately under all loading conditions and there was no tendency to sink on becoming airborne. When taking off with underwing stores it was recommended that one-third flap be used as this reduced the risk of tip stall should the aircraft unstick too early, and also shortened the take off run. During the climb out power needed to be as near maximum as possible (even in formation) although j.p.t. had to be watched carefully at heights above 30,000ft and had to be kept below 700–720°C. The first indication of a stall under all loading conditions was usually for a wing to drop but the aircraft recovered normally using standard technique. As already recorded, recovery from spins was straightforward, although considerable height could be lost if a spin was prolonged.

When descending in bad weather it was recommended that height be lost quickly by using dive brakes, but if fuel was a consideration, pilots were advised to descend without dive brakes with the engine throttled back to give better range and lower fuel consumption. For landing with external stores a normal power-on approach was considered appropriate, initially at 140kt IAS reducing gradually to a threshold speed 10–15kt above the stall. Care had to be taken if full flap was selected in one movement as a considerable forward pressure had to be applied to the control column to maintain the correct approach speed and the glidepath then became quite steep. The normal maximum landing weight was 11,930lb which could be achieved with various combinations of external stores and fuel, such as 4 x 60lb RP and 291 gallons of fuel, or 2 x 1,000lb bombs and 89 gallons of fuel. Overshoots were not difficult even with undercarriage down and full flap selected and an engine setting of 9,700rpm was found to be sufficient to allow a successful go around.

As a weapons platform the Venom was very similar to the Vampire. Due to its redesigned fin and rudder it showed less tendency to 'snake' although this particular characteristic was still noticeable in severe turbulence. The maximum diving speed of the Venom was greater than the Vampire and pilots found that they needed to pull back on the control column much more when recovering from dives. As a result extreme care had to be taken that the aircraft was trimmed correctly. With pull-out speeds in the order of 450–500kt IAS, loadings of +6g were not uncommon. As in the Vampire, the standard Mk 4 gyro gunsight was fitted and, again, this was positioned slightly lower than the pilot's head when in the normal flying position so that he was forced to crouch slightly when tracking a target.

For air-to-ground firing the best turn in height for training purposes was 2,500–3,000ft depending on the speed required at the pull-out point. Most dives were carried out at an angle of thirty degrees with an entry speed of 220–240kt at a height of 2,500ft and a throttle setting of 8,300rpm. The speed on pull out was about 360–370kt. With practice the aircraft became a very accurate gun platform although with its greater acceleration in the dive the firing time was somewhat shorter than with the Vampire. If dive brakes were used there was a tendency for the Venom to vibrate which made sighting more difficult, but if they were used momentarily speed could be reduced without the sight wandering too far off the target.

Rocket attacks were successfully carried out at dive angles varying from 20–60 degrees and speeds ranging from 350–500kt IAS. At the beginning of the trial a release speed of 350kt IAS was used which produced rocket accuracy comparable with the best results achieved with the Vampire. When speeds were increased to 450–500kt IAS the aircraft remained stable in the dive but in order to pull out at a safe height (750ft) the rockets had to be released at heights greater than 1,800ft above ground. As a result accuracy was considerably less during this type of attack due to the fact that the rocket motor burnt out before reaching the target. To avoid this situation rockets were released at 1,000–1,200ft but the pull-out height then became 400–450ft, at which height it was possible for the aircraft to be damaged by debris. It was recommended that this particular method should only be attempted by experienced pilots. During dives at speeds greater than 380kt IAS aiming accuracy was affected by 'snaking' in turbulence and pilots had to resist any temptation to correct with rudder as this only made things worse. Due to the heavy elevator control forces at high speed, care also had to taken not to impose too much loading on the aircraft during the pull out.

During the trials tragedy struck on 28 July when Flight Lieutenant M.E. Whitworth-Jones was killed flying WE261, his aircraft disintegrating during air-to-ground rocketing at the firing range at Holbeach South. Whitworth-Jones had taken off from West Raynham at 1650 hrs and had carried out two dummy attacks before being cleared by the range controller for his first live attack. His approach appeared to be perfectly normal, but he was seen to pass the usual point of release without having fired his rocket and continued his dive. At an estimated height of 4–700ft, the point at which he would normally have been expected to pull out, the aircraft broke up. As WE261 had not been embodied with mod.51 which provided for strengthening of the wing-root joints and fuselage crosstubes, the investigation centred on possible failure of one of the mainplanes.

It was quickly confirmed that the aircraft had crashed due to structural failure of the port wing, the primary failure having occurred in the bottom skinning at a point between Ribs 4 and 5 at the forward outboard corner of the under-carriage cut-out. A crack associated with abnormal stress concentrations initiating at this point had then progressed rapidly forward to the leading edge of the wing. This had caused the component to become unstable resulting in the mainspar failing completely in up-load. An impact mark on the leading edge forward of the aileron centre-hinge position showed that the wing had struck the tail assembly in the air after detaching. Although the aircraft was subject to the 6g limit, as signified by red wing bands and the provision of an accelerometer in the cockpit, there was no evidence to suggest that this loading had been exceeded. Whitworth-Jones was a highly experienced pilot who had just returned from an operational tour in Korea where he had flown

Two No. 11 Squadron Venoms low over Germany.

160 ground-attack missions with 77 Squadron RAAF flying Meteor F.8s.

Although there were serious doubts regarding the structural integrity of the wing, the Venom was cleared to enter squadron service subject to the limitation on g-loading mentioned previously. The first unit to fly the Venom was 11 Squadron, based at Wunstorf in Germany, which received the first of its new aircraft (WE271) on 11 August 1952, having previously had the loan of two AFDS machines for familiarisation. Over the next eight months the squadron carried out intensive flying trials which included an assessment under operational conditions during Exercise *Holdfast* in September. The improved performance of the Venom was immediately apparent but some snags were noted and adverse comment was made concerning high stick forces, and difficulties were also experienced during GCA approaches at the lowest minima. In terms of serviceability, problems were noted with respect to excessive tyre wear, leaking bag tanks, loose rivets, skin tears near the dive brakes and malfunction of the cold-air units. Many aircraft were sent to Germany in poor condition and on one occasion the ailerons in WE274 jammed during a roll when the control-cable tensioner fouled a wing rib. Only the strength of the pilot, who broke the rib in his efforts to restore control, averted a potential disaster.

Venom deliveries continued and by April 1953 No. 123 Wing at Wunstorf (5, 11 and 266 Squadrons) were fully equipped. No. 121 Wing at Fassberg was next in line, 14 Squadron receiving its Venom FB.1s in mid-1953. Squadron Leader (later Air Vice-Marshal) J.T. Lawrence recalls the changeover and some of the flying that the squadron carried out.

'I took command of 14 Squadron, which was then equipped with Vampires, on 18 May 1953. From then until we got our Venoms practically all our training was at low level. There were three squadrons at Fassberg (14, 98 and 118) and our speciality was a Wing rocket attack which we practiced on the range adjacent to the airfield. It involved a low-level approach in close tactical formation (6 x finger-four in line), a pull up to about 1,500ft and roll over on to the target. One had to wait for the aircraft ahead to pull out of the dive before firing. From the ground it was quite a spectacle.

We took delivery of the first of our Venoms on 5 July 1953 and were fully equipped by the end of the month. We were all delighted with its handling qualities which were not dissimilar from the Vampire, but its overall performance, particularly at altitude, was far superior. That August the squadron deployed to Ouston to take part in an air defence exercise – "Momentum". We were used, very successfully, on high level interceptions – up to 42,000ft – mainly against Canberras. The only concern was the tendency of the engine to produce a slight hydraulic "knock", often when about seventy-five miles out to sea.

All RAF Germany squadrons spent at least one month in the year at the Armament Practice Camp at Sylt. The main facility provided there was live firing on a drogue towed at 200kt. This involved positioning the aircraft parallel to the line of the drogue and making a "quarter" attack. It was rather an academic exercise, but very good training. In the summer there was at least one major deployment exercise. We were supposed to be fully mobile and to this end each squadron had 18 three-ton trucks to carry the ground staff, aircraft spares and tentage. Our dispersal airfield was Gütersloh where we would set up camp just outside the airfield perimeter. We were not allowed to use any of the permanent facilities except the runway and hard standings. These deployments were held in conjunction with major Army exercises. We would be on standby from before dawn to dusk for 4–5 days and the missions ranged from high-level interceptions, to low level recce and simulated ground attack.

Routine training at base included formation practice, night flying, instrument rating tests, aerobatics and air-to-ground firing (rockets and 20mm cannon) on the range. Also, in winter, the lucky ones were sent on a cold-weather survival course at Ehrwald in Austria. The F/GA role at that time was probably the most demanding in the service. We operated at low level without any aids except the Mk. 1 eyeball. On many occasions in poor weather the only airfield approach aid was a mobile "homer".'

Flying Officer Don Headley recalls his introduction to the Venom's high Mach number characteristics and another of its idiosyncrasies:

'The so-called "Death Dive", where you went past Mcrit got a very bad name for itself. One of the first things on conversion to the Venom, within the first 5–6 flights, was to go to high level and intentionally get into this problem so you would have confidence that it would recover. You went up to 40,000ft or thereabouts, turned it on its back and pulled through until you were coming down vertically. The speed built up rapidly and as it went past Mach 0.84–0.85, compressibility made you lose tailplane effect. The stick would thrash around in the cockpit, I can remember having to get my

No. 14 Squadron pilots. Back Row (LtoR) Steggall, Williams, Carder, Skidmore, Pettit, Sinclair, Peacock, ?, ?, Madgwick. Front Row (LtoR) Crook, Checketts, Bolger, Timilty, Lawrence, Simpson, Macpherson, Cross, Adams.

Venom FB.1s of No. 14
Squadron.

knees out of the way, and there was heavy juddering. Pulling back on the stick did not help, all you could do was sit back and wait until you got into denser air at about 20,000ft when control gradually came back again.

On start-up we experienced problems with torching so, before starting, a large asbestos blanket with a rope fastened to it was placed over the tail. The groundcrew then pulled the blanket off once you had started, whether you had torched it or not. The start-up sequence was automatic but if the igniters became soaked with excess fuel, the engine would fail to light up. This left a fair amount of fuel in the jetpipe which would set alight if you tried to start the engine again. Quite often the airmen would tip the tail down to let the fuel run out of the back and it depended on how much came out as to whether the aeroplane had to be moved.'

Although wet-starts posed no danger for pilots, for the groundcrew it could be a different story. SAC Eric Watson who served at Idris in North Africa, recalls one occasion when he was holding the asbestos blanket in place on the tail of a Venom when a particularly violent case of torching happened to coincide with an unfortunate change in wind direction. The flames gushing out of the jetpipe were blown towards him, but he managed to escape with only singed hair. The next time he was on tailplane duty he noticed that his Flight Sergeant had thoughtfully arranged for longer holding tapes!

14 Squadron's participation in Exercise *Momentum* in August produced a couple of incidents, although in the event neither were serious. Flying Officer

T.J. Bolger had engine failure at 41,000ft in WE367 but carried out a successful forced-landing at Boulmer, and Pilot Officer P. Harlen burst a tyre on landing which resulted in the undercarriage collapsing. Having returned to Fassberg, the squadron departed for Sylt on 5 September but a week was lost when all aircraft were grounded for the tail structure to be examined following a recent accident. Normal training was resumed in October although fog limited flying to 152 hours by day and ten hours by night, the airfield being at 'Red' seventeen times during the month.

Bad weather was to restrict the amount of flying that was possible for the rest of the year, and in November and December only 228 hours were possible. Despite this, a series of dive-bombing trials were commenced, and regular 'battle flight' duties were also carried out whenever possible. During December there were three minor accidents, Flying Officer Brian Pettit ran off the side of the runway due to failure of the port brake, Flying Officer Deluce landed wheels-up after the undercarriage refused to lower and Sergeant Stone stalled on approach and crash-landed in the undershoot area.

Throughout the year many new pilots had arrived at Fassberg and most were having their first taste of life on an operational squadron. Pilot Officer Geoff Steggall, who joined 14 Squadron in August 1953, recalls its make-up and some of the spirit that existed at that time between rival units:

'There had been a terrific intake of pilots into the RAF in 1951/52 as a result of the Korean War and many squadrons, including 14, were full of "first tourists". In my time only the C.O., Sqn Ldr John Lawrence, had previous experience and some of that was on flying boats! The two flight commanders were extended first tourists and the other twenty-two pilots were all straight from training. 98 and 118 Squadrons, also at Fassberg, were in a similar position, as were many other units in Germany. Compared to today's squadrons we were a shambles – flying discipline was very lax with unlimited flying, and the "bouncing" of other aircraft and formations was a daily occurrence. Trying to blow yachts over on Steinhude Meer was also considered good sport. A court martial after a "dummy attack" on a tank failed as the relevant Air Ministry Flying Orders "were not signed by authority".

On one occasion we received several lorry loads of camouflage netting, support poles, brackets, clips and wheels to cover our aircraft. No instructions were supplied and try as we did we could find no way of making a safe, mobile camouflage cover. In the end we gave up and decided that the components, minus the netting, could be fashioned into cannons. These took several forms and all used "thunderflashes" as the charge. The favoured indoor projectile was a box of Maltesers and outdoor missiles were either a second thunderflash or a Very cartridge (you will be surprised at the amount of damage a flying Malteser will do!). The AOC (AVM Hallings-Pott) was treated to a double thunderflash salvo during his station tour after his formal inspection.

Another cannon, which was made of wood and hardboard and about 4ft long, was a source of great rivalry between Fassberg and Celle, the

Not an ancient flying machine, but a contraption intended to camouflage 2 TAF Venoms. It proved a dismal failure, but the tubes and wheels were used to form makeshift cannons for frightening Air Vice-Marshals during station inspections.

nearest RAF station some twenty miles away. I cannot recall the exact origins of the cannon – a Mess Ball perhaps – but it used to be secreted in one officers mess or the other and the opposing team would try to capture it in a surprise attack. During one time that Fassberg had the cannon it was fixed to the chimney pots of the officers mess and surrounded with barbed wire. This was deemed to be provocative but safe as the mess roof was visible from the Guard house at the station entrance. One evening my wife and I were at the station cinema when I noticed a movement in the rows ahead of us. A message was being passed along each row in turn and husbands were leaving protesting wives. The message reached our row – "Celle are after the cannon!" – so I joined the home team. The Celle pilots were all over the mess roof. A fire engine was parked across the camp entrance so they could not escape and "battle" commenced. The order of battle is a little confused now; we chased them across the roof and there were several falls, but no injuries. I was wielding the mess fire-fighting hose but unfortunately it did not have the range to reach the chimney area. To cut a long story short the attack was successfully repelled and the cannon remained in our possession.'

Even though 14 Squadron was fully operational on the Venom FB.1, it still had a few Vampire FB.5s on strength which were mainly used for cine gun practice and general tactical training. This could lead to problems as a result of differences in cockpit layout as Pilot Officer Alex Carder recalls:

'When we re-equipped with the Venom we were still flying the Vampire and often would get out of one type and, next sortie, directly into the other. This caused the odd incident, particularly on air-to-ground range sorties. The press to transmit button was on the control column of the Vampire, but in the Venom it was on the throttle – the armament button being on the control stick. You don't need a vivid imagination to know what sometimes happened, much to the chagrin of the Range Safety Officer, when calling "Turning live" in the Venom, four rockets would depart heavenwards!

The Venom was my favourite aircraft; once I had climbed into the cockpit it became part of me and was like putting on a well worn glove. It handled well throughout the speed range, was an excellent, stable platform for rockets and air-to-ground gunnery, as well as being easy to fly during air-to-air firing. Comparing it to the Sabre, our main adversary at the time, it out-turned and out-climbed it, but was short on speed. I flew the aircraft above 40,000ft – it did get less manoeuvrable and the handling became washy, but nevertheless it was nice to be able to sit at height and watch other aircraft, particularly the Sabre, vainly trying to reach us. Although we operated as both a ground-attack and day fighter squadron, I felt the aircraft was more suited to the F/GA role because of its ease of handling, stability and manoeuvrability.'

The dive-bombing trials continued on the range at Fassberg during January 1954, the live attacks resulting in a distinct shortage of bombs by the end of the month. Initially the trials were of 'low-level' bombing which involved turning in at about 10,000ft with recovery by 2,000ft. This phase was completed by early March and was followed by 'high-level' bombing, the usual technique being to turn in at 18–20,000ft, dive at an angle of sixty degrees and recover by 10,000ft which was considered to be the minimum height to remain clear of anti-aircraft fire. The second phase had only been underway for two weeks when it was brought to a halt by the dramatic crash of WE368 on 23 March, an accident that occurred in very similar circumstances to that at CFE nine months before. Flying Officer Don Headley witnessed the event:

'On 14 Squadron we took it in turns to act as Range Safety Officer and on this particular occasion, I was on duty. Sam D'Arcy, whose call-sign was Blackspot 21, joined the range and having let him do a dummy, I cleared him for a "live". From the quadrant you couldn't see the aircraft turning in but you could hear the whine of the engine and the speed building up. I saw a 25lb practice bomb explode on the ground followed by three more in a stick going up the range and almost at the same time there was a very big bang which sounded a bit like a supersonic bang. Looking up there were bits coming down, one burning bit crashed into the ground and others floated down as always happens in aircraft disintegrations.

Having told base that we had had a crash, I got a three-tonner, drove across the range to the burning wreckage which turned out to be the cockpit and guns which were semi-buried in the ground. An airman said he thought he had seen a parachute open just above the pine trees about 200 yards away. We got in the wagon and thrashed across the pock-marked range looking for a parachute up in the trees when someone else said that he had seen someone dressed like a pilot on the other crash wagon heading back to the quadrant. We rushed back and found Sam standing at the top of the steps with a patch above his right eye. I said "Thank Christ you're all right Sam" – I was fairly shaken by the whole thing. Sam just looked at me and said "Hello Don, where did my bomb drop?" which has to be the coolest thing I have ever heard!'

Flying Officer Sam D'Arcy thus became the first pilot to successfully eject from a Venom, ejection seats having been incorporated in late production machines. In the circumstances his survival was remarkable as his departure took place at very low level and took him through the canopy, there being insufficient time for it to be jettisoned. D'Arcy later went to inspect the crash site together with several other pilots, including his C.O. Squadron Leader John Lawrence.

'The following day Sam and I were viewing the wreckage and found that the points where the cockpit, the ejector seat and Sam landed formed a five yard triangle – showing how close he was to disaster. Of all the pilots on the squadron only Sam could have got away with it – his reactions were always by far the quickest. Later that morning a long line of RAF Regiment airmen, equipped with wooden stakes were deployed on the range with instructions to mark every piece of wreckage. Sam called me over to see where one of the airmen with a warped sense of humour had put a stake through the top of his best Bates hat which he was in the habit of carrying behind his seat!'

Don Headley was another who witnessed the demise of D'Arcy's hat and recalls that he was more upset by this wanton act of vandalism than anything else!

As a result of the crash all Venoms were grounded so that checks could be carried out and all but two aircraft were found to have cracks in the wing structure. Rectification work involved strengthening the wings in the vicinity of the air brakes and undercarriage cut-out. While this was being done, the remaining Vampires were used as much as possible, but aircraft availability was reduced even further on 22 April when WG847 crashed shortly after take off following engine failure, Pilot Officer Stillwell escaping unhurt. As a result of this accident only two aircraft were left to carry out battle flight duties. Serviceability was again severely restricted in May as the de Havilland working party continued to patch up the Venoms and on 21 May two Vampires had to be borrowed from 98 Squadron. By the end of the month the situation had improved somewhat with five Venoms, three Vampire FB.5s and one T.11 available, but it was not until June that the squadron finally got back to something resembling normality when it flew 236 hours on Venoms.

Over the next two months the emphasis in training was placed on the interceptor role with an air firing detachment to Sylt and numerous tactical and cine exercises. Night flying was also resumed, although only a few sorties were flown as all pilots had to be checked before being allowed to fly solo. During the rest of the year there were a number of accidents of varying significance. Flying Officer Bolger's aircraft was hit by debris on a range exercise in August and the following month Flying Officer E.J. Cross (WE425) was seriously injured when he was involuntarily ejected after stalling and hitting the ground on a night overshoot at Wunstorf. WE410, flown by Flying Officer D.F. Madgwick, sustained Cat 4 damage during a force-landing at Fassberg in October after the engine cut (suspected front bearing failure), and in November Flying Officer Geoff Steggall (WE359) ended up on the grass at the side of the runway with a

Venom FB.1 WE359 suffers a collapsed nosewheel.

collapsed nosewheel as a result of hitting turbulence during a stream landing.

On 1 November all Venoms were grounded once again, this time as a result of two in-flight fires which had recently occurred at Fassberg involving 98 Squadron. Flying resumed again a week later but without tip tanks as these were thought to have contributed to the accidents. Throughout its life, in-flight fires were a particular hazard in the Venom, one of the first examples occurring in Canada on 22 January 1953 when WE266 was engaged on winterisation trials. During one test flight the fire warning light came on at 28,000ft and the pilot saw what appeared to be fuel streaming back over the starboard wing from the leading edge, just outboard of the air intake. On this occasion a safe landing was made and the fire that was burning in the tail cone and starboard flap bay extinguished.

The fire had primarily taken place in the lower portion of the rear engine bay and in the starboard wing flap shroud and was consistent with spillage of fuel from either of the No. 1 tank connections from where it would flow into the flap shroud and then into the engine bay. No satisfactory explanation could be found for the pilot's statement that fuel had been seen flowing out of the generator cooling air intake but such a discharge would be sucked into the wing in the region of the starboard flap shroud and the net effect would be the same as leakage from the No. 1 tank connection. Problems had also been experienced with the No. 1 wing fuel tank during the intensive flying trials carried out at Wunstorf. In the eight-month period of the trials, a total of eleven tanks had been changed due to leaks which were mainly caused by cracks at joints and corners, and rubbing on sharp points in the tank bay due to poor finish. There were also five cases of leaking connections to the No. 1 fuel tank. As engines were changed without the fuel pipes connecting the main tank to the No.1 wing tank being removed, it was possible that undue strain was being imposed on joints during such operations, leading to leaks or a fractured pipe.

Shortly after the trials were concluded Pilot Officer E.F.W. Gregory of 5 Squadron was killed on 2 May 1953 when attempting a crash-landing in WE271 following an in-flight fire. The pilot of a following aircraft saw flames appearing to come out of the cowling above the engine on the top starboard side. Although much of the aircraft was burnt out, it was thought that the fire had originated in the front starboard No. 1 tank coupling as there was blueing of the engine air casings and the cowlings above and below this point had burnt away.

To return to the incidents at Fassberg, the first occurred on 27 October and involved Flying Officer G.W. Schofield in WE365. Schofield had been cleared for an aerobatic sortie but, as there was no R/T contact after take off, the exact course that he took could only be surmised. Having taken off to the east he should have turned below 2,000ft to avoid flying into East Germany before continuing his climb to the north-west not above the cloud base, which was at 6,000ft. At some point during the aerobatic exercise it was thought that electrical failure occurred, possibly as a result of the fire. As the pilot did not use his fire extinguisher, he was probably unaware until a very late stage of the severity of the situation.

Schofield's aircraft was seen again thirteen minutes after take off approaching the crash strip to the left of the runway with its underside on fire. It passed the runway controller's caravan at a height of 6–10ft with undercarriage, flaps and dive brakes retracted and touched down well past the threshold. As its speed was too great it became airborne again before hitting the ground a second time causing various items of debris, including burning gun-bay doors, molten battery cases, cannon attachments and an assortment of electrical parts from the gun bay and starboard inner-flap compartment, to be strewn over a wide area. The Venom then left the ground and climbed steeply at an angle of forty-five degrees up to a height of 200ft when it rolled to the left and dived into the ground, disintegrating on impact. The pilot was killed instantly and a large fuel fire developed around the wreckage. Examination of the debris left in the two scrape marks showed that there had been a fierce fire in the gun bays and main fuselage tank bay and a fire of unknown severity in the starboard inner-flap compartment.

Just as the investigation was getting under way into this accident, Flight Lieutenant (later Air Vice-Marshal Sir) John Severne experienced an in-flight fire in WE377 during another aerobatic sortie on 1 November. At the top of a loop a loud bang was heard and immediately afterwards the fire warning light came on and the cockpit filled with smoke. Although pilots had been ordered to eject in such circumstances, as he was within easy reach of the airfield, Severne decided to carry out a forced-landing which he successfully accomplished, wheels-up on the grass. Fire crews were quickly on the scene and thanks to their prompt action, vital evidence was preserved which ultimately led to the cause of Flying Officer Schofield's crash being ascertained with a fair amount of certainty. For saving his aircraft, John Severne was later awarded the Air Force Cross (AFC).

After examining WE377 investigators concluded that the problem was caused by fuel venting through the vent drain-pipe at the bottom of the gun-bay doors and then travelling back with slipstream, or creeping back along the outer

Another landing mishap, this time involving WK486 of No. 118 Squadron. Lack of tip tanks suggest that this incident occurred in late 1954.

surface of the fuselage, to enter the forward-facing engine-cooling air intakes in the bottom engine-cowling. This fuel then vapourised in the engine bay and was ignited by the hot shroud ring after which it would flash to the gun bay and the starboard inner-flap compartment. As part of the inquiry into the crash a Venom fuel system was set up at Fassberg and during tests it became clear that fuel was much more likely to vent under conditions of zero or negative 'g'. It was also considered that the fire risk was made worse when tip tanks were fitted.

For the second time that year a working party from de Havilland arrived at Fassberg to carry out a series of modifications which, on this occasion, included reducing the air pressure that fed fuel from the tip tanks and forming drain holes in the top of the engine cowling. Operations continued to be restricted until the middle of January 1955 when aircraft began to return fully modified for inverted flight. On 14 Squadron, training got back to normal in February with air-to-ground firing, rocketing and tactical work ahead of a firepower demonstration on Fassberg range. During this period another aircraft was damaged by debris thrown up from the ground when recovering from an RP dive. Two other incidents occurred in the month, Flying Officer C. Allison experienced generator failure in the air and Flying Officer J.R. McEntegart made a dead-stick landing with a seized engine.

In March it became known that the squadron would shortly be converting to Hunters but in the meantime Venom flying carried on as before including two 'Wing Dingers', one a fighter sweep, the other a low-level strike on Diepholz. On 13 April Squadron Leader C.W. Beasley arrived to take over command and ten days later the squadron participated in a demonstration for the Italian Chiefs of Staff which involved the Venoms in rocketing and ground strafing with 20mm cannon, and the dropping of napalm by the unit's two Vampire T.11s. The emphasis throughout the month on ground attack illustrated once again the hazards of this type of operation when Flying Officer Alex Carder had his

Line-up of No. 14 Squadron Venom FB.1s at Fassberg.

canopy shattered on two separate occasions. It was thought that the damage was caused by spent cartridge cases ejected from the Venom flying in front of Carder's aircraft. On 23 May the ground party departed for Oldenburg where the squadron was to re-equip with the Hunter F.4. Before this, however, there was a fatal accident on 4 May when Flying Officer McEntegart crashed in WE357 six miles north-west of Munsterlager after hitting a tree during a low-level attack sortie.

Despite the modifications that had been carried out as a result of in-flight fires, accidents continued to occur and on 19 July 1955 Flying Officer Geoff Winspear of 145 Squadron had an extremely lucky escape during a cine gun exercise on a towed target over the North Sea from Sylt. His evidence to the Court of Inquiry details the sequence of events.

'I took off at 0515Z as No. 2 to F/O D. Brittain and we joined with the tug aircraft at 20,000ft at about 0530Z. I did a series of normal cine attacks on the flag but I do not believe that I applied more than +4 and −½ g during these attacks. At about 0545Z I noticed that my tip tanks, which were full on take off, had stopped feeding. Whilst manoeuvring for my last attack a few minutes later, I noticed a hot smell in the cockpit. I immediately checked the rpm gauge, fire warning light, j.p.t. gauge, oil temperature and fuel contents gauge. As everything appeared normal, I thought I was imagining the smell. I therefore turned in for my final attack but as I broke over the flag I saw the fire warning light come on. I tried to close the throttle but found it was jammed at 9,800rpm and next found that the R/T transmitter had failed. I heard one weak message and then my receiver failed too. Both the gunsight and the fire warning light also went out.

I pulled up steeply to gain height and lose speed during which time the fire warning light came on again. Whilst in level flight I pressed the extinguisher button but there was no apparent effect. I could see Sylt so set course for the airfield in a glide. There was a severe hammering from the engine and I had the impression that something had broken loose. After a minute or so this noise and vibration settled down to rather rough running. The ASI, altimeter, artificial horizon and fuel gauge all appeared to be u/s. I then jettisoned the hood but remained in the aircraft trying to reach the coast of Sylt but found eventually that I could no longer correct with aileron a roll to port. At the same time I saw F/O Brittain fly alongside me and draw his hand across his throat. I recognised this as the sign that it was time to leave and I then ejected. The seat worked perfectly and I landed by parachute in shallow water just off the beach south of Westerland, Sylt. In landing I sustained a mildly sprained right ankle.'

During the five-minute period that the Venom was on fire, Flying Officer Brittain attempted to formate on his No. 2 but had great difficulty in holding station as the other aircraft was flying so slowly. He saw what he took to be fuel vapour pouring back from the rear of the gun bay and this was followed by a short length of flame coming from the vicinity of the link ejector chutes on the starboard side. It appeared that the flame was under pressure. Not long after, the aircraft became a mass of flames stretching from a point just behind the canopy to the tailpipe. After Winspear ejected, his aircraft (WK469) commenced a tight, continuous series of barrel rolls until it hit the ground. When asked later why he had not ejected immediately, Winspear replied that he was a non swimmer and preferred to stay with his burning aircraft for as long as possible rather than bale out into the sea.

In all, 363 Venom FB.1s were built for the RAF and many went on to serve in the Middle and Far East. Some of those which had flown with squadrons in 2nd Tactical Air Force in Germany were replaced by a developed version, the FB.4, which flew for the first time on 29 December 1953. The new variant featured hydraulically operated ailerons with artificial feel for improved control at high Mach numbers, a redesigned fin and rudder which had a flatter top and increased chord, together with bullet fairings to the rear of the vertical surfaces as well as to the front to reduce buffet. One of the first evaluations was carried out by CFE who received WE260, a modified FB.1, on 13 May 1954. During the next twelve weeks it was flown by nine different pilots who accumulated twenty-three hours flying time, including eight hours on high-altitude interceptions during Exercise *Dividend.*

Due to the addition of powered ailerons pilots had to get used to a number of new controls. A hydraulic power selector was located low down on the port side of the instrument panel, consisting of a plunger which was pulled out and turned clockwise to select power 'On', and an adjustable spring strut, situated on the starboard cockpit floor, gave lateral spring 'feel' and trim adjustment. On the throttle quadrant a three-position electrically actuated trim switch gave lateral trim when hydraulic power was 'Off' (this was set to neutral in conjunction with a red position-indicator light on the top left-hand corner of the instrument panel) and there was also an aileron-tab motor circuit breaker mounted high on the port wall of the cockpit in case of runaway trim. Should hydraulic pressure drop below a certain value, a valve switched the hydraulic system 'Off' and the electric-tab circuit 'On' at the same time as initiating an audio warning. Manual power was then applied direct to the ailerons. Prior to taxiing, the recommended procedure was as follows:

Before start up	check audio warning 'Off' and aileron-tab motor circuit breaker 'In', ground/flight switch to 'Flight', check operation of position indicator light, leave trimmed 'Neutral' with lights out, select power 'On'
After start up	check operation of ailerons and that manual trimming switch is inoperative, select power 'Off', check audio warning and return to 'On', set adjustable spring strut to a position midway between the extremes of travel

During high-speed trials the powered ailerons gave good lateral control at all speeds up to limiting Mach number, although the elevator stick forces were still high and were accompanied by large changes in longitudinal trim as the aircraft accelerated beyond 0.85 IMN. The following trim changes occurred during forty-degree dives from 45,000ft:

0.80–0.84 IMN	No appreciable trim change after aircraft is trimmed into dive
0.84–0.86 IMN	Slight nose down change of trim, becomes stronger at lower altitudes
0.87–0.88 IMN	Strong nose up trim change – if a higher IMN is to be reached a firm forward pressure is required to produce full downward elevator deflection
0.89–0.91 IMN	These IMN figures may only be reached over 35,000ft and produce irregular wing drop and yaw. Ailerons remain effective and any tendency to drop a wing may be counteracted

At high IAS the powered ailerons again gave good control, with a high rate of roll, but it was felt that they did not measure up to those of the F-86 or Hunter. At the IAS limit the rate of roll was assessed as being comparable to the Venom fitted with spring tabs. Elevator stick forces during high-speed flight, however, remained heavy at all times. When flying in 'manual' the aircraft could be flown up to 525kt IAS or 0.84 IMN; lateral stick forces were heavy at all speeds but GCA approaches, landings and overshoots presented no difficulty. The CFE report concluded that the aircraft was much safer to fly at high Mach numbers at high altitude as it no longer suffered from the uncontrollable wing drop associated with the FB.1, but that due to the high longitudinal stick forces and strong trim changes experienced at high IMN, it was not an effective gun platform above Mach 0.85.

Of the fighter-bomber wings in RAF Germany only No. 123 Wing at Wunstorf, comprising 5, 11, and 266 Squadrons, was wholly equipped with the Venom FB.4 and the training routine showed little change from that carried out with the FB.1. As a very junior Pilot Officer, Chris Golds joined 11 Squadron in November 1956 and flew with them until the squadron was disbanded a year later.

'Our training included air combat, anywhere from 10–50,000ft, where we were up against a wide variety of opponents including Meteors, Sabres, Hunters and F-84Gs. The Meteor had similar speed to the Venom, and with its good acceleration it could give us a hard time, but not as hard as the Sabre which was an extremely dangerous "enemy" as it was faster and could turn hard. Thunderjets were hard work to "kill" as they were as fast and as manoeuvrable as we were. Even Canberras could be a problem, they were similar in speed and could turn well, but often they could not see us coming. The Javelin? Well, that was just a lumbering giant! Generally we could out-turn anything because of the Venom's large wing area, especially at 40,000ft plus. We flew a lot at this height and above, even doing (very gentle) battle formation at 50,000ft which was quite illegal for oxygen reasons.

We also flew low-level map reading exercises (250ft – 360kt), *Rat and Terrier* and low-level strikes in formations of up to twenty-four aircraft (including aircraft from other squadrons). Air-to-air gunnery was carried out from 5–10,000ft using single or four 20mm cannon, together with air-to-ground gunnery in 20–30 degree dive attacks against very elderly vehicles. Single cannon firing was scored, but four cannon was not. Air-to-ground rocketing consisted of firing 3in. x 60lb concrete heads (usually singly) in a twenty-five-degree dive at 800 yards range. We fired against old German Tiger tanks and on one occasion I scored a dramatic hit which blew the turret up into the air, but as it was a salvo, it didn't score! You had to allow for gravity drop which at 800 yards was 108ft. The gyro sight allowed some bank at the firing point but RP was very much a "seaman's eye" game. You could be very accurate with a static target, but against moving tanks (which would have been our prime target) I would doubt our accuracy. I seem to remember that someone worked it out that it would take 138 RPs, on average, to hit a moving tank. I'm sure that the Typhoon boys in World War Two would have been better.'

Like many other pilots, Chris Golds also had a fright during a compressibility dive in a Venom.

'Although I was only with 11 Squadron for a little over a year I had many opportunities to "drop myself in it". One day I was briefed by my Flight Commander to do some medium-level cine quarter attacks, each of us

Typical Venom start. A plume of smoke from the starter cartridge and a sheet of flame from the jetpipe. Note the worried look on the Airman's face.

being in turn fighter and target. Good gunsight training but rather dull for both pilots. Suddenly I was called into close battle position and heard the shout for "Buster", i.e. full power and climbing. Gerry [F/L Gerry Eades], my Flight Commander, had spotted a dogfight to the west of us and was itching to join in.

We climbed well above the top of the fight which seemed to have dozens of aeroplanes wheeling round and round and zooming up and down. One thing the Venom could do well was climb and usually to heights that other jet fighter-bombers could not reach. So Gerry took us up to above 45,000ft to look down and judge his entry dive to a nicety. At last he was satisfied, called "Black section rolling left – Go!" and peeled off quickly into his dive. I followed him but had to pull hard to keep up. Too hard in fact and I flicked rapidly to the right. Another thing the Venom could do well – flick! Eventually I sorted myself out at about 40,000ft by which time I was most definitely on my own.

Now what had I listened to in the mess bar night after night? – "Attack with height, out of the sun, pick a straggler, slash and burn, do not get involved if you are on your own, go through fast". So I looked down and at last spotted a singleton, also a Venom, about 15,000ft below me. Right, he is mine! I had by this time only been in a few "doggers" and those as a number two so I was being really brave – or stupid! As I rolled gently over into a dive I could see numerous other aircraft all in a fur-ball well below my quarry. I pulled down my goggles (unbelievably we still had Mk. 8 goggles attached to our brand new bone domes) and peered through my gunsight to search for my singleton. I was not conscious of how fast I was going downhill, but a glance at the Mach meter would have shown about 0.86 or 0.87 just as my aircraft rolled un-commanded to the right and the nose tucked under despite my heroic pulling on the stick. She was out of control and nothing I did would affect the plunge.

I throttled to idle and popped the airbrakes but still she plunged earthwards. I had of course exceeded the limiting Mach number for the aeroplane and this was quite plainly stated in Pilots' Notes which I ought to have read! My target whirled up towards me and passed above in a flash. Next I speared through a circling punch-up and as I glanced at my altimeter I saw about 25,000ft in an unwinding blur. By now I was distinctly un-brave and beginning to think of using the Mk.1 bang seat to escape this death ride. At last, as I got down below about 20,000ft, the stick began to have some effect and I pulled out, sweating with fear, at about 12,000ft, once more entirely on my own. With quite a lot showing on the also brandnew g-meter, I decided to go home as I had no idea where my leader was.

On the way back from Dummer Zee to Wunstorf I reviewed my situation and knew I was deep in the dung. So when I came across a battle formation pair of long-nosed Meteor night-fighters I thought that I could at least take home some cine film of them to salve my pride – after all they were almost bombers, weren't they? I attacked, they split, crossed, and sandwiched me between them. In no time at all they were queued up behind me holding my tightest turn and hosing me with their cine film. Nothing I could do seemed to shake them off until they decided to break off and go home. I landed and as I taxied in I saw my Flight Commander standing waiting at the open hangar doors. His de-brief set a pattern to be followed by others as the tally of my escapades mounted up and none of them are printable! Fourteen years later as a Squadron Commander myself, I could quite see his side of the argument – the miracle is that I survived to get that far!'

By the end of 1957 all single-seat Venoms had been withdrawn from 2nd TAF although the aircraft continued to serve with squadrons based in the Middle and Far East, the last unit being 28 Squadron at Kai Tak, Hong Kong which retired its FB.4s in July 1962 prior to converting to the Hunter FGA.9. Despite its various trials and tribulations, the Venom was a popular aircraft in RAF service, combining the fine handling qualities of the Vampire with the added power of the Ghost engine. For its day, the Venom's rate of climb and manoeuvrability were exceptional, its overall performance being close to the ultimate in terms of what could actually be achieved with a first-generation jet design. As it mainly served abroad, the Venom was never a common sight in the U.K. although, paradoxically, it can now be seen on a regular basis thanks to the preservation and display of former Swiss Air Force examples, aircraft that are a permanent reminder of the earliest days of jet-powered flight.

CHAPTER FOUR

NORTH AMERICAN
F-86 SABRE

By early 1952 war had been raging in Korea for more than eighteen months as U.N. forces attempted to overcome the Communist Chinese and North Koreans. The war had started like many localised conflicts but had escalated dramatically in October 1950 when forces of the Chinese People's Republic were committed to the land battles in large numbers. The following month MiG-15 jet fighters, flown by Chinese and North Korean pilots, were seen for the first time. The performance of the MiG came as a considerable shock to the Western Allies and prompted the rapid deployment of a Wing of USAF F-86 Sabres to counter the threat. Although no RAF fighter squadrons were involved in the war, reports coming out of Korea by RAF pilots serving on exchange postings with the USAF and RAAF were deeply worrying.

With first-line equipment still comprising the obsolescent Meteor F.8 and Vampire FB.5, and with the Swift and Hunter two or three years away from squadron service, it was clear that the RAF would be outclassed should any conflict occur in Europe in the immediate future. To try to restore its credibility in the short term, 430 Canadair-built Sabres were purchased via the Mutual Defense Aid Program, all aircraft to be delivered by the end of 1953.

The Sabre had begun life as the NA-140 in 1944 in response to a USAAF requirement for a medium-range day fighter. In its original form it featured a straight wing but was quickly redesigned with wings and tailplane swept to an angle of thirty-five degrees when German high-speed research data became available at the end of World War Two. The F-86A entered service with the 1st Fighter Group based at March AFB, California where Flight Lieutenant (later Air Vice-Marshal) W. 'Paddy' Harbison was serving.

'The first F-86A aircraft were delivered in early February 1949 and I checked out on one of the first four (FU-627) on 17 February. The aircraft were all early production models and they were still undergoing service acceptance trials. My first flight in the F-86 was exciting, but uneventful. I was one of the first in the Fighter Group to get airborne in the F-86 and without doubt the first serving RAF pilot. After cockpit familiarisation and briefing on emergency procedures, power settings, airspeed information, plus the new ejection seat limits, I was ready to start the J-47. It was a manual start, not much different from the F-80 power plant. The main message – do not hurry the process and monitor the jet pipe temperature. Start up went well and after chocks away, I taxied out of the ramp. The F-86 had nosewheel steering which was engaged by a button on the control column.

After clearance I lined up on the runway and absorbed the sight picture through the front screen. The F-86 sat much higher than the F-80 and the runway perspective was different. Take-off checks were completed and the engine run up to full 100% power on the brakes. Next came an emergency full control check and all was ready to roll. The throttle was advanced to full power again and the Sabre accelerated much better than the F-80. Slight back pressure on the stick brought the nose up and the aircraft unstuck cleanly. Wheels up, hydraulic pressure systems all OK and a turn made to the climb-out heading. The aircraft handled well and roll and pitch control was positive. Any first flight on type is a case of getting off the ground and getting back safely while hoping that nothing goes wrong. It is only later that the aircraft can be flown further into the envelope with more confidence. After lowering the undercarriage and flaps and trying the speed brakes (very powerful), I returned to the circuit for two approaches and overshoots. The landing was straightforward, and after completing my landing checks I taxied in to the ramp to answer my squadron colleagues questions – "What's it like?" There is an old adage that if it looks right it will fly right – it did!'

The possibility of the F-86 being flown by the RAF was discussed not long after the aircraft entered service, but it was to be another three years before the necessary approvals and funding could be arranged. In the meantime the Sabre's qualities were evaluated by CFE in October 1950 when two F-86A-5s (FU-91279 and FU-91296) were delivered to West Raynham from Burtonwood.

As a manual operation, start-up on the Sabre required full attention throughout and the most critical aspect was to avoid over-fuelling by excessive movements of the throttle as this was liable to send j.p.t. into the danger zone. On most occasions it was necessary to close the throttle slightly below the 'idling stop' position into the fuel cut-off range (equivalent to partially closing the HP cock on a Derwent 8). Here throttle movements had to be watched very carefully until approximately 23% rpm had been maintained. USAF technical orders stated that an engine change was mandatory if j.p.t. reached 1,000°C momentarily, or if it exceeded 850°C on a total of five starts. As a result of the level of concentration required on starting, other duties had to wait which meant that scramble times were slower (fifty-four seconds for the Sabre compared to thirty-seven seconds for the Meteor).

During taxiing the all-round view from the Sabre was excellent, nosewheel steering made changes of direction easy and the powerful foot-operated brakes were rated superior to those of any contemporary British fighter. With increased tyre and oleo pressures (tyre pressure 155psi), the springing was much stiffer than in a Meteor or Vampire. During take off, initial acceleration was slow but there was an improvement as speed was gained, the Sabre flying itself off at around 105–110kt IAS with a slight backwards stick force. Although the take-off run was not measured by CFE, American figures quoted 1,200 yards to clear 50ft. As flaps were raised there was a nose-up trim change which was easily corrected by use of the trimmer, but owing to the rapid acceleration when airborne, there was no tendency for the aircraft to sink. As the CFE trials were carried out in winter, times to 40,000ft showed a slight improvement over the figure of thirteen and a half minutes quoted by North American.

During dives the F-86 accelerated rapidly and quickly reached its (then) limiting speed of Mach 0.95, its controls proving to be fully effective throughout. Commencing at 40,000ft and using 100% rpm, the Sabre reached 0.95 TMN after a shallow dive of 2–3,000ft during which the aircraft could be easily held in the required nose-down attitude. At around 0.94/0.95 TMN wing drop was experienced, but variations were noted between the two aircraft tested, one having a tendency to drop its port wing, while the other was liable to drop either. In terms of overall manoeuvrability the CFE report made the following comments:

'Rate of Roll – The F-86 has an exceptionally fast rate of roll at all speeds and altitudes. At 10,000ft and approximately 0.60 TMN the rate of roll measured by CFE pilots was 150 degrees per second, decreasing to 110 degrees per second at 0.90 TMN. The manufacturer's report states that the maximum rate of roll is 210 degrees per second at 0.60 TMN. A very slight high-frequency buffet is felt when ailerons are rapidly applied.

Controls – In normal flight the tailplane trimmer is invariably used to match the elevator forces with those required to operate the light ailerons. The trimmer is well positioned and highly effective, so that the pilot automatically retrims while manoeuvring. This tends to mask a deterioration in control harmonisation at moderately high IAS and high MN. At these speeds the elevator forces become progressively very much heavier than the aileron forces. These large forces occur when boost assistance reaches maximum output at a pre-determined load. Further force is applied by pilot effort alone. This applies also at high MN where the elevators sustain a loss in effectiveness and require additional movement.

Effect of G Loading – The aircraft has a maximum "g" limitation of +6g and it is stressed to +7.33. At high altitude it stalls before reaching the limiting figure. On the approach of a high-speed stall, warning is given by mild airframe buffeting. Any attempt to increase the "g" loading aggravates the buffeting and either wing might drop. When "g" is rapidly applied, cable stretch may allow the aileron to up-float. The ailerons are of large area and are positioned well behind the C.G. The result is virtually an "elevator-up" effect which causes the aircraft to tighten the turn and increase the "g" loading still further. According to the manufacturer's report, in a 6g pull out, aileron up-float can provide an extra 4g. Although care should be taken not to exceed the limitations, the effect in practice is not normally noticeable to the pilot as the up-float merely serves to lighten the elevator forces.

Radius of Turn – It has not been possible to accurately measure turning radii. At 40,000ft and 300kt IAS, a 360-degree turn can be made in approximately 1 minute 35 seconds. During the turn speed is lost to around

215kt IAS. According to the manufacturer's report, the maximum usable "g" at this height is 2.2–2.4 up to 0.95 TMN. This figure increases to 3g at 1.0 TMN. In practice the available "g" for speeds in excess of 0.95 TMN can never be used at high altitudes. As the "g" loading is increased, so the rapid drag rise slows the aircraft to a speed where the available "g" is less. As a result the aircraft has a large turning circle even at moderate speeds and any attempt to turn at maximum rate on the verge of a high-speed stall will merely reduce the rate of turn.'

Deceleration on the approach was not one of the Sabre's better characteristics, half a circuit being required to reduce speed from 300 to 175kt even when dive brakes were used, the nose held up and a steep turn initiated. Care had to be taken as the use of dive brakes produced a marked nose-up trim change which was in contrast to a slight nose-down effect when flaps were lowered. As no indicator was fitted in the cockpit, flap operation had to be checked visually. Once again, excellent cockpit visibility meant that landing was easy and there was no tendency to swing.

Combat assessments were carried out against Meteors, the Sabre's speed and docility proving to be a complete contrast to what pilots had been used to. The Sabre was pleasant to fly, possessing more stability in turbulence and was regularly flown up to its limiting speed of 580kt IAS without discomfort. The Meteor on the other hand was extremely heavy and fatiguing to fly above 450kt IAS. One point which did emerge during simulated combat was that the harmonisation of the F-86's guns along its datum line resulted in the guns pointing slightly above the aircraft's line of flight and, except at very high IAS, attacks had to be made from below the target, which could be a little disconcerting, particularly at low level. In comparing the Sabre and Meteor, the CFE report commented as follows:

'A mock combat was staged between the F-86 and a Meteor. It was soon apparent that although the F-86 possesses the advantage in rate of roll, zoom climb, dive and level speed, it should not if possible be committed to close dogfighting with straight-wing aircraft owing to the disparity in best operating speeds. It should normally adopt a policy of attack and withdrawal, using its advantages to regain the initiative. When flown in mock combat against the Meteor the following points emerged:

a) The F-86 in line astern proved capable of following the Meteor through most manoeuvres. The minimum turning radii of the two aircraft appear to be almost identical, the F-86 being if anything slightly inferior to the Meteor at low and medium IAS, and superior at high Mach numbers.

b) In steep dives with dive brakes extended, the F-86 tended to overshoot the Meteor.

c) The minimum j.p.t. limitation prevented confident throttle movement near minimum rpm. There was invariably a reluctance to close the throttle firmly to idle stop without reference to the j.p.t. gauge.

d) The effect of the Meteor's slipstream was a fairly severe and sharp jolt, without a tendency for a wing to drop.
e) The elevator stick forces were often heavy because the rapidly succeeding trim changes precluded full use of the trimmer.
f) The need for attack and withdrawal tactics was even more pronounced when dogfighting with a Vampire at medium and slow speeds.'

Simulated attacks were also carried out on bombers during which it quickly became apparent that the Sabre offered a much greater degree of tactical freedom. Its higher limiting Mach number allowed diving quarter attacks to be made on targets flying up to 35,000ft without risk of encountering compressibility effects, and its manoeuvre boundaries at altitude were such that it was able to make successful attacks at 20–25 degrees angle off at 30,000ft and fifteen degrees angle off at 40,000ft. The Sabre's small frontal area also made it difficult for bomber crews to spot and its high rate of roll was put to good use after attacking by ensuring a more effective breakaway. Negative aspects of the F-86's performance were few. Its speed was a handicap when attacking relatively slow piston-engined bombers as pilots had to become accustomed to having a very short amount of time with which to fire their guns. The necessity of attacking in a slight climb was also commented on unfavourably. In addition, it was thought that six 0.50in machine-guns were totally inadequate for knocking down large aircraft such as the B-29 Superfortress.

Sabres for the RAF were produced at the Canadair plant at Cartierville and were equivalent to the USAF F-86E with power coming from a General Electric J-47 GE-13 jet engine of 5,200lb.s.t. Like hundreds of American aircraft that served with the RAF in World War Two, the problem of delivery was solved by flying them over the Atlantic. Pilots of No. 1 Long Range Ferry Unit (later 147 Squadron) commenced Operation *Beechers Brook* on 8 December 1952, the stopping-off points along the 3,100 mile route being Goose Bay, Bluie West One and Keflavik. Final destination was either Prestwick or Kinloss, but occasionally Stornoway was used if bad weather intervened. The ferry operation took just over a year to complete, with the final aircraft being delivered on 19 December 1953. Sergeant Graham Elliott was one of the pilots who took part.

'During the summer months there was no particular problem and the trips were made easier by the long northern days, giving us a bigger "window" in which to operate. During the winter, however, things were exactly the opposite. There were no diversion airfields until we arrived over Scotland, thus making it essential to have clear weather for arrival. This was vital for Bluie West One, and a low-level approach up the fiord was briefed, but fortunately not used, as fifty miles low level was probably impossible with the fuel available. I flew the route six times and several trips were one hour fifty minutes which is just about as far as we could go with our two 100-gallon drop tanks. Bluie West One only had one (uphill) runway and the USAF had a bulldozer ready to sweep any disabled aircraft off as there was nowhere else to go.

The procedure (also not used by the RAF) if the airfield suddenly became fog covered, was to set a certain course over the beacon at a certain altitude, at a specified rate of descent until sliding to a stop on the ice cap, when one would theoretically be within walking distance of a survival hut, to await rescue. We also used Royal Navy immersion suits for the crossings. These were very uncomfortable and were worn over long underwear and sweaters. We had two sayings – "The average immersion suit will hold four and a half gallons of seawater", also, "Nine out of ten pilots pulled out of the Atlantic have nothing to say." The pulling out would have to be done by the USAF Grumman Albatross flying boats which orbited at the quarter and three-quarter points along the track, the halfway point being occupied by an Ocean Station Vessel (weather ship) to provide a radio beacon for us. Luckily we did not need their services. On more than one occasion the Albatross (we called them "Duckbutts") was not there, having been forced to return due to icing. We, of course, were above that problem.

Navigation consisted of careful flight planning on forecast winds, and the use of the ship radio beacons to check ground speed en route, although what we could have done if we had been more than a few minutes late at the halfway point was not really considered. We flew in sections of four (or occasionally two, but never alone) at five-minute intervals, normally at 35,000ft. Flying in our survival clothing, perched on top of a parachute and dinghy, ration pack and even a dismantled .22 rifle, was not comfortable. I remember my "bone dome" hitting the top of the canopy on several occasions. We were in fact the first RAF squadron to wear these in place of the World War Two style leather helmet and goggles. Over the twelve months of the operation, we lost eight Sabres and three pilots, but none of them in the Atlantic. This was not bad considering that the route, although previously flown by USAF and RCAF Sabres, had not been attempted in the winter before the RAF came along.

XB626 of No. 67 Squadron.

On a general note, the Sabre was a pleasure to fly, it had very good visibility from the large canopy and a full air-conditioning system. It even had armrests on the seat, pure luxury after the Meteors and Vampires we had flown previously. The performance was, of course, vastly superior to the Meteor, except in rate of climb. The hydraulic controls were better even than the later Hunter and Swift. It was, however, somewhat sensitive in pitch, Pilot's Notes warning that, "The tailplane must be used with caution until its sensitivity and effectiveness becomes familiar . . . it is possible to set up a rapid porpoising movement". It would go supersonic (just) by pointing vertically downwards at 40,000ft at full power and without drop tanks.'

After the application of camouflage paint, Sabres began to replace Vampire FB.5s with 67 Squadron at Wildenrath, and went on to serve with 3, 4, 20, 26, 71, 93, 112, 130 and 234 Squadrons in Germany, as well as 66 and 92 Squadrons in the U.K. The Sabre was greatly liked by all pilots and almost without exception they took to it like a duck to water. Despite its advanced lines and high performance, it was largely vice free and a delight to fly. Of particular benefit were the hydraulically operated ailerons, which were of large area and produced an excellent rate of roll. The similarly operated 'all-flying tail' was found to be more than adequate to counter trim changes in the transonic region. Not long after the Sabre entered service, sonic booms began to be heard over northern Germany, although it did take considerable effort to go supersonic as Flight Lieutenant N.F. Harrison DSO of the RAF Flying College discovered.

'After a general check, the Sabre can be pushed at full throttle into a dive of about thirty degrees. The speed and Mach number rise rapidly. Nothing happens until about 0.94–0.95M when either wing starts to get heavy, but this can easily be held with a small aileron movement. The wing heavying tendency may transfer to the opposite wing after a second or so, but at no time does it become worrying. By the time 0.97M is reached this period is passed and no further lateral unsteadiness is encountered. In a thirty degree dive the aircraft will not accelerate much past 0.97M and to reach supersonic speed the aircraft must be clean, the dive must be started from at least 35,000ft and must be vertical, with the throttle fully open.

A dive of this sort is accomplished without approaching any of the aircraft's limits; during the whole performance the IAS remains well within the limiting speed of 600 knots. The only strain is that imposed upon the pilot's nervous system because, for the average cautious man, it takes considerable determination and mental effort to half roll, pull through to a vertical dive at full power, and then deliberately hold the aircraft in this unnatural attitude while the speed builds up.

The wing-heavy period shows up as a few sharp wing drops that occur and disappear almost before they can be corrected, after which nothing more happens except for a nose-up change of trim which is easily held and which can be trimmed out by blipping the trimmer, taking care not to over-control as all controls are very sensitive at these speeds. There is no indication that Mach one has been exceeded, the Machmeter itself may not read more than 0.98–0.99M, but once its needle has slowed down and eventually stopped, there is no point in pressing on as this movement represents the Mach number terminal velocity. The Sabre, in other words, can only just reach supersonic speed with its present engine.

Recovery can be made either by throttling back and using airbrakes or simply by pulling out of the dive. The latter method uses up more sky but is quite straightforward, level flight being resumed somewhere around, or a little below, the 20,000ft mark. There is one point that must be watched when opening the airbrakes, which, incidentally, are operated by a thumb switch on top of the throttle lever. The airbrakes are set so that on opening they cause a nose-up change of trim. This change is fairly strong at high indicated airspeeds and so must be anticipated and checked if necessary. The rate of descent at 30,000ft is somewhere between 50,000 and 60,000 feet per minute, and even though you are at a fairly high altitude you are uncomfortably aware of the fact that objects below are getting bigger noticeably faster. And, as the TAS is somewhere around 700 knots, the racket set up by the airflow is appalling.'

By the time the Sabre entered service in March 1953, a number of RAF pilots already had considerable time on the aircraft, having flown it on active service in Korea. Paddy Harbison (by now a Squadron Leader) was one of four CFE pilots who left the U.K. in January 1952 to 'observe and report on the air war'. The other pilots involved were Wing Commander Johnny Baldwin, and Flight Lieutenants Rex Knight and Brian Spragg. Once in Korea, Baldwin and Knight joined the 51st Fighter Interceptor Wing under Colonel Gabreski at Suwon, with Harbison and Spragg going to the 4th FIW at Kimpo commanded by Colonel Thyng. A complete pre-combat training programme was undertaken by all incoming pilots under the name 'Clobber College' which included instruction in escape and evasion techniques and a phased introduction to the F-86, including instruction in the various tactical formations flown. Sadly, Wing Commander Baldwin was posted missing on 16 March, command of the detachment passing to Harbison who had plenty of opportunities to assess the Sabre against the MiG-15 – the following is an extract from his report to CFE:

'Climb – The MiG-15 can outclimb the F-86 at any altitude. Below 20,000ft the climb superiority is not so marked, but between 30,000ft and 45,000ft it is most noticeable. The MiG can sustain a high angle of climb which can leave the F-86 at the point of stalling whilst the MiG is still climbing away. This is especially so above 40,000ft where the MiG can execute a steep climbing turn impossible to follow in the F-86 without stalling. The zoom climb of the MiG-15 is outstanding and when attacked, is one of its evasive manoeuvres. A slight dive by the MiG to gain speed, followed by a climb estimated to be between 50–60 degrees, is something which has to be seen to be appreciated. An F-86 attempting to follow such a climb is obliged to level off at an estimated 6–8,000ft before the MiG.

Dive – The MiG-15 can initially dive away from an F-86, but in a sustained dive at lower altitudes the dive performance appears to be fairly equal. At high Mach numbers the MiG appears to be extremely stable and without the aileron roll experienced in the F-86 at very high Mach. The MiG-15, however, seldom dives vertically when chased, the usual tactics being to roll over sharply, dive for a few thousand feet to gain speed and then level out or climb at a high angle. It is considered that the F-86 is superior to the MiG-15 in a sustained or near vertical dive. Nevertheless, MiG-15s have occasionally, and in exceptional circumstances, been seen to recover from positions not thought to be possible.

Speed Comparison – Above 20,000ft the MiG-15 can outrun the F-86. As the altitude increases so does the top-speed advantage of the MiG over the F-86. This is especially noticeable between 30,000ft and 45,000ft where the MiG-15 is definitely superior and can pull away easily. Below 20,000ft the F-86 and the MiG-15 are about equal in level speed, although the F-86 can usually close the range very slowly. MiG-15 pilots appear to be aware of this fact with the result that they commence to climb which rapidly lengthens the range once more.

Acceleration – The MiG-15 can, initially, out-accelerate the F-86 in the dive and, most noticeably of all, in the climb. I find it a somewhat more difficult matter, however, to compare the level acceleration qualities of the two aircraft. Perhaps the following extract from a combat report will give a better picture: "At 35,000ft a flight of F-86s entered into a shallow full-power dive upon a MiG formation some 3,000ft below. Before the range closed sufficiently to open fire the F-86s were sighted. The MiG formation started accelerating and the F-86 rate of closure ceased. Whilst still maintaining almost level flight, the MiG formation then pulled away out of range." The foregoing is not by any means an isolated incident. At lower altitudes, however, the F-86 can generally stay with the MiG, or close very slightly. Summarising therefore, it is considered that the MiG-15 can, initially, out-accelerate the F-86 in diving, climbing and in level flight noticeably above 20,000ft.

Deceleration – There have been occasions where MiG-15 pilots have extended dive brakes when fired on by F-86s with the result that the F-86 has overshot the MiG after extending his own dive brakes. However, in these circumstances it will be appreciated that the F-86 was closing the range and the pilot had to suffer the inevitable time lag between seeing the dive brakes of the MiG go out and selecting his own brakes. It is, however, generally conceded that the F-86 has superior deceleration qualities over the MiG-15.

Rate of Roll – The F-86 has a very high rate of roll and no difficulty has ever been experienced in following a MiG-15. This is especially so at high speeds. Moreover, the MiG has been successfully evaded by F-86s rapidly reversing their turn while under "g" and at high Mach numbers. The MiG-15 has been unable to follow this manoeuvre, which points to a higher rate of roll and a more efficient control system in the F-86E. (Note – The F-86A and F-86E models have different control systems. The "E" model can out-roll the "A" model at any speed and is a better aircraft at high Mach numbers.)

Ceiling – F-86s flying at 46,000ft have seen MiG-15s at an estimated 5,000ft above them. The MiG-15 definitely has a higher ceiling than the F-86. This suggests that the MiG must possess a most efficient pressurisation and heating system to fly consistently at these extreme altitudes.

Turn Comparison – At 40,000ft and above the F-86 will stall in attempting to turn level with the MiG-15. As the altitude decreases below 30,000ft, however, the F-86 will turn with, or out-turn the MiG-15. This is especially true if the turn is made diving and at high Mach numbers. This is the standard evasive tactic employed by F-86 pilots, namely a hard diving turn pulling maximum "g" on the Mach. Usually, the MiG will break away after one 360-degree turn, but aggressive MiG pilots, generally presumed to be Russian instructors, have occasionally been known to follow an F-86 right down to ground level. From my own experience, I have been followed by a MiG-15 from 27,000ft down to 5,000ft pulling maximum "g" at high speed. Indeed, so violent were the turns that both my oxygen mask and flying helmet slipped. In following me down the MiG was, however, unable to hit me as he could not get enough deflection, although he appeared to expend all his ammunition in trying to do so. Fortunately such aggressiveness on the part of MiG-15s is the exception rather than the rule.'

In his report Squadron Leader Harbison also commented on the effects of jet fighter combat on the pilot.

'Another important tactical lesson learned is the fact that the day of the "dogfight" is not over . . . every manoeuvre is done at high speed and high "g" loading, with the result that the pilot reaches the point of complete exhaustion. The evasive tactic employed by F-86 pilots is to spiral downwards at maximum speed pulling the maximum number of "g" possible. MiGs can, and in exceptional cases will, follow the F-86 down all the way.

XB634 broken down into its major components.

I personally have had this experience and my No. 2 was shot down by a MiG-15 which out-turned him during our downward spiral. F-86 pilots have returned to base after such encounters so fatigued as to require a rest before being debriefed and with little or no recollection of the trip home. After about six tight turns at high "g" there comes a feeling of not caring and of exhaustion. MiG pilots in similar circumstances have been seen to bale out without being badly hit.'

Harbison was given the command of 67 Squadron in early 1953 shortly before the unit introduced the F-86 to RAF service. The first three Sabres arrived at Wildenrath on 12 March and Harbison was temporarily attached to the neighbouring 3 Squadron to organise formation of the Sabre Conversion Flight. The short SCF course amounted to five hours flying time and during April, Flight Lieutenants A.H. Turner, J. Mellers, D. Mullarkey, Flying Officer P.K.V. Hicks and Pilot Officer Jimmy Reynolds successfully converted onto type with another six pilots beginning the process. Having flown Spitfire 16s and Vampire F.3s with 604 Squadron, Peter Hicks found the Sabre a quantum leap in most respects.

'After the Vampire and Meteor, the change of aircraft generation, design philosophy and ten critical years of development was as marked in many ways as changing from pistons to early jets. We had powered controls for the first time which were delightful and light and the initial tendency to over-control soon passed off. There was a very roomy cockpit with modern instrumentation, air conditioning even – not just "hot air" – indeed the "trombone" on your left could make you sweat or deliver ice crystals. It was good to have the comfortable thought of assisted ejection being available, since up till then we hadn't even considered ejection seats. We were therefore uncritical of the crude features of the seat compared with even the early marks of Martin-Baker seats. It had no drogue parachute to slow it down and stabilise it after leaving the aircraft and, just as importantly, had no automatic separation or parachute opening. It just bunged you out, tumbling and spinning into the airstream and left you to release your seat harness, push the seat away, find the ripcord and pull it.

The R/T on the Sabre was a tremendous improvement compared with anything previously experienced, but the RAF had still to distribute the new "Farnborough helmet" consisting of a cloth inner helmet with a bone dome over it, to replace the old leather helmets. The USAF kindly lent us bone domes and headsets (not nearly as good as the Farnborough ones) until they reached us. Of course, being one of the first two squadrons in the RAF to be equipped with aircraft capable of going transonic we could hardly wait to climb to 30,000ft plus and roll into a full-powered dive to make a supersonic bang. To let everyone know we had done it we aimed at the Technical Wing hangar, next to ours. When large cracks appeared in the hangar roof and walls we had to aim a little further afield!'

Pilot Officer Ian Forrester could not believe his luck that he had got the chance to fly one of the all-time classic fighters.

'Training on the F-86 was unbelievable, intensely exciting and enjoyable with most of our instructors ex-Korean aces. The F-86 was a battle proven classic from the same stable as the Mustang. When formating with other Sabres its beautiful lines were almost poetic, hardly a straight line to be seen, just delightful curves with the pilot in a large perspex bubble on top with complete all-round visibility. The controls and handling were also excellent, one of the early exercises to impress new pilots was to put the stick hard over to one side and see if recovery was possible before ten revolutions had been counted. This was also a good demonstration of the need for a bone dome when one's head banged against the canopy!'

67 Squadron took delivery of its first aircraft (XB674) on 12 May, the subsequent acceptance check being the first flight by a Sabre in any RAF squadron. By the end of the month sufficient aircraft had been received to carry out formation practice for the Queen's coronation flypast over Dusseldorf which took place on 2 June, Wildenrath supplying twelve aircraft, six each from 3 and 67 Squadrons. Formation flying was to be the squadron's lot for some time to come as the Sabres departed for Duxford on 20 June to commence preparations for the Coronation Review. Preparations for the trip included the crystallisation of radios so that they were compatible with U.K. frequencies and the checking of small compartments for contraband! Over the coming days a number of rehearsals took place, pilots taking great delight in planting sonic bangs over Duxford whenever they were not required for formation practice. The Review itself took place at Odiham on 15 July and was the biggest flypast ever staged by the RAF.

After returning to Wildenrath, 67 Squadron began preparing for Exercise *Coronet* which commenced on 23 July. Most sorties were of a defensive nature, intercepting Canadian and USAF F-86s and F-84s and formations of up to twelve Meteors simulating bombers, but occasionally offensive missions were flown, providing top cover for Vampires of 71 Squadron which attacked the airfield at Gros Tenquin. Attacks were also made on Laon and Champagne whose F-84s were conveniently undispersed and made ideal targets. As four pilots had not yet converted to the Sabre, the week-long exercise meant that those who had were forced to spend long hours at cockpit readiness. Despite operating a new and relatively advanced aircraft, flying for the month amounted to a creditable 336 hours from 376 individual sorties.

The work-up period on the F-86 was not without incident and there were a number of occasions when pilots got into trouble as a result of the Sabre's extremely sensitive longitudinal control. It was easy to set up a violent pitching motion or Pilot Induced Oscillation (PIO) as Peter Hicks discovered.

'As a flight commander I was the first to discover (unintentionally) that the Sabre, without a load of ammunition for its six 0.5in guns, was neutrally stable fore-and-aft. Selection of airbrakes (a thumbswitch on the throttle) resulted in a very marked nose-up reaction, about 2g stick free. This of course one normally countered with increased forward pressure on the control column followed by trimming out the pressure with the electric

XB627 of No. 67 Squadron.

trim button on top of the column. One morning, leading a formation of four in a descent at about 450 knots following a practice interception, I had a good (?) idea. As I called, "airbrakes, airbrakes, GO," I selected airbrakes with my left hand and simultaneously (but not quite!) trimmed forward with my right. Because the combined actions had not been perfectly synchronised (which was almost impossible) the nose had pitched up but had then been overtaken by the trim and pitched down. The result was astounding and disconcerting. Put yourself on the back of the biggest, strongest, most wicked bucking bronco let out of its stall at a rodeo and you're getting somewhere near it.

Due to the neutral stability, I had set up a phugoid which diverged and increased in intensity – the aircraft was off on its own. The accelerometer afterwards registered +11 to –4g. Arms, legs and head beat up and down like a rag doll and my horizon was lost. Since control wasn't effective I thought to eject but couldn't get my arms to stay on the armrests [the North American seat was operated by a small handgrip on each armrest]. In the seconds necessary to regain my wits I eased back on the control column, throttled back and eventually returned to normal flight. The other three, who had of course opened out and left me strictly on my own, were nearly as relieved as I was. We later found that this was known to the USAF as the "J.C. effect" from the first words spoken on experiencing it.'

Little flying was carried out in early August prior to 67 Squadron's departure for Sylt on the tenth for air firing. Twelve aircraft took off in the morning, although those flown by Squadron Leader Harbison and Flight Lieutenant Wilson were soon back at Wildenrath having leaking drop tanks attended to. Live firing got underway on 12 August but initial results were not particularly good as the radar ranging on some aircraft was uncalibrated and fixed-ring sighting had to be used instead. Further problems were encountered a week later when Group Captain J.E. 'Johnnie' Johnson (Wildenrath's station commander) had his nosewheel come down in flight. This prompted an immediate grounding for an undercarriage micro-switch test and following a similar incident at Geilenkirchen, all Sabres were limited to gentle manoeuvres until modified nosewheel locks could be fitted. As a result of the grounding, and poor serviceability due to lack of spares, the squadron's stay at Sylt was not a great success, a situation that was compounded when one of the pilots 'shot down' a Tempest tug. The events leading up to this unfortunate incident are recounted by Paddy Harbison:

'The APC gunnery instructor had told me that the pilot concerned had been opening fire out of range which also resulted in a low angle of attack. The pilot, myself and the PAI gunnery instructor reviewed the cine film of the attack and advised that he close the range before opening fire to some 300 yards. His next sortie was uneventful until the cine film of his attack was again reviewed. The opening view was not of the target sleeve, but a large black mass which turned out to be the black circle in the centre of the target banner. Frighteningly close, so close that there was insufficient time to reverse the turn and pass over the banner. To avoid hitting the banner, the pilot had pulled considerable "g", thus losing sight of the banner and the Tempest tug. He was advised that his pattern was much too close and to adjust it to the desired 300 yards. He was also advised that pulling through the target was dangerous due to the risk of collision with the banner or the tug.

Two sorties later he repeated his error and opened fire too late and too close to the target to reverse and go over the top. He had the misfortune to have a runaway gun after the trigger was released. A hot gun will do this and cook off a burst. Unfortunately his cine film revealed all. The banner came into focus and he ceased firing – too close to break away, his sight line passed through the Tempest tug aircraft. The runaway gun burst put some rounds into the engine and some into the cockpit. The throttle quadrant was shattered and one or two rounds creased the Tempest pilot's thigh and severed one of his parachute lap straps. With a damaged engine and an inoperative throttle, the Tempest force-landed on some mud flats near Sylt. The pilot was lucky to escape serious injury.'

Normal training was carried out for the rest of the year but the first Sabre was lost on 17 September when Flight Lieutenant Wilson was forced to eject from

Four of No. 67 Squadron's Sabres endure a typical north European winter.

XB683 when he was unable to recover from an involuntary spin. Worse was to follow when Pilot Officers E.J. Cooper and B.G. Pearse crashed a week later in the squadron's Meteor T.7 (WF792) when attempting to go around after an asymmetric approach. Both were killed instantly. In October, deployments to Zweibrucken and Florennes were badly affected by fog and another stint of gunnery practice at Sylt had to be cancelled. In the morning of 6 November 'A' Flight managed to get a fluid-six airborne to practice battle formation, and 'B' Flight put up four aircraft on a battle flight. During a similar sortie in the afternoon the No. 2s collided at 15,000ft during a formation crossover and both aircraft broke up. Pilot Officer Craig in XB690 ejected successfully but Pilot Officer A.F. Pollock (XB730) was killed. Although 67 Squadron's accident rate was no worse than that of other units, attitudes to safety were rather different to those of today as Pilot Officer Peter Hay recalls:

'Flight safety in those days was not as dominant as in later years due to a combination of factors. First, the transition from the more sedate jets to the supersonic Sabre. The Sabre Conversion Course took all of ten days under S/L "Danny" Daniels and F/L Martin Chandler (both ex-Korea). In this day and age of long conversion-to-type courses it seems an incredibly short period when moving from around Mach 0.8 on Meteors and Vampires to Mach 1.0+ on Sabres. Then the influx of USA-trained pilots who had passed through Nellis AFB ("Thru these gates pass the best goddamned pilots in the world" type culture) imbued with the "tiger" spirit of training for Korea. Also, our leaders were nearly all ex-WWII and naturally we followed their style of leadership which was more robust and accepted the odd prang more philosophically than today. G/C "Johnnie" Johnson was our Station Commander, Mike Le Bas was OC Flying with Al Deere as OC Admin.

I recall when I was the newly arrived "sprog" on the squadron when a formation of twelve Sabres was to be led by Johnnie Johnson and I was slotted in as No. 2. I was petrified initially at the thought of being wingman to this fighter ace and the brief to me was, "Stick with him at all cost and don't lose him". Thank God I didn't, but we managed to lose the rest of the formation. He spotted a target way down low (his eyesight was superb) and, without a word of command, peeled over and zoomed down on his prey with the rest of the battle fours wondering where the hell he had gone. We would also hassle with the US and Canadian Sabres from Bitburg and Zweibrucken when we got the chance, either when they came north to entice us up or we went south to do the same. I have to admit that they usually had the edge. When we exchanged detachments it was noticeable how committed they were to flying and their competitive streak. They talked, ate, slept and lived for flying and tactics. We thought that we led pretty hectic lives with our flying and "prolonged" bar debriefs, but they were in a class of their own.'

January 1954 got off to a bad start with all of 67 Squadron's Sabres subject to a grounding following the discovery of a number of cracked drives to the trim motors. On 24 January, of the twenty-two aircraft on strength, one had been returned with acid corrosion, one was Cat 3, four were A.O.G., three were on minor inspections with another two awaiting their turn, six were u/s with various minor defects and two were on intermediate inspections, leaving just three available for training. By early February the situation had improved sufficiently to allow the squadron to fly to Sylt but a combination of ice-bound runways, low cloud and bad visibility, together with an occasional out of limits crosswind on the main runway, severely limited the amount of firing that could be carried out. The treatment of runways and taxiways with sand also led to a number of burst tyres due to the relatively high proportion of sharp flints that the sand contained. 67 remained at Sylt until 11 March before returning to Wildenrath to resume normal training which included air-to-ground firing on the range at Monschau.

In recent months there had been several new arrivals including Pilot Officer Trevor Egginton who had trained in the USA and had flown the F-86E/F out of Nellis AFB near Las Vegas. He recalls his impressions of the Sabre:

'As a fighter the Sabre had great all-round visibility through the large bubble canopy, you could actually see the left-hand tailplane looking round to the right. The cockpit was well laid out with everything falling to hand. For the day, it had a good gunsight and weapon selection system, good for firing guns, rockets and bombs, although I only did the latter in the USA. The engine was reliable – it always got you back to base – but its biggest drawback was its lack of power, the Australian Avon-Sabres and the Orenda-powered Sabres were so much better.

The control system on the Sabre was vastly superior to the Hunter, particularly the earlier Mk.4s. It was developed for combat in Korea through the "A" to the "E" and "F". The "A" had a boosted hydraulic-jack system for the flying controls, but all the later variants used fully powered hydraulic systems with no manual reversion, but with a separate electric-powered pump as back up in the event of a main system failure. This was selected by a "T" handle which coupled the pump motor direct to the battery, irreversibly.

The airbrake on the Sabre was very effective and could be selected partially deployed if required. At high speeds it would throw you hard into the straps but it also caused a very sharp pitch up; you had to be careful when using it fully out although on one occasion this tendency got me out of a bit of trouble. I had been in the American zone and was returning with not much fuel left so a very rapid descent was made for a straight-in approach. Coming onto finals I found that I couldn't move the stick aft to flare for landing so used the airbrake deployment instead. Why I hadn't kept it out I know not, we normally landed with the brakes extended. It freed later but on inspection with the tail jack disconnected, the tail could not be moved by hand. The bearing tube had no lubrication (not called for in the servicing schedule). Presumably the rapid descent from –40 to +15°C had caused some differential expansion causing it to seize temporarily. The landing was a bit firm I remember. All our aircraft were checked and lubricated.' [Trevor Egginton left the RAF in 1973 and eventually become Chief Test Pilot at Westlands. In 1986 he took the World Speed Record for helicopters in the Westland Lynx.]

Over the next few months better weather and much improved serviceability allowed the monthly target of 500 hours to be exceeded on most occasions, although two more aircraft were lost in March when XB936 failed to take off and overran the runway on the fourth and XB600 bellylanded after electrical failure on the twenty-second. Both pilots escaped without injury. On 11/12 May the squadron took part in Exercise *Prune Two* which was designed to test the effectiveness of radio and radar jamming on controlled interceptions. The Sabres were used as fighters but also to simulate a bomber raid during which they were intercepted by Venoms. Little difficulty was experienced, although one VHF channel was blocked with H/F jamming, the other only suffered L/F jamming which was relatively ineffective.

In June, the emphasis in training was on cine quarter attacks and tactical formation work with a few practice forced-landings and QGHs thrown in for good measure. During the month serviceability reached an all-time high and on one occasion the squadron had seventeen aircraft airborne at one time. July brought participation in Exercise *Dividend* which was designed to test the U.K. Air Defence system. Over fifty sorties were flown simulating bombers and although the Sabres did not cruise above Mach 0.74, the number of successful interceptions by U.K.-based fighters were 'alarmingly few'. 67 Squadron also participated in a flypast for Princess Margaret who was on an official visit to 2 TAF. One of those who took part was Pilot Officer John Harrison.

'The formation was twelve Venoms, twelve Meteor NF.11s and twelve Sabres; Trevor [Egginton] and I were the last pair. The practice sessions went OK but on the day it was low cloud and poor visibility. As the weather was clearly unfit we thought it would be cancelled but some hero at 2 TAF HQ decided it should go ahead. The plan was to meet up over a small village (Wassemberg) and then fly to Cologne for the flypast. It was interesting sitting at the back watching thirty-four assorted aeroplanes take off and disappear into the gloom. As we took off we could hear the Venom pilots calling "Where are you?" – "Over Wassemberg." – "So are we," then a call from the Meteor leader – "Keep those PPIs going." I can't remember if the leader made a call for us all to climb above cloud or whether I chickened out and decided for myself, but we climbed up and saw six Venoms and four Meteors. We tagged on the end, the numbers increased with time but never achieved full complement. The "hero" decided to call it off and there was then the problem of getting this lot down into poor weather at Wildenrath. This was achieved by a chain QGH in which one delayed carrying out the controller's instructions by twenty seconds per place in the chain. As we were about the fifteenth pair this was a bit confusing. However we burst out of cloud over Wildenrath in poor visibility with aircraft everywhere. With a great deal of luck we managed to avoid hitting anyone and ATC did a fantastic job getting us all down.'

XB625 on a rain soaked apron at Wildenrath.

In August further problems were encountered when a pilot was unable to lock one of his mainwheels prior to landing. He re-cycled the gear several times and yawed the aircraft from side to side but the leg refused to lock and eventually collapsed on landing causing the drop tank to blow up when it hit the ground. A similar incident occurred on 12 August but on this occasion the wheel was successfully lowered by bouncing the good one along the runway. This particular snag was caused by corrosion of the down-lock pins and led to a temporary grounding. Engineering staff were even busier four days later after a Sabre lost the top of its fin, another had an engine overheat on shut down and a third suffered hydraulic pump failure. With these setbacks the serviceability situation never really recovered and the average number of aircraft available for the rest of the month did not rise above four. Despite such a handicap, 508 hours were flown in 489 sorties.

Lack of aircraft remained the major difficulty in early September, a situation that was not helped when Flying Officer 'Jock' Thomson crash-landed XB627 out of fuel near Kleine Broghel on the seventh having chased a B-47 too far over the North Sea. By the middle of the month, however, fourteen aircraft were able to take to the air for the Battle of Britain display held on the fifteenth. The only incident in September was an extremely rare engine flame-out, a successful relight being carried out. (Among its other fine qualities the Sabre was also good in the glide as 'A' Flight Commander Flight Lieutenant Peter Sawyer had already discovered in Korea. Having lost his engine at 45,000ft he was able to glide over 100 miles to make a successful dead-stick landing at Kimpo.)

In October all aircraft were on the ground again as two aircraft had their nose-wheel doors open when pulling out from dives during air-to-ground firing at Monschau. On both occasions the doors were torn off by the slipstream and caused minor damage. Further serviceability problems throughout the rest of the month meant that the target in flying hours was not reached.

The situation in November was no better as all aircraft were grounded for generator checks. It was thought (wrongly) that this had been the cause of a recent in-flight break up near Geilenkirchen (*see* page 114). When the squadron was cleared to fly again the weather took a hand and it was only by maintaining a high degree of aircraft utilisation that the target of 535 hours was surpassed. Owing to the small number of aircraft available it was not possible to fly tactical formations and most flying was carried out in pairs practicing quarter attacks at various altitudes. With the imminent arrival of winter, emphasis was also placed on GCA letdowns and I/F training. The weather in December was appalling but tactical formation flying was practiced whenever the conditions allowed. Towards the end of the month, however, many aircraft were limited to 15,000ft as their oxygen regulators were time expired and there were no replacements.

December also saw the departure of Pilot Officer John Harrison who had been lying flat on his back in Wegberg Hospital for two months with a prolapsed disc. For some, the seating position in the Sabre was not ideal as the back was slightly bent and great strain could be imposed during high-g manoeuvres, a situation that was not helped by the weight of early bone domes. Harrison had been having back problems for some time and his groundcrew had to help him out of his aircraft after each sortie. At Wildenrath there were differences of opinion with regard to tactics, Paddy Harbison favouring the vertical 'yo-yo' which conserved speed by pulling as little 'g' as possible whereas Johnnie Johnson was an exponent of the high-g horizontal turn. The former method of fighting suited Harrison better but eventually he had to admit defeat and was invalided out (he later flew for Dan-Air and Kuwait Airlines before becoming a simulator instructor with BAe).

In February 1955 several aircraft were sent to Geilenkirchen for modifications to the wings which involved replacement of the slats with a 'hard' leading edge and an increase in chord of 6in. at the wing root and 3in. at the tip. Generally known as the 6-3 wing, this was a product of experience gained in combat with MiG-15s in Korea and provided pilots with extra turning performance, albeit at the expense of a higher landing speed and a slight worsening of the Sabre's previously impeccable low-speed handling qualities, a fact that caught some pilots out as Pilot Officer Peter Hay recalls:

'We changed from the Sabre 4 to the hard-edged Sabre which improved performance, especially turns at height, but one had to be more aware of handling at low speeds, turns and stalls. One pilot on the hard-edged Sabre raised his nose too high on take off and careered through the overshoot and through the runway approach lights. Surprisingly he walked out relatively uninjured through the side of the cockpit, the nose having twisted round and opened out enough for him to clamber out. Also on the hard-edged Sabres the Boss of our sister squadron, 71 (Eagle), was notorious for his tight turns in the circuit at low speeds. His more junior pilots (US-trained) had told him so and would not risk their necks in following. He led in a formation of four in echelon starboard, broke into the left-hand circuit and promptly spiralled in for another "black box" trip to Cologne cemetery.'

During the process of wing modifications two of 67 Squadron's Sabres were found to have cracked mainplanes and further problems were encountered as most returned aircraft had defective compasses necessitating the relocation of the sensing unit which had previously been located near the leading edge.

By mid-March most aircraft were back on line and total hours for the month were 602 from 586 sorties. April began with excellent serviceability but this did not last as many aircraft were due for inspections, some of which revealed more cracked mainplanes. Sadly, there was another flying accident on 5 April when Flying Officer M.J.C. Grant was killed in XB634 after colliding with an Anson on final approach. The month also saw the arrival of Squadron Leader H.E. Walmsley DFC to take over command of the squadron from Paddy Harbison.

In May, 67 Squadron moved to Fassberg for three weeks although flying was restricted to preserve sufficient airframe hours for a forthcoming two-week deployment to Cyprus. The training consisted mainly of air-to-air and air-to-ground firing, full use being taken of Fassberg's range facilities and shorter sortie

Peter Hay equipped and ready to go.

John Perrott of No. 67
Squadron in front of
XB627.

times. The long journey to Cyprus began on 12 June when thirteen Sabres departed for Furstenfeldbruck before flying on to Ciampino (Rome) for a night stop. A further refuelling stop was made at Alevsis (Athens) where two aircraft went u/s, one having made a heavy landing necessitating a retraction test, the other suffering from a nosewheel that refused to retract. The remaining eleven aircraft arrived safely at Nicosia on 15 June.

With the exception of a two-day visit by four Sabres to Abu Sueir, flying for the rest of the month consisted entirely of air-to-air firing. Five banner targets were planned for each day with four aircraft firing on each in pairs. Apart from two days when early morning fog prevented the first target being flown, weather conditions were perfect. Even so, the first week was largely ineffective as in most cases the radar would not lock onto the target. The detachment provided virtually the first occasion when the squadron had used radar ranging and as a consequence the lack of experience in both maintenance and application had to be overcome. Towards the end of the two-week period radar unserviceability had been reduced to an acceptable level and pilots had become more confident in its use. The only complaints about the deployment were of its brevity, the Sabres returning on 4/5 July via Balacasia (Turkey), Larissa (Greece), Ciampino and Fürstenfeldbruck. As headwinds were experienced on the return journey, fuel was tight and Flight Lieutenant Peter Sawyer recalls one of the Sabres running out of fuel shortly after landing at Ciampino. Final destination was Bruggen which was to be 67's new base, the squadron forming part of No. 135 Wing.

Training resumed on 11 July and consisted mainly of tactical formation flying which had been neglected in recent weeks due to the Cyprus detachment. Sabres were flown without drop tanks throughout the month, this having the effect of reducing total hours, but sorties were carried out to much higher altitudes which gave pilots the opportunity to exploit their aircraft's capabilities to the full. August started off well, but fell away dramatically from the middle of the month when several Sabres were found to have fuel leaks caused by cracks in the fuselage tanks. All aircraft had to be inspected which resulted in only 2–3 being available at any one time.

In early September, 67 Squadron departed for Sylt once again, this time for five weeks. Improved GCI facilities allowed firing to take place up to 20,000ft, which was much nearer operational conditions than had previously been the case. Firing was possible above cloud which resulted in far fewer cancellations due to weather. All firing was carried out using radar ranging with the aid of spinner-type reflectors on the banners which proved very effective. By the end of the month the squadron average was just below 10%. Shortly before the end of the deployment, groundcrews were placed in the spotlight with a competition to see how quickly they could refuel and rearm. This involved four Sabres taking off with full fuel and ammunition which was expended on a glider target. After landing the times to replenish all four aircraft were taken, and the procedure repeated. When all the figures had been collated it was found that the average turn-round time was just over twelve minutes.

After returning to Bruggen, air-to-ground firing was carried out at Monschau on 17/18 October. All sorties were made under ground control, the aircraft being talked onto the range and the dive made through cloud if necessary. Procedures had, however, been revised and attacks had to be made using a twenty degree dive with a break-off point at 450 yards. This was in response to two fatal crashes which had occurred on the Meppen range in August, XB548 of 93 Squadron failing to pull out from a dive on the third, with XB808 of 20 Squadron suffering a high-speed stall during recovery on the sixteenth.

Flying hours for November amounted to only 130, a total that was partly attributable to bad weather, but also, once again, to extremely low serviceability. The squadron was suffering from an acute manpower shortage at this time and there were also problems with insulation around the VHF aerials breaking down which resulted in excessive static and rendered the radios u/s. The situation was no better in December and many aircraft were to be out of action for considerable periods. XB626 was reported with distortion on all radio channels on 5 December but, as there were insufficient personnel to carry out repairs, it was still on the ground at the end of the month. XB682 was in an even worse state, as it had been in the hangar since 23 August awaiting spare parts (five items). These eventually arrived after three months and work finally began on the aircraft at the end of December.

By now the Sabre was coming to the end of its life with the RAF as the Hunter was becoming available to 2 TAF squadrons. Towards the end of the year 67 Squadron was informed that it would shortly be converting and pilots attended lectures on the new aircraft when flying was not possible. The first Hunter F.4s were delivered in January but, for the time being at least, Sabre flying continued as normal with tactical formations, practice interceptions and cine quarter attacks. Arctic weather in February limited total sorties to thirty-one and by March there were sufficient Hunters available for the Sabre to be retired, the last aircraft departing on 26 March.

Even though 67 Squadron had received an aircraft that was much more powerful, many said goodbye to the Sabre with a heavy heart. Pilot Officer Peter Hay:

'Personally I was sad to move from the lovely Sabre to the Hunter 4. It seemed to be a retrograde step at first, the primary advantage being

XB727 'Y' of No. 234 Squadron.

increased speed but the controls were not so precise, particularly the elevator. Flying the Sabre through Mach 1, the all-flying tail always gave positive control and feel. I recall on my first sonic run to Mach 1 on the Hunter that the stick went slack and there was no apparent control (you could stir it as a pudding without result) until the denser air produced elevator control. Otherwise the Hunter 4 was certainly responsive and twitchier on the ailerons, especially on take off. We used to compare first-solo take offs on conversion to the Hunter and lay bets on who would twitch the most. All-round visibility on the Sabre was far superior to the Hunter. With its bubble canopy you could release your shoulder harness (still safely strapped in), crane your neck around to look up your tail for any threat. In the Hunter 4 your shoulders were locked in to the seat and you had to ease your straps and use the mirror; one felt more vulnerable.'

The Sabre was liked not only by its pilots, but also by those who looked after the aircraft on the ground. Tom Broomhead was a radar mechanic with 234 Squadron at Geilenkirchen.

'Our first two Sabres were a magnet for the ground crews who needed to climb on, in and under, but first of all we were reminded about the ejection seat and the need to check that the pins were inserted in the handles (at the end of the seat arms, not above the head) before climbing into the cockpit. Another feature of the Sabre was its live systems. The Vampire only came alive when a trolley acc was plugged in, but the Sabre had an integral power supply, ably demonstrated by one airframe mechanic who, on trying out the cockpit, managed to deposit two drop tanks on the hangar floor (luckily not full).

My servicing role was to pre-flight the gunsight. Primary inspections were a little more involved as we were supplied with a test rig – a large metal box into which we plugged various systems and a portable antenna. This consisted of a Sabre nose antenna mounted in a small wooden box with a flexible lead attached. We would remove the nose-radar panel (in front of the windscreen) and plug our equipment into the radar gunsight equipment therein. The aircraft nose-radar antenna would be substituted for the portable antenna and then we would wait for a truck or car to appear on the perimeter track across the runway at a known distance. Once "lock on'" had been achieved, it was possible to adjust the gunsight for ranging etc. All of this was accomplished on top of a high step ladder alongside the nose of the aircraft, and removal and fitting of the nose-radar panel could be quite an interesting experience on windy days.

As radar mechanics we tended to be underworked compared with the engine and airframe trades, who also got a lot dirtier, so we usually helped them out. To service the radio it was necessary to sit under the aircraft to access a small panel inside which was a handle. After releasing the radio compartment latches, the radio could be wound down (on four cables) for service. It tended to come down easily but, because of its weight, was very difficult to wind up. The answer was for one person, lying on his back, to push up with his feet, whilst the other person turned the handle until fully retracted and the latches closed. At other times we helped the instrument mechanic replenishing the oxygen lines and we also helped with refuelling. This could be a little tricky – especially in winter – because spilt fuel on the wings tended to become very slippery. Some airmen did fall off, but luckily it was no great height.

Our busiest time was during Armament Practice Camp at Sylt. It was fairly high pressure to turn the aircraft round and get them off again, so when they landed everyone moved in to do their allotted tasks. If the pilots

Another No. 234 Squadron Sabre, fast and low.

had got poor scores on the drogue, they blamed the gunsight, so we were hard pressed checking ranging and calibration etc. The guns were mounted either side of the fuselage, the barrels exiting at the nose about head height, and the armourer's first task was to check that all guns were clear. On one occasion a photographic-section erk had also decided to attend to the gun camera set in the nose-intake lip. There was a round in one of the guns, which fired and narrowly missed the photographer who later said he "felt the heat" as it went past his ear. He actually fell to the ground and eye witnesses thought he'd been shot!'

Another member of 234 Squadron, Flying Officer J.R. Pintches, recalls his memories of the Sabre:

'The climb to height took all day, it was very poor, but once there it was a beautiful aircraft to fly. Its rate of roll was fast. Moving the control column to its limit in roll would produce two and a half rolls before the control hit the stops. We regularly banged our heads on the canopy doing this. The rudder was not power controlled, it was connected by cables (this allowed the fuselage to be separated aft of the wings for engine changes) so often, when approaching Mach 1.0, it would be necessary to correct for yaw caused by the cables not being tightened to the same value. When this was done the Sabre would slip through the "sound barrier" quite smoothly. Limits on the Sabre, being American, were limits, there was no built-in safety factor as on British aircraft.

I flew the slatted version first, which was a pleasure, except when the slat on one side stayed in and the other extended on the approach to land. Later, we used the fixed leading edges on some aircraft which changed the slow-speed handling and required a higher landing speed. If the hydraulics failed, the undercarriage was lowered by pulling a handle at the base of the control column. This locked the undercarriage down, but not always. Occasionally, releasing the handle unlocked the gear again so the pilot ended up having to hold it while he flew the aircraft with his other hand as well as operating the throttles and flaps. Even on the ground his troubles were not over as he had to retain his grip on the handle while stopping the aircraft (fortunately the brakes were toe operated), retracting the flaps, stopping the engine, raising the canopy and transmitting, "Help"!'

During the three-year period when Sabres were operated by the RAF, fifty-nine were lost in accidents, approximately 14% of the aircraft delivered. Causes were many and included engine failures, collisions, in-flight fires, structural failures as well as a number of weather related accidents, including two occasions in 1954 when pairs of aircraft were lost. On 24 February XB643 and XB667 of 3 Squadron flew into high ground near Henri-Chappelle in Belgium on a GCA approach, and on 22 July XD707 and XD730 of 66 Squadron crashed on Kinder Scout, Derbyshire in cloud. Twenty-two RAF pilots lost their lives flying the Sabre, although some had luck on their side including a 234 Squadron pilot who miraculously survived a mid-air break up.

On 29 October 1954 Flying Officer Peter Underdown was required to carry out an air test in XB860 after a minor inspection. Weather conditions were good with 3/8ths cloud at 6,000ft, wind 200/14 and a visibility of 10nm. Underdown took off from Geilenkirchen's runway 27 at 1307Z and climbed straight ahead before levelling off at 2,000ft and turning onto a course of 320 degrees. Shortly afterwards his aircraft was seen to pitch up violently, followed by an equally dramatic pitch down at which point it disintegrated. Subsequent investigation showed that the wing and tailplane main spar sections had failed due to over-stressing caused by negative 'g'. The pilot was thrown out through the canopy during the bunt manoeuvre and fell in his ejector seat which had not fired, but broken loose. His parachute partially opened when near the ground but he would undoubtedly have been killed had his fall not been broken by apple trees on sloping ground which, fortuitously, coincided with his trajectory. He sustained serious but non-critical injuries, including severe concussion that prevented him from having any recollection of what happened. The main part of the wreckage fell about 500 yards away from the village of Wintraak, near Sittard in Holland.

As the winds at 2,000ft were blowing at 35kt, debris was spread over a wide area and not all of it was recovered. Some pieces turned up in a local scrap yard on the day of the accident and despite RAF and Dutch guards being posted, further bits disappeared before they could be marked and moved. From an investigation of the remains it was thought that the break up had been caused by full-up travel of the tailplane (full-down elevator) and attention was centred on the artificial-feel bungee which, in the case quoted, should have exerted a force of 56lb. During the inquiry into the accident it became known that the USAF had lost three F-86Es in similar circumstances. In these cases it had been concluded that the aircraft had broken up due to overstressing as a result of loss of the artificial-feel system. Although it could not be proved conclusively, it was felt that Underdown had failed to recognise that artificial feel had been lost and had over-controlled to the point of producing a violent pitching which induced aerodynamic loads upon the structure beyond the design ultimate. This was backed up to some extent by the discovery in other 2 TAF Sabres of a number of defective brackets which secured the bungee for the artificial-feel system.

Pilot Officer Roger Mansfield of 112 Squadron was another to have a lucky escape.

'On 16 June 1954 I was asked to do an air test on a Sabre (XB884) which had been in the hangar for some maintenance work. I taxied out and took off as usual, climbing through 4/8ths cloud at about 2,000ft. Turning south I climbed up to altitude to carry out the air test. After about ten minutes, when I was at 20,000ft, I noticed a funny acrid smell coming from the air conditioning system, shortly followed by thick grey smoke. I turned off the radio, generator and battery switches and gradually the smoke subsided. As I was on 100% oxygen I didn't have a breathing problem, but now I was left with no navigation aids for my return to base. I set course to the north hoping to spot some pinpoint which I could recognise, and eventually did so. I had no communications with Bruggen but the weather was clear with good visibility below cloud so they should see me approaching and be able to keep other aircraft out of my way. As the flaps were electrically controlled I would have to do a long straight-in flapless approach at a slightly higher speed than normal, but the runway was plenty long enough and this was no problem. The undercarriage was also lowered electrically on the normal system, however there was a standby system which involved pulling a lever which mechanically released the up locks allowing the gear to be pushed down by the hydraulics.

At about 500ft I lowered the gear and was nicely lined up with the runway ahead, but as I was passing about 400ft the hydraulic controls of the aircraft went solid. I now had no control over the aircraft at all, except for the throttle! Luckily the aircraft was well in trim when the controls failed and continued its shallow approach towards the runway although there was no way that I could have landed it without an elevator to flare it once it reached the ground. By this time I was down to 200ft and I thought that if I applied full power on the engine the nose might rise in response to the increasing speed in that trim condition, thereby giving me more height from which to bale out. As the speed increased the nose did rise, gently at first and then quite markedly, so that eventually the aircraft was climbing away almost vertically. I pulled the lever at the side of my seat, which blew off the canopy and cocked the ejection seat mechanism. I then turned my attention to the ASI which by now was showing a decrease in airspeed as the angle of climb increased. I was now approaching 1,500ft and when the airspeed fell back to 100kt I squeezed the trigger of the ejection seat and got an almighty kick in the pants, finding myself clear of the aircraft and tumbling over and over first seeing sky, then ground, then sky again.

The Sabre ejection seat was not as sophisticated as the Martin Baker seats which were to follow, these did everything for you once you had pulled the ejection lever, including separation from the seat and deploying the parachute. However in my case it was a "do it yourself" job once you were out of the aircraft. Firstly I undid my seat belt and pushed the seat away; now for the parachute "D" ring just under the left armpit, or that was where it should have been! Frantically I searched for it with the ground now approaching at an alarming rate. I realised that if I didn't find it in the next few seconds I would be dead. Looking back on it afterwards I realised that I was not even scared, things were far too serious for that, it was just a cold objective realisation of the finality of the situation. At last my fingers closed round the cold metal of the "D" ring, which had somehow been pushed right round towards the back of the parachute webbing strap, and with infinite relief I pulled it with all my strength and the beautiful sight of the parachute unfolding above me appeared before my eyes.

I was so low when the parachute opened that I only had about five seconds in the chute before I hit the ground, just long enough for the speed of my fall to be reduced so that when I landed nothing got broken. Actually this all took place over the middle of the airfield and was witnessed by some of my pilot colleagues from our hangar. In between them and me was a small ridge about ten feet high surmounted by pine trees and I had disappeared behind the trees without a parachute from their angle of view.

The story was that they were tossing up for my rather nice BMW sports car when they saw me emerge unscathed, walking towards flying wing headquarters. This is not quite the whole story as, when the parachute opened and slowed me down, the seat, which I had separated myself from some twenty seconds earlier and had been falling just above me, caught me up and crashed into my bone dome, cracking it and giving me a superficial cut on the head. I was very lucky that it didn't collapse the parachute on its way.

It was decided that we should adjourn to the Officers Mess bar and get ourselves a few pints of beer, which seemed an eminently sensible idea to me. After we had been in the bar for about an hour someone said, "Let's go and see where the plane crashed". So we all piled into a couple of Land Rovers and roared off to the south side of the airfield. We had to go outside the perimeter fence and I remember being driven through a sandy area with young pine trees dotted about. As we approached the spot where the Sabre had crashed we could still see small pockets of undergrowth smouldering away, although the main fire had been put out. There were quite a lot of people wandering about examining the wreckage which was strewn over an area of several hundred square yards, mostly broken into small pieces. My eyes were drawn towards one small piece of the aeroplane which was lying by itself. The force of the impact must have been immense, for there on its own, completely apart from the cockpit, was the handle that I had pulled to lower the gear by the emergency system. It was a short metal rod with a red emergency pull handle on one end and a jagged piece of the shattered instrument panel combing on the other, in all about six inches long. As I stood there my heart went cold for I suddenly knew exactly what had happened.

Situated on one side of the cockpit was the standby gear lowering lever and on the other side was the standby flying control change-over lever. Both had red handles and both were only ever used in the case of an emergency, however the undercarriage emergency lever was attached to a two-foot-long wire cable, whereas the flying control change-over lever was attached to a metal rod about six inches long! I had pulled the wrong lever and there it was lying accusingly at my feet. In normal circumstances it was only pulled after you had experienced hydraulic failure to the flying control surfaces, when the lever changed over to an electrically driven system which gave you back control again. However, in my case not only had I isolated a perfectly serviceable hydraulic flying control system, because there were no electrics to revert to, the flying controls had lost all their power and locked solid. All this flashed through my mind as I stared down almost unbelievingly at the lever. No-one else had noticed it at that time and it even crossed my mind to pick it up and dispose of the evidence, so great was my feeling of shame. Then I realised that I could never live with myself if I did this and so picked it up and walked over to my Boss, Squadron Leader Hegarty, gave it to him and told him the whole sad story.

Before we left the scene of the crime a few of us broke off some brushwood and, for the want of anything else to do, began beating out some of the small smouldering areas of vegetation round about. As I was doing this I heard a loud bang and felt something strike the base of my right thumb. It was one of the 0.5in machine gun bullets which had been strewn over the area when the plane had disintegrated on impact and which had been set off by the heat of the fire that I was trying to put out. As that was the third time I had nearly been killed in the last two hours, I felt that discretion was the better part of valour so returned to my room and went straight to bed.

Two interesting sequels happened with regard to this accident. The first occurred only a few weeks later when I asked my Boss to write a letter confirming my bale out so that I could apply for the much coveted Caterpillar Club badge which is issued by the Irvin parachute company to any pilot who has saved his life by using one of their parachutes. The letter he wrote was as follows:

"This is to certify that P/O R. Mansfield saved his life by bailing out of a Sabre 4 aircraft which was subsequently destroyed. The accident was entirely due to finger trouble on his part. Afterwards he was shot in the hand by an exploding machine-gun bullet, which served him jolly well right." Signed, Sqn Ldr F. Hegarty, C.O. No.112 Squadron.

I was very hurt when I first read this, but now I realise that it was exactly right, especially as this was the only repercussion that I had from the accident. I have always felt sadness and a certain amount of shame that I was the cause of the loss of such a wonderful aircraft, even in difficult circumstances, but it was only quite recently that the whole thing was put into perspective by a friend of mine when we were discussing aircraft accidents in general. He said – "Yes of course you do your best, but sometimes things go wrong. The main thing is that you walk away from it – to hell with the aircraft, they can make thousands more of them, but your parents could only make one of you!"'

XB920 of No. 112 Squadron with one of the unit's first Hunter F.4s.

By May 1956 all Sabres had been replaced by Hunter F.4s and the surviving aircraft ferried back to the U.K. Having been supplied under MDAP, they were returned to the USAF and many went on to serve with other friendly air forces. The only exception (XB982) was flown by Bristol Siddeley for development work in connection with the Orpheus jet engine. During its brief service life with the RAF the Sabre created a favourable impression with all who flew it and the strength of the various Sabre Associations today reflect its right to be included among the all-time greats. For one pilot it was 'the Spitfire of the jet age'. No tribute could be more fitting.

CHAPTER FIVE

SUPERMARINE SWIFT

At the end of World War Two, with the demise of the German aero industry, Britain was the world leader in jet-fighter technology. The Gloster Meteor had already been in squadron service for a year and the engine firms of Rolls-Royce, de Havilland and Metropolitan-Vickers were making excellent progress with centrifugal and axial-flow jets of up to 5,000lb.s.t. In contrast, the Americans had a few examples of the Bell P-59A in service, mainly to provide training for the USAAF pending the arrival of Lockheed XP-80 Shooting Stars, and the Soviets had yet to enter the field of jet-powered flight. Within a few short years however, Britain would rank a poor third behind both the U.S.A. and the Soviet Union.

Having emerged from war impoverished and exhausted, there was a deep desire to move on and leave the memories of the past six years behind. As if to reinforce that fact the General Election of 1945 returned a Labour Government whose policies regarding defence were to have serious implications for national security for many years to come. Once again it was assumed that there would be no European war for ten years and there was a huge cutback in the country's military forces so that by 1946 the RAF could muster only twenty-six fighter squadrons. Research budgets were slashed and the Miles M.52 supersonic research aircraft was cancelled, the official reason that it was 'too dangerous' proving to be cruelly ironic as many test pilots were to be killed over the next decade as aircraft manufacturers attempted to make up for the time that had been lost.

In the immediate post-war years two factors dominated the quest for speed, British proficiency in jet-engine technology, and German research into advanced aerodynamic shapes to delay the onset of compressibility. During the war the Americans and British had freely exchanged information and examples of the early Whittle engine had formed the basis of the jet-turbine industry in the U.S.A. As it happened the British were also responsible for the foundation of Russian expertise in this area with the extraordinary 'gift' of Rolls-Royce Nene jets in 1947, engines that were quickly copied to power the MiG-15. The significance of German aerodynamic research was quickly appreciated by the Americans to the extent that the XP-86 (*see* Chapter Four) was redesigned to employ a thirty-five degree swept-wing to produce the incomparable Sabre. The story was the same in the Soviet Union whose design bureaux were quickly experimenting with designs featuring highly swept wing and tail surfaces. Of the major powers, only Britain failed to take full and immediate advantage of the data coming out of Germany, a policy which ultimately had serious implications for its defences.

The complacency which existed in Britain after the war did not last long. In 1947 Winston Churchill warned of the 'Iron Curtain' which had descended over Eastern Europe and the following year crisis in Europe was only averted by the use of air power to transport supplies into Berlin to overcome the Russian blockade. In 1949 the Soviet Union exploded its first nuclear device and in 1950 war broke out in far-off Korea. As a result of these events Britain belatedly realised that the new world order was far from stable and that the RAF's current fighters were rapidly becoming obsolescent in comparison with second-generation aircraft already in service elsewhere. Contracts were eventually awarded for the development of advanced aircraft and associated weaponry but the lost years had placed Britain's aircraft industry in an extremely difficult situation. In the U.K., one of the first products of the 'Cold War' was the Supermarine Swift, an aircraft that was developed into an excellent low-level photo-reconnaissance machine, but was an abject failure in its intended role of high-altitude interception.

Supermarine's first attempt at jet-fighter design resulted in the Type 392 which married Spiteful laminar flow wings to a somewhat portly fuselage containing a Rolls-Royce Nene. The prototype, TS409, was flown for the first time on 27 July 1946 and was developed into the Attacker which entered service with the Fleet Air Arm in 1951. In 1946 Supermarine were asked to construct two aircraft based on the Type 392, but with swept flight surfaces, to Specification E.41/46. As the research programme was seen as being low cost, its granting still owed as much to Treasury penny pinching as to any great desire to explore the realms of high-speed flight. Despite the fact that the new aircraft was based heavily on the Attacker, it was still over two years before Chief Test Pilot Mike Lithgow was able to take the first Type 510 (VV106) into the air at Boscombe Down on 29 December 1948.

The Type 510 featured a forty-two-degree swept wing but retained the tailwheels of the Attacker. It was immediately much faster than anything that had gone before and easily attained speeds of up to Mach 0.90. At speeds in excess of this figure there was a marked deterioration in lateral stability to the point where full right aileron was needed to prevent the port wing from dropping. At the other end of the speed scale serious tip stalling was experienced at low speeds during the approach. Another worrying feature was an erratic yawing motion which was eventually traced to turbulence created in the engine intakes.

The second aircraft to E.41/46, Type 528 (VV119), flew for the first time on 27 March 1950. It was soon back at the manufacturers for extensive modification work, which included an extended nose to carry a nosewheel undercarriage, a new and larger swept wing and the fitting of an afterburning Nene 3 jet engine. The latter also required alterations to the air intakes, rear fuselage and the carriage of additional fuel. Redesignated Type 535, VV119 took to the skies again on 23 August 1951 but it quickly became apparent that the longer nose had adversely affected directional stability and a dorsal fillet had to be added to increase fin area.

The pace of development suddenly quickened following the outbreak of war in Korea and two pre-production prototypes based on the Type 535 were

Supermarine Type 535 VV119.

ordered on 9 November 1950. More re-engineering took place installing a Rolls-Royce Avon RA7 of 7,500lb.s.t. and the first of two Type 541s (WJ960) flew on 1 August 1951. Unfortunately it was soon in trouble. Mike Lithgow had to land without power on 3 August after severe vibration led to the fuel cock breaking, and another engine failure on 8 September resulted in Lieutenant Dave Morgan force-landing short of the runway when on approach at Chilbolton. A number of similar failures were to dog the Type 541/Swift over the next two years. The trouble was eventually traced to the compressor-blade root fixings of the Avon engine itself, but not before much time had been wasted trying to solve the problem by changes to the inlet ducts.

By now the manufacture of the first two production Swifts was well under way at Supermarine's experimental section at Hursley Park, while the works at South Marston geared up for full production. The second pre-production prototype (WJ965) was flown for the first time on 18 July 1952 and was quickly followed by the first production example (WK194) on 25 August. Further changes had been incorporated into the design including modified nose contours, increased fuel tankage and a revised wing position in relation to the fuselage. In addition, the thickness of wing skinning was reduced to save weight.

First service evaluation of the Swift F.1 occurred on 8 November 1952 when Squadron Leader C.G. Clark DFC of A&AEE flew WK194 at Chilbolton. His report was not favourable and highlighted several major handling problems including a lack of stall warning and associated wing drop, pitch-up in the turn and aileron flutter at high speed. Already aware of these characteristics, the company set in motion a modification programme which included a variable-incidence tailplane, wing fences and fully-powered ailerons. In the event only eighteen Swift F.1s were produced.

Whereas the Swift F.1 was armed with two 30mm Aden cannon, the F.2 had

121

double the firepower, although this was to lead to a considerable worsening of its handling problems. The guns in the Swift were positioned under the engine intake ducts and to cater for the increased ammunition for the extra pair of Aden cannon, the leading edges of the wings adjacent to the fuselage were extended. Unfortunately this brought about a marked deterioration in pitch-up. Numerous modifications were to be made to the wing in an attempt to eliminate the problem, including wing fences and dogtooth extensions to the outer wings, but the ultimate cure was to move the C.G. forward by adding ballast to the nose, a drastic measure which ruined the aircraft's high-altitude performance. The Swift F.2 turned out to be even less numerous than its immediate predecessor, only seventeen being produced.

There were also doubts about the Swift's stall/spin characteristics, especially after the loss of WJ965 on 10 November 1953. The aircraft was being flown by Squadron Leader N.E.D. Lewis of A&AEE to test various stall conditions and ten minutes after take off it was seen flying slowly at around 3,000ft with wheels and flaps up. Witnesses stated that the engine appeared to be making a loud 'crackling' noise. Later, the Swift was seen flying between 3–5,000ft when the engine noise died away, at which point it entered a flat spin to the right from which it did not recover. Although fitted with a Martin-Baker Mk. 2 automatic ejection seat, Lewis made no attempt to abandon the aircraft and was killed. The accident occurred during or following Lewis's investigation of the stall in the landing configuration, with power off. It was established that full nose-up trim had been applied.

The assumption was later made that the odd engine noise was likely to have been caused by surge at the high angle of attack necessary to place the aircraft in the correct landing attitude, although during a subsequent investigation by Rolls-Royce no evidence of surging could be found. When the nosewheel was extended, the Swift showed a directional trim change to the right and the theory was put forward that engine surge had distracted Lewis to the point that he had failed to correct with rudder leading to a spin developing from which there was insufficient height to recover. The slow, flat nature of the spin was put down to the influence of flap.

The first production Swift F.1s to be evaluated at Boscombe Down were WK201 and WK202, which arrived in January 1954. Due to the need to get the Swift to the RAF as quickly as possible service release was soon granted, albeit with a long list of flight restrictions. These included non-operational use only, speed limits of 550kt below 5,000ft and Mach 0.90 at heights between 5–25,000ft and a maximum height limitation of 25,000ft. Intentional spinning was also forbidden. Other limitations included a maximum take off weight of 17,200lb (max landing weight 16,000lb), and loadings were not to exceed +6g.

Such severe restrictions were the result of some worrying deficiencies in the Swift's performance which echoed A&AEE's previous findings with WK194. Above 25,000ft severe pitch-up was encountered at high Mach numbers to the extent that it occurred even during relatively moderate low-g manoeuvres. Turns were also limited by the onset of buffet. Criticism was made of the elevator controls which were generally heavy and lacked effectiveness above Mach 0.91. There was also a marked nose-down trim change when the air brakes were used

Swift F.1 WK195 landing at Farnborough. (*RAF Museum Hendon*)

at speeds of Mach 0.94 and above, and a pronounced wing drop was noted between Mach 0.92 and 0.94. Engine surge was an ever-present hazard, and during fully developed stalls there was a marked tendency for the aircraft to depart into a spin. An assessment of the Swift was also carried out at CFE and three aircraft (WK206, WK211 and WK212) were delivered to AFDS on 13 February, with WK205 going to the Handling Squadron on the same day. By the end of April, 109 hours had been flown, WK211 achieving the highest total with forty-one hours.

For pilots who had been used to the roomy cockpit of the F-86 Sabre the limited amount of space in the Swift was somewhat disappointing, although the reduced number of instruments and better layout meant that the display could be memorised more easily. Start-up was fully automatic and took around twenty seconds to reach idle after pressing the starter button. Taxiing proved to be extremely easy, the view was excellent, throttle response was good and the powerful and effective brakes made steering straightforward. Prior to take off the aircraft could be run up against the brakes to around 7,400rpm and during the run itself there was no tendency to swing. Any direction changes that were needed to counteract cross-winds had to be made with differential brake until the rudder became effective at around 50–60kt. Acceleration was rapid and the Swift flew itself off at 135kt, the best climbing speed of 415kt being achieved one minute fifteen seconds after brake release. With an AUW of 16,732lb the length of runway required to clear 50ft was 1,400 yards. No change of trim occurred as flaps and undercarriage were raised and there was no tendency to sink. The only slightly disconcerting aspect of the take off was a distinct thump as the nosewheel retracted.

Rate of climb varied from 9,000ft/min at sea level to 1,500ft/min at 40,000ft, and although a maximum altitude of 44,500ft was achieved, there was no useful climb performance available at this height. Times to height (min/sec) compared to the Sabre 4 and Venom were as follows:

Height	Swift 1	Sabre 4	Venom
20,000ft	3.00	4.30	4.00
40,000ft	9.45	14.00	9.00

With regard to high altitude dives at high Mach number, the CFE report made the following assessment:

'The Swift Mk.1 accelerates rapidly in a dive from 40,000ft. At an angle of thirty degrees it quickly reaches 0.96 IMN which is a TMN of 1.00. As speed increases the control column moves progressively aft of the central position and the elevator control becomes less and less effective. Response to the elevator is extremely slow as 0.92 IMN is approached. At speeds above 0.92 IMN the elevator is tactically useless, since with the stick fully back the nose will rise only gradually and the pilot must sit and wait for the response. The elevator effectiveness decreases with increasing altitude as well as increasing speed. If the airbrakes are operated above about 0.93 IMN during a dive, a nose down pitch is produced and the dive angle may be increased by fifteen to twenty degrees with no trim change. Slight buffeting is felt. Above 0.93 IMN it is doubtful whether the airbrakes are effective. It is felt that under these circumstances, their use will not help during the recovery phase and are liable to aggravate the situation.

Throughout the dive little trim change is felt and the stick forces are so light that little use need be made of the trimmer. As 1.00 TMN is reached there is a slight tremor on the elevator which might be accompanied by the stick moving slightly fore and aft. For recovery the throttle should be closed and the stick held firmly back until the denser air is reached when the elevator feel begins to return. A slight push force may then be necessary in order to prevent the aircraft tightening up of its own accord and stalling from excessive "g" during the pull out. In a dive from 40,000ft during which 1.00 TMN is reached, the aircraft will regain level flight at approximately 25,000ft. This loss of 15,000ft is tactically unacceptable. The highest Mach number achieved with a vertical dive at full throttle from 40,000ft was 1.13 TMN. The aircraft was rolled on its back at 0.80 IMN and pulled through to a vertical dive with full throttle. 1.00 TMN was immediately exceeded. At 25,000ft with an IAS of 440kt, the throttle was closed and the pull out was achieved at 17,000ft.'

In acceleration the Swift showed a marked superiority over the Sabre and in a comparative test at 0.80 IMN at 35,000ft the Swift overcame a 300 yard deficit in forty-five seconds when full power was selected. It then continued to accelerate away at an estimated speed advantage of 10–20kts.

At the stall, the aircraft developed a strong judder and a high rate of sink before the actual stall itself, anything up to 1,500–2,000 ft/min. With continued back pressure on the stick this rate could be increased until one wing became heavy and the nose dropped. At 10,000ft with wheels and flaps down, the stall occurred between 110–125kt depending on fuel load, but these figures were raised considerably with only a moderate increase in 'g' loading. Height loss in a fully developed stall was usually around 2,000ft. Although experience of spinning was limited, CFE pilots found the aircraft reluctant to spin, full rudder and back stick being needed to produce a breakaway at 150kt at 18,000ft. Recovery began immediately the controls were centralised, although it was important to ensure that the ailerons were kept neutral. Height loss during the spin was around 2–3,000ft per turn.

During aerobatics the Swift proved to be a delight, although pilots were warned to check hydraulic pressure before starting manoeuvres to guard against sudden, unexpected reversion to manual control. Loops were commenced with an entry speed of 430–450kt and, provided full power was applied when vertical, the Swift went safely over the top, speed having decayed to around 230–250kt. With its light ailerons, the aircraft's rate of roll was high at all speeds and exceeded that of the Sabre at high IAS, although this was not translated into radius of turn which was rated as poor against the Sabre and even worse when compared with the Venom.

As the trials proceeded problems were encountered with the powered ailerons which were operated via a mechanical linkage to a Fairey booster situated one at each aileron. Operated hydraulically, they provided fully-powered operation, with feel being provided by spring loading on the control column. Should hydraulic pressure fail, or the pilot select 'manual' control, the boosters disengaged automatically leaving the ailerons directly connected to the controls. When power was reselected the boosters were re-engaged by two hydraulically operated pawls which entered slots in the jack rods. On a number of occasions, however, only one pawl engaged, which meant that one aileron was in power while the other was still in manual. If such a situation arose it was necessary to forcibly move the stick through its full lateral travel until the other pawl engaged, not an easy task as the force required to move the ailerons in manual was three times that needed when in power. In operation, the power controls were not as positive or well harmonised as those of the Sabre and the artificial feel was described as being 'spongy', particularly at high altitude when considerable movement of the control column was necessary to change the attitude of the aircraft.

One of the Swift's main deficiencies at altitude was a basic instability, especially above 20,000ft. During the climb constant attention had to be paid to the ASI to maintain the correct speed, and flight at 40,000ft required an excessive amount of instrument flying during which it proved to be impossible to trim the aircraft to fly accurately straight and level. During high-speed stalls there was a tendency for the Swift to flick out of the turn, and at low speeds with airbrakes out there was a slight lateral wander giving 2–3 degrees yaw in either direction that could not be counteracted by stick or rudder. Use of maximum 'g' at altitude led to a rapid decrease in airspeed and if 'g' was increased in a turn above 20,000ft, the aircraft began to judder and was liable to suddenly tighten into the turn. If this occurred the pilot had to move the stick forward rapidly to avoid a high-speed stall.

During high-altitude testing, a wide variety of compressor stalls were experienced and the loss of height before effective use of the engine could be regained varied from 2–8,000ft. Most of these occurred at very low temperatures coupled with high rpm and high angle of attack and usually occurred when in the buffet above 28,000ft. On some aircraft it was possible to produce the characteristic banging noise in the engine but if the pilot reacted quickly enough by closing the throttle the engine remained alight. The aircraft then had to be dived in order to increase airspeed to around 200–250kt when the throttle could be opened and normal thrust regained. A number of intentional flame-outs led to the worrying discovery that relights could not be guaranteed above 20,000ft.

On the approach, it was recommended that the downwind leg be flown at around 230kt, the aircraft's most disconcerting habit being its tendency to yaw when the undercarriage was lowered. As deceleration in the landing configuration was rapid, it was suggested that the turn onto finals be made at no less than 160kt with as little flap as possible, full flap being left to the later stages of the approach. Speed over the boundary could be reduced to 125–135kt depending on weight, but it was recommended that power be kept at 6,000–6,500rpm due to the fact that airspeed fell away rapidly with the engine throttled back. Engine acceleration was also extremely slow. It was also discovered that the aircraft was prone to 'g' stall at low speeds if mishandled. If conditions were poor with a low cloudbase, the Swift was by no means the ideal aircraft with which to carry out a bad weather circuit due mainly to loss of elevator effectiveness and rather sloppy controls at low IAS. Its large turning circle meant that almost full-back stick was required to stay near the airfield boundary.

The landing itself was easy, touchdown occurring at around 120–125kt with fifty gallons of fuel remaining. Thanks to its extremely effective brakes the landing run could be as little as 1,200 yards under ideal conditions. Care needed to be taken when landing on wet or icy runways however, as intermittent wheel grip due to the aircraft's relatively wide undercarriage track could lead to a swing developing.

During simulated scrambles the Swift was airborne from the ORP in fifty seconds, a time that was bettered only by the Venom, and with full tanks (475 gallons) it took just under ten minutes to climb to 40,000ft. This could be reduced to just over seven minutes if fuel was reduced to 300 gallons, but radius of action was reduced from 250nm to 160nm. To ascertain the aircraft's suitability for medium-altitude attack, a small number of sorties were flown against B-29s, the Swift's high rate of climb and lightness of aileron control making all types of attack possible, although care had to be taken in high astern attacks as speed built up quickly, and the undesirable high Mach characteristics mentioned previously could lead to the pilot being unable to bring his guns to bear. At heights above 30,000ft the Swift's large turn radius (4.4 miles at Mach 0.80 at 40,000ft) severely hampered successful interceptions – at best it called for very accurate GCI, and at worst (at speeds of Mach 0.90 and above) the pilot was unable to manoeuvre sufficiently after sighting the target to be able to set up an attack.

In combat with other fighters the Swift could gain success if it achieved an element of surprise and used its superior speed to the full. However, should it be drawn into a dogfight, it stood little chance of manoeuvring into an attacking position and was more likely to be shot down itself because of its poor turning circle and the fact that it lost speed rapidly during turns. This became apparent during mock combat with Venoms and Sabres, which also had the advantage of having a superior operational ceiling.

In conclusion, the CFE report highlighted four main shortcomings – poor manoeuvrability at high Mach number, inadequate operational ceiling, compressor surge during steep turns at low IAS and high angle of attack, and poor rearward visibility. The Swift was considered to be effective against targets such as B-29s and Canberras flying at heights up to 35,000ft, but above this height the chances of success against targets such as the Ilyushin IL-28 became increasingly unlikely.

While the CFE trials continued, 56 Squadron at Waterbeach became the first (and last) user of the Swift in the interceptor role, the first aircraft (WK209) joining the unit on 20 February 1954. By the end of the month two more aircraft had been delivered and the squadron's conversion was aided by Supermarine test pilot Dave Morgan, who spent a week at Waterbeach, together with a whole host of Air Ministry 'boffins'. The Swifts initially formed 'B' Flight, with 'A' Flight continuing to fly Meteor F.8s, the intention being to replace the Meteors when sufficient aircraft had been delivered, although in the event this was never achieved.

For most of March serviceability rates were abysmal and it was only at the end of the month that more than one aircraft could be flown at the same time. By contrast the following month saw the Swifts fly 137 hours but, despite optimism at the time, this proved to be a false dawn. April also brought 56 Squadron's first in-flight emergency when Captain Jack Brodie USAF experienced hydraulic failure during a night flying detail on the fourteenth. The undercarriage was eventually lowered by the back-up pneumatic system, but the aircraft had to be landed under manual control as the aileron hydro-boosters were also inoperative. This was a portent of things to come as trouble with the Swift's power controls would be the major engineering headache during its brief service life. As no more aircraft had been delivered during the month, several pilots who had converted onto type were forced to revert to flying Meteors with 'A' Flight.

Having shown a certain amount of promise in April, flight trials of the Swift were soon thrown into complete disarray. During the first week in May, Flying Officer A.D. Harvie diverted to Coltishall with a defective fuel gauge, Flying Officer J. Hobbs made an emergency landing following a hydraulic leak, and Wing Commander K.C.M. Giddings (O.C. Flying Wing) had his ailerons lock on final approach. Considering what was to happen over the next few days it is worthwhile looking at this last incident in some detail. The following comes from Mike Giddings' incident report:

'On 4 May 1954 I flew Swift WK208 on a *Rat and Terrier* exercise. On rejoining the circuit downwind I noticed that the controls had reverted to manual although the hydraulic pressure gauges were both showing normal pressures (approx 3000psi) and the aileron power switch was still in the "power" position. After selecting "manual" and then reselecting "power" on the aileron switch, the controls went back into normal power operation. Just as I was levelling out at about 250ft, but when I still had a little port aileron on, I selected full flap whereupon the aileron power dolls-eye immediately started to flicker. At this moment I found that I could not move the stick at all. As I was down to fifty gallons I was loath to overshoot but opened the throttle to approximately 7000rpm. Airspeed at this moment was 150kt.

By this time I had slightly overturned the runway and applied slight starboard aileron (about 1in. stick movement) to realign. I then attempted to centralise the stick but could not do so. To keep the wings level I was forced to apply full port rudder. By this time I was more or less in line with the runway at approximately 150ft, airspeed 165kt. I then selected the power control switch to "manual" but still could not move the stick to port but continued my descent with the stick still about 1in. starboard of central and with almost full port rudder applied. Being in a suitable position to land and unwilling to overshoot with the small fuel load, I throttled back and pushed the aircraft onto the runway touching down at approximately 160kt. Immediately before touching down I centralised the rudders and landed without undue stress.

The hydraulic power gauges were registering 3000lb just after touchdown. The runway was wet (a storm had just moved away from the airfield) but I had little trouble in pulling up after about 1800 yards. It was necessary to use brakes very sensitively to avoid lock on the wet surface. The stick was still solid laterally during the landing run except for about 1in. play to starboard. At the end of the runway I reselected "power" and put both hands on the stick but could not move it to port until I loosened my straps and half standing up, obtained more leverage when the stick reverted to normal power operation. Taxiing back to dispersal I reselected "power" and "manual" several times without any difficulty.'

Although a thorough inspection was carried out no fault could be found and following a successful air test, WK208 was put back on the flight line where it was scheduled to be flown by Flying Officer Neil Thornton on 13 May on what would be only his second flight in a Swift. His detail required him to take off at full throttle, climb at 7,750rpm to 20,000ft after which he was to accelerate to 0.91 IMN before initiating a sequence of dives, zoom climbs and steep turns. This was to be followed by a QGH procedure to 2,000ft, visual approach, overshoot and single landing. Weather was ideal with 1/8th cloud at 5,000ft, wind 140/5kts and a visibility of 7nm. Thornton took off from runway 05 at 1500Z and immediately after becoming airborne began a very slight turn to port before climbing away in a normal manner. Approximately fifteen seconds later he called up stating that the aircraft was uncontrollable and that he was baling out. At a height of 600ft and two miles from the airfield, the cockpit canopy was jettisoned, after which the aircraft was seen to snake slightly before diving into the ground at an angle of forty-five degrees. It exploded and disintegrated, killing Thornton instantly.

As a result of the accident all Swifts were immediately grounded pending investigation of the aileron control systems. The Court of Enquiry brought to light the fact that this was not an isolated incident as similar problems had been experienced at Boscombe Down and West Raynham. Only three months before, Flight Lieutenant L.A. Coe of the Handling Squadron at Boscombe had experienced a situation remarkably similar to that which had confronted Neil Thornton, as his report testifies:

'On 22 February 1954 I was authorised to carry out a familiarisation flight in Swift Mk.1 WK212. It was my second flight on type; whilst performing cockpit checks after starting I noticed that the aileron power indicator was at white – indicating that the locking pawls were not engaged. I attempted to engage them by moving the control through its full lateral travel. The indicator remained white but the control column appeared to have full free movement indicating that the aileron power was successfully engaged. Knowing from experience that the dolls-eye type of indicator was inclined to occasionally stick I decided that the indicator was unserviceable and to take off. I was wrong.

As soon as the aircraft became airborne I realised that I had aileron direction in one direction only. The aircraft started to roll slowly to starboard and I was unable to prevent it with a maximum two-handed force on the control column. I thereupon reduced power and selected aileron power off. I was able to regain control immediately and continued to make a circuit and land in "manual". After landing I was able to re-engage aileron power quite easily by switching on and moving the control column smartly from side to side until the pawls were felt to engage and the indicator went to black. I took off for a second time and continued the flight without further incident.'

On 29 April WK212 was being flown by Flight Lieutenant H.S. Carver of AFDS at West Raynham when control problems were again experienced.

'Before taxiing, aileron and elevator controls were checked to be engaged in "power" and a further check was carried out just before entering the runway in use. A check was made both visually of the ailerons and of the warning blinker. A full-power take off was then commenced and on becoming airborne the ailerons were found to be locked solid. Lateral control was maintained by use of rudder. A delay of about twenty seconds followed before the pilot selected manual control on the ailerons. On selection it appeared to take about ten seconds for the hydraulic aileron control to disengage. However, manual control was then obtained. Four attempts were made to reselect aileron power control – using 7000rpm and 350kt – but neither aileron engaged during any attempt. The aircraft was then flown for thirty minutes in manual to use up fuel and a manual circuit and landing carried out.'

Flight Lieutenant Carver, a highly experienced pilot, later described the incident as 'frightening' and it is significant that a considerable period of time elapsed before he made the decision to switch to manual control. Largely as a result of the evidence of previous problems with the power control system in the Swift, it was concluded that the most likely cause of Thornton's crash was jamming of the ailerons.

In fact WK208 was not the first Swift to be lost in squadron service, as Squadron Leader G.J. 'Twinkle' Storey had been forced to eject from WK209 on 7 May after carrying out practice stalls in the landing configuration at

25,000ft. His aircraft entered a violent spin to the right and no amount of control input or variations in power could make it recover. Having tried all possible techniques Storey ejected safely at 10,000ft. The only other mishap to occur to the Swift before the grounding came into effect involved Flight Lieutenant D.P.F. 'Mac' McCaig who burst both tyres on landing and ended up on the grass at the side of the runway.

With the Swift temporarily out of action, 56 Squadron had to take delivery of an additional batch of Meteor F.8s so that 'B' Flight pilots could maintain their proficiency. No Swift flying took place at all during June as modifications continued, the main work involving the fitting of a positive hydraulic selector for aileron power, together with a warning light. At the same time as this work was being carried out, several other mods were incorporated including an audio warning of hydraulic failure and Maxaret brakes.

By the end of July the first modified Swift was air tested by Supermarine test pilot Les Colquhoun and was then flown by Squadron Leader Storey on the twenty-fourth. Over the next few weeks all four of the squadron's Swifts took to the skies again but serviceability was again so bad that it was virtually impossible to plan a flying programme. Most of the pilots that had already flown the Swift managed to reconvert but single sorties were the order of the day as aircraft invariably went u/s after each trip. Some high-level cine gun sorties were at least possible during which it quickly became apparent that the Swift was not as stable a gun platform as the Meteor due to its highly sensitive controls.

In the morning of 25 August only WK213 was pronounced fit to fly but very soon it was spread all over a wood near Six Mile Bottom, a small hamlet to the south-east of Waterbeach which was fast becoming popular as a final resting place for out-of-control aircraft. Flying Officer John Hobbs took off at 0917 hrs to carry out a practice for a forthcoming Battle of Britain flypast to be followed by simulated forced-landings, but on rejoining the circuit he was confronted with

Swift F.2 WK242 of No. 56 Squadron.

130

a single red light on lowering the undercarriage. A low-level flypast over the tower confirmed that although the nosewheel door was open, the wheel was fully retracted. With fuel now down to fifty gallons the emergency button was pressed to try to blow the nosewheel down, but this too failed. Hobbs was then instructed to climb to a safe height and abandon the aircraft as it was thought that a landing with the nosewheel retracted might result in a wingtip 'digging in' and a cartwheel developing.

Having jettisoned the canopy at 1,500ft, Hobbs continued to climb through cloud to 8,000ft where he levelled out. By now four fuel tank 'dolls-eyes' were showing white, as was that for fuel pressure. He experienced difficulty in trimming the foot loads off the rudder and then throttled back prior to reaching up with his left hand for the ejection handle, his right hand still grasping the stick to keep the wings level as the aircraft was flying right wing low. As he attempted to grab the handle his hand was sucked out of the cockpit by the slip-stream and he experienced great difficulty in bringing it down again, losing his wristwatch in the process. After finally getting hold of the handle, he pulled hard only for the blind to descend no further than eye level. A further tug succeeded however, and he was ejected out of the aircraft. Initially the seat started spin-ning, but it soon stabilised itself and just as he was about to reach for the override D-ring, he and the seat parted company and the parachute opened. Not long after, a safe landing was made in a cornfield less than a mile from his aircraft's crash site. (Hobbs' difficulties in initiating the ejection sequence were shared by others and led to the firing handle of later versions of the Martin-Baker seat being located at a much lower level.)

With Swifts becoming distinctly scarce at Waterbeach, one of West Raynham's remaining pair of F.1s was delivered to 56 Squadron on 26 August to be followed four days later by two camouflaged F.2s direct from South Marston. A temporary grounding following Flying Officer Hobbs' accident was lifted on 7 September which allowed some pilots to visit the SBAC Display at Farnborough although Flying Officer A. Martin suffered a flame out on finals and only just made it to the undershoot area of runway 23. Back at Waterbeach, the increased risk of pitch-up with the F.2 was immediately apparent and Wing Commander Giddings ruled that the new aircraft were only to be flown by pilots possessing adequate experience on type. The policy in future would be to convert pilots onto the F.1 initially, and then, after 5–10 sorties, onto the F.2. In addition to the previous list of limitations, the F.2 was also restricted from carrying ammunition or ballast in lieu.

On 9 September two more Swifts arrived, an F.1 from West Raynham and an F.2 from South Marston. Around this time the Meteor Flight became 'B' Flight, with the Swifts forming 'A' Flight (also known unofficially as 'Test Pilots' Flight). With more aircraft on strength formation flying could at last be contemplated and on 13 September five Swifts flew in Vic formation in preparation for a fly-past over London for Battle of Britain day. This event took place at 1700 hrs on 15 September (having been put back from midday due to bad weather) and involved Wing Commander Giddings, Squadron Leader Storey, Flight Lieutenant McCaig, Flying Officers Hobbs and Martin, the latter having taken over from Flight Lieutenant Gledhill who had to drop out with an R/T problem.

Waterbeach had its own 'open day' on 18 September and during rehearsals on the seventeenth Flying Officer Martin experienced hydraulic failure when in close formation, but later made a successful (manual) landing. At least the usefulness of the hydraulic failure audio warning system was proved as it allowed him time to break formation before reverting to manual control. In addition to displaying the Swift at Waterbeach, Flight Lieutenant Gledhill flew over to Biggin Hill where he had to be escorted from his aircraft by service police to prevent him from being mobbed by young boys wanting his autograph! Thereafter he was referred to, somewhat disparagingly, as the 'Chief Test Pilot'. On 25 September total Swift flying time for the day amounted to eleven hours which was far in advance of anything previously achieved, and on the twenty-sixth several aircraft began power, range and endurance tests up to the restricted height of 25,000ft.

Just when it seemed that the Swift was at last making progress there was another serious incident involving the aircraft's power controls. During a flight in F.2 WK244 on 1 October, Flight Lieutenant G.F.W. Hoppitt had an aileron go into 'manual' and lock there, a successful landing eventually being made thanks to the pilot's flying skill (and strength) in overcoming the problem. All Swifts were immediately grounded once again but just as before, ground tests, including high speed taxi runs in WK244, produced no obvious defects. This particular aircraft left 56 Squadron on 23 October to undergo further testing at Boscombe Down.

Flying recommenced with the Swift on 15 October, the opportunity having been taken to modify the aileron manual selector handle to make it easier to grasp in an emergency. With little apparent progress being made with the Swift,

ACM Sir Dermot Boyle signs the Form 700 at Waterbeach on 25 October 1954. (*RAF Museum Hendon*)

Fighter Command's Commander in Chief, Air Marshal Sir Dermot Boyle KBE CB AFC, visited Waterbeach on 25 October to make his own assessment of the aircraft's potential during a brief sortie. Unfortunately his visit was marred by another emergency landing. On returning to Waterbeach, Flying Officer R.A.J. Carrey found that he was unable to lower his nosewheel and diverted to Duxford where he considered carrying out a belly landing. On this occasion the emergency system lowered the offending leg before such drastic action was needed.

By the end of October, 56 Squadron had twelve Swifts on strength but could still only manage a total of sixty-four flying hours for the month. At least half of the available aircraft were having snags rectified in the servicing hangar at any one time, and as average sortie length was only 40–45 minutes, hours built up very slowly. In November the squadron departed for Armament Practice Camp at Acklington. Aircraft were flown whenever available but serviceability was still extremely poor. The only mishap occurred when Wing Commander Cooper (Acklington's W/C Flying) ran off the perimeter track and bogged down resulting in Cat 2 damage.

In October it had been decided to form a third Flight ('C' Flight) to undertake all repair and rectification work on the Swifts, formed from 'A' Flight personnel and seven technicians from the Air Servicing Flight, Technical Wing (all major and minor servicing still to be carried out by ASF). Due to the detachment to Acklington this plan could not be implemented until the New Year and although it led to an improvement in serviceability, high level decisions had already been made to withdraw the Swift from the interceptor role.

In January 1955 'A' Flight spent much of its time on the ground, not due to technical problems, but bad weather. Runways and taxiways were icebound for much of the month and flying was only made possible after the application of sand to clear snow and ice. Operations with Meteors went ahead as normal but it was felt that such material would be easily ingested into the Swift's Avon engines and could cause damage. The enforced lay-up at least gave servicing crews plenty of time to rectify outstanding snags so that February would see the second-highest monthly total in terms of hours flown. Ironically this was the month when it was announced in the House of Commons that the Swift would be taken out of service and replaced in the fighter role by the Hunter. By the end of February all 56 Squadron's pilots, except three newcomers, had converted onto the Swift together with several of 63 Squadron's senior pilots. 56 continued to use the Swift until 15 March when the type was officially withdrawn, the aircraft being ferried to 33 MU at Lyneham. They were replaced by Hunter F.5s which began to arrive in May 1955.

The following table shows 56 Squadron's use of the Swift in the thirteen month period in which it flew the type:

Period	Number on strength	Flying hours (hrs/mins)
22–28/2/54	3	10.00
3/54	5	13.02
4/54	5	137.39

Period	Number on strength	Flying hours (hrs/mins)
5/54	4+	27.08
6/54	4	--
7/54	4	3.11
8/54	4	44.40
9/54	6–10	79.23
10/54	10–12	63.59
11/54	10–12	55.31
12/54	10–12	49.06
1/55	10–12	60.01
2/55	10–12	105.27
1–15/3/55	10–12	70.50

Total hours amounted to 781.23 in 1,086 individual sorties.

During the Swift's brief service in the fighter role a total of thirty-four pilots of 56 Squadron flew it as follows:

S/L G.J. Storey	F/O R.A.J. Carrey	F/O J. Hobbs	F/O M.J. Withey
Capt J.L. Brodie	F/O R.E. Chitty	F/O A. Martin	F/Sgt Herbert
Capt C.G. Gillespie	F/O C.M. Christie	F/O Marvin	F/Sgt Tindal
F/L J.P. Gledhill	F/O H.L. Crawley	F/O K. Mills	Sgt Mitchell
F/L G.F.W. Hoppitt	F/O J.M. Daulby	F/O H. Munro	
F/L D.P.F. McCaig	F/O G.S. Drury	F/O R. Rimington	
F/L E. Richards	F/O R.C. Fenning	F/O D. Stringer	
F/L I.A. Simmons	F/O M.P. Gower	F/O S.A. Sumner	
F/L R.E. Webster	F/O A.D. Harris	F/O P.H. Sykes	
F/O R.F. Byrne	F/O A.D. Harvie	F/O N. Thornton	

In addition 56 Squadron also supervised the conversion of thirty-two other RAF pilots onto the Swift.

Although the days of the Swift as an interceptor were over, testing continued and on 16 March 1955, the day after the type's official withdrawal, WK220 was flown by Flight Lieutenant John Crowley of A&AEE to test engine relights above 25,000ft. During the flight a loud bang signified a serious problem with the Avon and several attempts to relight the engine all failed. Rather than eject, Crowley elected to carry out a wheels-up landing at Boscombe Down but lost control when the aircraft swung through ninety degrees and left the runway. Fortunately it remained upright and eventually came to a halt without injury to its pilot. When damaged fuel pipes had been replaced, the Avon was started up and ran perfectly, even performing several successful relights. In a situation reminiscent of the power control problems, no defects were found and the reason for the in-flight failure remained a mystery.

Two more fighter variants of the Swift were produced, the F.3 and F.4, but neither got any further than service evaluation by A&AEE. The F.3 was essentially similar to the F.2, except that it had an Avon RA7R offering 9,500lb.s.t. with reheat, although its use meant that sortie time was reduced to a wholly unacceptable 25–30 minutes. Pitch-up was still present but was more controllable due to the fitting of vortex generators above and below the tail surfaces. Twenty-five F.3s were produced (WK247–271) and after testing, most ended their days as ground instructional airframes.

The F.4 featured further improvements intended to improve the Swift's handling characteristics, the three principal modifications being the use of saw-tooth outer leading edge extensions, a taller fin to allow the carriage of a ventral fuel tank and a variable incidence tailplane. Tests were carried out at A&AEE on F.4 WK272 in February 1955 but unacceptable longitudinal control and engine characteristics led to its return to the factory for further modifications. The report on the Swift F.4 was eventually finished after the aircraft's return but, once again, the conclusions were mostly negative. It was assessed as being effective up to a height of only 38,000ft but due to a general lack of manoeuvrability, it was considered that the Swift would be outclassed by other fighter types at all heights above 15,000ft. Adverse comments were also made about the aircraft's lack of endurance.

With the F.4 in full production at South Marston, cancellation of the Swift fighter could have threatened Supermarine's very existence. As they were also responsible for development of the Scimitar carrier-based fighter for the Fleet Air Arm, such an eventuality would clearly have been unacceptable and so the decision was taken to adapt the F.4 to the low-level high-speed tactical reconnaissance role as the FR.5. with a lengthened nose to accommodate three cameras for forward and oblique photography. All-round vision was improved by a frameless clear-view canopy and there were also wing hardpoints for the carriage of up to 2,000lb of bombs or rockets. The Swift F.R.5 replaced the Meteor FR.9s of 2 and 79 Squadrons and served as part of 2nd Tactical Air Force in Germany from January 1956 until early 1961.

During this period the FR.5 proved to be an excellent performer at low level, its robust airframe, speed and stability being ideally suited to the fighter-reconnaissance role. Unfortunately, space does not allow a discussion of the Swift in the FR role and in discussing only pure fighter variants, it may well be that this book has presented a rather bleak view of the aircraft. Anyone wishing to learn of the Swift's successes in its later life should look no further than Nigel Walpole's comprehensive history *Swift Justice* (Astonbridge Publishing).

Although the FR.5 was to spend much of its time on ultra-low-level reconnaissance sorties over Germany, it was tested at CFE to ascertain its capabilities as an interceptor, despite the fact that the decision had already been taken to cancel further development of the Swift in the fighter role. As the FR.5 was closely related to the F.4, which was to have been the main fighter variant of the Swift, the CFE report gives a good insight into the reasoning behind its cancellation.

During the trials the Swift FR.5 was compared with a Hunter F.6 which proved to be superior in nearly every respect. One of the few areas in which the Swift held an advantage was in rate of climb as it took seven minutes to reach 45,000ft when operated clean which compared to a figure of eight minutes for the Hunter. To attain this figure however, the Swift had to be flown in reheat which resulted in a much higher fuel burn, 1,470lb compared to 880lb for the Hunter. If a ventral fuel tank was carried, the Swift's time to height was reduced to eight minutes fifty seconds, although this was still faster than the Hunter when fitted with underwing tanks. The times to height in minutes and seconds from wheels rolling and fuel used were as follows:

Height	Hunter 6 clean	Fuel used lb	Hunter 6 2 tanks	Fuel used lb	Swift 5 clean reheat	Fuel used lb	Swift 5 ventral reheat	Fuel used lb
35,000ft	5.00	665	5.30	760	4.30	1190	5.05	1300
40,000ft	6.00	755	7.00	850	5.17	1300	6.31	1420
45,000ft	8.05	880	10.00	1000	6.58	1470	8.50	1680
48,000ft	10.15	980	13.00	1130	9.30	1720	12.30	2010
50,000ft	12.20	1030	—	—	—	—	—	—

Once at altitude the Swift's weakest point, its basic lack of manoeuvrability, soon became apparent. To obtain reasonable manoeuvring performance the aircraft had to be operated in reheat above 37,000ft which imposed a crippling fuel penalty of 100lb/min, compared with 45lb/min for the Hunter. The manoeuvre boundary of the Swift was so low that it proved to be extremely difficult to measure 'g' accurately with the pilot's instruments, and if the aircraft was pulled into the buffet above 40,000ft the induced drag rise was so large that even reheat would not prevent speed falling and height being lost. A small pitch-up was also experienced at 0.2g beyond the buffet, but this was easily controlled. With a ventral tank fitted it was not possible to maintain height in gentle turns at 35,000ft without exceeding max continuous rpm, and in a comparison of turn performance at 40,000ft, the Hunter was able to get on the tail of the Swift in one 360-degree circle having started the turn with the situations reversed. At the same height, and at 0.9 IMN, the Swift's radius of turn was 5.2nm, almost double that for the Hunter.

Such limitations meant that it was extremely difficult to work out how the Swift could best be used to attack a hostile aircraft with any degree of success. Assuming a target flying at Mach 0.85 at 45,000ft it would have had to be flown clean on one of the following profiles:

a) Reheat climb to 40,000ft followed by cruise at max continuous rpm with the final climb to 45,000ft included in the ten minute reheat allowed for combat. This particular profile would have depended on faultless GCI.

b) Reheat climb to 45,000ft followed by cruise in reheat to the target ignoring the engine limit of ten minutes. The radius of action for this sortie would have been approximately eighty-four miles.

Although the use of reheat allowed the Swift to be operated to 45,000ft (ventral) and 46,000ft (clean), problems were encountered in that the reheat often commenced a gentle surging which tended to get progressively worse until it had to be cancelled. In most cases it could be relit at 45,000ft but this procedure was not 100% reliable and tended to vary from one aircraft to another. Without reheat the aircraft would lose height from 45,000ft if any turn was attempted. As the whole operational value of the aircraft depended on the successful use of reheat, its lack of reliability was extremely serious.

Another performance aspect where the Swift did have a slight edge over the Hunter was its manoeuvrability in the longitudinal plane which allowed it to recover from a forty-five-degree dive at 1.05 IMN within 5,000ft on elevator alone, assuming that recovery was initiated by 35,000ft. If the variable incidence tailplane was used, recovery was more rapid still and a pull force of 4½g could be attained. It was thought, however, that little tactical advantage could be derived from this ability considering the Swift's shortcomings in performance and its lack of manoeuvrability in the lateral plane. In terms of level speeds the Swift in reheat (clean or with ventral tank fitted) was slightly inferior to the Hunter at all altitudes.

Largely due to the need to operate the Swift in reheat, its radius of action was significantly worse than that for the Hunter as illustrated by the following figures:

	Hunter 6 – 2 tanks	Swift 5 – ventral	Hunter 6 – clean	Swift 5 – clean
Cruise altitude	45,000ft	35,000ft	45,000ft	40,000ft
Cruise IMN	0.90	0.87	0.90	0.87
Radius of action	358nm	253nm	163nm	111nm
Fuel cons 10 min	520lb	1000lb	520lb	900lb
Combat	full power	full reheat	full power	full reheat
Combat altitude	45,000ft	40,000ft	45,000ft	45,000ft

Overall, the Swift was considered to be tactically and operationally unsuitable for the role of interceptor fighter due to its poor level-speed performance in dry thrust and excessive fuel consumption when reheat was used, the unreliability of the reheat system at altitude, and its unacceptably low manoeuvre boundary. In addition, its restricted radius of action when compared to the Hunter F.6 led CFE to conclude that the Swift was not capable of adequately dealing with a threat flying at Mach 0.85 and 45,000ft.

The final Swift variant to fly was the F.7, of which twelve were manufactured, following the cancellation of the unarmed PR.6. The F.7 was used in development trials of the Fairey Blue Sky (Fireflash) air-to-air missile with 1 Guided Weapons Development Squadron at Valley where it was regarded as the best Swift of the lot. Its long-span wings and slab tail improved handling and it also featured the much-improved Avon 116 with reheat. Unfortunately, the type's basic lack of agility remained and even with the benefit of hindsight, the decision to drop the Swift from the interceptor role in favour of the Hunter was undoubtedly correct. The last Swifts to be used were two pre-production F.7s – XF113 which flew with the Empire Test Pilots School at Farnborough until 1962, and XF114, which was used by Bristol Siddeley at Filton for wet runway trials in the same year.

CHAPTER SIX

HAWKER HUNTER

enerally regarded as one of the classic jet fighters, the Hawker Hunter had its fair share of problems during development and, despite being awarded super-priority status (as was the Swift), three years were to elapse from first flight to service entry. Even so, the first production examples were chronically deficient in terms of endurance and air-firing was initially restricted at altitude as this often led to surge in the Hunter F.1's Avon engine. This at a time when the Swift F.2 could not carry ammunition because it was likely to induce pitch-up!

As Chief Designer at Hawkers, Sydney Camm was as aware as any of early developments in the field of jet turbines but at first took the view that the early centrifugal engines had insufficient power and did not offer any performance advantage over the latest piston-engines. It was not until Rolls-Royce began working on the B.41 Nene in 1944 that he began to take real interest, one of his first studies resulting in a jet-powered Fury (P.1035). This was quickly dropped in favour of an all-new design, the elegant P.1040, which was developed into the Sea Hawk for the Fleet Air Arm.

Just as Supermarine had been encouraged to begin high-speed research with the Type 510, so Hawker received an instruction to build two swept-wing proto-types to Specification E.38/46. This led to the P.1052 which was essentially the same as the P.1040 but with wings swept to an angle of thirty-five degrees. The two prototypes were serialled VX272 and VX279, the former flying from Boscombe Down for the first time on 19 November 1948. Speeds of Mach 0.90 were soon being attained although the aircraft was prone to Dutch roll, an uncomfortable motion involving roll and yaw which afflicted many early swept-wing types. The second P.1052, VX279, flew on 13 April 1949 but was soon back in the works for extensive modifications, which included swept tail surfaces and a straight-through jetpipe instead of the bifurcated system of its immediate forebear. Although the RAAF was keen to purchase the resultant P.1081, the Air Staff showed no such interest, favouring axial-flow turbo-jets over the centrifugal Nene/Tay. With no backing from the RAF, the Australians withdrew and chose the F-86 instead. VX279 continued to fly until 3 April 1951 when it crashed, killing Hawker's Chief Test Pilot Squadron Leader T.S. Wade.

In parallel with development of the P.1052/1081, Sydney Camm had also been wrestling with Specification F.43/46 which was an attempt to provide the RAF with a Meteor replacement. Camm found it impossible to satisfy the speci-fication's varying requirements and instead started work on a scheme based on the new Rolls-Royce AJ.65 axial jet (later to be named Avon). Given the designation P.1067, the design began life in 1947 and exhibited a wing of 9.5% thickness/chord ratio and 42.5 degree sweepback, a nose-mounted air intake and a straight tailplane mounted on top of the fin. This proved to be of sufficient interest for Specification F.3/48 to be written around it in March 1948 and over the coming months the design was gradually adapted to become the shape familiar to all as the Hunter. Three P.1067 prototypes were ordered, the first two (WB188 and WB195) to be powered by the 7,500lb.s.t. Avon, the third (WB202) by the 8,000lb.s.t. Armstrong Siddeley Sapphire. The use of the Sapphire was mainly to provide back-up for the Avon in case the latter hit trouble.

WB188 was flown for the first time on 20 July 1951 from Boscombe Down with Squadron Leader Neville Duke at the controls. First impressions of the aircraft were favourable, although a high-frequency vibration was noted at high subsonic speeds. This was found to be caused by breakdown of airflow at the base of the rudder and was cured by the inclusion of a reversed 'bullet' fairing at the junction of the vertical and horizontal tail surfaces. WB188 was followed by WB195, which flew for the first time on 5 May 1952 and featured the Aden gunpack and radar-ranging gunsight. The Sapphire-powered prototype joined the test programme on 30 November.

By now the P.1067 had been named Hunter and had been ordered into full production at Kingston and Blackpool (F.1) and at Armstrong Whitworth's plant at Coventry (F.2). The Hunter was typical of British military aircraft programmes of the period in that testing was carried out by a small number of prototypes with production machines being ordered before the snags had been sorted. Although it was generally performing better than the Swift, the Hunter was not immune from trouble itself and the first major problem concerned the air brakes. Early aircraft incorporated landing flaps which doubled as air brakes but, when used at high speed, a nose-down trim change was experienced which would have been a severe handicap during air combat. Various modifications were tried, but the use of wing-mounted brakes was eventually abandoned in favour of a large ventral air brake under the rear fuselage.

The other, more serious, problem to afflict the Hunter has already been referred to, the susceptibility of the Avon to surge, particularly when the guns were fired. This phenomenon was characterised by a violent breakdown of airflow in the compressor, which could lead to a reversal of flow and the engine flaming out. The Sapphire, as fitted to the F.2, was not affected in this way and as the early gun-firing trials had mainly been carried out by the Sapphire prototype, the trouble only became apparent very late in the development programme.

Early examples of the Hunter F.1 arrived for testing at CFE within days of the activation of the first operational unit, 43 Squadron at Leuchars, in July 1954. The first three aircraft (WE577, WE578 and WE579) were collected from Dunsfold on 5 July, and these were followed by two more (WE588 and WE591) a week later. Trials continued until the end of September, by which time 237 hours had been flown.

For take off, power was increased to 7,000rpm against the brakes, but contrary

Hunter F.1 WT622 of No.
43 Squadron at Sylt in 1955.

to recommendations by Hawker, CFE advised setting the tail trim one degree
nose-down rather than neutral to reduce the amount of trim change after take
off. After brake release, power was increased to maximum rpm (7,900) and
the aircraft accelerated rapidly to 70–75kt, at which point the rudder became
effective. The nosewheel could be raised at about 105kt and the unstick speed
of 135kt was reached soon after. There was little trim change as the undercarriage was raised and the aircraft's best climbing speed of 430kt was reached
one minute twenty seconds after commencing the take-off run. Here a nose-up
change of trim was experienced, but this could easily be countered by trimming
one and a half degrees nose down. Aileron control was extremely light and effective which caused most pilots new to the Hunter to over-control at first,
producing a slight lateral rocking.

The Hunter's rate of climb showed an initial 11,000ft/min at sea level, falling
to 2,600ft/min at 40,000ft. The highest altitude recorded was 52,500ft which
was achieved eighteen minutes after take off. Manoeuvrability at all altitudes was
excellent, the only criticism being the elevator control which became heavy
at high IAS and ineffective at 0.96 IMN. Above this speed initiation of manoeuvres in the longitudinal plane was limited by the rate of trim on the
variable-incidence (V.I.) tail. Comparative trials showed the Hunter to be
capable of out-manoeuvring the Sabre 4 at all altitudes, although the Sabre
retained a slight advantage in the initiation of manoeuvres which was particularly noticeable at high IMN.

When flying in power the aileron stick forces were constant for a given deflection throughout the speed range, but those for the elevator varied and the
trimmer had to be used to prevent the forces becoming unreasonably heavy.
Very high rates of roll were possible at high speed and in order that the ailerons
were not over-stressed, the hydraulic jacks were designed to 'stall' within a safe
aileron load. During all normal manoeuvres this load was not reached, but a
determined effort could produce a jack stall which limited aileron movement,
the stick coming up against an apparent stop just short of normal full travel. In
manual, the controls became quite heavy even in the low-speed range, and this,
together with a slow response to control input, meant that manoeuvrability was
severely restricted. Despite this, QGH and GCA procedures were flown with
little difficulty, although in turbulent conditions both hands were needed on the
stick to maintain adequate lateral control.

At high speed the Hunter was pleasant to fly up to limiting IAS at low altitudes (620kt), provided that weather conditions were not excessively turbulent. At high altitudes Mach 1.0 could be reached in a shallow dive using full power, elevator stick forces becoming very high above 0.96 IMN, although aileron control remained light throughout. There was a marked lack of compressibility effect in the transonic speed range and the aircraft showed no tendency to drop a wing. With the elevator ineffective, recovery from high-speed dives had to be made by the tailplane trimmer, although care had to be taken due to trim reversal as speed decreased. As the nose came through the horizon, the aircraft had to be trimmed from the zero position to 1.5 degrees nose-down to counteract a strong nose-up trim change as it left the sonic speed range. It was found that a clean pullout could be made without the use of airbrake, which only served to increase height loss, recovery from a forty-degree dive at Mach 1.05 being completed within 7,000ft.

Rates of roll were excellent all the way up the speed range and aileron effectiveness did not begin to drop until speeds in excess of 500kt IAS were reached. In comparison with the Sabre, the Hunter had more effective ailerons above 380kt IAS, although the Sabre had a faster rate of roll below this speed. Tests showed the Hunter and the Swift to have very similar performance in the rolling plane. In terms of acceleration, the Hunter generally performed well at all altitudes up to 40,000ft being particularly impressive in shallow dives. It was, however, important for pilots not to lose speed during manoeuvres, as acceleration times from Mach 0.75 and below were poor unless speed was gained by diving. The under-fuselage airbrake performed satisfactorily under all normal conditions and it was considered that the Hunter's deceleration was roughly comparable to the Sabre 4, although not up to the standard of the Swift 1. The airbrake could be augmented by use of flap although the marked nose-down trim change that this produced was described as being 'most unpleasant' above 350kt IAS.

Stall warning took the form of a general airframe vibration, together with a slight directional breakdown 8–10kt before the primary stall which was gentle and accompanied by wing drop. Up to this point height could be maintained, but thereafter the rate of descent increased rapidly. The tendency for a wing to go down could be held by aileron down to the fully developed stall after which no amount of control input could prevent the aircraft rolling off in the direction of wing drop. Recovery was immediate, however, once back pressure on the stick was released and ailerons returned to the neutral setting. At 10,000ft with undercarriage and flaps down, the primary stall occurred at 105kt IAS with the full stall following at 95kt IAS. Recovery from high-speed stalls was considered to be normal for a swept-wing aircraft and was easily effected by forward movement of the controls. A certain tightening at the 'g' stall was experienced but as there was adequate warning, this was deemed to be tactically acceptable.

For approach and landing, the circuit was joined at 300–320kt IAS, speed being reduced by throttling back and use of airbrake, together with twenty degrees of flap, when below 250kt. Cockpit checks when downwind at 200kt were – Airbrake In, Flaps forty degrees, Undercarriage Down and Three Greens, Brakes Off (check pressure) and Harness Tight. Full flap was lowered on final approach, by which time speed had been reduced to 150kt IAS, but it was recommended that power be kept above 4,500rpm until committed to landing. Under normal conditions the boundary was crossed at 120–125kt with 5kt being added for every 100 gallons of fuel carried above the normal landing figure of 100 gallons. Touchdown occurred at 110kt and with light elevator stick forces, care had to be taken to avoid scraping the tail bumper along the runway. Braking action was extremely powerful and it was relatively easy to lock a wheel when landing on wet runways. One characteristic that had to be allowed for concerned undercarriage extension, which took longer than other fighters and varied considerably depending on power. With 6,000rpm selected the extension sequence took eleven seconds, increasing to fifteen seconds at 4,500rpm and twenty seconds at idle.

During the trial five sorties were flown against a Sabre 5, powered by an Orenda Mk.10 of 6,300lb.s.t., which showed the two aircraft to be closely matched. The Hunter's rate of climb was superior up to 30,000ft, but from this height the Sabre held a slight advantage and was only 600ft below the Hunter on reaching 48,000ft. Thereafter the Sabre was able to continue up to 54,000ft, compared to the Hunter's absolute ceiling of 52,000ft. In acceleration, the Hunter was appreciably faster than the Sabre if speed was kept above 0.85 IMN. Below this speed there was little to choose between the two, the Sabre having a slight advantage below 0.80 IMN.

Both aircraft had similar turning capability at altitudes over 40,000ft, although if the Hunter was forced to reduce speed to below 0.82 IMN it tended to lose ground. When pulling 5–6g at lower altitudes, care also had to be taken with the Hunter to avoid 'tuck in' at high IMN. In dives the Hunter initially had the edge, though the performance of both aircraft around 0.95–0.97 IMN was similar, the exception being when the Sabre remained at 0.97 when induced drag due to wing drop allowed the Hunter to pass. If speed was kept above 0.85 IMN the manoeuvrability of the two compared very closely, the Sabre having an advantage in initiating manoeuvres due to its superior longitudinal control at high IMN, whereas the Hunter possessed a superior rate of roll at lower altitudes at speeds in excess of 380kt IAS.

As the CFE assessment continued, the first Hunter course at the Day Fighter Leaders School (DFLS) at West Raynham got under way. Impressions of the aircraft were generally similar to those of AFDS pilots, although there were more cases of power loss due to engine surge, especially during tight turns at full throttle when OAT was lower than –56°C. Comment was also passed that the rearward view from the Hunter was unacceptable due to the harness of the Martin-Baker ejection seat preventing the pilot from twisting his shoulders to look behind. The view to the rear was also not helped by the canopy design dictated by the aircraft's dorsal spine. The airbrake came in for particular criticism, as did the R/T, especially air-to-air transmissions. Other than these grumbles however, the Hunter was rated first class!

222 Squadron, based at Leuchars, became the second unit to fly the F.1, its first aircraft arriving in December 1954. One of its pilots, Flying Officer Brian Carroll, recalls his introduction to the Hunter and some of its early limitations:

'Before any of us flew the Hunter we were personally briefed by Neville Duke and Bill Bedford who came to Leuchars to give us the low down on this sleek new aircraft. There were no dual versions in those days, so everyone simply went solo. Bill Bedford supervised my first trip, he assisted me to strap in, patted me on the head and said, "have fun," which I did! The Hunter was quite one of the most delightful aircraft to fly. The controls were well balanced and harmonised, roll rates were very impressive and easy to handle, apart from the first solo when we all found that the ailerons were so sensitive after the Meteor that every pilot was seen gently "wagging" the wings as the aircraft climbed away.

My first sortie was on 2 March 1955 in WT619 and lasted thirty-five minutes which was just about the limit of what could be achieved with the fuel we had. This was a big failing with the Hunter Mk.1 and, indeed, the Mk.4 which was only marginally better. The Mk.1 carried 337 gallons of fuel which could be used up totally at low level in eleven minutes. Admittedly this was by achieving and maintaining high speed, say around 5–600 knots, but it meant that any effective low-level exercise was very limited, although we did some tactical low-level work. Realistic training was seriously curtailed and over the eight month period we flew the Mk.1s, I averaged only twelve hours a month, nowhere near the level to be fully operational and totally conversant with the aircraft.

The Hunter did suffer from engine surge in the early days although I only once had an engine flame-out during air firing. After a short pause one would press the relight button for a hot start and the engine would usually catch and perform as normal. If the initial relight action failed, the HP fuel cock would be turned off and after a short period of time to allow any excess of fuel that might have accumulated in the engine/jet pipe areas to drain away, the HP cock would be turned on and the relight pressed. The system was very reliable and relights were virtually guaranteed. A modification was eventually introduced to briefly reduce the fuel flow to the engine when firing the guns – this virtually eliminated the surge problem and flame-outs became a thing of the past. Gun firing did have another effect on the early Hunters. The vibration would cause the withholding bolt on the nosewheel door to shear so that on selecting undercarriage down for landing, only the main wheels would lower, the nosewheel door remaining firmly locked in place. A foam strip would be laid along the runway by the fire service and after coming to a stop, the aircraft would be jacked up and the nosewheel lowered. This fault was resolved by fitting stronger bolts, but for a while was somewhat embarrassing.'

Not surprisingly, the arrival of the high-performance Hunter took some getting used to and inevitably there were mishaps for the unfortunate few. Brian Carroll recalls some of those he witnessed during his time at Leuchars:

'I was waiting to take the active runway 27 as the leader of a pair about to fly off to Leconfield. A 43 Squadron Hunter was just turning from the downwind position so we were holding until he landed. Unknown to me at the time he was carrying out a recovery in "Manual". Watching him come round finals he looked to be too tight and I thought that he would overshoot and try again, but he continued and I really thought that he would crash into my aircraft. I was undecided as to whether to use the ejection seat just before he hit me (in those days seats were not zero-zero capable), or slam on full power and try to move out of the way. In the event I did neither as he hit the ground some 300 yards short of where I was parked, striking the ground with his port wing. The fuselage broke into two halves, but he walked away, shaken, stirred, but still alive.

Another incident involved the Northern Sector Commander, an Air Commodore, who was based at Turnhouse and had his own Hunter which he flew only on very rare occasions. Again I was waiting to line up for take off, this time on runway 09, when ATC called that a Hunter was on short finals for runway 27. Looking towards the east I saw a Hunter that by this time was halfway down the runway, but looked to be travelling so fast that I assumed it was taking off, and was not the one reported on short finals. He went past me at a fair clip, continued into the overshoot area before hitting a great burst of power that sent mud, clods of earth, stones and other debris flying as he taxied out to park up on our squadron dispersal. I took off, completed my sortie and on return went into the crew room and immediately asked, "Who was that idiot that went into the overshoot?" The Air Commodore stood up, introduced himself and said, "It was me, may I get you a coffee?" Somewhat taken aback (I was a Flying Officer at the time) I accepted his kind offer and asked what had caused the problem. "As you probably know," he said, "I don't fly very often and I could not remember the correct approach speed. I knew it was either 130kt or 230kt and so I opted for the higher one."

In the early days of the Hunter it had an unnerving habit of allowing the jet pipe to detach itself and hang out of the back end of the fuselage. This occurred to one of our pilots who was about to eject due to a fast rising j.p.t. and a certain loss of thrust. I happened to be in his immediate area and was able to carry out a visual inspection of his aircraft. There was no sign of fire, so I suggested that he should make an attempt to recover to base – we were only some twenty miles away and I would follow to advise him if anything exciting looked like happening. All went well and he landed successfully, though the jet pipe finished up on the runway.

The final incident involved one of our pilots during air-to-ground firing on the range at Tentsmuir which is situated right off the eastern edge of Leuchars. He had carried out a couple of attacks firing cannon when a ricochet shot him down – complete engine failure and a fire. He ejected, landing in the Tay estuary, fortunately close to a sandbank. I say fortunately since he had omitted to connect his dinghy to his Mae West. The punch line being that he was our survival expert, giving regular briefings on flight safety in all its aspects. He took a very long time to live that one down!'

Flying Officer (later Group Captain) Peter Vangucci was another who began flying the Hunter shortly after it entered service.

'As with all RAF fighters, on first entry into service one seemed to be short of fuel as soon as, if not before, you were airborne. I never flew the Hunter in action so the main problem was the shortness of time available to achieve a useful sortie, especially when everything and everyone had worked so hard to launch the sortie in the first place. Every minute was precious and there was no time to loiter to overcome failings and delays in the system – air defence, air traffic control or whatever. Only the Lightning was shorter on fuel.

The handling was excellent with the exception of running out of tailplane at awkward moments, usually in air combat and especially at night. The all-flying tail eventually cured the problem but it was ironic that the Sabre, which the Hunter replaced, already had one. We all got pitch-up, the symptoms were "soggy" controls and lack of effectiveness, but to the best of my recollection, I did not experience it ever again after the saw-tooth leading edge was introduced. In a dogfight the Hunter behaved very well up to a point. At low to medium altitudes it could out-turn many of its contemporaries (F-84, F-86, F-100 etc.) but before the follow-up [tail] it ran out of tailplane, especially in the vertical above 25,000ft. As fishtailing was very effective for losing speed, it was good in scissors manoeuvres. It was a very clean aircraft and you could overtake targets very quickly with the element of surprise even if they were theoretically faster (e.g. F-100).'

The Hunter F.2, powered by a Sapphire 101 of 8,100lb.s.t., entered service with 257 Squadron at Wattisham in November 1954 quickly followed by 263 Squadron, based at the same Suffolk airfield, two months later. These two units were to be the sole users of the F.2 which is something of a surprise considering the Sapphire's performance advantage over the Avon and the fact that it was surge free. The increased power of the F.2 greatly improved times to height as the following figures show (times in min/sec):

Height	Hunter F.1	Hunter F.2
20,000ft	3.40	2.50
30,000ft	7.48	6.20
40,000ft	10.30	8.40
50,000ft	16.00	13.15

Acceleration was also much more rapid than the F.1, the best climbing speed of 450kt being reached 1 minute 5 seconds after brake release, an increase in performance that was maintained at all heights.

The next Hunters to be tested at CFE were the F.4 (Avon) and F.5 (Sapphire) which were evaluated between April and June 1955. Results were a little disappointing. Although fuel capacity had been raised from 337 to 414 gallons to increase the aircraft's radius of action, weight had gone up as a result, together with a forward shift of C.G. As the machines delivered to CFE were early production examples fitted with the same RA.7 Avon and Sapphire 101 as fitted to the F.1 and F.2, overall performance was down, in particular times to height,

Hunter F.4 WV367 of No.67 Squadron.

turn radius at high altitude, and acceleration times. Stick forces per 'g' were also higher. On the plus side the changed C.G. position reduced the aircraft's 'pitch up' tendency and manoeuvrability and level speeds were similar to the earlier aircraft. Although the CFE assessment was that the F.4 and F.5 were inferior to their predecessors, this was somewhat misleading as modification states were in a constant state of flux. Over the coming months incorporation of the more powerful Avon 115 (RA.14) in the F.4, the long-awaited 'all-flying tail', and mod 228 to allow the use of 100-gallon drop tanks on all four under-wing pylons, would transform the aircraft's operational capability.

The trials did highlight a particular problem when it came to out-of-wind landings. It was found that with crosswinds in excess of twenty knots practically full rudder was required to kick the aircraft straight for touch down, and nearly all braking had to be accomplished with the 'downwind brake' to overcome the Hunter's strong tendency to weathercock into wind. When operating from flooded or icy runways relatively small crosswind components were likely to be unacceptable and provision of a braking parachute was strongly recommended (this was eventually incorporated in the F.6A and FGA.9).

Despite the Hunter's early tribulations it quickly became apparent that at long last the RAF had a fighter capable of taking on the very best, although when it came to air combat, the skill and experience of the pilot was still a major factor in determining the outcome. Flying Officer Brian Carroll recalls his impressions of the Hunter as a dogfighter:

'It handled well, was very manoeuvrable, had good visibility, and it was easy to keep a good lookout in one's "six o'clock". I had the opportunity to mix it against Sabres and generally speaking the odds were pretty even, though the F-86 had more fuel (sore point) so could stay around longer than we could. The Hunter's airbrakes were a joke, they had very little effect and were of no use in combat. However the flaps were something else, the phrase "barn doors" comes to mind. In the Mk.1 they caused a severe pitch down when selected, and in the circuit when preparing to carry out pre-landing checks you really had to grab hold of the stick to stop the aircraft entering a terminal dive. With the all-flying tail, this was easier to combat and the flaps could be used in combat to increase the turn rate. Being fully variable made them very useful, and full flap effected a marked deceleration with the intention of forcing a fly-through. The Javelin had tremendous airbrakes which were fully variable and when fully extended generated a 1g deceleration. I attended the All-Weather Combat School at West Raynham (on Javelins) and we flew several sorties against Hunters. The Hunter boys soon realised what a problem the Javelin's airbrakes caused them and were quick to utilise their flaps to try and match the deceleration. They failed, but it did help them a little. At the end of the day honours were about even which surprised the day fighters who thought that they would beat the pants off us.'

Reference has already been made to the early Hunter's lack of endurance and this was highlighted in the worst possible way in early 1956. In the morning of 8 February, eight Hunter F.1s of DFLS at West Raynham were prepared to carry out a 4 v. 4 dogfight at 45,000ft but low cloud, together with extensive mist and fog, caused the exercise to be postponed. The weather forecast was for a gradual improvement from the north and by 1050 hrs conditions had improved sufficiently for the Hunters to take off. Cloud extended up to 11,000ft but above this the air was clear.

After twenty-five minutes the Hunters returned to West Raynham's overhead at 20,000ft in four pairs, but the weather had deteriorated since their departure and cloud base was now around 400ft with visibility estimated at 800–1,000 yards. The decision was taken to divert the aircraft to Marham, ten miles to the south-west, despite the fact that the worsening weather was heading in that direction and the airfield's CRD/F was temporarily unserviceable. Having carried out a QGH procedure down to 2,000ft over West Raynham, the Hunters set off for Marham with twenty seconds between each pair, but by the time they arrived fog had begun to form there as well. Although Marham's CRD/F was quickly back on line, the controller was unable to identify the aircraft to effect control and the only possible alternative was to bring them in on GCA. This type of procedure, however, required a spacing between each pair of two minutes and by now each Hunter was down to around ten minutes of fuel.

Red 1 and 2 eventually broke cloud at 500ft and, despite becoming separated in the poor visibility, both landed safely, Red 1 running out of fuel as he taxied in. Yellow 3 and 4 also descended to 500ft but were unable to locate the runway due to irregular cloudbase and mist. Shortly afterwards Yellow 3 ejected when his engine flamed out and the pilot of Yellow 4 was killed when his aircraft crashed four and a half miles north-east of Swaffham. The other two members of Yellow section descended to 250ft but were unable to find the airfield, Yellow 2 having to climb to 2,000ft and eject when his fuel ran low. Yellow 1 in the meantime had remained at low level and at one point had to climb back into

Flying Officer Trevor Egginton of No. 67 Squadron.

cloud to avoid trees. On dropping down again he picked up the runway but, before he could begin his approach, his engine flamed out and he was left with no alternative but to force-land straight ahead. The remaining pair, Red 3 and 4, both ejected when they ran out of fuel.

With over 400 hours on the F-86, Flying Officer Trevor Egginton converted onto the Hunter F.4 with 67 Squadron at Bruggen in March 1956 and later flew with 222 and 43 Squadrons at Leuchars. Having been used to the Sabre's superb flying controls the Hunter proved to be a bit of a disappointment.

'I think we were all a little sad to see our Sabres go to be given a more powerful but very much inferior combat aircraft in the Hunter 4. The Sabre had a fully flying tail and you always had full control regardless of Mach number. When you pulled the stick back the aircraft responded. Some of the first Hunter 4s had boosted controls to an elevator with a very slow tailplane trim system to the forward section of the tail. Quite a few of us got a bit of a fright at times when in a steep dive at high Mach numbers (usually diving to bounce some unsuspecting USAF Sabres). You pulled the stick back and nothing happened; the tail jack stalled. You then tried trimming aft on the tail trim, but it was very slow. At about 10,000ft in the denser air you then did about a 6g pull-out with the stick full forward, frantically trimming the tail forward. Harry Walmsley our boss at the time, caused a stir at Group by declaring all our boosted system Hunter 4s non-operational. Fortunately they were replaced by the fully-powered versions (still with a single hydraulic system and manual reversion) and latterly the electric follow-up tailplane which you didn't have to trim manually. Still it was not as effective as the Sabre's all-flying tail.

As most pilots in 67 Squadron had been trained in the USA we had many friends at Bitburg and used to beat them up frequently, sometimes joining forces with the Canadians in what was known as the "Brits and Colonials" against the "God Damns" and "You Alls"! We almost convinced the Bitburg crowd that the Hunter was supersonic in level flight. One morning we dived from altitude, went supersonic pointing at the airfield, levelled out at low level over the runway about the time that the sonic booms arrived, the illusion made more believable with the condensation over the wings showing up the shock waves. The illusion didn't last long!

In my view the fitting of a manual reversion system in the Hunter was a poor choice and bad design. It's a pity that Sir Sydney Camm didn't look at Sabre development when designing the Hunter. I had an accessory-drive failure at Leuchars in not too good weather, thereby losing generator and hydraulic pump, the controls reverting to manual. I remember well doing a straight-in approach with my forehead on the gunsight pad, hunched over, the stick gripped with both hands braced, snatching a hand off to adjust the throttle. I was bushed on landing – never had to work so hard in all my life. At higher speeds the ailerons would float up and the loads were very heavy. You would be a dead duck in a combat situation.

The other fiasco with the Hunter was the 30mm Aden cannon. At least with the Sabre's 6 x 0.5in. machine-guns you stood a chance of hitting and killing the target at 1,500ft, although considerably closer was recommended. The low velocity 30mm on the Hunter could be seen floating out in front of the aircraft on firing and dropping away sharply. Unless you were right up the target's backside, it was doubtful whether the round would have sufficient impact velocity to penetrate the target, let alone explode the round. The later high-velocity rounds were better, but you still had to get close for effect and still needed large deflections in turns. At least when you fired the guns on the Sabre the engine kept running and there was little change in trim. When we first fired the guns on the Hunter, the engine flamed out in turns, during flag firing for example. We rapidly learned that if you pulled back the throttle a bit as you fired the engine kept running. Rolls-Royce mechanised this with a bleed valve which opened when you fired, bleeding air from the compressor and reducing rpm [automatic "fuel dipping" was also incorporated to reduce fuel flow].

When all four guns were fired the gas flow affected the trim, the nose pitching down sharply – not an ideal situation for a fighter relying on its guns as it spoilt your aim a bit. Around 1957, blast deflectors were fitted to deflect the gas flow downwards, counteracting the pitch down. This worked at medium and low levels, however at Leuchars we were doing operational turn-round exercises: take off, climb to altitude, fire the full load from four guns, land, rearm and take off again as soon as possible. As the squadron PAI, I thought it would be a good idea to fire at high altitude as we had done it only at 20,000ft or below on flag firing sorties. So we went off to 48,000ft or thereabouts. All four aircraft pitched down noticeably when the guns were fired (into the sea I hasten to add). It was reported to Fighter Command but I don't think they wanted to know.

Hunter F.4 XF317 of No.67 Squadron being towed to the hangar at Bruggen.

One other problem with the Avon engines in the Hunter was its tendency to flame out in tight turns (combat manoeuvres) at altitude. There was a critical air temperature and the only saving grace was that the engine relit easily – throttle back to idle, hit the relight button and away you went. We got very blasé about it and when someone flamed out he was not allowed to relight until someone else had formated on him so that a combination of power/flap/airbrake could be determined to simulate an engine failure for practice. I think we must have done more relights than landings.'

From the earliest days, thought had been given to developing the Hunter by increasing wing-sweep and installing more powerful engines to create a truly supersonic fighter. Under the impetus of increased tension created by the Korean War, Hawker produced the P.1083 which featured a fifty-degree swept wing and Avon RA.14R, but with the end of the conflict in 1953, official encouragement ceased and the project was cancelled when the prototype was about 80% complete. This left the possibility of extracting more performance from the Hunter by installing larger engines but, due to the design of the airframe, it could never be supersonic in level flight. The resultant Hunter F.6 quickly followed on from the F.4 and utilised the 200-series Avon of 10,000lb.s.t. which employed much of the compressor technology developed for the Sapphire to cure the Avon's habit of surging at high altitude. Early production F.6s (XE603, XE606 and XE 608) were tested at CFE over a three-month period commencing in July 1956.

The new Hunter weighed in at 17,600lb, a full 1,600lb heavier than the F.1, and featured an extension of the airbrake angle from sixty to sixty-seven degrees, artificial spring feel of the ailerons to allow trimming in flight to give zero stick force, and a start up sequence initiated by liquid fuel instead of by cartridge. It also possessed four under-wing pylons for 100-gallon overload tanks, or it could be configured to carry 1,000lb bombs on the inner pylons with 12 x 3in. rockets outboard. The 'large-bore' Avon more than made up for the increase in weight as the following times (in min/sec) to height show:

	20,000ft	40,000ft	45,000ft	50,000ft
Hunter 6	3.00	6.00	8.05	12.20
Hunter 4	4.30	8.35	11.05	18.00
Hunter 5	3.20	7.40	10.25	17.30

Although overall manoeuvrability was similar to earlier aircraft, turn radius showed a marked improvement at high altitude, the F.6 using up 3.8nm at 45,000ft and 0.91 IMN, compared to 4.5nm for the F.4/5. Acceleration times (min/sec) from 0.70–0.92 IMN were also much better as the table indicates:

Height	Hunter 6	Hunter 4	Hunter 5
1,000ft	0.22	0.42	0.28
5,000ft	0.23	0.42	0.28
10,000ft	0.28	0.42	0.35
15,000ft	0.31	0.46	0.40
20,000ft	0.36	0.50	0.45
25,000ft	0.41	0.50	0.54
30,000ft	0.46	1.03	0.57
35,000ft	0.59	1.17	1.12
40,000ft	1.17	1.45	1.40

Despite the fact that the airbrake now extended to sixty-seven degrees, this made little difference to deceleration times below 40,000ft but there were notice-able trim changes which, in conjunction with the sensitivity of the elevators, could lead to over-controlling at high IAS. The change of trim was nose down initially, becoming nose up during the last few degrees of extension. Pitch up was not appreciably different from previous marks and was considered to be more of an embarrassment than a penalty. Buffet allowed adequate warning of a high-speed stall and recovery could be easily effected by easing the pull force. As the aircraft tested by CFE did not have the 'all-flying tail', comments regarding poor longitudinal control above 0.93 IMN were the same as those for previous marks. (Later Hunters were fitted with an electric follow-up tailplane. After two degrees of elevator movement micro-switches changed tailplane inci-dence at the rate of 0.7 deg/sec. Opinion on the revised tail was divided. Due to the delay in operation and the fact that the follow-up operated at the same speed as the manual trimmer, some pilots flew with it switched off, preferring to use the thumb-operated trim on the control column.)

Recommended speeds on final approach and at the threshold were 160kt and 135kt respectively at normal landing weight. Due to the increased landing speed, greater weight and greater residual thrust, tyre and brake consumption

WV391 of No.20 Squadron in the air.

was three times that of early Hunters, indeed CFE pilots found great difficulty in pulling up within 2,000 yards when the runway was wet.

During the trials, pairs of Hunters were scrambled within forty-five seconds but due to the increased fuel consumption of the big Avon, the F.6 was even less suited to the low level interceptor role than the F.4/5, having a combat radius of only 60nm when operated clean, assuming five minutes combat at full power and a 620lb landing reserve. With two drop tanks fitted, radius of action could be increased to 137nm. For high altitude interceptions, the F.6 showed a considerable improvement over the F.4/5, its better climb performance giving the control organisation much greater flexibility and allowing a bomber to be intercepted 24nm farther from base. Radius of action at 45,000ft, allowing for ten minutes combat and 620lb fuel reserve, was 163nm (clean) and 358nm (drop tanks). Overall, the Hunter F.6 was found to be well suited to intercepting a target flying at Mach 0.85 at 45,000ft, given that it received precise ground control.

The introduction of the F.6 into service allowed some of the older marks to be transferred to second-line duties and by mid-1956 several Hunter F.4s were being used by the Central Flying School so that staff instructors could remain current on first-line types. It was at CFS that Flight Lieutenant Peter Hicks experienced what is arguably a pilot's worst nightmare.

'The morning of 24 August 1956 was dry and bright with the sky obscured by 8/8ths altocumulus, base about 10,000ft, tops about 11,000ft, with good visibility below and above. I did two sorties in XF980 in the morning and it is noteworthy that no ATC clearance was necessary to penetrate cloud, nor could it be obtained since no frequency was allocated to obtain radar clearance. The incident which was about to occur was one important piece of ammunition which, following Boards of Inquiry, was to cause vital change as more and faster aircraft filled the airspace.

On my third sortie I took off on the westerly runway at Kemble and climbed straight ahead at 430kt. I entered cloud momentarily at about 10,000ft and very soon shot into the clear. Simultaneously there was the mother-and-father of bangs. A "bang" is a pretty inadequate description of 15,000lb of Hunter at 430kt impacting 38,000lb of Javelin at, I believe, 500kt descending. In the event, the Hunter broke in two somewhere aft of the cockpit, and the navigator of the Javelin who also survived, saw the floor splitting beneath his feet. With the bit of Hunter I was sitting in tumbling and rolling, there was little doubt as to what to do next. I was very lucky to be able to do it; afterwards it was established that my bone dome was severely smashed in on the left side by a piece of aircraft structure and that there was a hole in the seat frame about 6in. behind my ear. Nice timing at the closing speeds involved!

In what was a dazed dream I gave up the idea of jettisoning the canopy (it was smashed anyway), reached up and back with my right hand and pulled the seat firing handle. So far so good – a clean ejection in spite of damage – but then the result of the damage to the seat started to become evident. Instead of the drogue in the top of the seat deploying half a second after ejection, it remained firmly packed. The reason being that the drogue withdrawal line had been cut so that the drogue bullet fired and took only a few inches of line into space. So no drogue, no deceleration and no stabilisation. Because of the speed at the time of ejection the resulting extreme buffeting and rotation of the seat was so severe that this, I decided quite objectively, was it, whether there's anything beyond or not, it will be wonderful when this violence stops. The violence, however, didn't stop and, almost as though I was alongside myself watching, I saw that my right leg was sticking out straight behind me and flailing like mad. No sense, no sensibility – I didn't feel a thing. Although being in an early Mark 2H seat with no leg restraints, my leg had blown up and back and had snapped on contact with the thigh guard on the seat.

Still partly conscious and "relaxed", I must have passed 10,000ft, to which the barostat mechanism was set. Here three things should have happened with Jimmy Martin's most excellent seat, if undamaged. First, the harness buckle attaching pilot to seat should rotate. It did. Next, the lug attaching the drogue and its lanyard to the seat should open, releasing the drogue which should now jerk on the deckchair-like strip on which the pilot is sitting and pitch him out of the seat. Then, drogue pulling on deckchair, pulling on parachute harness should open the parachute. Result – happiness! In my case, however, the only "should" which occurred was the rotation of the harness buckle. I must have fallen out of the seat in the parachute, which was still attached to the seat by the release cord, and so the 'chute opened. I looked up and saw it open, with a tear in it, but the seat (pretty heavy) was dangling over my head, still attached to the apex of the parachute by the release cord. Such was my semi-conscious state at this stage that I thought to climb up the rigging lines to release it. It was just as well that I became unconscious, which spared me the thought of worrying about the seat and my leg on landing at a higher rate of descent than normal.'

Peter Hicks eventually returned to the Examining Wing at CFS after three months in hospital at RAF Wroughton followed by a further three months rehabilitation at Headley Court. The navigator of the Javelin (XA644), which was on a test flight from Moreton Valence, escaped with a minor injury to his arm, but the pilot was killed. A report subsequently submitted by Martin-Baker noted that it was remarkable that two airmen escaped safely in what were exceptionally difficult environmental circumstances.

Although pitch up had been encountered with the Hunter from the very beginning, the lack of manoeuvre in pitch at high IMN imposed by the original V.I. tail had tended to mask the problem, and it was not until the arrival of the all-flying tail that the phenomenon became a serious handicap. The hoped-for solution lay in extending and drooping the outer wing leading edges, as had been tried on the Swift and a number of other jet fighters of the period. This produced a marked vortex at the point of discontinuity which inhibited the spanwise flow of air, a major factor in tip stalling. It also had the effect of decreasing the thickness/chord ratio of the wing's outer portion which, in turn, raised Mcrit. Another advantage was that the wing's mean Centre of Pressure was moved forward, which meant that when the tip did eventually stall, forward movement of C.P. was less marked and the magnitude of pitch up, was less.

Comparative tests were carried out at CFE in the last two weeks of July 1957 to ascertain the performance advantage of the extended leading edges, XE628 (modified) and XE608 (unmodified) flying a total of fifty-three sorties. Turns were carried out in XE628 at medium and high altitudes with an initial speed of 0.88–0.92 IMN. It was found that, if turns were entered gently, a stalled or nearly stalled condition could be reached without encountering pitch up, whereas if the turn was initiated as rapidly as possible, as in a break, it could still be induced. This was not significant at high altitude since the aircraft stalled at low 'g', but it was possible to reach the limiting figure of 7g at medium altitude. Approach to

F.6 XJ638 of No.4 Squadron viewed from a No.2 Squadron Swift FR.5.

the pitch-up point was accompanied by very heavy airframe buffet, an extremely rapid reduction in airspeed, together with an apparent lightening of the pull force just before the pitch up occurred. Buffet during tight turns was noticeably more intense than in the unmodified aircraft. In all cases the overshoot 'g' could be checked by forward movement of the controls. This recovery action resulted in an immediate reduction in 'g' but full recovery was often prolonged for several seconds in a well developed case.

On one occasion the aircraft entered a spin following a hard turn at 160kt IAS at 36,000ft with full nose-up trim. During the turn heavy buffet had been experienced together with longitudinal porpoising and lateral rocking. Standard recovery techniques over five turns had no effect, as did subsequent use of in-spin aileron. The hood was jettisoned at 18,000ft and the aircraft came out of the spin at 10,000ft apparently of its own accord. (Over the years there have been several similar incidents leading to the assumption that turbulence from the open cockpit affects airflow over the tail so as to aid recovery.)

Overall, there was little difference between the two aircraft at high altitude. The leading edge extensions delayed onset of buffet by 0.2g, but increased buffet thereafter meant that there was no apparent increase in useable 'g'. At medium and low levels, however, the modified aircraft had a clear advantage and was able to turn inside the standard aircraft until the latter pitched up or stalled. Although the severity of buffet with the revised wing was a disadvantage, a reduction in lateral rocking was noted when the two aircraft flew identical turns at low IAS. The improvement in manoeuvrability was continued to ground level, although structural limitations were likely to result in a pilot not being able to take any advantage. Nevertheless, it was thought that delay in the onset of buffet would provide an additional safety margin when pulling out from a misjudged attack.

During service with 43 Squadron, Flying Officer Trevor Egginton had reason to curse the Hunter's air conditioning system during a detachment to Cyprus, but found that the additional power of the F.6 made up for many of the inadequacies of the earlier marks.

'A pet hate of mine of all British fighter aircraft was the extremely poor heating and ventilation systems fitted. I remember waiting for take off at Nellis AFB with runway temperatures of 120°F, sitting comfortably with the cooler in the Sabre blowing snowflakes at me. At the hot setting it would cook you. We never had trouble in rapid descents from high level with the screens freezing over or misting. This was a complete contrast with the Hunter in Cyprus in the summer of 1958; the cooling system could not be used at low level – it just burnt out after a few minutes. On low-level sorties you just had to sweat it out, literally needing windscreen wipers on your eyebrows to keep the sweat out of your eyes and having to lift your oxygen mask periodically to drain out the sweat and stop the gurgling. It was very uncomfortable and at times you had to break off the sortie to climb into cooler air or crack the canopy back at low speeds. The heating system was about as effective and one had to use the "flood flow" to keep warm and keep the screens clear during rapid descents [cockpit ventilation was improved in the Hunter FGA9].

I did actually enjoy flying the Hunter in spite of its failings as a fighter. The power in the Hunter 6 was impressive for its day. At Leuchars we did air tests after a minor [inspection] without drop tanks. Normally we carried two or four for ferry flights. After doing the test and monthly mandatory exercises, we returned low on fuel and just about one to one on power to weight ratio, so everyone did an overshoot after a touch and go. At full throttle you just pointed the nose skywards and could reach 10,000ft by the end of the runway being forced back hard into the seat. I won't mention radio sets with the forty-four-channel equipment. If all four aircraft in a formation got onto the same frequency after a channel change it was time to put the flags out. The Hunter 6 was a nice aircraft to fly and built like a brick-built chicken house, as the saying goes. Its strength saved many a pilot. We had one come back with the "g" meter at full scale (+12g). The wings were a bit wrinkled and the wing securing bolts a bit disturbed but at least the wings stayed on.'

Flying Officer Dennis Keys flew the Hunter F.6 from Gütersloh.

'In my opinion the Hunter was a gem, a real gentleman's machine. In three years with 14 Squadron I never experienced a single system failure. During dogfights, twenty degrees of flap was a great help in tight manoeuvring but one had to remember to lift them before entering a dive because the aircraft would not recover from a supersonic descent with any flap down. I seem to remember that the first supersonic ejection from a Hunter was brought about by this situation. With a high cockpit workload it was easy to forget about the fuel gauges which were down on the right consol. I once neglected to read them in a dogfight with a bunch of Sabres, got the "bingo" warning and only just made it back to base (to a good rollicking!) I also found that the saw-tooth leading edge extensions greatly improved the Hunter's performance in simulated air-to-air combat.'

The supersonic ejection referred to by Dennis Keys was also the first example of the Hunter's own particular 'Phantom Dive' and took place on 3 August 1955. Flying Officer Hedley Molland of 263 Squadron was carrying out a practice cine attack in WN989 at 37,000ft when he followed the target aircraft into a forty-degree dive. As he was descending through 31,000ft the angle of dive steepened appreciably and no amount of control input or nose-up trim could deflect the Hunter from its downwards plunge. With the Mach meter registering 1.1, Molland ejected successfully at 25,000ft. At first it was thought that the accident had been caused by structural failure of the tailplane, but further crashes over the next few years began to point the finger at the use of flap at high Mach numbers.

On 14 February 1958 an F.6 (XG236) of 66 Squadron at Acklington bounced a pair of Hunters during practice interceptions at 40,000ft. As it was manoeuvring to attack it entered a vertical dive from which it did not recover and eventually crashed near Kielder in Northumberland. Six months later, on 21

August, a 74 Squadron pilot was killed when his aircraft (XF448) fell out of a loop and crashed into the sea near Winterton, Norfolk. A further accident occurred on 30 May 1960 when XF507 from 65 Squadron at Duxford was seen to enter a steep descent at 28,000ft when attempting to get on the tail of two Hunters. As in the previous cases it did not recover and crashed near Thrapston in Northamptonshire, killing its pilot.

These fatalities prompted a test programme to be carried out at Dunsfold which highlighted the problem of elevator-jack stall and tailplane actuator clutch slip. In such a situation it was possible to experience catastrophic tailplane runaway which made recovery impossible and it was recommended that the flaps should be modified to retract automatically at 0.87 IMN. The Air Ministry concluded, however, that the cost of modification would be too high and Pilot's Notes were merely amended to include a limitation on the use of flap of 300kt IAS/0.90 IMN. At first it appeared that the message had got through, but eventually more flap-related accidents began to occur. On 15 January 1969 XF517, an FGA.9 of 54 Squadron, dived into the sea off the Norfolk coast during simulated air combat and later the same year a trainee pilot from Lebanon was killed in XG204 shortly after taking off from Valley. After climbing to 2,500ft his aircraft entered a dive which gradually became steeper until it crashed at Rhosneigr in Anglesey. The accident was put down to mishandling and a failure to raise the flaps after take off. Amazingly, pilots continued to get into trouble as late as the 1980s, even though the problem had been identified two decades before. On 28 May 1980 an F.6A of 2 TWU at Lossiemouth (XG261) crashed after control was lost during aerobatics near Dufftown, Banff – the student pilot had lowered twenty-three degrees of flap and had subsequently forgotten to raise them. At least this particular incident had a happy ending as a successful ejection was made.

From the mid-1950s the Hunter was the RAF's premier day fighter, a position it retained until the arrival of the English Electric Lightning in 1960. If it had had to go to war in Europe at that time its most likely adversary would have been the Russian MiG-19, the first examples of which had entered service in late 1954. Powered by two afterburning Tumansky RD-9B engines of 7,165lb.s.t., the MiG-19 had a top speed of around Mach 1.35 which put it in a similar class to the F-100 Super Sabre. In the summer of 1959 CFE carried out comparative trials with a Hunter F.6 pitted against the F-100C/D to ascertain the tactics that could be used by RAF pilots should they be faced with a rival who had the benefit of supersonic performance.

With its superior speed, the Super Sabre invariably held the initiative, but there were certain aspects of performance that the Hunter could use to embarrass its opponent. In terms of initial acceleration the Hunter had the upper hand but after approximately 0.82 TMN, the F-100C in reheat began to pull away. The F-100D although superior at altitudes below 35,000ft, lost its advantage above that height due to its greater weight when compared to the F-100C. It was also discovered that, at matched speeds, the Hunter could out-turn the F-100 at all altitudes between 15–40,000ft whether or not the latter used reheat. This advantage became more pronounced as IAS was reduced. It was, however, possible for the F-100 to out-run the Hunter sufficiently to obtain and hold deflection at 40,000ft when it had a speed advantage of 0.2–0.3 TMN over the Hunter's 0.85–0.94 TMN.

During high-speed bounces by the Hunter, the F-100 was able to engage reheat and out-run its adversary, but only if the pilot reacted quickly enough. If the selection of reheat was delayed until range was down to 2,000 yards the Hunter was able to close to firing range before the F-100 could accelerate away. When the situations were reversed the Hunter was also able to force the F-100 to break off its attack, but due to its lower overall performance it was unable to gain the initiative. One of the Hunter's biggest advantages was its ability to decelerate much more rapidly, which was of use in setting up low speed manoeuvres in which it usually came out on top.

When attacked from the rear it was recommended that Hunter pilots should initiate a turn at a separation of about 2,500 yards to maintain angle off and when range had been reduced to 1,000–1,200 yards, begin a hard break with maximum deceleration in an endeavour to draw the opponent into a scissors manoeuvre. The Loughberry, or diving spiral, was not preferred as a means of escape except when altitude was below 30,000ft and the attacker was at a stabilised separation of not less than 500 yards. Another manoeuvre to be avoided above 30,000ft and 0.92 IMN was the high 'g' barrel roll due to the Hunter's poor elevator control at high Mach number and lack of available 'g' compared to slab-tailed fighters.

The best 'last ditch' manoeuvre for the Hunter was a violent turn-reversal (scissors), allowing time for the turn to develop between each successive reversal. It was advised that the pull force on the controls should not be released during the reversal and full rudder should be applied in order to achieve the maximum rate of roll. The turn could be either normal or underneath (Derry turn) according to circumstances. In general the reversal should be normal when the intention was to gain height and reduce speed and underneath when it was intended to lose height and increase or maintain speed. The Hunter in RAF service was never to fly in aerial combat for real, however a few years later it was engaged on operations of a very different sort.

From a very early stage in the development process it had been recognised that there was likely to be a requirement for the Hunter to operate in the ground-attack role carrying a variety of external stores. Over the period 1957/8, trials were carried out at CFE to assess how the aircraft coped with various combinations of stores commencing with the carriage of up to 24 x 3in. rocket projectiles on the outer-wing hardpoints. It immediately became apparent that the Hunter's crisp handling qualities had been adversely affected, as it was sluggish and difficult to fly accurately, particularly at altitude. The stores also moved C.G. aft, which made the aircraft slightly tail heavy. Although the pitch-up tendency could still be controlled by the use of elevator alone, great care was required in hard turns. Pilots also found that sudden arresting movements in the rolling plane were liable to bend rocket fins and that flight in excess of 500kt led to the possibility of the RP leads becoming detached.

The tactics, as recommended by CFE, were a low-level approach to the target at 480kt with a 3g pull up to 3,000ft and turn through 90–120 degrees. This would result in an initial attack speed of 360kt IAS increasing to a firing speed of 440kt with a fifteen-degree angle of dive, or 460kt when the dive was increased to thirty degrees. Both resulted in a 6g pull out with a safety height of 800ft AGL. The withdrawal could either be carried out at low level (420kt) or, if the tactical situation permitted, at high level. Radius of action when carrying RP and two overload tanks was 123nm at low level and 186nm when the outward and return flights were carried out at optimum range altitude. For landing the approach speed with RP fitted was the same as for the clean aircraft (160kt IAS) but the recommended speed over the threshold was 140kt IAS. If rockets were retained after gun ammunition had been expended, C.G. moved well aft and there was insufficient nose-down trim available for landing with full flap. In such cases not more than thirty-eight degrees of flap could be used. Landing with asymmetric load in 'power' was not a problem, but when landing in 'manual', speed had to be maintained above 180kt IAS or lateral control was likely to be lost.

With the conclusion of the rocketing trials, CFE then evaluated the Hunter in the bombing role flying 102 sorties during which seventy-four bombs were dropped. As all-up weight had increased to 21,585lb, great care had to be taken when taxiing to avoid undue strain to the undercarriage, as well as excessive tyre wear. During take off the aircraft behaved in similar fashion to those equipped with RP. When taking off in a pair the recommended engine setting was 7,800rpm which resulted in a clean unstick at 150kt IAS after a roll of 1,200 yards in still air. The preferred flap setting was thirty-eight degrees together with an initial trim setting of one and a half degrees nose down. Once in the air handling was found to be similar to the aircraft when fitted with RP.

For dive-bombing, three types of attack were evolved depending on weather and the tactical situation on the ground. The first required a cloud base of 20,000ft or higher and involved a high-level cruise to the target at 40,000ft followed by a descent to 20,000ft, ten miles before the point of entry into the dive. This was carried out at an angle of sixty degrees, commencing at 380kt IAS rising to 520kt IAS at the time of bomb release, at 10,000ft. The steep angle of dive was a little disconcerting at first and some difficulty was experienced in achieving and holding the required sight picture, but this was overcome with practice. The recovery was completed by 7,000ft with loadings of 5–7g.

Although most of the pilots involved in the trial had little recent practice, the general level of accuracy was good, 84% of bombs falling within ninety yards of the target, 52% within fifty yards, with two direct hits. Incorrect estimation of the dive angle led to the greatest bombing errors, five degrees out producing a lineal error of up to 144 yards, although the dive angle could be gauged to some extent by grease-paint markings applied to the side of the canopy. As aircraft used in the trial were all fitted with the follow-up tail, pilots had little difficulty in recovering from dives, but it was suggested that unmodified aircraft would be likely to suffer from jack stall. This could be anticipated by trimming back to zero degrees ensuring a positive recovery by 6,000ft.

The second method of attack was for a cloud base of 8–20,000ft and again consisted of flying to the target at 40,000ft, this time followed by a descent to

8,000ft. As before, this was flown at 0.87 IMN converting to 400kt IAS with an engine setting of 6,500rpm and speed brakes out. After a level run of 10nm, the dive was commenced at 450kt IAS and thirty degrees to a height of 3,000ft where the bomb was released at 530kt IAS. Throughout all of this the aircraft handled normally, the recovery being completed by 2,000ft without pulling excessive 'g'. All bombs released cleanly and did not alter the trim of the aircraft in any way. The final profile involved flying at 250ft until ten miles from the target, after which a full power climb was made to 8,000ft and a thirty-degree dive attack carried out as described above. The 10nm level run-in was the most vulnerable period, but it was considered that this was the minimum distance to allow for speed stabilisation, target identification and the selection of armament switches after descending through cloud. During this phase of the attack speed had to be kept as high as possible to try to reduce the risk of being engaged by ground fire.

In addition to bombing from medium levels, consideration was also given to shallow dive attacks from low level. These could be used where pinpoint accuracy was required, or where operations were being carried out in a limited war in the face of less than effective ground defences. This type of attack commenced at a height of 3,000ft and consisted of a 20–30 degree angle of dive with an entry speed of 250kt IAS. Bomb release height was 4–500ft, by which time speed had increased to 380kt IAS. Due to the low level at which the aircraft recovered, bombs needed to be of delayed action type.

When carrying 100-gallon drop tanks, the radius of action when cruising to and from the target at 40,000ft was 291nm, dropping to 141nm if the approach and withdrawal phases were carried out at 250ft. When flown clean these figures were 110nm and 71nm respectively. In turbulent conditions it was recom-

FGA.9 XG256 of the Khormaksar Strike Wing armed with sixteen 3in rockets.

mended that bombs should be jettisoned before landing; if this was not possible, great care had to be taken as the Hunter's lateral control was noticeably inferior to that of the clean aircraft. In the unlikely event of a reversion to manual occurring together with an unjettisonable bomb, the pilot was left with no alternative but to eject.

The abilities of the Hunter with regard to ground attack were ably demonstrated in the Middle East during operations in the Radfan area of Aden. By late-1963 tension within the Western Aden Protectorate had reached a peak due to Egyptian-backed border incursions from neighbouring Yemen and subversion within Aden itself. In early 1964 Operation *Nutcracker* was launched, whereby Hunter FGA.9s carried out attacks on rebel positions with 30mm cannon and 3in. rockets. Conditions were far from ideal. The Radfan mountains consist of a complex of jagged peaks and sheer sided cliffs rising to 6–7,000ft with deep wadis or ravines in between. Most targets were in these narrow, steep sided valleys, many of which also ended in a sheer rock-face forming a cul-de-sac. Cloud could also form in these mountainous areas with astonishing rapidity, cumulonimbus often rising to over 40,000ft, and pilots also had to contend with severe turbulence and sudden changes in wind direction.

Sand was another problem, especially during the hot season, as it was blown into every crack and opening, coating cockpits with a thick layer of dust and sand-blasting windscreens to the point where they suffered serious discolouration. In the air visibility was often reduced to less than a mile and flying in such conditions with a sand-blasted windscreen was more akin to instrument flying. Ground crews were hard pressed to replace damaged windscreens and heat and dust made life extremely difficult. Group Captain John Jennings, leader of the Strike Wing in Aden, recalls the Hunter in the ground attack role and some of the missions that led to the award of a Distinguished Flying Cross (DFC):

'I took command of the Tactical Strike Wing in Khormaksar, Aden, from March 1963 (to April 1965) just before things started to hot up. Within the Wing I had three Mk.9 Hunter squadrons, Numbers 8, 43 and 208, plus a Mk.10 Hunter Recce Flight [1417 Flt] together with Shackletons, Whirlwinds and Belvederes. During the tour I flew over 200 operational sorties covering all types but the bulk of these was in the Mk.9 against selected targets or in support of ground forces. I cannot speak too highly of the Hunter Mk.9. I had flown every RAF ground attack aircraft from the Hurricane onwards, including the Mustang, Tempest and Venom, and in my book the Hunter was the number 1. It was rugged (I was struck several times by ground fire), reliable, highly manoeuvrable and a superb weapons platform. There were some operating restrictions – no use of all four guns, no 230-gallon tanks, no flap use above 300 knots and a maximum speed of 450 knots below 10,000ft, a speed reached at the bottom of a rocket dive-attack. This latter restriction was due to instances of runaway tail-trim which had resulted in accidents and deaths, but not during my tour. I did experience this myself (fortunately at altitude) and recovery was made without undue difficulty.

The Mk.9 was equipped with four 30mm Aden guns which made it the heaviest gun-armed fighter in the world at that time. Each gun had 135 rounds and a rate of fire of about 1,250 rounds per minute, a switch in the cockpit enabled one to select either two or four guns thus providing the opportunity to double the duration of fire. Unfortunately when we were given the authority to use four-gun firing I conducted a trial shoot and the result was that I lost all electrics – the circuit breakers popped and the radar failed. This was attributed to the effect of vibration and four-gun firing was vetoed whilst a modification programme to strengthen bulkheads etc. was introduced. I refrain from comment as to my views on those responsible for introducing the aircraft into service without adequate weapon-firing trials. The 30mm cannon was extremely accurate within a comparatively short range (800 yards) and with its high rate of fire was devastatingly effective against soft targets. Such targets rarely, if ever, were involved and we were constantly presented with hard-skinned targets i.e. stone-built sangars, buildings etc. As the only ammunition available to us was the High Explosive (HE) shell there was a constant hazard of ricochet from our own shells and rock splinters.

The only other weapon at out disposal was a World War Two weapon, the 3in. rocket. These could be carried in a two-tier arrangement of eight under each wing, i.e. sixteen in total. These weapons were notoriously difficult to aim. They required a steady tracking time of four seconds before release, had a long time of flight and a large gravity drop. In experienced hands remarkably good results were achieved but Squadron Commanders had to exercise great care in how they "bloodied" their pilots, feeding them into operations of increasing difficulty only as they gained experience. It speaks volumes for the care exercised that the loss of aircraft and crews was avoided.

With the need to initiate rocket attacks 4,500ft above the target and the speed of about 450 knots attained in the dive, great skill and judgement was necessary to close to the 800 yards release point, achieve the accuracy required, and effect a 6–7g pull-out safely. Another drawback to the use of this weapon was that only High Explosive Semi-Armour-Piercing rocket heads were available. On our early missions I quickly discovered (having been accused by Headquarters that we had missed the target) that the S.A.P. head was going straight through the front of a building leaving a comparatively small hole and exploding at the back wall. We really needed a squash-head rocket that would knock down the front wall, but here again no stocks were available. Another factor to consider was the heavy drag penalty flying with these rockets underslung and even in the 8xRP configuration, the radius of action was reduced by 20%. This may seem of little importance but the lack of diversion airfields and the ever present threat of sand dust-storms meant that fuel margins had to be carefully monitored and a close watch kept on wind changes.

I led the attack by eight aircraft on the fort at Harib in the Yemen on 28 March 1964 when quite fortuitously the aiming point I had chosen proved to be the magazine and the fort literally blew apart when my rockets struck. I was also instrumental in coming to the aid of an SAS patrol that was trapped and under attack on 30 April and provided support to within

Gp Capt John Jennings
when SASO Air Forces
Gulf, Muharraq 1968.

twenty-five yards of a party of beleaguered paratroopers. The close air support provided by the Hunters has received unrestricted praise both from the troops involved and their Army Commanders at all levels. They have left no-one in any doubt that casualties to troops on the ground would have been very much higher without that support. Although this is a tribute to the expertise of the pilots, it is also a real tribute to the aircraft that provided the weapons platform.'

Operations continued until the rebels capitulated on 18 November 1964 and on that date all operations in the Radfan ceased. In the two-month period from 30 April to 30 June which represented the height of the offensive, the Hunter FGA.9s of the Khormaksar Strike Wing flew 527 sorties and fired 2,508 rocket projectiles and 176,092 cannon shells. In addition the Hunter FR.10s of 1417 Flight flew 115 sorties and fired 7,808 cannon shells.

With its outstanding handling qualities, the Hunter quickly became popular for solo and formation aerobatics, and several squadrons formed four-aircraft aerobatic teams including 54 Squadron at Odiham in 1955. The following year they became known as the 'Black Knights' and were led by Captain R.G. Immig (USAF). At Leuchars, 43 Squadron formed the 'Fighting Cocks' under Flight Lieutenant P. Bairsto and 111 Squadron's 'Black Arrows' came into existence led by Squadron Leader Roger Topp AFC who achieved fame by looping twenty-two Hunters at Farnborough in 1958. The 'Black Arrows' were the RAF's premier aerobatic team from 1957 until replaced by the 'Blue Diamonds' of 92 Squadron in 1961. During their four-year reign, 111 transformed the art of display flying by using much larger formations, special paint schemes and smoke generators to greatly increase visual impact. Flying Officer Roger Hymans, who flew with the team from 1958 to 1960, recalls the build-up to the twenty-two-aircraft loop and some of the techniques that were evolved:

'The boss (S/L Roger Topp) started off with twenty aircraft and the original intention was to have a Vic of five with three aircraft behind each in line astern, a formation that was going to called the "Top 20". We tried that but found that the chap at the back behind the No. 3 in echelon was such a long way from the leader that he was liable to lose position, as the leader was further round the loop. After a lot of fiddling we went to a front row of seven with two behind each forming three Vics of seven. We then had one more behind the boss so there were four in the middle to bring the number up to twenty-two. We brought in a load of pilots who were not practiced at formation aerobatics so those of us who were regulars did line-astern formation and loops with five or six of them, as that was all they would have to do on the day.

We had a cine camera mounted in one of the aircraft and a chap on the ground took pictures with a G90 camera, which we used afterwards so that we could sort out the distances that we would have to fly apart. One of the problems is that if you have a big formation with people in line astern, what tends to happen is that the ones at the back sometimes stray too close to one another. When we flew the twenty-two we actually flew it wider than we normally would and it was actually something like 300ft across. For the Farnborough show we did two loops in twenty-two-aircraft formation and after the second we broke away a lot of those in the line-astern positions to leave sixteen for a roll. After this another seven broke away to drop down to a nine-ship which then became five after another four broke away. This all happened in about seven to eight minutes.

For display flying everyone flew either on the right or the left; we would never swap sides. I was always on the right so might move around from 2 to 4 or 6 which were all on the right-hand side, but would never go over to 3, 5 or 8 which were on the left. When you are formating on someone errors tend to build up. You get what we called a "yuck" where someone would drop a little bit low then pull up into position and the chap next to him would accentuate the effect so that if you were on the outside, by the time it got to you it was quite a big movement. After a while we developed a technique where we all flew on the boss so that the movements were damped out; if the aircraft next to you started bumping up and down, you just ignored him. Obviously if he moved out towards you, evasive action had to be taken because there wasn't a lot of distance between the aircraft.

We used ten degrees of flap for displays to improve handling at lower speeds and also to allow the use of more power by the leader so that we could be in a more responsive part of the throttle range, thereby allowing us to make quicker and more accurate position changes. If you were going through those 2–300rpm where the variable guide vanes of the Avon engine were clicking in and out you got variations in thrust, so to get out of that range we put the flaps down which gave us a bit more drag as well as lift. The boss would fly with a throttle setting of around 6,900rpm, which was about three-quarter power on the Avon, so that we wouldn't have this

Hunters of the Black Arrows in immaculate formation. (*Ministry of Defence*)

problem with throttle control. It is much easier to fly in close formation if you keep a steady g-loading so as far as possible our display was one flowing manoeuvre. We would come out of a loop, pull up into a wingover, down for a barrel roll and back into another loop, so it was a continuous g-pull varying from 2–4g. It's a big advantage to be pulling "g" when going through bumps, in fact I've always felt that straight and level flypasts are more difficult than doing aerobatics.'

Throughout his three years with the team Roger Hymans flew something like 600 formation aerobatic sorties (including practice displays), a figure which includes 150 shows. One of the most memorable occasions took place at Le Bourget during the Paris Airshow where the dimensions of the main runway made it possible for the team to take off in diamond-nine formation, a piece of one-upmanship which left the crowd singing their praises. In marked contrast, various members of Fighter Command's hierarchy were less than pleased and afterwards a lot of questions were asked that began with, "What if . . .". Unlike the full-time aerobatic teams of today, 111 Squadron retained an operational commitment and took part in gunnery practices and exercises at various times throughout the year. As all pilots had at least one previous tour on Hunters, results obtained during air-to-air firing were well up with the standard set by other squadrons, despite the fact that much of the unit's time was taken up by display flying.

While the 'Black Arrows' stole the show at Farnborough in 1958, one of the stars in 1959 was Hawker test pilot Bill Bedford who regularly performed thirteen-turn spins in a two-seat Hunter T.7. Despite the fact that the Hunter did not suffer any undesirable spin characteristics, intentional spinning was prohibited during its service with the RAF although Pilot's Notes did contain information on what could be expected should a spin occur and the action that was necessary for recovery. Those for the Hunter F.4 were as follows:

'The behaviour varies between spins to the left and spins to the right. The aircraft is reluctant to spin to the left unless pro-spin controls are applied at the stall, in which case the nose will rise, the left wing drop, and the aircraft will hesitate before falling into a spin in an attitude approximately forty degrees nose down. The first one or two turns may be steady, but during succeeding turns the rate of rotation, which is slow, becomes unsteady and there is marked pitching and rolling. Periodically, the nose rises and the rate of rotation momentarily ceases, the aircraft then falls and rotates rapidly through approximately sixty degrees before nosing up and hesitating again. In comparison the aircraft spins more readily to the right. The attitude is steeper and the rate of rotation, though faster, is steadier. When spinning in either direction, the ailerons should be held neutral as out-spin aileron will cause the spin to become erratic.

Normal recovery action is effective, particularly if it coincides with the aircraft's hesitation. However, when rotation ceases the controls should be centralised immediately, otherwise the aircraft may enter a spin in the opposite direction. This is important when recovering from a spin to the left. If a spin occurs with undercarriage and flaps down they should be retracted. Care should be taken during recovery action to ensure that the ailerons are central as out-spin aileron may hinder or prevent recovery. In-spin aileron is powerful in checking the spin, but great care must be taken to prevent development of a spiral in the same direction or spin in the opposite direction.'

For most pilots, converting onto fast jets meant a very steep learning curve, but perhaps not quite as steep as that experienced by Roger Hymans at Chivenor in 1956, as he encountered pitch up, a flame-out and a spin in a single flight.

'I had just finished my wings training on the Vampire and was now converting to the Hunter. At the time there were no two-seat aircraft and no simulator, so the training staff relied on briefings and a supervised start up before first solo. One evening in the bar one of the younger tactics instructors advised me to try climbing to high level, increase speed to around 0.94 Mach and then really pull it into a steep turn. He was joking but was unaware that he was talking to a nineteen-year-old immature youth who did everything he was told. The next day on my fourth trip in the Hunter I climbed to a height of 40,000ft, accelerated to 0.94 Mach and pulled the aircraft into a high-g turn. It juddered and then pitched up violently, full-forward stick failed to move the nose down and

166

the airspeed quickly decreased to below the first marking on the ASI.

The aircraft then rolled to the right and entered a fast and uneven spin, the roll rate and pitching moment changing all the time. The standard recovery drill I had been taught in the Vampire did not appear to work, so for some reason I cannot understand, I put the stick and rudder into a position to make the aircraft follow its erratic path, i.e. stick forward and to the right, plus right rudder. I then moved the controls back to the central position and the aircraft immediately recovered. I later realised that the reason for the recovery was because I had unwittingly done the right thing by applying in-spin aileron. The Hunter had very large ailerons and the smallest amount of control movement in the wrong direction would keep the wing stalled and prevent recovery from a spin. I had lost 25,000ft before regaining level flight and at that stage I realised that the engine had flamed out. The engine was started again and I returned rather shakily to Chivenor. On landing I told no one of my problems because I assumed it was my entire fault. It took me some time on a Hunter squadron before I could take the aircraft to its limits in high-level practice combat.'

Hymans also recalls that the violence of the manoeuvre tended to fling his hand to the outside of the spin and in so doing induced him to apply out-spin aileron which, as already noted, inhibited recovery. Some effort had to be made to overcome this effect and move the controls in the opposite direction.

Other than the manufacturers, the only place where Hunters were regularly spun was at Boscombe Down as part of the course at the Empire Test Pilots' School. Here two T.7s, XL564 and XL612, carried out erect and inverted spins to acquaint students with the characteristics of swept-wing jet fighters during and after departure. The aircraft were modified to include a special spin panel in front of the left-hand seat to provide the pilot with additional attitude information, as inverted spinning in particular could be extremely disorientating, even for those with plenty of fast-jet experience. As the Hunter was reluctant to spin, positive action had to be taken to produce an auto-rotation, consisting of full rudder in the desired direction, together with full-back stick with the ailerons held neutral. Typically a four-turn erect spin from 40,000ft would lead to a height loss of around 10,000ft, plus another 5,000ft during a 3.5g pull-out from the subsequent dive.

For inverted spins there were two entry techniques, out-spin aileron applied at a roll-rate hesitation during an erect spin, and an entry from a full aileron roll. For the latter method the aircraft was set up at about 175kt IAS in level flight and then full aileron was applied with slight forward pressure. When a good rate of roll had developed (after about 270 degrees) full opposite rudder was applied with the stick maintained in its fully deflected position. At the end of the first roll a pitch/yaw coupling could be felt and by the end of the second roll a spin was usually fully established. During the second roll the stick was centralised at a position slightly aft of neutral while the rudder was held fully deflected throughout. The inverted spin in the Hunter was found to be less oscillatory than the erect spin but it was faster, with each turn taking 3–4 seconds. For the pilot the predominant sensations were negative 'g' (usually –1 to –2g) together with a high rate of yaw. Recovery actions were the same as for the erect spin, although a more determined effort had to be made to apply and hold full rudder, and full-forward stick was usually needed before the aircraft recovered.

Like most thoroughbred military aircraft, the Hunter served far longer than originally envisaged and the last large-scale user (No.1 TWU at Brawdy) only gave up its Hunters on 25 July 1985, an event that was marked by a nine-ship formation display led by former Red Arrows leader Wing Commander Brian Hoskins. Thereafter T.7s were used for pilot continuation training by the Buccaneer force until the disbanding of 208 Squadron at Lossiemouth in 1994, forty years after the arrival of the first Hunters at Leuchars. With 6,500 hours on type, including six years as leader of the Royal Navy's 'Blue Herons' aerobatic team, Derek Morter is well qualified to sum up the Hunter's characteristics:

'It was so delightful to fly that one cannot recall any terrible faults, it was just sheer pleasure to handle; any problems, let go of the stick and the aircraft would sort itself out. You wore the Hunter like a favourite pullover, it was full of character, fly it sedately or turn it inside out, fly it accurately or play about, aerobatics were a dream, it reflected your mood. The controls were well balanced and seemed almost effortless after you had built up muscle from years on Meatboxes. It was also a great gun platform, especially in the ground-attack role. Leading formation aerobatics with ten degrees of flap and the throttle set to give 350kt in level flight, one could then go through all the aerobatic manoeuvres without having to change the power setting except for take off, box landing and the undercarriage loop (gear and flap over the top of the loop). A blown exterior windscreen like the F-86 or a wiper like the T.7/T.8 would have been helpful when landing in heavy rain and, of course, more internal fuel instead of external tanks, two x 100 gallons were reasonable, but four were a bit of a bind, especially at high altitude. However, in my opinion the aircraft is a classic, meaning as much to we pilots of the 1950s and 1960s as the Spitfire did to WW2 chaps. Just imagine the capability of a version with reheat!'

Part Two

Night/All-Weather Fighters

CHAPTER SEVEN

ARMSTRONG WHITWORTH METEOR NF.11–14

At the beginning of the Second World War Britain was well protected from daylight attack, possessing day fighter aircraft and an associated ground control system that were second to none. Paradoxically, it was virtually defenceless against attack by bombers at night. Although the use of Airborne Interception radar was pioneered by the Bristol Blenheim 1F in 1940, it lacked the necessary performance and it was not until the introduction of the Beaufighter 1F, equipped with A.I. Mk. IV radar, that the RAF could deploy a capable night fighter. During the war years radar technology advanced rapidly, so that by the end of hostilities Fighter Command's standard night fighter was the de Havilland Mosquito XXX which was fitted with the American-manufactured centimetric-wave A.I.10.

In the immediate post war years the parsimony which afflicted British defence spending as a whole resulted in the venerable Mosquito remaining in front-line service as a night fighter until 1951, by which time it was patently obsolete. The first attempt to provide a replacement, Specification F.44/46 issued in January 1947, was as confused as its day fighter equivalent and was superseded the following year by F.4/48 which ultimately led to the Javelin. Of the firms involved in the quest for a successor to the Mosquito, Gloster proposed a version of the Meteor based on the airframe of the two-seat T.7, but as the company was already fully committed producing other Meteor sub-types, design work for the night-fighter variant was passed to Armstrong Whitworth Aircraft Ltd.

The performance of the proposed Meteor NF was set out in Specification F.24/48 and work began on an aerodynamic prototype at Armstrong Whitworths's experimental works at Bitteswell in January 1948. This was a conversion of VW413, the fourth production Meteor T.7, which was flown on 23 December 1948 with wingspan increased to 43ft by incorporating long-span wings similar to the earlier F.3. The nose was extended by 4ft to accommodate A.I.10 radar and a series of test flights carried out which, apart from a little directional instability, were entirely satisfactory. The last major modification to the airframe was the fitting of an F.8 tail assembly that increased overall length to 48ft 6in.

In 1949 AWA were awarded a contract to build three prototypes and 200 production examples of the night fighter Meteor (now designated NF.11), the first prototype (WA546) flying for the first time on 31 May 1950. Armament still comprised four 20mm Hispano cannon but due to the installation of radar in the

171

View from a Meteor T.7 emphasising the amount of metalwork in the T.7/NF.11 canopy.

nose, these had to be relocated to the wings and were mounted outboard of the engines. The two-man crew had the benefit of cabin pressurisation, a cabin pressure of 8p.s.i. allowing an equivalent of 24,000ft to be experienced by the crew when operating at 40,000ft. Endurance was also increased thanks to a ventral tank of 175 gallons and two underwing tanks each of 100 gallons, which supplemented internal fuel capacity of 325 gallons.

The first production NF.11, WD585, was delivered to CFE at West Raynham on 18 November 1950 for service trials and flew a total of 130 sorties by day and twenty-three by night. The aircraft featured spring tab ailerons, A.I.10 with 'Lucero' facilities (a device for tracking and measuring distance from ground beacons), two TR 1934 ten-channel VHF radios, Gee 3, IFF Mk.3G and a radio altimeter (AYF). The hood was a multi-framed one-piece structure, similar to that on the T.7, and was hinged along its starboard side to allow access to the cockpit. Unfortunately it inherited one of the T.7's weaknesses in that the hood was liable to part company from the aircraft in flight, an event that posed a distinct threat of decapitation for the crew. Another NF.11 flown by CFE (WD594) lost its hood during a trials sortie but on this occasion the pilot and navigator did not suffer any injury.

At the normal take-off weight of 18,300lb, the NF.11 accelerated fairly rapidly, although a little more slowly than other marks of Meteor, and a pronounced stick movement was necessary to raise the nosewheel. This occurred at about 90kt and the aircraft flew off readily at about 115kt. The undercarriage could be raised immediately after take off without change of trim or loss of height. At maximum take-off weight of 20,100lb (ventral and underwing tanks plus full ammunition) the nosewheel lifted at 100kt, the aircraft becoming airborne at 125kt, although not as cleanly as at the lower weight. It also took longer to reach safety speed and the ailerons were noticeably heavier. Take-off characteristics could be improved by using one-quarter flap and the average run in light wind conditions was approximately 1,500 yards.

During aerobatics no undesirable characteristics were noted, the aircraft appeared to be vice free and loops could be carried out without inducing excessive 'g'. With ventral tank fitted, rolls took around 6–7 seconds at 250–330kt, and eight seconds with underwing tanks. There was a slight heaviness about all controls compared with other marks of Meteor, which meant that all manoeuvres were carried out somewhat slower, but this did not detract from the overall experience and aerobatics were easy and pleasant to perform. Stalls were also straightforward; some tail buffeting together with a slight pitching motion and aileron snatch were experienced at 5–10kt above stall speed which occurred at approximately 105kt undercarriage and flaps down and 120kt clean, depending on altitude. At speeds approaching limiting Mach number, a slight nose-up change of trim became evident around Mach 0.77 and as speed increased further this led to a progressive left wing and nose down tendency. No snaking was exhibited and the aircraft could be held straight and level even at Mach 0.80.

On the approach, the dive brakes were satisfactory although deceleration was not as rapid as on other marks of Meteor. The biggest problem experienced during the trials was one of visibility. The prominence of metal in the canopy was compounded by the build up of ice and/or mist which seriously affected the pilot's ability to plan his descent. In conditions of rain, forward visibility became virtually nil. During one particular flight an experienced pilot made three unsuccessful approaches and on his fourth attempt finished up forty yards into the overshoot area. Landings generally produced very little float, the correct procedure being a flat approach with touchdown at around 110kt. If aerodynamic drag was needed to slow down, a positive pull force was needed to hold the nosewheel off the ground. No problems were encountered during crosswind landings. In the case of an overshoot the NF.11 lifted off easily even when full flap had been selected. Stick forces were light and no difficulty was experienced in climbing away.

Under asymmetric conditions, it was possible to maintain directional control until the aircraft was almost stalled when using climbing power (14,100rpm) and at this setting a speed of 250kt could be achieved in level flight. At cruise power (13,500rpm) it was possible to fly at 190–210kt at 10,000ft without losing any height. Critical speed at full power was 140kt, increasing to 150kt with underwing tanks. In terms of general handling, the NF.11 was assessed as follows:

'The aircraft is pleasant to fly and is quite stable except in conditions of turbulence when it develops a pronounced snaking, particularly with dive brakes out. Overall, manoeuvrability was quite satisfactory for the night-fighter role.

Stick forces in the medium height and speed range are slightly heavier than those in the Meteor 4 but at greater heights and speeds, aileron controls are comparable due to spring tabs which have been incorporated in the ailerons. The elevators are effective but require greater stick force at height where continuous steep turns and the following of hard evasive actions cause some fatigue. Rudder control is satisfactory in all respects.

At heights above 35,000ft the controls all become noticeably less effective. The rate of roll is moderate but acceptable, being a little less than that of the Meteor 8. The maximum rate of turn achieved at 35,000ft and at 420kt TAS was 360 degrees in approximately one minute ten seconds, although with some loss of speed during the turn. This corresponds to a radius of turn of 1.25nm. With underwing tanks fitted the aircraft is generally heavier on the controls with a marked heaviness on the ailerons. At heights above 30,000ft with underwing tanks the manoeuvrability is reduced considerably. There is a pronounced tendency to "wallow" in turns and considerable height can be lost inadvertently. The rate of roll is a little slower. The maximum rate of turn obtained with underwing tanks at 35,000ft was 360 degrees in one minute thirty seconds at 410kt TAS, corresponding to a radius of 1.6nm. Limitations imposed on CFE are 5.4g without tanks and 4.8g with, and maximum permitted stick force is 60lb at speeds above 375kt.'

Throughout the trials a considerable number of tactical climbs were carried out in the course of high-speed interceptions during which the aircraft averaged eleven minutes to reach 35,000ft. Thereafter climb rate began to deteriorate, another four and a half minutes being required to get to 40,000ft. With underwing tanks the time to 35,000ft was reduced to fourteen minutes and rate of climb then fell away rapidly. Although the aircraft could be coaxed up to 40,000ft, it was deemed operationally unacceptable above 36,000ft. All climbs were carried out with a full war load. During level speed runs at 35,000ft, the maximum achieved with underwing tanks was Mach 0.74 but acceleration above Mach 0.70 was slow unless a shallow dive was used to build up speed. Fuel consumption was measured at 430 gal/hr at high altitude, increasing to 520 gal/hr at low level, so that with ventral tank only, sortie lengths varied from forty minutes at 0–10,000ft, to sixty minutes at 25–40,000ft.

When it came to tactical handling the NF.11 showed itself to be a stable gun platform in still air but in turbulence there was a tendency to snake, which caused some difficulty in holding a steady aim. At high altitude adequate vision was again one of the major headaches as internal frosting invariably occurred, a situation made worse by lines of mist which formed in the quarter panels between the heater wires. Instrument flying posed no great difficulty except in cases of snaking, which became worse if dive brakes were used. At high altitude, particularly at high speed, considerable concentration was needed to fly accurately as height could be rapidly gained or lost during hard turns. It was considered that sixty degrees would be the maximum angle of bank that an average squadron pilot could usefully employ.

As regards radar performance the following contact ranges were achieved:

Average Maximum Range at Medium/High Level			
10–15,000ft	Mosquito	4nm	
20–25,000ft	Mosquito	4.5nm	Fair
	Meteor	6.5nm	Good
	Washington	6.75nm	Unacceptable
25–35,000ft	Meteor	4.5nm	

Maximum Range at Low Level		
Below 2,500ft	Mosquito over land	13,700ft
	Mosquito over sea	17,000ft

Minimum Ranges			
B Scope	500ft – av	C Scope	400ft – av.
	400ft – best		200ft – best

In conclusion the NF.11 was considered suitable as a night fighter, but not for the all-weather role, as its lack of an air-interpreted approach aid meant that it was dependent on GCA and was subject to the same weather limitations as a day fighter. From the point of view of intercepts in cloud, doubts were cast as to whether the A.I.10 equipment could bring pilots close enough to obtain a visual identification. It was conceded that the NF.11 could not be expected to survive combat with escort fighters and could therefore only operate successfully against unescorted bombers above the weather. The most serious reservation concerned the ability of the pilot to see his target and then effect a successful recovery to base. This situation was summed up as follows: 'Were it not for the urgency of the re-equipment of the night-fighter force, the vision of the Meteor NF.11 might well have been termed unacceptable.'

Although the Meteor possessed a considerable improvement in performance over the Mosquito NF.36, its A.I.10 radar was rapidly becoming obsolescent as the contact ranges quoted above would indicate. Its lack of sophistication also meant that the navigator's job was extremely taxing and could only be mastered with considerable experience. The radar display was presented on two screens. The right hand screen, or B Scope, gave range in feet along a vertical scale, and the relative angle of the target to left or right of the night fighter's heading on the horizontal scale. The other display, known as the C Scope, comprised a radial-grid pattern which showed whether the target was above or below.

The most straightforward intercept was for the ground controller to manoeuvre the defending fighter onto a course so that the target's flightpath crossed that of the fighter at ninety degrees. This would result in an angle between the two aircraft of forty-five degrees which, if speed and height were equal, would result in the two flying a collision course. As range decreased, the nav/rad in the night fighter would see the target blip move down the B Scope on the forty-five-degree line. He would then position a movable strobe line on the blip to make sure that the selected target echo appeared on the C Scope, the blip on this screen giving angular displacement above or below the tracking aircraft. To set up an attack, a turn would have to be made towards the target (the exact timing to be determined by rate of closure) until the blip was almost dead-ahead, at which point the turn would be reversed so as to bring the night fighter round in a curve of pursuit. With the target now directly in front, speed would be increased to reduce range and, hopefully, allow visual identification.

The above example illustrates the basic method of night interception under ideal conditions, but hostile aircraft would be unlikely to fly straight and level for very long and the fun usually started when the target began to take evasive action in an attempt to throw the fighter off. In such a situation the target aircraft would have an advantage in that its pilot would be able to put on full bank before the navigator in the following aircraft would see any deviation of the blip on his screen. His first indication would be to see the blip suddenly rush off to one side of the 'B' Scope or the other. Even if the navigator told his pilot to turn hard, there was still the very real possibility that the blip would disappear off the screen altogether. After the initial turn the target might then initiate a maximum-rate turn in the opposite direction so that the hard-working back-seater would be faced with the blip suddenly changing direction and heading rapidly towards the other side of his display. If these changes in direction were not spotted immediately the chances of a successful interception were slim.

Following its evaluation at CFE, the Meteor NF.11 entered service with 29 Squadron at Tangmere on 20 August 1951 to commence a period of intensive flying to ascertain any potential defects that might affect the aircraft and its associated equipment, and the adequacy of scales of servicing, spares and ground equipment. The trial was initially to comprise 1,000 hours which was to be flown with eight NF.11s over a three-month period, but during familiarisation it became apparent that the lack of a direct-vision panel in the windscreen severely affected the aircraft's capability. As a result the test was delayed until the end of November pending modifications. In the intervening weeks, however, 500 hours were flown and it was decided to utilise this experience and reduce the intensive period to a further 500 hours comprising high-level interceptions (150 hrs), low-level interceptions (100 hrs), air firing (110 hrs), Broadcast control (50 hrs), navigation (50 hrs) and airtests (40 hrs). This was completed within five weeks with each aircraft flying at a rate of fifty-eight hours per month.

During the trial there were no incidents or accidents, and on completion all aircraft were still serviceable. Several difficulties were highlighted. There were sixty-one failures on start-up, mainly caused by fouling of the torch igniters, and 12% of the sorties had to be abandoned due to unserviceability of the AI radar. The most serious handicap however, was a very high cannon stoppage rate which was so bad that the chances of having a 'clean shot' with all four guns was only 4%. The majority of the stoppages were caused by broken belts and late feeds. As a result a lot of shooting was done with uneven firepower which made it impossible to achieve any degree of accuracy.

NF.11 WD625 of No. 85
Squadron visits Horsham
St Faith in May 1952.

   High-altitude practice interceptions were carried out without difficulty and
Broadcast control utilising Gee 3 was seen to be the best way to intercept mass
raids or even a concentrated raid of ten-plus bombers. Gee simplified navigation
and was of great value for accurate positioning prior to carrying out a GCA,
which, in view of limited fuel reserves, took much of the anxiety out of letdowns
in bad weather. Practice interceptions over the sea at low level were much more
demanding. With a target at 1,000ft and the fighter slightly below, contact only
occurred at around two miles, although even this depended on sea state. The
target blip was also difficult to follow due to the presence of stronger blips from
ships and buoys. Interceptions were attempted down to 100ft but these proved
to be impossible on a really dark night and 3–400ft was a more realistic limit for
experienced crews. The effect of hitting slipstream at 2,000ft range at 100ft AGL
would almost certainly have been fatal. It was also found that low-level coverage
from land based radar stations had many blind areas which put more pressure
on the nav/rad to effect a successful interception.
   By the end of the year three further squadrons had begun conversion, 141 at
Coltishall, 85 at West Malling and 264 at Linton-on-Ouse. In early 1952 Meteor
NF.11s began to arrive in Germany, with 68 and 87 Squadrons at Wahn forming
No.148 Wing. Both units had been reformed on 1 January but nearly a year was
to pass before they could be considered fully operational. 68 Squadron was
commanded by Squadron Leader D.S. Leete whose initial responsibilities were
decidedly ground based. Over the coming weeks new crews continued to arrive
but the only flying to be had was in the squadron's T.7, the first three NF.11s
only arriving in March, by which time Wahn could boast GCA facilities, but no
A.I. radar servicing!
   It was not until May that reasonable progress was made; the delivery of
more aircraft allowed fifteen crews to convert to the NF.11 and the A.I.10
radar could at last be used with the arrival of radar mechanics to join the ground
crew. These points were offset, however, by concern over the accuracy of
Wahn's homing facilities and the value of its GCA. By July, total flying hours
had risen to a healthy 409 (140 at night), time enough for crews to be apprecia-
tive of the aircraft's relatively docile handling characteristics and improved
performance compared with the Mosquito. Most would have echoed the
following assessment by Flight Lieutenant Bruce Spurr who joined the squadron
in 1956:

'The Meteor was a stable aircraft, with no yaw when the throttles were manipulated and there was no lack of engine response; the power was there, it just took longer to become effective, but one soon became familiar with this. The foot loads on the rudder when doing asymmetric overshoots were similar to a Mosquito, however, the Meteor had a greater amount of power available and from the recommended decision height of 400ft and 140kt one could go around on one with no loss of height. A Mosquito under the same conditions would require most of the height to be converted into speed while the aircraft was being "cleaned up" and the single-engine climb speed of 160–165kt achieved. The loss of an engine in normal flight posed no problem for either aircraft, both were capable of aerobatics in the rolling plane on one engine.

Approaching the stall in the Meteor there was buffeting, probably orig-inating from the high-set tailplane and the nose would drop at the stall itself. Occasionally one wing or the other would drop but not as violently as, say, the Harvard. In the stall the height loss was rapid and recovery action, although what one would class as "normal", needed the fairly rapid opening of the throttles to keep height loss to a minimum. There was adequate warning of an approaching stall and easing back-pressure on the stick and applying power gave a rapid recovery. With undercarriage and flaps down, or with airbrakes out, the pre-stall buffet was more pronounced.

Handling was not much different to the other marks of Meteor – perhaps a slower rate of roll and slightly heavier aileron input, but it was as aero-batic when the nav/rad had locked the A.I. scanner dish. The cockpit was roomy enough, but might have been tight if ejection seats had been fitted. As it was the crews sat on their parachute/dinghy packs and I seem to remember that it was always the CO_2 bottle or paddles which were in contact with one's bum! Perhaps it was a good thing that endurance was so short.

After a prolonged period at height there was a tendency for the wind-screen to ice up when descending to commence a GCA or to join the circuit. Lack of fuel usually precluded waiting for it to melt, but many units provided a glycol soaked rag in a small linen bag to wipe off the ice (or use one's gloved hand). Rain on the approach was usually blown clean off the screen at the start of the approach, but as speed was reduced to below about 120kt for the touch-down, it then collected enough to impede vision. One unit tried a silicone polish on one half of the screen, but the results were not noticeably any better.

With over 1,500 hours on type, the Meteor has to be my favourite aircraft. On my very first sortie I was flying it more precisely than the Mosquito on which I was quite experienced – it had the typical solid "Gloster" feel and there was no backlash in the controls.'

The operational adequacy of the Meteor night fighter depended very much on the height and speed of the target it was tasked to intercept. Pilot Officer Howard Fitzer describes some of the flying that he undertook with 68 Squadron and a few of the problems encountered:

178

Pilot Officer Howard
Fitzer with navigator
Pilot Officer D.B.
Collins.

'We could get up to about 41,000ft (after a very long climb), but at that altitude it felt like trying to balance a plate on the point of a needle and the
slightest turn induced a loss of altitude which made interceptions at
anywhere near that height impossible. The Meteor could cope with
Lincolns, B-29s and B-36s, but the Canberra was another matter. I recall
trying to intercept one at night during a NATO exercise. At approximately
36,000ft every time the Meteor reached 0.78 Mach, the port wing dropped
quite violently making directional control difficult. After a futile eighty
mile chase I was forced to abandon the interception due to fuel shortage.

Displaced head-on attacks at or above target level was the more usual
method on interceptions, mainly because the potential targets had broadly
similar performance and long tail-chases were therefore usually imprac-
tical. The use of window by target bombers posed quite a problem,
although in some instances it could be utilised as an indication of target
position. In most cases, however, it seemed to simply swamp the radar.
The main problem for the pilot was to obtain visual sighting of the target
at night – at that time a pre-requisite to engagement with guns – the worst
condition being a clear night without cloud or moon and over the sea (no
light source or background and nothing to reflect it).

Among the hazards were heavy bombers trailing aerials and any that
were piston-engined. The low speed of the target meant that a fighter could
be caught in the slipstream and thrown about at speeds perilously near the

stall. This was a particular danger to those squadrons which had a night "anti-minelayer" commitment. Mine-laying aircraft typically flew at heights below 500ft above sea level and at very low speeds, and since it was necessary to approach the target from below to avoid swamping the radar with "sea-returns", the task was sufficiently dangerous to cause the loss of aircraft. One other rather unpleasant habit was for the targets (usually Lincolns) to install microphones in their engines and tune-in to interceptor frequencies – a delightful noise at full power!

I particularly remember the sequel to a NATO night exercise when sufficient aircraft had been gathered together to simulate a "1000 bomber" raid against the U.K. At the appropriate time a number of night-fighter squadrons were launched to intercept them head-on, all participants being instructed to operate with navigation lights switched off in the interests of realism. At the end of the exercise all aircraft were asked to switch on their navigation lights prior to return to base, at which point the sky seemed to be lit up like a Christmas tree. I've never seen so many aircraft at night in my life – it was quite a sight!'

68 Squadron departed for its first air-firing detail at Sylt in August but the results were far from encouraging. At the end of the deployment the best marksmen were Flight Lieutenant Bob Smythe and Flying Officer Davis with a score of 2.2%. Pilot Officer Howard Fitzer recalls some of the difficulties:

'The Meteor itself was a stable flying platform but suffered from two salient problems typical of wing-mounted gun installations. The first was wing twisting, the severity of which varied with "g" loading. This, of course, induced altered gun alignment and consequent sighting inaccuracy. The second concerned harmonisation. For the Meteor NF this was set at 400 yards, at which range gun-pattern density (concentration of fire) was at its greatest. It follows that at lesser or greater ranges than 400 yards (i.e. before and after trajectory convergence) there was a consequent 'scatter' effect, particularly at greater ranges.

There are those who would argue that the resultant wide scatter of shot, despite loss of concentrated fire, would be a decided advantage in the

Three of No. 68 Squadron's Meteors in echelon.

night-fighter role. Others would argue that the usual additional commitment to a day-fighter role would put the NF Meteor at a disadvantage in a combat environment that implied high "g" loadings and difficulty in bringing to bear concentrated fire at a precise range. Although the parallel fuselage-mounted guns of the day fighter also suffered a degree of pattern spread with increasing range, it was considerably less than wing-mounted installations, thus permitting higher concentration of fire at virtually any range. Results tended to speak for themselves, as was apparent from the air-firing results I obtained with the Meteor F.8 whilst attending the Pilot Attack Instructor (PAI) course at the Fighter Weapons School at Leconfield. My average air-to-air firing scores were consistently higher (up to ten times higher) than those I ever obtained in the NF versions – a result which tends to highlight the airframe/harmonisation problems inherent in wing-mounted gun installations.'

In September, 68 Squadron took part in Exercise *Holdfast*, during which it operated from dispersals under canvas, and also Exercise *Ardent* when eight crews flew out of Tangmere. Throughout the rest of the year numerous *Bullseye* exercises were flown against Canberras and Washingtons, the only problem being a persistent R/T fault that only became apparent in the air. The first two months of 1953 brought the usual bad weather, ice on the runway causing two aircraft to end up in the overshoot area and low cloud resulting in five aircraft diverting to Wildenrath where one suffered minor damage when it hit the approach lighting. The highlight of March was Exercise *Jungle King* in which the squadron attempted to intercept high-flying Canberras, but the month also saw the unit's first accident when Flying Officer K.J. McLeary was killed in WD676 when his aircraft crashed after entering an inverted spin, possibly as a result of hypoxia. His navigator, Flying Officer H.A. Lake, baled out successfully.

In April the squadron practised formation flying for a visit by the Chief of Staff after which twelve Meteors deployed to Sylt for more air-to-air gunnery. Results were again disappointing, so much so that three new pilots and three 'duffers' were ordered to stay behind for further practice when the squadron returned to Wahn. This had the desired effect and Pilot Officer Paterson proceeded to out-score everyone else with 29%. After much display flying in June, a return was made to operational flying in July with Exercise *Coronet* when the squadron operated 'in the field' at Beauvechain. Intruder operations were carried out against F-86s, B-29s and Lincolns but on the twenty-eighth Flight Lieutenant Duff and Pilot Officer Miles were killed in WM222 when they flew into trees at night near Soulme in Belgium.

Following a deployment to Coltishall in August for Exercise *Momentum*, 68 Squadron returned to regular training at Wahn in September although problems were experienced with poor serviceability and flying was eventually curtailed for five days while all outstanding modifications were cleared. From the beginning of November to the break for the Christmas holidays however, 739 hours were flown of which 516 hours were at night (mainly practice interceptions), but by the end of December the festivities had taken their toll on most

No. 68 Squadron Meteor NF.11s in formation.

aircrew and the general level of physical fitness was assessed as 'extremely low'!

Flying quickly got back to normal in January 1954 although two incidents tended to spoil an otherwise excellent month. Flying Officers Smith and Evans crash-landed WM233 near Bonn when they ran out of fuel in bad weather on the eleventh, and Flight Lieutenant Smythe's aircraft was hit by a ricochet during air-to-ground firing on the range at Monschau two weeks later. Further bad weather over the next two months severely curtailed operations but flying time hit an all-time high in April when 399 hours were flown by day and 227 at night.

After spending two and a half years building the squadron up from nothing, Squadron Leader Leete was posted out in August to be replaced by Squadron Leader Dickie Goode, although his tenure was to be extremely short as a month later it was announced that all night-fighter units were to be commanded by officers who held the rank of Wing Commander. Goode was moved to become Wahn's Squadron Leader Ops and his place as boss of 68 was taken by Wing Commander E. James DFC AFC who had previously been OC Flying at Ahlhorn. During the year two detachments were made to Sylt, Flying Officer L. Jones winning the coveted 'Winged Bullet' as the squadron's best shot with a score of 10.3%.

In the first half of 1955 a series of exchanges took place with 723 Eskadrille of the Royal Danish Air Force at Aalborg, providing an opportunity for the two units to share experiences with the NF.11, and in April, 68 Squadron participated in Exercise *Sky High* in which it claimed twenty Canberra kills at night. Towards the end of the month trials began with a new Gee system which, it was hoped, would allow pilots to position for a GCA or visual let-down from thirty miles, the aim being to waste as little time and fuel as possible when large numbers of aircraft needed to be on the ground quickly.

By now, flying hours had been considerably reduced and in May total time amounted to 286 hours, of which only eighty-eight were at night. There is no explanation for this in the official records although complaints were made at various times throughout the year regarding the level of spares back-up. In June 68 Squadron moved to Brusthem in Belgium for *Carte Blanche*, a large NATO exercise in which war conditions were simulated as closely as possible. Many sorties were flown against 'enemy' bombers, and the unit's Meteors were also used in the intruder role against bomber airfields at night and on daylight sweeps. The following month 68 were back at Sylt for gunnery practice, excellent weather allowing 454 firing details to be flown. At the end of the detachment the squadron's average was 4.6% with Flying Officer Godden leading the way on 9.8%.

The squadron's excellent safety record going back twenty months came to an end on 26 September when a collision took place over Bonn during a night P.I. at 21,000ft involving Flight Lieutenant Appleyard and Flying Officer Saunders in T.7 WH236 and Flying Officers Jones and Ansdell in NF.11 WD682. Both aircraft spun away out of control, and although the T.7 caught fire, all four crew members managed to bale out safely, the only injuries being a broken collar bone for Jones and a cracked rib for Ansdell. One of the aircraft demolished a house as it hit the ground but there were no casualties. Normal training continued for the rest of the year at the end of which, Wing Commander 'Jimmy' James left the squadron to be replaced in January by Wing Commander F.W. Davison.

The New Year got off to a good start with 370 hours being flown, but practice in February was severely affected by bad weather and an ice-bound runway. Another detachment to Sylt in March saw the squadron's average improve to 6.3%, and on return to Wahn the following month the opportunity was taken to use the facilities at Monschau for air-to-ground firing. Although problems were still evident when it came to air-to-air firing, some prodigious scores could be chalked up when firing at ground targets as Flying Officer Barry Holmes recalls:

'The NF Meteor was never a successful air-to-air platform mainly because the guns were wing-mounted. Bearing in mind that in the firing pattern the aircraft was in a steep turn and that the vertical dimension of the flag was only 6ft, thus subtending an angle of less than half a degree at firing range, the fact that the guns were some 20ft apart was very significant. There was also the theory that the wings flexed under "g" in the firing pattern. Some people tried to combat this supposed problem by pushing negative "g" round the pattern to "unload" the flex; others took to trying wide patterns to reduce the "g" at the firing point. I don't believe either method ever worked or resulted in improved scores, except that in the latter case, flag-tow pilots took grave and understandable umbrage at the bullets tending to whistle past their ears!

Unlike the day-fighter version, the night-fighter Meteor had no tendency to snake and this was proved during air-to-ground firing. Very few night-fighter squadrons carried out air-to-ground; 68 was, I believe, one of only two in 2ATAF which did. Because we had a range conveniently situated, we tended to carry out air-to-ground one morning every week. The target was a 15ft square and the NF was rock steady in the firing dive, "g" of course was not a consideration. Thus, while my scores air-to-air were in the 1–20% range, with a mean of around 12–14%, my air-to-ground results produced scores of 50–70%, with one shoot producing 107%! (caused by ricochets).'

By now the squadron had adopted a shift system with 'A' and 'B' flights active on alternate nights. This was intended to ease the task of the ground crews and resulted in flying hours increasing once again to just over the 400 mark. Until the intervention of bad weather in December the usual training routine of GCA letdowns, practice interceptions, formation flying and cine gun was broken only by the requirement to take part in two exercises (*Whipsaw* and *Stronghold*), both held in September. The only incident during this period involved WD734 which sank back after take off and ended up in the overshoot area.

Although all personnel at Wahn were committed to getting the most out of their rapidly ageing Meteors, if war had come in the mid-1950s it is doubtful whether they would have had much success in their primary role considering the progress that had been made by the Soviet Union in its offensive capability. Flight Lieutenant Bruce Spurr, a recent arrival who had completed two instructing tours in the U.K., comments on the Meteor night-fighter's effectiveness:

'When I joined 68 Squadron the RAF's training systems had been developed to a fairly high standard, and most crews were fairly competent and professional and able to operate the aircraft to its limits. It was a pity that they had to work with an aircraft that was obsolete in terms of speed, range and endurance, and with a radar that was a decade behind those in service with some other air forces. The Meteor was inferior to most of the aircraft against which it might have had to operate and combat successes would

Night marshalling scene at Wahn.

have been few except against training, transport or maritime reconnaissance aircraft.

We did have a secondary ground-attack role, and in addition there was a requirement for the squadron to be able to load its ground-servicing equipment into road vehicles and be on the move in about three hours, the aircraft to operate from selected stretches of autobahn. For this we had a pool of some twenty or more vehicles including three-and-a-half-ton-load Magirus trucks, some with seven-ton trailers, a mobile crew room, a Leyland Hippo radar servicing truck (the bodies of these opened out to triple their area), a mobile battery-charging vehicle, a VW Kombi crew bus, the C.O.'s Beetle and various trolleys for oxygen, ammunition, weapons etc. We didn't take the tractors because Land Rovers could tow the aircraft about the dispersals. Fortunately it never came to this, and we regarded the twice-yearly trips to APC at Sylt as sufficient rehearsal.'

In the aftermath of the Suez crisis, flying was strictly rationed in early 1957 with crews being restricted to twenty-two hours each and fuel restrictions were not lifted until March when 338 hours were flown including 192 practice interceptions. During the month use was also made of the Siegburg range for air-to-air firing practice ahead of another trip to Sylt in April. This additional practice appeared to have a dramatic effect, as Wing Commander Davison later scored 54%, the highest 'A'

The Moonrakers pull up into a loop.

flight scorer being Flight Lieutenant Noel Davies on 24% with Flight Lieutenant Johnson leading 'B' flight on 21%. Firing was also carried out on glider targets, several of which were blown to bits. Not to be left out, the armourers took part in a rearming exercise which prompted the Armaments Officer at Sylt to comment that their performance was the most efficient that he had yet seen.

Around this time inter-crew rivalry at Wahn expressed itself in a competition to see who could get the Meteor NF.11 to the greatest height. Flying Officer Mike Butt managed 51,000ft but was soundly beaten by someone who claimed to have made 53,000ft. This particular episode emphasised the Meteor's almost total lack of manoeuvre at height and during one of his attempts Butt ended up in an inverted spin at around 48,000ft. His aircraft began to revolve very lazily around its axis but was eventually recovered having lost about 8,000ft.

May was an extremely busy month that saw 68 take part in Exercise *Vigilant* during which the squadron was tasked to provide a protective radar-screen at 35,000ft to intercept incoming bombers. During this period a record was set when fourteen aircraft were recovered to base in six and a half minutes. From the twentieth two crews were allotted to 'battle flight' which involved being held at 15 minutes readiness, and the month also saw the setting up of a four-ship aerobatic team called 'The Moonrakers' under the leadership of Flight Lieutenant John Parker and his navigator, Flight Lieutenant Barry Blakeley. The main inspiration for the team's formation was to give a display on the occasion of 68 Squadron's departure from Wahn which was scheduled to take place in July. The rest of the team comprised Flying Officers Graham Jones and Mike Boggis as No. 2, Flying Officer John Davoine and Flight Sergeant MacMillan as No. 3, with Flying Officers Barry Holmes and Derek Blundell occupying the box position. Flying Officers John Holdway and George Pearce flew the reserve aircraft, the latter being the team photographer. This was a particularly difficult job in the Meteor NF.11/T.7 as the large amount of metalwork in the canopy often got in the way of a good picture, requiring some unusual control inputs on the part of the pilot to clear the view. Thanks to practice formation flying, a series of long distance cross-countries flown with under-wing tanks (code-named *Guest*), excellent serviceability and good weather, total hours for May were up significantly at 554.

The closure of Wahn as an RAF base occurred on 13 July with 68 Squadron moving to Laarbruch. At the same time its official establishment was reduced from sixteen to twelve aircraft although the number of crews remained at twenty. Ceremonies on leaving Wahn included a Garden Party held outside the squadron hangar and the first (and last) public appearance of 'The Moonrakers', some team members, including leader John Parker, leaving the squadron for postings in the U.K. shortly after. Problems were initially experienced at Laarbruch in obtaining spares and other equipment and there were also difficulties with ATC in adjusting the Meteor's approach patterns with those of local Canberras and RF-84Fs. As there was no twenty-four-hour ATC available at the station, Meteors allocated to 'battle flight' had to operate during the night from Wildenrath.

Towards the end of the year there was increasing concern over a growing list of airframe unserviceabilities which occasionally led to postponement of the

Pilots and navigators of the Moonrakers aerobatic team (LtoR) F/L John Parker, F/L Barry Blakeley, F/O Graham Jones, F/O Mike Boggis, F/O John Davoine, F/Sgt MacMillan, F/O Barry Holmes, F/O Derek Blundell.

flying programme. Despite the antiquated equipment at his disposal, Flying Officer Barry Holmes still has fond memories of the Meteor and recalls some aspects of its operation:

'In the normal configuration (with ventral tank fitted) fifty minutes was an average sortie length. If the two wing tanks were on, this was extended to 1 hour 30 minutes, but the performance penalty was so great that we avoided this fit as much as possible. It was sometimes imposed on us, however, by C.O.s trying to improve squadron hours!

The normal type of interception practised was the ninety-degree profile with, ideally, the target crossing about a mile ahead, or less at low level. The difficulty was created by the limitations of A.I.10. On a very good day this might have a range of some four miles, but more often was only two miles. Moreover, the antenna rotated through 360 degrees and was not stabilised; its coverage in elevation relative to the aircraft was controlled by the navigator using "tilt" switches which controlled the upper and lower limits of its elevation scan. So every time the aircraft banked, the "tilts" had to be used to hold the target in scan. This called for very good co-ordination between pilot and navigator, especially when trying to follow an evading target. Nevertheless, good crews achieved excellent results, even on some of the more esoteric exercises such as night low-level (250ft) or night intruder, when we would intercept targets in the airfield circuit.

Almost all our practice interceptions were against other Meteor NFs. The normal procedure was to take off as a pair, then alternately, one would act as fighter, the other as target under the direction of GCI. Only during exercises were we likely to meet other types of target; at night these were most likely to be Canberras. These were extremely difficult to get a "kill" on at 40,000ft; I can recall following one for 150 miles about 1,000 yards behind, unable to close to gun range. I would put the nose down to pick up speed, get within range, pull back up to get to a firing position and just drop back to 1,000 yards again! I found the Meteor NF a very pleasant and easy aircraft to fly; difficult to get the best out of it as an operational night fighter, when it could be frustrating from a radar and aircraft performance point of view; but I look back on it with a great deal of affection.'

In November 68 Squadron flew to Sylt once more for one of its most successful exercises in air-to-air gunnery. At the end of the detachment the squadron average stood at 20.7% with Flight Lieutenant J.K. Jennings leading on 35.5%. Back at Laarbruch a combination of bad weather and poor aircraft serviceability reduced the amount of flying that could be carried out and it was not until April, when 345 hours were flown, that the squadron got back into its stride, thanks to excellent work on the part of the groundcrews in ensuring sufficient aircraft were on line. In May, hours were still a respectable 321, the highlight of the month being a scramble on the thirteenth to investigate an unidentified aircraft which turned out to be a USAF T-33 which had become lost having flown too far to the east. At the end of the month Wing Commander Davison was replaced as C.O. by Wing Commander M. Scannell DFC AFC.

For the rest of the year routine training was mixed with occasional exercises including *Sunbeam* in October, which represented Fighter Command's major test for 1958. During night hours 68's Meteors acted as 'bombers' but reverted to the fighter role during the day, intercepting Canberras returning from simulated attacks on the U.K. As a result of the squadron's commitment to *Sunbeam*, it was unable to practice prior to another trip to Sylt which resulted in the unit's average falling to 15%. As 96 Squadron (Meteor NF.11) had achieved 26% immediately before, this performance did not go down well with Wing Commander Scannell. Although 68 Squadron had been rather erratic at air-to-air gunnery throughout the years, its ability to consume alcohol had never been in doubt and during one particular bash at Sylt, sixty-one bottles of champagne (the entire Mess stock at the time) disappeared in a little over two hours.

In December word was received that 68 would shortly be disbanded and renumbered as 5 Squadron. This event took place on 20 January 1959 and the final flight was an air test carried out by Flight Lieutenant S.G. Knight and Flying Officer W.D.G. Blundell. In the event the Meteor NF.11 continued to be used by 5 Squadron at Laarbruch until replaced by Javelin FAW.5s in 1960.

In all, 341 NF.11s were produced for the RAF and the last (WM403) left Armstrong Whitworth's Baginton plant in May 1954. During the production run a batch of forty (WM308-WM341 and WM362-WM367) were converted to NF.13 standard for use in the Middle East and featured a cold air unit to regulate cockpit temperature, aerials on the outer wings for Distance Measuring Equipment (DME), and a radio-compass loop fitted under the rear of the canopy.

The first NF.13 was flown on 23 December 1952 and it went on to serve in Egypt, with 39 Squadron at Fayid and 219 Squadron at Kabrit. Following the abrogation of the treaty with Egypt, however, 219 Squadron was disbanded on 1 September 1954 and 39 Squadron transferred to Luqa in Malta in January 1955. With the nationalisation of the Suez Canal by Egypt, 39 Squadron moved to Cyprus in August 1956 flying in support of Anglo-French operations during Operation *Musketeer*, and was eventually disbanded on 30 June 1958.

Although the NF.11/13 was to soldier on into the late 1950s, it did so in tandem with the NF.12/14 which featured the American APS-57 radar in a nose lengthened by a further 17in. Despite the fact that the aircraft's all-up weight had been increased, its overall power-to-weight ratio remained more or less the same thanks to the use of more powerful Derwent 9s of 3,800lb.s.t. The longer nose resulted in fillets being added to the fin above and below the tailplane bullet to restore adequate directional stability and the bulge under the nose that had protected the lower mounting bracket of the radar on the NF.11 was no longer required. The ultimate Meteor night fighter, the NF.14, also featured a redesigned windscreen and two-piece blown canopy which slid backwards instead of being side-hinged, spring tab ailerons and a yaw damper.

Carrying the British designation A.I.21, the new radar operated in X band and provided IFF facilities as well as the ability to operate in the ASV role. The antenna was mounted in the front of the nose on a special mounting frame and was accessible for servicing by the removal of the radome which was of solid fibre glass 0.31in. thick. The radome itself was attached to the airframe by ten quick-release toggle fasteners. The nose of the aircraft aft of the antenna was divided into upper and lower compartments by an anti-magnetic screen, the upper level accommodating the radar modulator and synchroniser, with the receiver-transmitter located underneath. Power supply was mounted forward of the modulator, above the rear of the antenna, and hatches were provided in the fuselage for access to these units for servicing. The navigator's cockpit contained the radar control-panel, strobe unit and console, all the operating controls being mounted on the front panel of the console, which in turn was located on a removeable tray in front of the nav's seat. Visors for the two cathode ray tubes were stowed on the port side of the cockpit.

The Meteor NF.12 entered service with 25 and 85 Squadrons at West Malling in March 1954, the two units converting from the Vampire NF.10 and Meteor NF.11 respectively. Early experience showed that the new radar out-performed A.I.10 by an appreciable margin, Meteor targets being picked up at 10–11 miles above 25,000ft and 6–7 miles below 5,000ft. This increase in pick-up range, together with the PPI presentation, allowed good initial turns to be carried out leading to successful intercepts, even when the attacking Meteor had only a small speed advantage over the target aircraft. Another advantage of increased AI radar performance was that the need for accurate positioning by GCI was not as great and crews were able to employ freelance tactics to achieve a 'kill' once they were established in a bomber stream. The news was not all good however, problems with the elevation tilt control and a poor blip repetition rate meant that it was difficult to follow a target which employed hard evasive action.

Flight Lieutenant Don Headley converted onto Meteor NF.12/14s at North Luffenham and subsequently completed a tour with 64 Squadron.

'The first thing you were taught at OCU was that the smooth CFS-style instrument flying technique that you had been used to was no good! There had to be no finesse, no easing into a turn, the stick had to hit the stop, left or right. This was due to the fact that the navigator had to pick up the target on the radar, assess what it was doing and then instruct the pilot which way to go, by which time the target had moved a considerable distance, either across you or towards you. If he said go starboard, you put thirty degrees of bank on; if he said go starboard hard, it was sixty degrees; and if he said go starboard as hard as you can, then you hauled it around just off the buffet, but it all had to be done very quickly because of the built-in lag in the system. At OCU it was also stressed that you formed a team with your navigator; you had to regard it almost like a marriage and get on with each other come what may. On a really nasty night it was not unusual to have to get in to 200 yards behind a target, and all the time you were trusting the chap in the back because everything you did was based on what he was telling you. At that sort of range it was not unusual to hit the slipstream and be turned on your back at 30,000ft or more.

I found the long-nose Meteor very nice to fly, particularly on instruments. Doing a GCA, which invariably you were at night in bad weather, you could set it up on the glidepath at five miles and it was just like sitting on railway tracks, it was so stable and just sat there rock steady. Of course it had the same asymmetric problem as any other Meteor so if you did have an engine failure then you just made sure that you kept the speed up an extra ten knots on the approach to keep clear of the critical speed. You then had to have a decision height, my own personal height was 500ft, and if I was below that I made sure I was going to land.'

The last Meteor night fighter (NF.14 – WS848) came off the production line in May 1955 and the new variant replaced most of the earlier NF.11s within Fighter Command. Its period of service, in the U.K. at least, was to be relatively short, as it was progressively replaced by the Javelin which entered service with 46 Squadron in February 1956. Requirements further afield led to a stay of execution as 60 Squadron at Tengah swapped its Venom FB.4s for NF.14s in October 1959 as the unit's role was changed to night/all-weather defence. To facilitate this a refresher course was held at 228 OCU, Leeming, in April to convert crews prior to their departure to the Far East. The NF.14 was involved in the Malayan Emergency which ended in August 1960 and the last sortie by a Meteor occurred on 17 August 1961. After its operational demise the aircraft's versatility led to the NF.14 being used by No. 2 Air Navigation School (ANS) at Stradishall until 1965 and retired NF.11s were converted into TT.20 target tugs for use by No. 3 Civilian Anti-Aircraft Co-operation Unit (CAACU) at Exeter until 1970.

Despite its relatively modest performance the Meteor night fighter was popular in service and many former pilots have fond memories of it including

No. 46 Squadron crews in front of Meteor NF.14 WS830.

Pilot Officer Malcolm de Garis who flew NF.11s with 29 and 125 Squadrons.

'It was a rather stately carriage in comparison to its day equivalent . . . on the debit side the hood was dreadful in terms of all-round visibility, far too much metal, plus its locking mechanism left a deal to be desired, as did its method of checking. It was known to unlock in flight with often disastrous results for the unfortunate crew. The radar was a disaster which, even at peak condition, could barely cope with head-on contacts given the true airspeeds experienced at altitude. However, I much preferred the Meteor to the Venom NF.3 that replaced it, a truly nasty little aeroplane whose only redeeming features were its side-by-side seating and A.I.21 radar. I enjoyed the NF.11, always felt safe in it and still have a strong affection for the aircraft, the Derwent, and the night-fighter trade as a whole.'

In all, thirty-eight examples of the Meteor night fighter have survived (out of a total 592), including NF.11 WM167 (G-LOSM) which is flown out of Bournemouth-Hurn. Although it carries the colours of 141 Squadron which flew the type from Coltishall between 1951–55, WM167 never flew with an operational squadron and was used as a trainer by 228 OCU until 1960. After its retirement from this role, it was converted to TT.20 standard and spent ten years with Flight Refuelling Ltd at Tarrant Rushton and Llanbedr on trials work. After being put up for sale in 1975, it was purchased by Doug Arnold at Blackbushe before passing to Brencham Historic Aircraft at Hurn in 1984. Currently operated as part of the Bournemouth Aviation Museum, WM167 is a popular performer at airshows where it is flown as part of the Heritage Pair with Vampire T.55 G-HELV, formerly U-1215 of the Swiss Air Force.

Chapter Eight

DE HAVILLAND VAMPIRE NF.10

T he Vampire NF.10 served with the RAF in the early 1950s in small numbers and did so almost by accident. As manufacturer of the Mosquito NF.36, the RAF's principal night-fighter in the post-war period, de Havilland was well placed to investigate the possibilities of transferring the existing radar technology to their Vampire jet fighter. In 1949 the company produced a private venture development of the Mark 5 which featured an enlarged nacelle capable of housing a crew of two, together with an A.I.10 radar installation and its associated cockpit displays. The Vampire night fighter (often referred to as the 'Screaming Kiddy Car') was armed with four 20mm Hispano cannon (150 rounds per gun) but unlike the NF version of the Meteor, its design was such that these could be retained in their original position, under the fuselage pod. Two prototypes were built (G-5-2 and G-5-5), the first taking to the air on 28 August 1949, piloted by Geoffrey Pike.

The Vampire NF was given the designation DH.113 and was intended for export, particularly to those countries that had already bought the Vampire day fighter. It was powered by a 3,350lb.s.t. Goblin 3, which gave it a performance comparable to the single-seat version, and it also shared excellent manoeuvrability, with light and responsive controls and general handling characteristics similar to the FB.5. Initially it suffered from directional instability brought about by the increased keel area of the extended nose, but this was cured by heightening the tips of the rudders to smooth the airflow and provide increased moment arm. At the same time the elevator trim tab was also enlarged and the tailplane area increased by extending the horizontal surfaces outboard of the twin fins.

The first order for the DH.113 was for twelve aircraft for the Egyptian Air Force but this was cancelled by the British government in October 1949 when a ban was imposed on the export of military equipment to Egypt. With the deterioration in east-west relations it was decided to transfer the aircraft to the RAF as a temporary stop-gap until the more versatile Meteor NF could be brought into widespread use. As it was normal RAF policy to operate twin-engined aircraft in the night role, the willingness to use the Vampire as a night fighter gives an indication of the state of Britain's night defences at that time. Limited production was undertaken at the de Havilland plants at Hatfield and Chester which between them accounted for ninety-five machines serialled WP232-265,

WM659-732 and WV689-691. In RAF service the Vampire night fighter was known as the NF.10 and equipped 23, 25 and 151 Squadrons from 1951-54.

From the crew's point of view, the Vampire NF.10's cockpit was not for the squeamishly claustrophobic, but was certainly no worse than that of the Mosquito. The pilot was seated on the left and all flight and engine instruments were situated on a single panel directly in front of the control column with a somewhat antiquated GM2N reflector gunsight mounted on the coaming above. All other controls including throttle, flap selector, elevator trimmer, under-carriage selector, fuel cocks etc. were positioned within easy reach along the left, hand side of the cockpit sidewall.

The navigator's seat was set 15in. behind and to the right of the pilot to allow room for the cockpit components of the A.I.10 radar installation, which were mounted on the right-hand side in a vertical tier extending forward of the main panel. The radar indicator was mounted above the control box and synchro-niser, and comprised two separate screens surrounded by a viewing shroud to prevent light from the displays affecting the pilot's night vision. The right-hand screen indicated target range in azimuth (direction), and the left-hand screen showed the target in terms of zenith (height above or below).

Having already been flown by A&AEE at Boscombe Down, G-5-2 was deliv-ered to CFE on 15 January 1951 to assess whether it was suitable to be introduced as a night fighter, but soon after its arrival it had to be returned to de Havilland for rectification work on its G4F compass. It was returned to West Raynham on 5 February but as the loan agreement ran out on the seventeenth only eleven sorties were possible amounting to seven hours forty minutes flying time. Despite such a limited period it was deemed that this was sufficient to obtain a general impression of the aircraft.

Cockpit layout was considered to be generally satisfactory although it was noted that the elevator trimmer was not visible at night and had to be illumi-nated by the navigator's torch or felt for by hand. The ASI was also partially obscured and no markings between 100–200kt could be seen which meant that accurate speed control during the approach, particularly at night, was extremely difficult. The pilot's seat was set too low and although all-round vision was fairly good for the night-fighter role, there was some distortion through the curved transparencies. In rain, forward vision was considerably restricted but it was possible to see sufficiently to carry out a circuit and landing by looking through the side panels or opening the direct vision panel at speeds below 200kt. The cockpit heating system of ducted hot air was well liked and little or no external or internal icing troubles were experienced.

Engine starting was simple and reliable, no wet starts were experienced and the average time for idling rpm to be achieved was eighteen seconds. During taxiing, the Vampire NF.10 was easy to handle, although the Goblin's response to movements of the throttle was slower than that for the Rolls-Royce Derwent engines of the Meteor. It was found that G-5-2 tended to crab to port when taxiing, though this was not as marked as with the Venom NF.2 which had been tested a few weeks before the Vampire's arrival (*see* Chapter Nine). The aircraft could be run up on the brakes to at least 10,000rpm prior to take off but acceleration proved to be slow compared with the Meteor NF.11 and Venom NF.2. A definite stick force was required get the Vampire airborne and this usually occurred at about 105kt. The distance to clear 50ft in still air without use of flaps was estimated at about 1,400 yards and there was no marked change of trim when the undercarriage was retracted.

Once in the air the Vampire's performance was disappointing, especially for those pilots who had already flown the Venom NF.2, times to height being particularly poor. Climbing power was restricted at first to 10,250 rpm and with this setting it took seventeen minutes from 'wheels rolling' to reach 35,000ft. Later, clearance was given to use 10,500rpm which reduced this figure by three minutes and it was felt that this could be improved still further as the trials were conducted when the tropopause was lower than normal. Subsequent tests by de Havilland also showed the engine to be slightly down on power. In the limited amount of time available, only two level speed-runs were recorded; at 10,750rpm at sea level a speed of 465kt was obtained with 415kt being achieved at 10,000ft at the same power setting.

High-speed dives were carried out at 20,000ft and the Vampire appeared to be quite steady up to its limiting Mach number of 0.78. As speed was increased the nose tended to drop and there was some aileron snatching, but when dive brakes were extended, recovery was immediate. No attempt was made to trim out the nose-down tendency as this would make for a violent change of trim on recovery. During the assessment of low-speed handling characteristics, only straight and level stalls were investigated, the clean stall proving to be quite straightforward with no tendency towards wing drop. Little warning was felt but a gentle vibration preceded the stall which occurred at about 110kt. With wheels and flaps down there was minor buffeting from 100kt down to the stall at 90kt with an occasional slight tendency for a wing to drop. Following general handling tests up to 30,000ft the Vampire was described as being 'delightful' although its controls became progressively 'sloppy' above that height and its rate of roll was noted as being inferior to that of the Venom NF.2.

For the approach and landing the view from the cockpit was good and with the exception of the ASI, all instruments and indicators could be seen easily. It was discovered, however, that the Vampire's dive brakes were not particularly effective in producing sufficient deceleration, and some forward trim was required when full flap was selected before landing. The approach was normally flown at 110kt at not less than 5,500rpm. On landing there was little tendency to float and the touchdown in the fully stalled condition occurred at 90kt. There was no swing or nosewheel shimmy and the aircraft was brought to a halt by moderate braking within 1,400 yards. Throttle response on overshoots was adequate provided engine revolutions were maintained at a figure not less than that quoted above.

The limited number of sorties flown did not allow for a full examination of interception techniques but two points did emerge which, it was thought, would adversely affect high-altitude sorties. Acceleration to combat speed at 35,000ft was slow, even allowing for the fact that the engine was slightly down on power, and compared with the Meteor NF.11 and Venom NF.2, the dive brakes were

Vampire NF.10 WM659. (*RAF Museum Hendon*)

much less efficient. It was thought that the ineffectiveness of the dive brakes would result in navigators having to give instructions such as 'throttle back' or 'brakes' in good time if an overshoot of a slow moving target was to be avoided. Although dive brakes would probably not be needed against faster targets, should their use be necessary, great care would have to be taken to retract them in good time in view of the aircraft's sluggish acceleration at altitude. The view was expressed that these shortcomings would probably make speed control in approaching a target the most critical part of a high-altitude interception.

Vision for the crew was adversely affected by the considerable amount of metal work in the canopy structure, together with distortion of the glazing, although the hot air demisting system was rated a great improvement on the electrically heated panels of the Meteor NF.11 and during descents to low altitude only the top part of the windscreen became obscured. Only one air-firing sortie could be carried out during the trials, but at speeds of Mach 0.75–0.76 at 35,000ft, the Vampire proved to be an excellent gun platform with only a slight tendency for the nose to drop during a long burst.

The most serious criticism of the Vampire NF.10 was reserved for the inadequate means of abandoning the aircraft in an emergency. As ejector seats were not fitted the only means of escape was through the opening left by the rear-hinged top panel which could be jettisoned by a lever mounted above the windscreen, but it was thought that the chances of the pilot and navigator hitting the tailplane on their way out were extremely high. Even if the aircraft could be inverted for the crew to drop out one after the other, the positioning of the navigator's station behind the rear edge of the canopy hatch meant that this was not a very attractive proposition either. Despite such reservations the CFE report concluded with the following statement:

'The DH.113 is a very pleasant aircraft to fly and will be a most valuable means of familiarising night-fighter crews with the problems of operating jet night-fighters. Its performance, whilst inferior to both the Meteor NF.11 and the Venom NF.2, is a considerable advance on that of the Mosquito. It will prove an invaluable intermediate step in the transition from the Mosquito to the high-performance Venom.'

The first RAF unit to receive the Vampire NF.10 was 25 Squadron at West Malling which began to replace its Mosquito NF.36s in July 1951, this unit being followed two months later by 151 Squadron at Leuchars and 23 Squadron at Coltishall, the latter receiving its first NF.10s on 11 September. The build up of new aircraft for 23 Squadron was extremely slow and initially only 'A' Flight, commanded by Flight Lieutenant C.F.P. Hughes, flew the new machines with 'B' Flight continuing to use the Mosquito NF.36 for another nine months. The overall situation was made worse by a serious shortage of ground staff, and at one point the squadron had only three engine fitters to carry out all first and second line servicing. In December, total flying hours with the NF.10 amounted to a pitiful nineteen (day) and five (night). Serviceability problems were eventually overcome, but it would be many months before the squadron managed to fly more than 200 hours which, with fifteen pilots on strength, allowed a mere 13–14 hours each per month.

Having previously flown Mosquitos with 39 Squadron at Kabrit in Egypt, Pilot Officer Noel 'Snowy' Davies joined 23 Squadron in January 1952. He recalls his first impressions of the Vampire NF.10:

'The Vampire was not very powerful, but it was manoeuvrable, and having only one engine, it was quick to start and scramble. On 23 Squadron we used to time our "scrambles" by stop watch, and rather impolitely used a calendar to measure the scramble times of the Meteor NF.11s of 141 Squadron next door! The Vampire armament, being centre mounted was more flexible and simpler to use effectively than the wing-mounted guns of the Meteor NF.11. I remember no real vices in either the Meteor or the Vampire, though the latter was much lighter to the touch.

Although cramped, the cockpit accommodation was adequate for most, the side-by-side seating being preferred to the tandem version in the Meteor. It was surprising for me to get into a Vampire cockpit after, say, Sergeant Jackson had flown it (he was a tall, lanky man, and I was, and still am, 5ft 7in.). I would descend further than I wished on to his seat, which was lowered fully, try to save myself by treading on the rudder pedals, only to find that they had been moved fully forward, out of reach. I soon learned!

The Vampire "D" doors sometimes caused trouble as they were operated by cables that withdrew small securing bolts, which allowed the doors to be released before the wheels came down. This cable could stretch preventing the door from opening and forcing a belly-landing. The Vampire design was such that this usually caused virtually no damage on grass, and the aircraft could be lifted and its wheels lowered with no ill-effects. Conversely the nosewheel "D" door was sprung only, being pushed open as the wheel was lowered, springing closed again as the wheel retracted. It was possible for this door to spring shut early, preventing the wheel from retracting, whilst the force of the hydraulic retraction was enough to damage the door, jamming it in place – shut! Whilst the wheel could be lowered safely, flights had to be abandoned on more than one occasion.'

Flying Officer Ted Hooton, of 23 Squadron's 'B' Flight, began flying in the NF.10 in June 1952 and recalled his thoughts on the Vampire in 'Nocturnal Navigator', a series of articles written for *Aeroplane Monthly* magazine.

'Our establishment of Vampires on 23 Squadron slowly grew to a total of twelve. I would not have cared to go to war in them; their unsuitability soon became apparent. I was dismayed that they were less well equipped than the Mossies we had discarded. For a start we lost the radio altimeter. Admittedly it had never worked that well in the Mossies, but I think it could have done. Also, there was no radio countermeasures gear, so we lost a valuable operational capability. On the plus side, the Vampires did have Gee Mark 3. It worked in the same way as Gee 2 but was more accurate, as well as being easier and quicker to use [23 Squadron's Mosquitos had been equipped with either *Hookah* or *Bat* – the former was a device that homed on to aircraft attempting to jam ground-radar frequencies, whereas the latter homed on to VHF radio jamming].

To operate above 20,000ft, A.I.10 had to be fitted with a pressurised radio frequency line to feed pulses to the scanner. Without it, severe arcing would occur at high altitudes. It was standard equipment, but it was no surprise to discover that it had not been fitted to our Vampires before delivery. Until the lines could be found and installed, our aircraft were limited to heights below 20,000ft. The final straw was the gunsight. While the Americans were into radar-ranging gunsights, our Vampires had simple reflector gunsights, the same as in the Mosquito. There was no room in the cockpit for the larger gyro gunsight which was, at least, fitted to the Meteor NF.11.'

In addition to its shortcomings in the air, Hooton recalled an embarrassing episode which could have had serious implications in the event of the Vampire NF.10 being involved in a real shooting match.

'The whole squadron was slated to go up to the Armament Practice Station (APS) at Acklington and, if we were not to appear as incompetents, our pilots needed a lot of air-to-air gunnery practice beforehand. We arranged for some Meteors to tow drogue targets off the Norfolk coast, and a week of intensive gunnery was planned but as soon as the Vampires were loaded with 20mm shells, their nosewheel oleos collapsed! I assume that someone at D.H. had forgotten the additional weight of the nose AI, and figured that the ordinary day-fighter oleos would be all right. With long faces, our engineering officer and our resident D.H. representative rushed around to find a cure. Although they fixed the problem that time, there was a sequel.

Months later, during the annual air exercise, four Vampires were on the hardstanding at the end of the runway, awaiting a night scramble. Crews were strapped in the cockpits and, to make matters more realistic, all four cannon were fully loaded – unlike the earlier panic, when only two cannon had been loaded at any one time. The order to scramble never came, and time dragged by. To avoid condensation within the cockpits we all had our top hatches open, but it was cold, and boredom set in.

Suddenly, the still of the early morning hours was disturbed by a yell followed by furious oaths from one of the aircraft. Torches probed the darkness, and guffaws followed when the crews in the other three could see a Vampire tipped up on its nose. The nosewheel oleo had collapsed under the strain of all those hours of waiting with the full ammunition load. The laughter soon turned to oaths all round as slowly but surely, one by one, the other three Vampires silently sank on to their noses. What a fiasco. The entire night defence of eastern England grounded in ignominious disarray!'

By mid-1952 the activities of the Vampire NF.10 units were extremely varied and included day and night practice interceptions at varying heights, low-level cross countries often acting as 'Rats' for day fighters, formation flying, air-to-sea and air-to-air firing, together with practice instrument letdowns using QGH and GCA procedures. Despite being designated as a night-fighter squadron, 23 Squadron flew approximately a 70/30 split in favour of daytime sorties. In addition, Vampires were frequently employed in exercises with Lincolns and Washingtons of Bomber Command. Ted Hooton again:

'*Bullseye* exercises were a feature of my time on Vampires. Bomber Command was still enamoured with "stream" tactics as previously used against the Germans, and liked to practice them occasionally. We were added to the scenario to attack the bombers. One night we were scrambled and given a vector by Neatishead. Then, right on cue, the VHF radio jamming began; those ghastly Merlins raging in our ears. With no radio countermeasures (RCM) gear in the Vampire we could not even find the noise-makers. Eventually my pilot (P/O Alan Rowe) switched the radio to a guard channel, and silence reigned. While we maintained the vector given to us by the GCI, I kept watch on the AI radar. Suddenly, right at the top of the B Scope at ten miles range, a mass of blips appeared, coming head-on. I quickly checked the heights on the C Scope, and they were above and below us. Hell! Go up or go down? No time for that, stay at the same alti-tude, cross your fingers, pray hard, and do a quick 180-degree turn.

Our guardian angels were on the ball, and we turned around in the middle of the stream of bombers without a tremble of anyone's slipstream to jolt us, or a terrible bang that would have signalled our demise. It tran-spired that most of the attackers were Avro Lincolns and, as we began to creep up behind, we realised how vulnerable the similar Lancasters must have been to German night-fighters during the war. The glowing exhausts of each bomber were visible for miles. After completing each attack we made our claim by flashing the navigation lights. If the rear gunner saw you first he was supposed to flash his aircraft letter in Morse using an Aldis lamp, but it never happened; they never saw us first.

The rear gunners of Lincolns were quite good. After we signalled, they would usually reply. The Washingtons were hopeless, and minutes of our flashing lights would go unacknowledged. Some years later I heard that Bomber Command had too few gunners to man all the positions in each Washington. So they forgot about the tail turret and put two gunners in the central fire-control position where they could not have had much of a downward view.

Not long afterwards, life became more traumatic for us. On a rainy, grey day, with low cloud and miserable visibility, we flew around the North Sea trying to intercept a wretched Lincoln simulating minelaying at about 600ft. The AI was not very good at low altitudes due to ground returns, and nor was a Vampire trying to fly at about the same speed as a lumbering old Linc, with a radar pick-up range of about five miles at that height. We earned our money that day.

As the Autumn air exercise was coming up, we started practising another form of GCI. It was a technique used earlier by the *Luftwaffe* against Bomber Command and was known as "Broadcast Control". The ground controller would call out the position of the bomber stream by grid reference, their direction and speed. He provided updated information every minute or so. In the fighters, we were left to navigate our own way to the stream by using Gee, and the well established Principle of Equal Angles. I used the technique only once during Exercise *Ardent*, and then we were recalled just as I obtained my first radar contact.'

Exercise *Ardent* took place in October 1952 during which 23 Squadron flew a total of forty-six sorties (thirty-six at night) and claimed thirty-eight 'kills', including twenty-three Washingtons and ten Lincolns. Shortly before *Ardent*, four crews from 23 were detached to Fassberg for a seventeen-day period which included participation in Exercise *Holdfast*. During their time in Germany the Vampires were employed in trials to determine whether the NF.10 could be used in the night ground-attack role. A little closer to home, the evaluation of the Vampire in the night intruder role was to lead to an altercation with the media. Ted Hooton was one of those who took part:

'The job had to be tackled with some sort of scientific approach, and thus it came to involve me, a Land Rover plus MT driver and the wartime USAAF 8th Air Force airfield at Hethel – deserted in 1952, but still with its runways fairly intact. I was despatched in my Land Rover with a schedule of manoeuvres to perform at specified times. Drive up runway X with full-beam headlights for X number of runs, repeat on low beam, repeat with no lights etc. While the driver carried out his task on my instructions, we were to be attacked by the Vampires, one by one, after sunset. My driver rubbed his hands with glee at the prospect, and I must say I was looking forward to an evening of exciting, if noisy, entertainment.

Meanwhile, back in the mess, some members of the squadron who were not flying that night were slumped in their chairs in the anteroom, with the BBC Home Service providing an aural background. "We now bring you *Any Questions* from the small town of Wymondham, out in the quiet countryside of Norfolk. Our panellists tonight are . . ." A couple of blokes in the mess sat up. "Isn't that just down the road from Hethel?" asked one of them. It was indeed, and I need not describe the racket that followed as 23 Sqn's screaming kiddycars (crews and i/c target Land Rover blissfully unaware) wrecked the programme. Furthermore, one of the panellists was one Gilbert Harding, renowned for his bad temper. As the noise went on he became incandescent, and publicly vented his fury on the RAF. Frantic telephone calls from listeners to the BBC, then from the BBC to the Air Ministry were to no avail. By the time some poor duty officer had traced the racket, we had all packed up and gone home.'

A further detachment was undertaken from 3–13 November when four Vampires were flown to Takali in Malta to take part in Exercise *Longstop*, and on the tenth two aircraft departed for Leuchars for low-level anti-minelaying exercises with Bomber Command Lincolns. On 25 November Exercise *Garage* consisted of practice attacks carried out on MTBs in the light of flares dropped by ASV aircraft, a task that was carried out only by the most experienced 'A' rated crews as fine judgment was required to operate at low level at night. By now however, there was a worrying shortage of aircraft following two Cat 3 accidents the day before. In the first of these, Flying Officer T.A. MacKenzie ran out

Line-up of No. 25 Squadron Vampire NF.10s at West Malling. (*RAF Museum Hendon*)

of brakes in WM674 and had to raise the undercarriage to stop, and Flight Lieutenant A.A.V. Maxwell scraped the port wing of WM706 along the runway when landing in a snowstorm.

Although the Vampire NF.10 had only moderate performance compared to some of its contemporaries, the strains imposed on both aircraft and crew could still be great as Pilot Officer Noel Davies recalls:

'On many occasions we flew *Rat and Terrier* exercises which involved flying at low level all over East Anglia, usually with the most dreadful forms of steer. We would be over Kings Lynn and they would say, "We have a target for you at Lowestoft", or we would be at Bury St Edmunds and they would say, "Try Skegness". The result of this was often that there was much dependence on the ROC who were very good at following aircraft much more accurately at that height than the radar. On one particular afternoon we were being thumped all the way across Norfolk. It was very hot, very bumpy and very uncomfortable indeed. When we got down we found that the stress on the aircraft had been so great and the airflows had been so massive that the camouflage paint on the wings looked as though it had been dragged by a giant comb leaving streaks of yellow primer all the way back from the leading edges.

Another time we carried out an unscheduled high-quarter attack on a bomber we found during an exercise. It was at such a height that we had not got our normal height advantage from which to dive on it; instead of 3,000ft as we would expect to have for a dive attack of this nature, we only had 1,500ft. I just pulled to get round as tight as I could, but went out like a light due to excessive "g". On recovery the effect was like coming back in a completely different world. I didn't know what was happening at all and had to start from scratch and think, "Where am I?" – "I'm flying", "Am I the right way up?" – "Yes", "What's that feeling in my right elbow?" – "Oh, it's the navigator stabbing me with his ruler trying to wake me up." It's that sort of unconsciousness, it's total and it's like a complete brick wall between the then and the now. It has to be experienced once, but after that you do not do it a second time.

Attacks on bombers at night could also be difficult. One of our chaps in a Vampire fitted with drop tanks got behind a bomber at around 25,000ft but got into its slipstream, which for a little thing like a Vampire could be quite significant. It flipped him over onto his back but at first he didn't realise this as his instruments showed that he was still flying straight and level, and his speed was constant. A few seconds later his VSI told him that he was beginning to descend quite rapidly so in those circumstances what do you do? – you pull up, but of course he was flying upside down so he actually went right through the bottom half of a loop which took him way beyond the speed that he should have been doing. When he landed there were about 3,000 hours worth of damage to the aircraft, one of the drop tanks had nearly been ripped off and the tail fin kingpin had severed and was 4in. to one side of where it should have been.

On one occasion two Vampires were carrying out practice interceptions at night, one aircraft as target, the other fighting. In such a situation you always came in underneath and behind so that the radar and visual pictures were as clear as possible. They were about 50–60ft apart in zenith when another unknown target passed between the two of them on a reciprocal course. This was extremely unusual and was probably a result of GCI as they always had problems with blind areas in their coverage, which meant that they couldn't always see everything that was going on. I also recall an incident when one of our pilots took off at night with the pebble guards still attached to the air intakes. These were triangular shaped devices used on the ground, as the Vampire sat very low and it was easy to suck in stones or other debris during engine runs. He actually managed to get up to about 15,000ft before he realised that something was wrong and on returning, found out what it was!'

Bad weather in January 1953 was not the only cause of a severely restricted flying programme, as numerous minor snags with various pieces of ancillary equipment were badly affecting overall serviceability, a situation that became worse on the twenty-second when Flight Lieutenant J.H. Hedger had the hood detach in flight resulting in Cat 2 damage to the tailplane of WP236. This was the third occasion that a canopy had departed without warning on the Vampire NF.10 and there would be more such occurrences over the coming months. In nearly all cases the hood hit the tailplane but, fortuitously, the resultant damage did not lead to loss of control. (Damage to the horizontal stabiliser caused by jettisoning the hood prior to a forced landing did result in the fatal accident of a Venom NF.2, *see* page 210.)

Pilot Officer Noel Davies recalls a situation when he tested the Vampire's somewhat suspect canopy to the full:

'On one occasion they had an Open Day at RAF Newton near Nottingham which has a grass runway of about 1,200 yards with a fifteen degree kink in the middle. We went from Coltishall to show off our aeroplane to the assembled masses of ATC cadets and ROC people. Landing is always a hazard on a short grass runway, but with a sharp left-hander halfway up it made it even more dicey. The demonstration itself was mainly static and we stood by the aircraft answering questions, or rather failing to. All the ATC cadets knew everything about it, how many pop rivets it had, how many blocks there were on the tyre tread, who made the headlights etc., we knew virtually nothing about it apparently, except how to fly it – all rather chastening!

After take off from this "kinky" runway we had been told not to go below 500ft and we were not allowed to do anything other than fly straight past, so of course everyone came down to about 150ft and did a roll or something on the way out. As we had been there overnight we had full luggage and I did my duty roll (quite a good one really) but I forgot about the negative "g" that it created. As a result the luggage, ladders and all the dirt and debris underneath us went walloping onto the canopy. How it didn't come undone I'll never know. Again it was one of those flying experiences that you do once and never again.'

February was much better from a weather point of view and 213 hours were flown, of which seventy-six hours were at night. Duties consisted of air-to-air and air-to-ground firing, battle and close formation work, bomber affiliations, navigation exercises and practice interceptions, in addition to air tests and instrument flying. During the month two *Kingpin* exercises were flown during which Flying Officers Chris Brooksbank and R.F. Gratton successfully attacked a Canberra flying at 40,000ft. The only mishap occurred on 26 February when Sergeant I.T. Rutter suffered a flame out in WP247 when in formation and had to land wheels-up which resulted in Cat 4 damage.

In April 23 Squadron flew a relatively high proportion of air-firing sorties, a situation that was brought about by the fact that new crews continued to arrive without any experience of live firing and with very little cine practice. If this were not enough, it turned out that of two new pilots who had arrived in February, one had an expired instrument rating! During the month an average of five air-to-air shoots were carried out per pilot, the average being 5.1%, a low score which reflected the inadequacies of the old GM2 gunsight and the fact that the Vampire did not have a camera gun fitted. An aircraft was lost as a result of engine failure on 11 May when WM722, flown by Flight Lieutenant A. Wright, lost its flame at 250ft during a low-level cross-country, the subsequent forced landing and impact with a dyke causing sufficient damage to ensure a write-off.

Four weeks later a more serious accident occurred when WM671 crashed near the village of Frettenham, three miles north of Norwich. Flying Officer G.H. Smith was carrying out practice interceptions on the night of 8/9 June with Flying Officer J.S.G. Weir, but due to a predicted cloudbase of 500ft, Smith had been instructed to carry out a restricted procedure on return, entailing a QGH to be followed by a straight-in approach from the inward vector. If he was in any doubt as to whether he could make a safe landing he was to make use of the GCA facilities at nearby Horsham St Faith. On a restricted type approach it was normal practice to call out ranges at frequent intervals to assist ATC in spacing aircraft for landing, these ranges to be obtained from Gee or the A.I.10 radar.

At 0255 hrs Coltishall ATC received a call from Smith (call-sign Reject 22) that he was returning to base and he was asked to orbit for two minutes to allow the required separation from the first two 'pipeline' aircraft. His approach was monitored on CRD/F and at sixteen miles he was still at 1,500ft on the QNH pressure setting of 1017mb. He was instructed to descend below cloud but contact was lost at 0306 hrs at a range of seven miles. The aircraft had in fact come down two and a half miles short of the runway and had ploughed through a hawthorn hedge before bouncing and skidding into an earth bank where the front portion of the Vampire had disintegrated. Smith and his navigator, Pilot Officer G.C. Baghurst, were severely injured in the crash and both died shortly after assistance arrived. The post-crash fire destroyed much of what remained of the centre section of the aircraft, and all that survived from the engine were the flame tubes, main shaft, turbine unit and jetpipe. From the scorch marks in a field of corn leading up to the crash, it appeared that the engine had been running prior to impact.

It was concluded that Smith had allowed his aircraft to get too low on the approach either through pilot error, or some unknown cause. As the Vampire NF.10 had a pronounced tendency to sink when full flap was raised, the theory was put forward that he had misjudged his rate of descent and had tried to reduce flap to flatten his approach, only for this action to increase height loss. A report from a witness of loud engine noise may have indicated a sudden increase in power, which would have accounted for the fact that initial contact with the ground had been relatively gentle. Although agreeing with the overall assessment that Smith undershot through an error of judgement, Air Vice-Marshal R.L.R. Atcherley, AOC 12 Group, made the following comment:

'As an older pilot I am shaken to find that a pilot of such tender experience, with a total of 308 hours solo but only seventy-seven hours total night flying, should be considered safe to operate in marginal weather conditions of this kind and with a ceiling at the time and place of the crash of slightly below 500ft. I fully appreciate that he had all the qualifications which are now required and which are obtained by test, yet none of these in my opinion make up for that extra 100 hours or so flying experience which I feel he needed. I cannot blame anyone for authorising the flight because it is currently held by best opinion that pilots of this experience are fully capable of operating in such conditions. I can only say that I certainly wasn't in my day and that, based on my experience, I feel we are today pressing all-weather training far too fast. In my opinion we could well have afforded to wait for F/O Smith to gain that little extra experience in better weather conditions which might well have saved not only this accident, but the valuable lives of these two officers.'

An improvement in serviceability and an increase in aircrew establishment in June brought about a marked improvement in flying hours to 360, a figure which was also boosted by the use of drop tanks allowing sorties of two hours or more to be flown. The vast majority of flying in the first half of July comprised day formation as the squadron prepared for participation in the Coronation flypast at Odiham which was scheduled for the fifteenth. Noel Davies recalls some of the preparations for the big day:

'The only drawback to the side-by-side seating arrangement in the Vampire NF.10 came when we had to do formation flying such as that for the Coronation Review in 1953. We drew lots, the "losers" doing the final rehearsal, which was the filmed version. It involved very precise close formation at low level in hot, bumpy weather for nearly one and a half hours – very hard work, especially for the left-hand wing man, with the cockpit offset to the left, he had to lean over to the right throughout the entire flight. The whole thing was done by map-crawling, with references every fifteen seconds struck off across the flight path. More than fifteen seconds adrift meant withdrawing – no one ever did!'

A formation of Vampire NF.10s, made up of aircraft from 23 and 25 Squadrons, was led by Coltishall's Wing Leader, Wing Commander J.W. Allan

WP233 of No. 25 Squadron returns after a night exercise.

DSO DFC who had the responsibility of leading the entire jet contingent. His job was made particularly difficult as the Vampire's speed of 265kt was considerably more than the 170kt of three Hastings transports which brought up the rear of the piston-engined section, just ahead of the Coltishall formation. At the saluting base a gap of one minute had to have been established, the NF.10s then being followed by twenty Wings of Meteors, Vampires, Canberras and Sabres which had all slotted in behind so that they passed over Odiham at thirty-second intervals. Weather conditions were reasonably kind for the event and to the relief of everyone, the whole operation proceeded according to plan.

In August total flying amounted to 337 hours of which a much increased figure of 153 hours were flown at night. This was largely due to participation in Exercise *Momentum* which commenced on the night of the fourteenth when twelve aircraft scrambled at various times to intercept targets flying at heights ranging from 5–40,000ft. During the second night eight Vampires were scrambled but WP254 was seen to dive vertically into the ground shortly after take off and the crew, Sergeant J.B. McLeod and Flight Sergeant P.J. Cull, were both killed. In addition to night intercepts, four aircraft acted as day fighters on the sixteenth and successfully engaged a section of Meteor F.8s at 30,000ft.

During the night of 19 August weather conditions deteriorated to such an extent that only the most experienced 'A' and 'B' rated crews were allowed to fly, but a subsequent improvement allowed the exercise to reach its climax on the twenty-second when eighteen night sorties resulted in forty 'kills', mainly Lincolns and Washingtons, thanks to very efficient Broadcast controlling by Eastern and Metropolitan sectors. Such excellent results were achieved despite the fact that eleven out of seventeen crews had been with the squadron for less than eight months. Noel Davies was one of those who took part in *Momentum* and recalls some particularly bad weather:

'On exercises you usually stretched the rules more than you would normally do and one night we were scrambled in very bad weather with massive thunderstorms all over East Anglia. We went up into cloud and I'd never seen anything like it before, in fact it cured me of being frightened by lightning for life. There was St Elmo's fire everywhere, usually it only came across the windscreen perhaps a third of the way from the outer frames, but this looked like it had been painted all over. We were being banged around all over the place, something wicked. There was no way that you could look out at all, you had to put the seat down and lower your head so you didn't get blinded too much. All the cabin lighting had to be turned right up otherwise you would not have been able to adjust your eyesight, and the noise was appalling. I never want to fly like that again!

Eventually we were all diverted to West Raynham which was the only airfield open at that time so aircraft were coming in from all over the place. We got into the crewroom there at about three o'clock in the morning, all completely exhausted. The Wing Commander Flying came in and announced that his airfield was rather unusual in that it had left and right hand circuits and that because of this, everyone should read the flying order book. All we wanted to do was to get out of the place so there was nearly a riot, until that is someone actually opened the book to discover that it contained one of the best collections of pornographic photos that anyone had ever seen!'

By now the Vampire NF.10 was coming to the end of its service life as a first-line fighter and on 25 November the first of 23 Squadron's 'long awaited' Venom NF.2s arrived courtesy of C.O. Squadron Leader A.J. Jacomb-Hood DFC who, in the absence of any ferry crews, flew the aircraft over from the de Havilland factory at Hawarden himself. Conversion to the Venom gathered pace in December and the last NF.10 sorties took place during the first week of the month comprising investigation of low-level slipstream effects when flying behind a Lincoln at 1,500ft, and long-range night interceptions in conjunction with Langtoft and Neatishead GCI stations. As 23 Squadron began their evaluation of the Venom NF.2, 25 and 151 Squadrons soldiered on with the Vampire for a little while longer, 25 converting onto Meteor NF.12/14s in April 1954 with 151 Squadron swapping its NF.10s for Meteor NF.11s shortly after.

Following the Vampire NF.10s retirement from first-line service a number were offered for export and after overhaul and the removal of certain internal equipment these were delivered to the air forces of India and Italy, those for the latter being designated NF.54. A small number of Vampire NF.10s were retained by the RAF for use as advanced navigational trainers, which involved the removal of the A.I.10 radar and the addition of extra navigational gear including Rebecca 3. Without the weight of the nose-mounted radar, ballast had to be fitted to keep the aircraft's C.G. within limits and the aircraft also retained their armament, again for reasons of loading. During conversion, the opportunity was taken to fit a revised canopy similar to that of the Venom NF.2a and the aircraft carried standard trainer markings of yellow bands on wings and tail booms. The Vampire NF.10 flew with No.1 ANS at Topcliffe until April 1959 and with No.2 ANS at Thorney Island until June 1959 when they were replaced by Meteor NF(T).14s.

CHAPTER NINE

DE HAVILLAND VENOM
NF.2 AND 3

J ust as the Vampire NF.10 had resulted from a private venture prototype, so the Venom NF.2 and NF.3 were the result of de Havilland's decision to fund a two-seat version of the Venom fighter-bomber. Carrying the B-Scheme registration G-5-3, the first Venom Mk. 2 flew from Hatfield on 22 August 1950 shortly after the outbreak of the Korean War, the fall-out from which was to have a profound affect on the aircraft's subsequent history. Indeed its very inclusion in the RAF's inventory was the outcome of increased tension brought about by this particular conflict. The Venom was destined to be relatively unpopular during its brief service life, one former pilot describing it as 'a tightly packed bag of tricks which was fine as long as everything worked'. Unfortunately things tended to go wrong rather too often.

The Venom Mk. 2 retained the wings and tail booms of the FB.1 which were mated to a wider fuselage nacelle, similar to that of the Vampire NF.10, accommodating A.I.10 radar and a two-man crew seated side-by-side. A preliminary assessment of G-5-3 was carried out by CFE, the aircraft arriving at West Raynham on 22 November 1950, two months before the Vampire NF.10. Minor servicing troubles, including two failures of the nosewheel to extend, led to it being returned to the factory for repair as a result of which the trial period was extended into January the following year. Due to the urgency and importance of the trials the aircraft was delivered before certain engine and airframe work had been completed, and it had to be operated with a temporary electrical starting system, a limitation on maximum power of 10,150rpm (normally 10,250rpm) and without cockpit pressurisation. No tip tanks were fitted as these had yet to be cleared for flight.

The Venom Mk. 2 was faster, more manoeuvrable and had a better rate of climb than the Meteor NF.11, indeed the overall assessment was that it had better performance than any fighter, single or two-seat, in squadron use at that time. The Venom's rate of roll was classed as 'delightful', although this may have been influenced by the lack of tip tanks. The elevators were a little heavy but considered satisfactory. Due to the lack of pressurisation, no flying was carried out above 40,000ft, this height being achieved in around ten minutes. The main criticism of the Venom concerned its poor means of emergency exit, which showed no improvement over the Vampire. There was also little room in the cockpit for ancillary equipment such as Serrate or ILS and the cramped conditions of the

207

radio and radar equipment made first-line servicing a difficult and lengthy process.

The first production Venom NF.2 (WL804) was flown from Hatfield on 4 March 1952, but the production line was then set up at Chester which delayed deliveries until early June 1953 when WL816 and WL818 were flown to CFE for a more comprehensive series of tests than had been possible with G-5-3. The trial was stopped on 28 May 1954 after 167 sorties owing to problems with both aircraft. Serviceability was described as being 'unbelievably bad', both aircraft suffering numerous snags including jammed nosewheel doors, a down-on-power engine in WL816, and a long list of instrument and electrical problems. In spite of these problems a full assessment was carried out which, in many cases, was less than complementary.

The amount of space in the cockpit was deemed ample for pilots and navigators of average size but a tall pilot found that his knees came into contact with the instrument panel, and a navigator of similar stature had his head hard against the top of the canopy. Ejection seats were not fitted (nor would they be) and the escape hatch was rated as entirely inadequate. Cockpit heating was efficient provided that the engine was operated above 9,500rpm.

In contrast to the electrical start fitted to G-5-3, the engine was now set in motion by a cartridge-fired system which proved to be very quick. The usual technique was to pre-select all necessary switches to 'On' with the ground/flight switch set to 'Off' and the throttle about half open. On the scramble order being given the pilot only had to turn the ground/flight switch to 'On' and press the starter button. As the engine accelerated the only concern was to keep j.p.t within limits, which could be achieved easily by retarding the throttle. If the engine failed to light up immediately the cartridge had been expended, it was important to cut the high pressure cock as quickly as possible to prevent a late light up which could result in excessive j.p.t. and turbine blade stretch, together with torching of the tailplane.

During taxiing the Venom showed a marked tendency to weathercock into wind and continual corrections had to be made with brake. This was also apparent during crosswind take offs and slight touches of brake were required until the aircraft had accelerated sufficiently for the rudders to become effective. Heavy back-pressure had to be applied to the stick to lift the nosewheel. Once airborne, there was no noticeable trim change on retracting the gear, although slight back-trim was needed as the flaps were raised. The aircraft's manoeuvrability was described as follows:

'The rudders are spring-operated self-centring. The rudder trim changes noticeably with IAS. With the fixed trim-tabs adjusted to give no slip at intermediate speed, the slip needle shows a left slip at low speeds and a right slip at high speeds. At the extremes, since there is no rudder trim control, accurate flying demands steady foot pressure. Since this is against the spring of the self-centering device as well as aerodynamic forces, this can be very tiring. If one adds the possibility of battle damage to one wing giving aerodynamic drag, the foot pressure required might become overpowering. The aircraft would be greatly improved by the addition of rudder trim.

Aileron control is delightful and produces a good rate of roll with reasonable stick forces. Unfortunately the elevator control at present fitted is much too heavy, the stick force per "g" being at least 20lb. The elevator trim, in consequence, is in constant use but, being somewhat stiff in operation, requires continual adjustment in unaccelerated flight with steady power. For example, in making a 360-degree turn at maximum speed at 30,000ft, it has been found impossible to reach the pre-stall buffet with one hand on the stick without trimming back; trimmed fully back, the buffeting condition can be reached with full back pressure by one hand but the aircraft then tightens in its turn, loses speed, and has to be trimmed forward. Again, at 10,000ft, a maximum speed, maximum rate (untrimmed) turn took one minute to complete 360 degrees, a comparable turn in a Vampire NF.10 took thirty-four seconds. It seems to be impossible for the pilot to pull enough "g" in the Venom NF.2 to black himself out.

For level instrument flight, the heavy elevator may have some advantages but for combat purposes its present weight is quite unacceptable. This statement applies not only to the day-fighter role but also to the night-fighter role at medium and low levels, as the maximum rate of turn of which the aircraft should be capable just cannot be achieved by a pilot of normal strength.'

The maximum rate and radius of turn at varying heights are given in the accompanying table (speeds quoted are IMN):

Height	Entry speed	Exit speed	Bank	Time taken	'g'	Radius of turn
10,000ft	0.78	0.72	80	30 sec	4.5	1.2m
30,000ft	0.83	0.81	70	42 sec	2.5	1.7m
45,000ft	0.82	0.79	60	60 sec	1.75	2.3m

In comparison with the Meteor NF.11, the Venom showed much better performance in the climb and could reach 40,000ft in 12.3 minutes with tip tanks fitted (10.3 minutes without), although to achieve these times it was found that very accurate speed control had to be maintained. The Venom was also capable of operating up to 45,000ft (tip tanks) and 47,000ft (clean). At these heights the aircraft needed very careful handling and the maximum angle of bank that could be applied without losing speed was thirty-five degrees. It also appeared to be very sensitive to outside air temperature and on one occasion, when the air at altitude was relatively warm, the Venom only managed 45,000ft having first been accelerated to full speed at 40,000ft. The maximum level speed achieved at 40,000ft was 258kt IAS or Mach 0.84.

As the Venom did not reach its critical Mach range in level flight, investigation of its handling characteristics at high Mach numbers was carried out in dives from 45,000ft and these characteristics were described in the following terms:

'At about 0.82 IMN, a slight but definite nose-down tendency is experienced; with further increase of IMN, a nose-up tendency occurs which requires steadily increasing forward stick pressure and/or trim to correct. Ultimately, at about 0.86 IMN, a wing roll develops. At first this can be held, but eventually aileron control will be lost and the aircraft will roll despite full aileron correction. Elevator control loss then follows and the aircraft will descend, out of control, in a spiral dive, recovery being effected around 20,000ft in the denser atmosphere. In dives below 30,000ft, the same sequence of events occur, but without loss of control. The carriage of tip tanks brings on the wing roll at about 0.015 IMN lower than with the clean aircraft. In a straight dive, throttling back produces quicker recovery from the wing roll condition than the use of dive brakes, in fact, there are indications that the premature use of dive brakes may accentuate the wing-rolling tendency and speed up the resultant rotation in the spiral dive. Use of dive brakes at high Mach number produces a fairly rapid oscillation in the fore-and-aft trim during deceleration from 0.86 to 0.82 Mach.'

As a day fighter, the NF.2 was found to compare reasonably with the Venom FB.1 up to 35,000ft, but thereafter stick forces became increasingly heavy so that combat manoeuvring became extremely tiring. Visibility was very poor, especially to starboard and to the rear owing to distortion through some panels and excessive 'ironwork', and the pilot's seat on the left-hand side of the cockpit caused great difficulty when it came to flying in battle formation. In addition to assessing the Venom's capabilities at high level, it was also evaluated against low-level targets such as might be employed on minelaying duties. Here it proved to be less suited to the role than the Meteor NF.11 as it was unpleasant to fly at slow speed in turbulent conditions and did not possess a radio altimeter. The view was also expressed that the crew would be most unlikely to survive should the engine fail over the sea.

In summing up, CFE came to the conclusion that the Venom's disadvantages rather outweighed its good points. Although its rate of climb and speed at height were excellent, it was not a pleasant aircraft to fly, its elevator control being particularly tiresome. Its single Ghost engine vibrated considerably and the cockpit was extremely cramped which made it difficult to enter (or leave) in a hurry. It also made for a working environment that was inferior to that offered by the Meteor NF.11. The biggest criticism remained that of emergency evacuation, as it was considered very doubtful whether a crew would be able to bale out and survive if the need arose. This situation remained throughout the life of the night-fighter Venom, despite the fact that ejection seats were successfully fitted to the Navy's equivalent Sea Venom.

Following the trials at CFE, the Venom NF.2 was introduced to active service by 23 Squadron at Coltishall in December 1953 and by the end of the month most 'A' and 'B' rated crews had successfully converted from the Vampire NF.10. There was to be an early tragedy as Flying Officer A. Towle was killed on 29 December when ferrying WL829 from Hawarden to Coltishall. Towle was part of a formation of three aircraft which departed Hawarden at 1425 hrs, but

Four Venom
NF.3s of No. 23
Squadron near
the Norfolk coast.

ten minutes into the flight he reported that he was experiencing engine trouble and was unable to get more than 5,000rpm. Weather conditions were not particularly good with visibility down to 3,000 yards and his last message stated that he was about to carry out a forced-landing. Witnesses saw him approach a suitable field but at a height of around 200ft an object was seen to fall from the aircraft after which it nosed down, hit the ground and burst into flames. The crash site was near Tuxford in Nottinghamshire.

A preliminary investigation noted pieces of perspex from the pilot's jettisonable hatch scattered up the wreckage trail, and the leading edge of the tailplane bore crushing damage and marks which were matched by similar distortion on the remains of the hatch. The major portion of the hatch was found lying beneath the tailplane in a deep ditch. It was clear from the jettison mechanism and strut release pin that the hatch had been released, but the evidence of the rear hinge pins indicated that it had failed to lift clear and had hinged back, tearing away the hinge brackets. The hatch had then struck and embedded itself in the leading edge of the tailplane. As this had happened at a critical point in the forced-landing it was clear that this had been the primary cause of the aircraft diving into the ground. As was the case in many Vampire/Venom accidents, a post-crash fire destroyed the centre section of the aircraft, including much of the engine, and it proved to be impossible to discover what had caused the initial loss of power.

23 Squadron's total flying for January 1954 amounted to a mere sixty-three hours mainly due to serviceability snags and the fact that many aircraft delivered from MUs were not up to date in terms of modifications. On 14 January 151 Squadron arrived from Leuchars to take part in a *Kingpin* exercise, but due to technical difficulties 23's contribution comprised a single aircraft which flew two successful sorties before having to be retired on the third when the radar went u/s.

On the morning of 21 January, Squadron Leader Jacomb-Hood and Pilot Officer A.E. Osborne took off to carry out a weather recce to see if conditions were suitable for the day's flying. A layer of stratus with a base of 600ft was producing occasional light rain and drizzle, and the wind was from the east at eight knots. Visibility was estimated at five miles and the risk of icing was classed as moderate. Flying as 'Sweetmeat 14', Jacomb-Hood was seen near West Raynham flying in and out of cloud as though assessing the cloud base. Not long after, several building workers saw the aircraft dive out of cloud at an angle of about thirty degrees and crash into the ground behind some trees. Both crew were killed.

Although little of the aircraft remained, the Court of Inquiry pointed the finger of suspicion at the flight instruments, in particular the artificial horizon, which was electrically operated and depended on an inverter to convert DC electricity to AC. Incorporated between the DC circuit and the inverter was a resetting-type circuit breaker, located on the starboard cockpit wall, which was designed to break the circuit between the battery supply and inverter should it become overloaded. Problems had already been experienced with the inverters in Venoms and it had also been discovered that the navigator could inadvertently trip the circuit breaker with his sleeve while operating the AI set. If the electric supply to the artificial horizon failed, it took around six and a half minutes for it to show signs of inaccuracy, but even then it was not immediately apparent as the errors were small, being in the order of 3–5 degrees. Even so, after suffering such a failure an aircraft would soon be completely out of control, and could well become inverted before its pilot became aware of the situation.

With the death of Jacomb-Hood, 23 was taken over by Squadron Leader M.H. Constable-Maxwell DSO DFC, a World War Two 'ace' who had flown Hurricanes with 56 Squadron in the Battle of Britain and, later, Mosquitos and Beaufighters with 264 and 604 Squadrons. He was occasionally referred to as the 'Mad Monk' as, prior to his arrival at Coltishall, he had spent four years as a novice at Ampleforth Monastery in Yorkshire.

The Venom's first major exercise took place in the first week of March when 23 sorties were flown during *Magna Flux* resulting in thirty claims, but the month brought another sad loss when Sergeants P.B. Jackson and H. Drabble crashed into the sea three miles off Cromer in WL830 on the sixteenth. They had been with the squadron for two and a half years and, as well as being exceedingly popular, were a highly experienced crew. On a brighter note, seventy-five hours were flown in the last week of March, which hinted that serviceability problems might soon be a thing of the past.

Unfortunately this level of utilisation could not be maintained and in April the squadron's two Vampire T.11s had to be used to their maximum potential to provide I/F training and to act as targets for Venoms during practice interceptions. One of the most worrying aspects of the Venom's problems was that pilots were lacking operational flying practice and were well below the annual training commitment of 240 hours. In terms of servicing, one of the biggest headaches was the fact that the AI radar could not stand multiple sorties. On another *Kingpin* exercise held on the nights of 7/8 April results were good on the first night but by the second, most radars had gone off line and only Flying Officer Morgans had success, claiming four Canberras and a Lincoln in two sorties. There was a further setback on the twenty-sixth when all Venoms were grounded following the discovery of cracks on the upper portion of the flaps of one aircraft. After inspection only three aircraft were cleared to fly, the others all requiring rectification work.

In May, 156 hours were flown by day and seventy-three hours by night, thanks mainly to the increased usage of serviceable aircraft and flying longer sorties. By now 23 were flying higher and faster than ever before with the introduction of 40,000ft as the normal height for practice interceptions, increasing to 48,000ft whenever the control system was able to cope. As crews became more skilled at handling the Venom there was a marked improvement in confidence and morale was also boosted by the fact that the aircraft were now cleared for air firing. During the month 23 Squadron also welcomed Squadron Leader P.S. Englebach as its new C.O.

Air-to-air firing was carried out in June, the average being 7.7% with Flight Lieutenant Welfare topping the list with a score of 17%. The following month the squadron took part in Exercise *Dividend* flying thirty sorties in the first phase and eighty-five in the second. Overall serviceability was much better and at the beginning of the second phase, nine aircraft were available. Turn-round times also showed considerable improvement, the average being six minutes. The only mishap occurred to Flying Officer Langstaff who had a tyre burst on landing and was forced to raise the undercarriage to stop, resulting in Cat 4 damage to his aircraft.

In response to the less than successful entry of the Venom to squadron service, a programme had been initiated to modify remaining production NF.2s to include dorsal fins similar to those of the Vampire T.11, kidney-shaped fins and rudders as on the Venom FB.4 and a new clear-view canopy. Carrying the designation NF.2A, two of the modified Venoms arrived at Coltishall in August and these were followed by another four in September. By October 23 Squadron had ten of the new machines, which generally were in a much better modification state than the old ones.

During this period incidents continued to occur although none were serious. During a minor inspection, WL831 was found to have a cracked burner-can which had burnt through the leads to the fire warning light rendering it unserviceable and also causing Cat 3 damage to the airframe. Another aircraft on a high-level cross country at night developed a severe engine vibration and had to divert to Wattisham where it was later discovered that the rear bearing had burnt out due to oil starvation, and there were two mishaps on landing, one Venom losing a tyre and another suffering a flame out just after touch down.

Just as the squadron was looking forward to increased utilisation, a further restriction was imposed in early November when all tip tanks had to be removed, thereby limiting sorties to a maximum of fifty minutes. This was as a result of a number of in-flight fires that had recently occurred on single-seat Venoms (*see* Chapter 3). Looking on the bright side however, the removal of the tanks resulted in a considerable improvement in the Venom's rate of climb and interceptions were regularly carried out well in excess of 40,000ft. Air firing was also restricted initially, although crews were allowed to resume firing their guns into the sea the following month. There were a few close calls in December, but again there were no injuries. One aircraft lost a turbine blade at night, but by throttling back the pilot managed to make a safe landing; there was yet another case of a tyre being lost on landing, and on the thirtieth Flying Officer Newman suffered a flame out at 30,000ft. Three attempted relights were all unsuccessful but he managed to glide thirty miles back to base thanks to positioning by CRD/F and fixes obtained by his No. 2, Flying Officer Gayer. The dead-stick landing was judged to perfection and no damage was sustained.

The first two months of 1955 were characterised by bad weather and much flying had to be abandoned due to low cloud and ice-bound runways. In January all aircraft were cleared to be refitted with tip tanks, and during the month the only incident involved Flying Officer K.S. Dixon who had a flame out on the approach, but made a safe landing. In February however, 23 Squadron suffered the loss of another C.O. when Squadron Leader Englebach and Flying Officer M.J. Wright were killed in WR781 on the fifteenth. Using the call-sign 'Gasring 14', Englebach, in company with two other Venoms, had diverted to West Raynham in the evening and had just taken off to return to Coltishall when his aircraft hit a tree at Tithe Farm, one mile from the end of runway 22. A greenish-white flash was seen, after which the Venom climbed slowly, turned to port and crashed in a field one mile south of Rougham at 2157 hrs.

As a large amount of debris was found near the tree, and there were branches embedded in the port air-intake duct, it was clear that the Venom had struck the tree well below its top. This initial contact caused a fire to break out in the engine bay and starboard wing root and several witnesses stated that the engine noise faded out before the aircraft went down. Although it remained at low level throughout its brief flight, the crew did try to bale out and the canopy was located one and a half miles beyond the tree. The body of the navigator lay seventy yards from the point of impact with the ground; that of the pilot was located still in the cockpit.

There were no obvious technical reasons for the crash and the investigation considered that the most likely cause was the preoccupation of the pilot in changing radio channels shortly after take off to the extent that he neglected to ensure that the aircraft settled into the correct climbing attitude. The pilots of the other two aircraft which departed shortly before, stated that they had been forced to go onto instruments before leaving the end of the runway and that there was no visible horizon below 1,000ft. During the Court of Inquiry, Air Commodore (later Air Marshal Sir) John Grandy commented that ejection seats were a must in modern aircraft and had they been fitted, the navigator, if not the pilot, may well have saved his life.

With 23 Squadron now commanded by Squadron Leader C.R. Winter DFC, the emphasis in training in March was on air-to-air and air-to-sea firing although there were still plenty of opportunities for practice interceptions. During an exercise with Canberras on the tenth, Flying Officers Dunwoody and Sawtell were dismayed to find that no Venoms were available so took the initiative and borrowed one of the Vampire T.11s. Although it had no radar and was a relatively poor performer at altitude, a combination of good airmanship, night vision and excellent ground controlling allowed a Canberra to be successfully intercepted at 45,000ft. A week later three crews claimed a Valiant flying at 47,500ft, the first time that the RAF's new bomber had been intercepted by an operational squadron.

Air firing continued to be the main priority in April ahead of a deployment to Acklington which took place at the end of May. Before this, however, there were a number of mishaps. Flying Officer J. Dickson's canopy departed at the top of a loop, an incident which occurred a few days after he had suffered an engine cut on finals, and Flight Lieutenant Eric Knighton lost a tip tank whilst on an air test. Safe landings were made on each occasion. The APC at Acklington took place between 23 May and 16 June and saw a gradual improvement in results, Flight Lieutenant Knighton leading with a score of 20%. Serviceability was excellent and despite the short duration of most sorties, total hours for June amounted to 335. (Eric Knighton was also responsible for the squadron's NF.2s being adorned with the names of snakes including WR791/A 'Adder', WL822/D 'Diamond Back', WR779/G 'Gaboon', WR784/R 'Rattlesnake' and WR781/V 'Viper'.)

In July the squadron overshot its target for the first time, daytime flying amounted to 444 hours thanks mainly to hard work by the groundcrews of the Technical Wing, and the squadron's first involvement in Exercise *Fabulous* which involved crews being held on standby during daylight hours and numerous scrambles. Rapid landing trials were also carried out at West Raynham to evaluate the practicalities of getting large numbers of aircraft of differing performance on the ground as quickly as possible. During the month Wing Commander A.N. Davis DSO DFC was posted in to take over command.

Having finally sorted the 'bugs' out of the NF.2, 23 began making preparations in August to receive the Venom NF.3. Three Brigands arrived from Colerne on 16 August and over the next few days each navigator flew five trips to become accustomed to the new radar. The Brigand was capable of accommodating three students and an instructor on each sortie, with Venoms acting

Venom NF.3 WX795 of No. 141 Squadron at Coltishall. (*via Ralph Feather*)

as targets. As conversion continued, the rest of the squadron took part in more rapid-landing trials and Exercise *Bentback* in which they flew sorties against aircraft dropping 'Window'. Three incidents were recorded during the month, two engine cuts were experienced during aerobatics – successful relights being carried out on each occasion – and Flying Officer J.S.G. Weir was forced to retract his undercarriage on landing at Leconfield when the brake lever came adrift. In September 23 Squadron completed its conversion onto the NF.3 and continued to fly this variant until March 1957.

The Venom NF.3 featured the longer-range American Westinghouse APS-57 radar (A.I.21), power-operated ailerons, an up-rated Ghost 104 of 4,950lb.s.t., and Maxaret brakes. Three Venom NF.3s (WX804, WX807 and WX808) were delivered to CFE at the beginning of June 1955 for trials prior to the aircraft entering squadron service. The NF.3 weighed in about 1,000lb heavier than its predecessor so that, despite a modest increase in power offered by the Ghost 104, its overall performance was not as good. The new engine also had a Dowty fuel system instead of the Lucas system as used on the Ghost 103. On start-up, slow running rpm was achieved in approximately twenty-five seconds and throughout the duration of the trials no wet starts were experienced. Handling during taxiing showed a slight improvement over the NF.2 and turns could be made either way without difficulty, even in a fair crosswind. On take off the aircraft could be held easily against the brakes although it was recommended that this only be carried out on concrete surfaces as tarmac runways might be damaged by jet blast. During the take-off run the nosewheel was found to be extremely hard riding and considerable drumming was experienced until it could be lifted off at 100kt, the aircraft becoming airborne at 120kt, twenty-three seconds after brake release.

Largely due to the increase in all-up weight, the figures for rate of climb on the NF.3 were considerably down on those achieved by the NF.2 and were roughly comparable with the Meteor NF.12/14. With tip tanks fitted the NF.3 made it to 40,000ft in sixteen minutes, 3.7 minutes longer than the NF.2. Engine behaviour in the climb was also deemed to be unsatisfactory, as above 30,000ft continual throttle adjustments had to be made to keep within the 10,100rpm limit that was mandatory when climbing above 25,000ft. Engine revs tended to creep up or down and great difficulty was experienced in achieving the correct setting as small throttle movements either way caused too large a change in rpm. Although the NF.2 could easily get to 45,000ft or higher depending on temperature, the NF.3 could only manage 42,000ft.

The aircraft's top speed was also down on the NF.2 due partly to the redesigned radome of larger frontal area to accommodate the A.I.21 radar. At 40,000ft, Mach 0.795 was achieved, which was 0.045 lower than the NF.2. Acceleration times were not particularly inspiring either and at 40,000ft the NF.3 took three minutes fifty seconds to accelerate in level flight from climbing speed to maximum level speed (0.62M–0.795M). To check the aircraft's characteristics during high-speed stalls, steep turns were carried out at various heights above 20,000ft with an entry speed of Mach 0.78. On tightening the turn the Venom commenced buffeting and if the turn was continued a lateral rocking set in, followed by wing drop. This was not vicious but could occur in either direction, irrespective of the direction of turn. No 'pitch up' was detected during these maximum rate turns.

Manoeuvrability was adequate, controls were well balanced and the aircraft was generally pleasant to fly, however the aileron break-out force in power was regarded as being too high and rudder control was heavy due to the powerful self-centring springs incorporated in the control system. There was also a marked oscillation in yaw after turns (especially at altitude) which the spring system failed to correct. It was thought that this could affect firing accuracy and a rudder trimmer, or better still a yaw damper, was recommended. At 35,000ft (Mach 0.78) and above, the elevator became increasingly ineffective with increase in speed and the rate of turn suffered accordingly, but as soon as the aircraft decelerated to Mach 0.78 or below, it suddenly became effective again and comparatively small turning circles could be achieved. In 'manual' the ailerons were extremely heavy and the aircraft could not be considered a fighting machine in that condition, although it was perfectly possible for a QGH or GCA to be flown in reasonable safety.

The Venom NF.3 could operate up to 275 miles from base assuming a climb to 42,000ft, ten minutes combat and return at best range speed. This flight profile allowed sixty-five gallons of fuel for landing and would have taken approximately one hour thirty minutes. For maximum range the NF.3 could be flown at a constant IAS of 165kt and during a descent from 40,000ft to 2,000ft the distance travelled was just under 100nm. This type of descent led to problems with windscreen icing and during prolonged periods of cruising at low rpm for maximum range the whole canopy was liable to ice up. If this occurred it was necessary to apply full power for ten minutes for it to clear, assuming that sufficient fuel was available. It was also found that the windscreen frequently misted over immediately after landing.

Prior to landing the Venom NF.3 took slightly longer to lose speed than the Meteor NF.14 as its airbrakes were not as effective, this inadequacy being especially marked below 200kt where the Venom's brakes provided no assistance at all. Undercarriage extension was rapid and produced virtually no change of trim. The emergency lowering system was not too difficult to operate although it required 115 strokes on a handpump to be performed by the navigator (who else!). On lowering the flaps a large amount of nose-down trim was needed, as had been the case with all previous marks of Vampire and Venom. The threshold was crossed at 110kt and, being heavier, the NF.3 remained firmly on the ground when stalled onto a smooth runway. With its Maxaret brakes it could be brought to a halt in about 1,000 yards.

Should a go-around be necessary, 9,000rpm was found to be adequate for climbing away even with undercarriage and flaps down, although with the increase in power the aircraft had to be trimmed nose down. No trim changes occurred when the undercarriage was retracted, but nose-up trim was required when the flaps were raised. The Venom's behaviour at low speeds and at low level depended on the amount of turbulence experienced, and in bumpy conditions it yawed continually which was a great hindrance when attempting to fly an accurate instrument procedure. In terms of engine handling, the throttle could be used coarsely at any height and the engine would not flame out, but extreme care was needed to avoid exceeding engine limitations at height owing to the extreme sensitivity of the throttle. A very small amount of movement was likely to result in a difference of nearly 1,000rpm.

During the trials a number of scrambles were carried out, the average time for the Venom NF.3 to get airborne being one minute. This compared unfavourably with the NF.2 which took forty seconds and was due to slower throttle-opening on start up enforced by the Dowty fuel system. Air firing was carried out at 40,000ft at speeds up to Mach 0.84 – no stoppages were experienced and there was no effect on the aircraft's Mach characteristics. Several firing sorties were flown at lower levels at speeds between 350–420kt and on each occasion the radome sustained damage.

Overall, the performance of the Venom NF.3 was only slightly better than the Meteor NF.14 in terms of maximum IMN, operational ceiling and times to height, although it could be forced 'somewhat unwillingly' to a greater absolute ceiling. It was also handicapped by being directionally unstable at altitude, which affected simulated night attacks when accurate sighting was often impossible. In conclusion the report considered that the Venom NF.3 was likely to be effective against targets flying up to Mach 0.72 and 41–42,000ft, and although it could do better, the probability of success grew rapidly less.

141 Squadron at Coltishall became the first operational unit to receive Venom NF.3s in June 1955 and by the end of the year, 23 Squadron, also at Coltishall, 151 Squadron at Leuchars and 125 Squadron at Stradishall had begun to convert. Flying Officer Guy Woods recalls his introduction to the Venom:

'Following a dozen hours in the Vampire NF.10 at Shawbury for jet experience, I did radar training on the Bristol Brigand prior to converting onto the Meteor NF.12/14 at the Night and All Weather OCU at North Luffenham. I completed about 100 hours on this delightful machine before being posted to my first squadron, 151 at Leuchars, which had just completed conversion from the Meteor NF.11 to the Venom NF.3. It had the same American radar as the NF.12/14 so my conversion wasn't quite as detailed as my pilot's had to be.

The Venom was a nice aircraft to fly in, the side-by-side seating arrangement was very popular and its performance was superior to the Meteor. It had a higher limiting Mach number and with power-assisted ailerons was quite a nippy number, but they all varied a bit depending on which team of DH apprentices built it! One of our pilots on 151 reputedly got one up to about Mach 0.89/0.90 in a steep dive from 40,000ft where he got into compressibility problems and everything went solid on him until he got down to lower altitude. Its main drawback was its twin-boom layout and lack of ejection seats which made abandonment in flight highly problematical. The Venom proved to be quite lethal in service and many were lost, together with the crews. The main problem, as I recall, was caused by failures of the single engine at *moments critique*, i.e. just after take off and on final approach to land.

Although we had no fatal accidents on 151 Squadron, there were a few incidents, mainly on the ground, which was the best place to have them! We Cat 5'd (wrote off) a Venom when the undercarriage would not come down forcing the crew to do a wheels-up landing on the runway at Leuchars. There was a flash fire caused by fuel leaking from the fuselage scraping along the runway. The pilot hopped over the side smartly but the navigator took his time, much to the consternation of the pilot. The fire badly burned one of the booms and damaged the pod. We were all horrified to see that what was scorched on the fuselage was painted fabric covering the plywood skin of the aircraft. Beneath its exterior it was more Mosquito than any of us had imagined! This airframe was deemed not worth repairing and was replaced by a brand new one out of the Maintenance Unit. It was in service for such a short time prior to re-equipping with the Javelin that I don't think they even bothered to paint squadron markings on it.'

89 Squadron re-formed at Stradishall on 15 December 1955 under the initial command of Squadron Leader J.W. Valentine, and began flying NF.3s the following month. One of its founder members was Flying Officer Paul Hodgson, a first tourist who had also trained on Meteor NF.12/14s at North Luffenham.

'The Venom NF.3 was the most unpleasant aircraft that I have ever flown and, perhaps, the least suited for its intended role. An all-weather fighter with only one engine that would sometimes flame out for no reason was not a prospect to fill one with confidence. The NF.3 had a Dowty fuel system unlike the NF.2 which had a fuel system by Lucas, which was reckoned to be far more reliable. No ejection seats were fitted and the possibility of leaving the thing in extremis was doubtful. As a night-fighter the Venom was far from ideal, the side-by-side seating made for a very cramped cockpit, wearing the then new bone dome meant that you were squashed under the low canopy and the visibility was poor. In any rain the forward visibility was nil since water built up on the windscreen instead of blowing off. This gave rise to the situation where the Hunters at Stradishall could operate quite successfully while we were grounded till the rain eased. Some all-weather fighter!

The NF.3 was fitted with power ailerons which did give it a fine rate of roll but unfortunately they had a slight break-out force before operating which made the aircraft twitchy in roll. The flying controls were not nicely balanced, unlike the Vampire T.11 which had beautifully matched control responses. The Venom was not naturally stable, unlike the Meteor and Javelin, and this, combined with its control responses, made it tiring to fly for long periods on instruments. For high-level interception exercises it was an improvement on the Meteor, it could turn quite well without losing too much speed and had quite a good Mach number, although it would flick out of control if this was exceeded. The air brakes were poor which made speed control difficult. The A.I.21 radar could give quite good results when working properly, but serviceability was never good. Altogether, the Venom was not my favourite aeroplane!'

Paul Hodgson's views on the Venom NF.3 are shared by another of 89 Squadron's pilots, Flying Officer Malcolm de Garis:

'It only had one engine which had an alarming propensity to cease functioning, the canopy was prone to mist up at altitude, the windscreen was likely to ice up on return and it was also fond of cracking. At one stage the RAF ran out of spares and some bright spark at the "Airbox" suggested we could make up and use aluminium sheets of suitable strength. We turned down his kind suggestion. With its narrow high-pressure tyres it was a bit of a handful on a wet runway with a crosswind. The fuel gauges were fond of telling "porky pies" and were probably only accurate during pre-flight. We were issued with tables to compare gauges with elapsed time airborne to give a best guess as to how much remained.

The aircraft would cheerfully lose height in any turn unless the pilot kept his eye on the instruments, there being no external clues to this height loss, which would be greater the steeper the bank angle. The engine-fire warning system was just a teensy bit unreliable in that it had a habit of shouting FIRE when there wasn't one. The problem was that the engine was right behind us and 90% of it was out of sight. Also the fuselage consisted of a great deal of fuel-soaked wood. If there WAS a FIRE and if the fire extinguisher did not discourage it, the good book encouraged you to vacate the machine pronto. How to tell if there WAS a FIRE? Simple. The same sort of helpful gent at the "Airbox" told us to whip the aircraft into a 360-degree turn and if we found ourselves flying into smoke then there was a fair chance we were on fire. We didn't have the heart to tell him that we were night-fighters and that the old adage of "red sky at night means the engine's alight" would probably cover the situation!'

89 Squadron received its first Venom NF.3s in January 1956 but did not receive its full complement of aircraft until March. Personnel continued to be drafted in during this period including Wing Commander David Simmons AFC who took over as C.O., and Squadron Leader Sid Munns DFM who became Nav/Rad Leader. During the conversion programme airframe serviceability was extremely good, but the AI radar gave a lot of trouble. The monthly target of 400 hours was exceeded in April, thanks mainly to emphasis being placed on cine combat training which meant that radar snags did not handicap the flying effort as it might otherwise have done. Night flying was also carried out, including circuit work and cross-countries, and the first of the 'hard noses' arrived which, it was hoped, would solve air-firing problems that had been experienced at CFE. By the end of the month all pilots had practiced quarter attacks on banners towed by the unit's Meteor F.8s. During night interceptions it was found that the Venom's small size meant that it was difficult to see and it was therefore decided that the target aircraft would switch on its nav lights when the attacker was at 1,000ft range. In addition, evasion would cease when the attacker was within 1,500ft as difficulty was experienced in controlling close-in targets on A.I.21. These precautions were adopted as a temporary measure until crews gained more experience with their new equipment.

Although the NF.3 had only been in service for a short time, its reputation was already suffering and some of the system failures that occurred produced potentially dangerous situations. The following rather understated account by Wing Commander David Simmons of an electrical failure at night tends to disguise a superb piece of flying:

'We briefed for a night cross-country at 30,000ft and got into an aircraft in which one alternator was u/s, although this didn't show up because the warning light bulb had blown. We took off and climbed through 20,000ft of cloud into bright moonlight but somewhere over the south coast the radar packed up and was switched off. We had one red light staring at us but were not unduly worried as we thought we had a second alternator. However, things then started to go quiet! We turned on a reciprocal heading and after some time started to let down when we estimated we should break cloud over the North Sea. By now the cockpit lights had gone dim, we couldn't see our wing-tip lights, the intercom was dead and the artificial horizon was spinning, so I concentrated on turn and slip and airspeed. We actually broke cloud at about 500ft indicated over land and I saw a small town ahead and circled it. I recognised the cinema and knew where we were. I followed roads back to base and buzzed the caravan at the end of the runway. There were no green lights, of course, so I counted three clunks when we lowered the gear, landed safely and got out to meet the reception committee at the end of the runway.'

During May two-weeks' air firing was carried out at Acklington, resulting in an average score of 7.6% and a stoppage rate of 1-in-4,020 rounds, figures that, at the time, were appreciably better than any other unit. The highest individual score was 28.3% by Flying Officer Jack Fuller and the highest average was 13.9% by Flying Officer F.K. Lundy. On return to Stradishall however, it was no great surprise to discover that not a single radar installation was in working order. As a backlog of STIs and modifications (which had been postponed due to the Acklington detachment) had to be attended to, total hours for June amounted to only 115 by day and forty-four by night, a situation that was not helped by

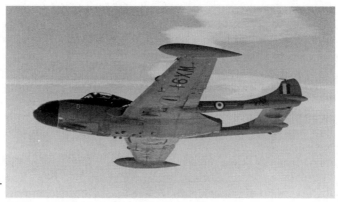

NF.3 WX911 of No. 125 Squadron.

inadequate spares backing. As a result, crews were not getting enough flying to maintain proficiency or even, in many cases, to attain it. To try to get around the problem the unit's two Meteor F.8s were fully utilised, as was the Vampire T.11, for instrument training and the renewal of lapsed ratings. Towards the end of the month three crews and aircraft departed to Waterbeach on the squadron's first *Fabulous* detachment.

In July the main flying effort was directed towards AI training. Whenever possible aircraft were not sent up unless they were fully radar serviceable, though occasionally this meant that only two out of sixteen aircraft on the squadron was airborne. A general improvement allowed a satisfactory number of practice interceptions to be achieved towards the end of the month but there were further radar problems in August. On the tenth, 89 suffered its first fatal accident with the Venom when Flying Officers J.D.H. Hammett and R.E.G. Hickling were killed during a night overshoot in WX884.

They had been carrying out practice interceptions with an aircraft flown by Flying Officer P.C. Evetts and had returned just after midnight to carry out a GCA letdown to Stradishall's runway 07. Weather conditions were good with no cloud below 10,000ft and a visibility of four miles, but other aircraft had reported unusually severe internal icing. From his first approach Hammett overshot into a visual circuit and, although he touched down after his second attempt and seemed to be in a reasonable position to complete the landing, he decided to go around. His climb-out seemed to be unusually flat and when still very low, he began a turn to port that led to a shallow descent which was continued until the port wing hit the ground and broke off. The main body of the aircraft continued through a hedge and became airborne again for about 250 yards before striking the ground heavily, probably inverted, and bouncing another fifty yards into a wood. A fire broke out which, by the time that the crash crews arrived, had turned into a magnesium fire which could not be extinguished and continued to burn for the next four hours, destroying much of the wreckage.

Various possibilities were put forward as to the cause of the accident, including that of oxygen failure. Since March 100% oxygen had been used at all times instead of the previous routine of using 'normal' oxygen for take off and landing and switching to 100% above 25,000ft. The Mk.17 regulator was known to be temperamental and the one in WX884 had a history of faulty operation, although it was found to be serviceable when tested. It was noted that Hammett's oxygen bottle had been used but it was not known if this had been activated by the pilot or had merely discharged as a result of the crash. If the regulator had failed at a critical point on take off the pilot would not have been able to breathe.

It was also suggested that internal icing may have been a factor as Flying Officer Evetts had experienced severely restricted vision and had been forced to lean forward to scrape ice from the windscreen with his glove. If Hammett had done the same after his overshoot he may have inadvertently allowed his aircraft to descend too low. Another explanation was that he may just have been anxious to get down quickly, as a civilian witness noted that the aircraft turned unusually early into the circuit. The Venom had been heading 002 degrees at the first point of impact (runway heading 070), so assuming speed to have been in the order of 220kt, sixty degrees of bank would have had to be applied to generate that amount of turn. Shortly after the accident Mr J.W. Wilson, deputy Chief Test Pilot at de Havilland, visited Stradishall to speak to the crews after which a 'lively discussion' took place on the performance and serviceability of the Venom and its handling characteristics.

Total flying for August was 244 hours, a disappointing figure caused mainly by A.O.G.s for time-expired oxygen regulators and problems with the engine Air Fuel Ratio Control Unit. Several examples of the latter had to be replaced and four new units, received direct from the manufacturers, were also found to be unserviceable on fitment. In September 89 Squadron took part in Exercise *Stronghold* which was divided into two parts. Each crew did a daily twelve-hour shift with 'B' Flight on duty midnight to midday, followed by 'A' Flight, these roles being swapped during the second phase. For the exercise the Venoms were scrambled from the ASP so that a Meteor night-fighter unit, which did not have the advantage of cartridge start, could use the ORP adjacent to the runway. Even so, scramble times for the Venoms averaged a respectable two minutes. The squadron flew thirty-six sorties during *Stronghold*, the highest interception being a Valiant by Flying Officers R.L. Watson and J.M. Cole at 44,000ft.

Concern over the reliability of the Venom's single Ghost engine was re-inforced on the night of 23/24 October when WX907, flown by Flying Officers D.W. Walters and J.M. Larkin, crashed after undershooting. They had been carrying out mutual practice interceptions with Flying Officer Jack Fuller and Pilot Officer Peter Desmond in WX896 and were approaching runway 25 at 800ft when engine rpm dropped, picked up for another thirty seconds, before failing completely one mile from touchdown. Height was lost rapidly, the aircraft coming down in an orchard in a level attitude but with a fifteen-degree angle of descent. After bouncing and demolishing numerous fruit trees, it came to rest about 220ft after the initial impact, catching fire as it did so.

Both crew members were severely injured in the crash. Despite having a broken back and first-degree burns to his arm and leg, Walters managed to get out, but was unable to free his navigator who died after being trapped inside the burning aircraft. When his body was examined later, it was found that both legs were fractured just above the knee, injuries that had probably been caused by contact with the AI console. This was a particular hazard during Venom crash-landings and the injuries were identical to those received by the navigator in the previous fatal accident in August. Once again fire had destroyed much of the wreckage, including all except the steel parts of the engine, but there was strong circumstantial evidence to suggest that the engine had failed due to fuel star-vation. Much trouble had been experienced with the Dowty fuel system, in particular the Air Fuel Ratio Control Unit, which was prone to leak due to block-ages caused by foreign particles, with subsequent loss of main fuel supply.

For the rest of the year, practice interceptions remained the priority with some crews being able to begin the next phase in their training, the intercepting of targets evading in elevation as well as azimuth. Thirteen crews departed to Waterbeach for the unit's second *Fabulous* exercise on 16 November but during the week only four scrambles took place and of these, three were aborted.

Serviceability for the period was only 40%, caused in part by a general lack of manpower, especially engine mechanics (25% below establishment) and instruments mechanics (50% below).

In January, hours improved to 209 by day and 114 by night which allowed all pilots to move onto the next phase in the squadron training programme whereby all interceptions were carried out under GCI control, with height differences of up to 8,000ft between fighter and target. This situation was not set to continue as flying was restricted in February due to the national fuel-economy drive brought about by the Suez crisis and pilots were only allowed twelve hours apiece. Despite this, several exercises were carried out including a 'Bombex' on the fourteenth when two out of four Venoms flew without tip tanks as the targets were expected to fly high and fast. These two aircraft managed to intercept a Valiant but another with tip tanks was unable to close to 'kill' range before it was forced to return to base.

89 Squadron were on *Fabulous* duty again in early March, this time at Wattisham, the detachment proving to be the most arduous yet as crews were required to remain in the cockpit at two minutes standby throughout the night from 1800–0700hrs. Those taking part also had to stay a day longer than planned as a blocked runway at Leuchars meant that 151 Squadron were not able to take over. March also saw a large influx of crews from the recently disbanded 125 Squadron. One of the new arrivals, Flying Officer A.J. 'Hank' Prosser, recalls his feelings for the Venom and some of the incidents that occurred during his tour:

'There were many things about the Venom that I disliked. The cockpit heating and demisting system was laughable. Glycol rags were necessary

WX877 of No. 125 Squadron (note airbrakes deployed).

and frequently used to de-ice the inside of the canopy at high altitude, and I also recall having to crouch down and squint through the only clear piece of misted windscreen – about a couple of inches at the bottom – to see to land on many occasions. Some squadrons I understand fitted inner bicycle tubing to a louvre on the nav's side so that he could spray the windscreen with hot air on the descent to demist it. The NF.3 had a wide, flat windscreen but was not equipped with wipers. The chemical rain-repellent system was a poor substitute, if applied with care it worked for a short time. In practice, landing in rain was often an added difficulty, exacerbated by the flat design. All Venom squadrons used the Vampire T.11 as their instrument rating and general handling trainer so it therefore seemed very bad engineering to transpose the functions of similar levers on the throttle quadrant. On one it was the high pressure fuel cock (operation of which immediately stopped the engine), on the other it was the air-brake selector which was used much more routinely in the air to less dramatic effect. The air-conditioning temperature selection wheel between the two seats also operated in opposite senses.

Our interception practices were normally set up by GCI as 180 or 90 degrees with the target 2,000ft above or below. They were generally high level at 30–40,000ft and on the climb out we would compare altimeter readings for a safety check. Directions would continue until the nav/rad said he was confident to take over direction of the interception. We did not do much work at low level, but were conscious of the very high casualty rate of the Coltishall-based squadrons who did many more low level tasks than us.

I was fortunate not to have any major incidents on the Venom, although on my very first trip at night my seat fell to the bottom of its adjustment as I rotated for take off and I seem to remember holding the control column at about the level of my nose and gazing up at the instrument panel rather than down. On another occasion I was doing a high-speed run at 400kt+ over the runway at Stradishall after a short ferry flight from Wattisham when the canopy blew out. All rather disconcerting! I also recall our station commander who used to turn up at the squadron for a flight. This, of course, involved "borrowing" a navigator from us. Our navs found this deeply worrying as his abilities in the air were somewhat alarming. On one occasion he landed without the nicety of rounding out, making such firm contact with the runway that the nav's knees made forceful contact with the radar display. Another time, when on an air-to-air sortie against a towed banner target, he managed to catch the towrope with the twin booms.'

In April cine training took precedence prior to the arrival of instructors from the Fighter Weapons School who stayed at Stradishall for three days, during which air firing was carried out on the low-level range at Lowestoft and also at high altitude near Trimingham. The FWS team carried out a demonstration on the latter form of attack as the squadron had not previously fired on banner targets above 7,000ft. The rest of the month was taken up with an exercise known unofficially as 'Chinese quarter attacks'. This took place at 35,000ft and consisted of an attacking aircraft being positioned 1,000 yards behind and 1,000ft above another Venom. On being told to evade, the target turned either left or right losing 750ft, then reversed its turn and climbed through 1,500ft. Turns of sixty degrees were used throughout and the pilot of the attacking aircraft had to close range to 200 yards, ranging and tracking the target throughout the manoeuvre.

The highlight of May was Exercise *Vigilant* from the twenty-fifth to the twenty-seventh, during which 89 Squadron flew sixty-four sorties by day and thirty-one by night. Once again the shortcomings of the Venom's performance made the interception of high flying targets difficult and tedious, and on some occasions pilots found that they were completely out-performed. Despite this, 87 claims were made, of which 80 were later confirmed. The most successful crew was Flight Lieutenant J.M.C. Morgans and Flying Officer Peter Desmond who collected a mixed bag comprising two Canberras, four F-84s, one Meteor PR.10 and two Canberra B.8s one of which was intercepted over Holland. During *Vigilant* the squadron operated as two flights, each flying alternately, the crews appreciating that standby periods had been considerably reduced compared with the last major exercise the previous year. Bad radio contact with GCI stations was experienced on occasion and effective jamming meant that some crews had to freelance, but generally the level of controlling was of a high standard. Only one incident took place, Flying Officer J.H. Adams experiencing a slow-burning cartridge in WX912 during start-up which led to severe burning of the tailplane, sufficient for the aircraft to be written off.

The NF.3 continued to be flown by 89 Squadron until October when the unit began to re-equip with the Javelin FAW.2. The final public appearance of 89's Venoms took place on 13 October during an Open Day at Stradishall, although bad weather meant that only four could take part instead of the twelve aircraft formation that had been intended. Nineteen of the squadron's Venoms were ferried to Shawbury shortly after, leaving just one aircraft u/s in the servicing hangar after an airborne argument with an unknown bird.

By the end of 1957 all night-fighter Venoms had been replaced by the Javelin, which provided crews with the luxury of twin engines, ejection seats and a well laid out, comfortable cockpit. Although the Venom had suffered a fair amount of criticism during its brief service life, it had at least taught many the basic skills of night fighting, techniques that were to serve them well when flying more advanced types of aircraft. Flight Lieutenant Guy Woods went on to be a navigator in F-4 Phantoms but learned his trade flying in Venoms with 151 Squadron.

'For normal training we operated in pairs doing interceptions turn and turn about, doing maybe three each in a one hour twenty minute sortie. Occasionally we would do what were known as mutual interceptions without radar control from the ground, setting up the intercepts ourselves. We conducted these from a variety of track crossing angles from 90 degrees every 30 degrees through to 180 head-on. Track separation was designed to be such that our turning circle fitted it nicely so that we could turn round neatly to roll out 1nm behind the target. This was fairly easy on the lower

No 151 Squadron crews pose for the camera.

track angles, but a 180 left you very little time to make a complete adjustment. Having got in behind, the target was told to evade and the next phase of the attack initiated. This would be either to close in for a simulated guns kill or to close in down to 100 yards to visually identify the target. We did ident runs at night against evading targets with their lights off, something we certainly would not do in this day and age! Two student crews did collide at night on my OCU course on Meteors and unfortunately one of the pilots was killed when he hit the fin after bailing out.

During these exercises the poor old navigator was having to work like the proverbial one-armed paper hanger. The radar was not roll stabilised, so every time bank was applied the scanner had to be moved up or down to keep painting the target. This was done using a little joystick on the radar control panel with the right hand. Scanner control could get quite frantic at close range against an evading target and many is the joystick that was actually snapped off at the hilt. Meanwhile the left hand was kept busy adjusting a strobe control which transferred the PPI range and azimuth display to the elevation tube while simultaneously adjusting the gain control. All the time the navigator was assessing what was going on, giving his pilot commands to go up/down, port/starboard, more speed/less speed as required to complete the interception, and giving a running commentary on where the target was and what it was doing. All of this without a radar lock-on facility. Looking back on it I find it difficult to believe that I could actually do this at one time!

Our main operating height band was 25–35,000ft with the odd target at 40,000ft. We did very little low-level work and virtually nothing over land apart from the occasional *Rat and Terrier* exercise. These were carried out visually since the radar was swamped out with ground returns. The radar itself was quite sophisticated. It was a multi-mode affair with a variety of scan patterns available to the operator. The main range azimuth display was a PPI with a coverage of eighty-five degrees either side of the nose. For normal operations full 85/85 was selected with an elevation raster scan of something like ten or twelve degrees. This wedge of coverage could be moved up or down as required in order to see targets at levels other than yours. The scanner could be motored from about thirty degrees down to about fifty or sixty degrees up, so the possible radar coverage was quite high. Pick-up ranges depended very much on target size. On something like a B-36 you might see it at twenty-five miles, but on a Venom sized target 10–15 miles would be more like it.

Another useful mode was ground mapping which gave a very good map picture out to 150–200 miles, particularly useful against the U.K. coastline. As a change from Venom v. Venom practice interceptions, we had several group-and-command exercises which gave us a much greater variety of targets. These could be Canberras (with the odd Lincoln doing ECM work) and USAF aircraft including B-45 Tornados, B-36s, B-47s and F-86s. Two or three times a year we would set aside a week concentrating on air-to-air gunnery against a towed target. We would fire from one gun only and the navigator had little to do but keep the contents of his stomach under control. If one had any tendency towards airsickness the often violent manoeuvring carried out during a guns pass could bring it to the surface so to speak! Without a radar lock-on facility the nav could not give the sighting system any ranging information. Once in a while we would load up all four guns and fire them out. This shook the airframe more than somewhat and I recall that on one occasion the pilot's instrument panel came adrift from its mountings. Unfortunately there were no overseas deployments during my time with this particular aeroplane – I believe we were not allowed to take the radar out of the country for security reasons, and also their "lordships" were not happy to let a fairly unreliable aeroplane get out of their clutches!'

Guy Woods maintains that the techniques he learned back in 1955 still hold good but with the vastly increased range of modern radars, he feels that there is much greater scope to sort out the cock-ups made by ground controllers! Flying Officer Ivan Logan was also a nav/rad on Venom NF.3s with 23 Squadron at Coltishall.

'The Venom NF.3 with more advanced radar and airframe improvements was, nevertheless, slower, and had a lower ceiling than the Mk. 2 which could get up to 50,000ft reasonably easily. Most of our interceptions were practice interceptions, Venom against Venom. We would get initial contacts at around 13–14 miles, a big improvement over A.I.10. Such ranges enabled us to use "long range" procedures to position behind, rather than turning hard at zero range and hoping to pick up the target after a blind turn. For PIs we would split at about 40,000ft and work up to 47,000ft staying airborne for around one hour forty-five minutes.

During Exercises we often operated against USAF B-66s – they were no problem, they were usually around 38,000ft, and left their lights on at night! We never did, even when evading. I remember once picking up a B-36 at twenty-eight miles on A.I.21 and we would get something like a Valiant at about eighteen miles. We had trouble getting up to Canberras who were often around 50,000ft – I remember one of our crews following a Canberra for 120 miles before getting his "splash". We sometimes sat below them and recorded their numbers, but that was cheating!

Following evading targets at close range on A.I.21 was not easy as our azimuth scope was a PPI. On A.I.10 and A.I.17 the timebase was expanded right across the tube so that collisions came straight down rather than towards the centre of the timebase. Most low-level interceptions were carried out over the sea to avoid the problem of ground returns but they caused us problems and LLPIs, particularly at night, were very hairy.'

There was only one successful bale-out from a Venom, an event which occurred on 21 November 1956 and involved Flight Lieutenant F.A. Mallett and

No. 151 Squadron Venom NF.3 with Hunter F.1s of 43 and 222 Squadrons.

Flying Officer D.N. Hodges of 253 Squadron. The crew were briefed to carry out a series of cine quarter attacks on a banner towed by a Meteor F.8 and took off from Waterbeach at 1135 hrs, meeting up with the Meteor between base and the range at Winterton. On his fourth attack Mallett commenced a dive from 1,800ft above the target but during his descent he realised he was getting too close and had to tighten his turn to port producing an estimated 4½–5g. The attack was abandoned at about forty degrees angle off and a pull up initiated at around 330kt IAS to clear the target. Immediately after this and without warning, the aircraft lurched and rolled rapidly to starboard, completing at least three rolls before the pilot knew what was happening. Mallett instinctively applied full left rudder, but it also took full port aileron to stop the roll and keep the starboard wing up. Despite full back stick the Venom continued to lose height, the situation quickly becoming critical as Mallett reported in his evidence to the Court of Inquiry:

> 'At the beginning of the violent rolling the navigator's R/T connection had become disconnected, now, however, we regained contact so I informed him that we would abandon the aircraft. I jettisoned the canopy which came off cleanly. I allowed the aircraft to invert by a slight relaxation of pressure on the aileron control and when inverted pushed forward on the control column creating some negative "g". I maintained full port rudder throughout as I was convinced that any relaxation would recommence the uncontrolled rolling. The navigator left the aircraft before it was completely inverted after about 150 degrees of roll. He went cleanly and I followed immediately. As my feet were still on the rudder bar, I did not go cleanly. My right knee was cut and my left leg scratched and bruised. This must have affected my exit for my lower back caught in something in the cockpit, probably the Gee set, and I was stretched back by the slip-stream. I wriggled and at about 1,700ft fell clear, missing the tailplane and fins which I vaguely remember seeing. I landed safely before my navigator showing that the aircraft was probably losing height rapidly during my short period trapped in the cockpit.'

After Mallett baled out, his aircraft performed another one and a half rolls before crashing in a field three quarters of a mile from the village of Forncett St Mary, near Norwich. Most of the larger components of the Venom were located in a 6ft deep crater, with smaller pieces of debris about 50 yards further forward. The canopy was found one mile west of the crash site and the starboard tip tank was 200 yards to the south-west. The latter find proved to be crucial as it was later proved that the violent rolling was caused by the tip tank becoming loose and twisting up at an angle of about forty degrees. This was caused by incorrect maintenance, an additional plain washer having become trapped end on, which prevented the fixing nut running the correct distance down the attachment bolt.

CHAPTER TEN

GLOSTER JAVELIN

In the late 1940s Britain finally woke up to the fact that it needed to spend more on air defence and embarked on numerous projects with varying degrees of success. A large slice of the available revenue was taken up by the urgent need for a night/all-weather fighter and two designs, the de Havilland DH.110 and the Gloster G.A.5, were ordered in prototype form to compete for the role.

One of the problems facing the aircraft designer of the period was a basic lack of experience with regard to which aerodynamic shape was best suited to fulfilling the requirements he had been asked to achieve. Should he go for a radical design as suggested by some of the research that had come out of Germany at the end of World War Two, or would a more conservative approach be just as good? Many British designers favoured the former course of action which tended to lengthen development periods, a situation made worse by the small numbers of prototypes ordered and constant changes to requirements and specifications by the customer. Looking back, it is surprising that anything was finished at all. Ironically the most successful British combat aircraft of the 1950s, the English Electric Canberra, was of relatively conventional design, yet it out-performed most first-generation jet fighters, especially in terms of speed and manoeuvrability at height.

Gloster prepared several schemes to Specification F.44/46 for a two-seat night fighter, initially along the lines of a developed Meteor, but their proposals were progressively redefined and several featured wings of delta planform. This owed much to research carried out in Germany by Dr. Alexander Lippisch who had begun experimenting with delta wings as early as 1930.

The basic delta shape was well suited to high-speed aircraft as it combined sharp wing-sweep with low thickness/chord ratio to satisfy the aerodynamicist. At the same time the structural engineer was happy as aspect ratio was kept low (thereby keeping bending moments to a minimum) and this, together with the wing's overall proportions, allowed the use of thinner, lighter material. The volume within the wings was sufficient to accommodate fuel, guns and associated ammunition bays and the main landing gear. Specification F.44/46 was superseded by F.4/48 in February 1948 by which time design evolution had moved on to the P.272 which had a delta wing and high-set tailplane, also of delta planform. This was a most unusual feature which allowed the trimming out of possible longitudinal stability problems. It also meant that wing flaps could be used to reduce the angle of attack on landing. By the spring of 1949 design work was complete and on 13 April Gloster was ordered to proceed with the construction of four prototypes, a figure that was reduced to two the following year, only to be raised to six in 1951!

The first G.A.5 (WD804) was flown on 26 November 1951 by Gloster's Chief Test Pilot, Squadron Leader Bill Waterton AFC. The flight was marred by severe rudder buffet caused by interference of the jet efflux and airflow over the rear fuselage and led to the first of several extensions to the fairings surrounding the jetpipes which gradually raised the buffet boundary to an acceptable level. Test flying continued with WD804 until 29 June 1952 when severe elevator flutter was experienced on a high-speed run between Oxford and Gloucester which led to both elevators breaking away. A degree of longitudinal control remained thanks to the tailplane trimmer, which allowed Waterton to carry out an emergency landing at Boscombe Down, but the aircraft was caught by a gust of wind on touchdown, causing it to crash on the airfield and catch fire. Waterton managed to escape and was subsequently awarded the George Medal for saving his valuable aircraft. The missing elevators were later found in a field near Witney.

With the demise of WD804, the development programme came to a halt until 21 August 1952 when WD808 flew for the first time from Moreton Valence. Despite the dramatic failure of the prototype's tailplane, the Ministry of Supply ordered the G.A.5 into quantity production with a super-priority classification, also officially naming it Javelin. A third prototype, WT827, flew on 7 March 1953 and was the first to be equipped with the proposed armament of four wing-mounted 30mm Aden cannon. It was also the first to carry AI radar in the nose radome.

During early testing it had become apparent that high-altitude manoeuvrability was inadequate and a modified wing planform was devised whereby sweepback of the outer panels was reduced from 39.5 degrees to 33.8 degrees. This produced a marked 'kink' at mid-span, the increased chord at the tip reducing the spanwise flow of air and improving the wing's stalling characteristics. The new wing was fitted to both WD808 and WT827, but within weeks the former was written off in a crash that killed Peter Lawrence, Gloster's deputy Chief Test Pilot. Lawrence had been carrying out various types of stall to test elevator response when the aircraft failed to recover from a stall with flaps down. The post-crash investigation revealed evidence of a new phenomenon, that of the 'deep stall' in which the wing, at high angles of attack, blankets the tailplane so that rudder and elevators are ineffective. As a result of the crash, restrictions were imposed on the use of flap, and eventually a stall warning system would be fitted that triggered a warning alarm in the cockpit.

Development continued throughout 1954 with two further prototypes, WT830 and WT836, joining the test programme, although another emergency landing had to be made at Boscombe Down when the controls failed on WT830 on 5 March. This was the first Javelin to feature full power controls, previous aircraft having hydraulic power assistance only. The pilot was Squadron Leader

J.A. Sowrey of A&AEE, the first time that a serving RAF Officer had flown the Javelin, but on this occasion a safe landing was made.

The first production Javelin FAW.1 (XA544) was taken into the air for the first time on 22 July 1954 by Wing Commander R.F. 'Dicky' Martin DFC AFC who had taken over as CTP from Bill Waterton. Over the next two years many early production aircraft were used to carry out development work including the testing of twin ventral 'bosom' tanks of 250 gallons that supplemented internal fuel capacity of 765 gallons, an all-flying tail, with the elevators acting as anti-balance tabs, and initial trials with four under-wing de Havilland Firestreak air-to-air missiles.

The programme suffered a further setback on 21 October when XA546, flown by Flight Lieutenant R.J. Ross of RAE, was lost over the Bristol Channel. The flight was intended to obtain trim figures for various combinations of engine rpm and airspeeds, but eleven minutes after take off Ross radioed to say that he was attempting to recover from a spin over the Severn. Several eye witnesses saw the aircraft diving steeply whilst rotating slowly about its longitudinal axis until it crashed into the sea. Despite an extensive search by the Navy, and later by the manufacturers, only small pieces of wreckage were found.

Following Ross's accident, a programme was initiated to ascertain the Javelin's spin characteristics which were found to be unusual, to say the least. The aircraft was eventually awarded a restricted CA release on 30 November 1955 that did not allow aerobatic manoeuvres in the vertical plane, and laid down a minimum speed of 125kt, flaps up or down. Concern over spinning was heightened on 8 December when Squadron Leader (later Air Vice-Marshal) David Dick found himself in a flat spin after exploring the buffet boundary in a 3g left-hand turn at 39,000ft. The spin was unlike any previously experienced as the speed of rotation was high and there was little variation in pitch. Attempts at recovery, including trailing the anti-spin parachute, all failed and Dick was left with no alternative but to eject which he did at 8,000ft over the Isle of Wight. The Javelin (XA561) crashed near Ashley and was burnt out.

The Javelin FAW.1 was tested at CFE over an eight-month period from January 1956 using XA565, XA566 and XA568. A total of 258 hours were flown, including thirty-four hours at night. On start-up, the Mk.12 cartridge proved to be extremely unreliable, the failure rate being in the order of 30%, but during successful starts scramble times from the ORP took around fifty seconds. If the aircraft was scrambled from a lower state of readiness however, the length of time taken for the crew to strap in, together with difficulty in manhandling the crew access ladder, raised this time to six minutes. For take off it was not necessary to use full power against the brakes as the take off run was well under 1,000 yards. With zero degrees tail trim, lift off occurred at 125kt IAS with very little stick movement, the actual moment of leaving the ground being hardly perceptible. There was virtually no trim change as the gear was raised, although a progressive forward trim was needed as the aircraft accelerated to climbing speed.

Climbs were carried out at 400kt/0.85M and 450kt/0.87M, with the following average results (fuel figures include taxi time from the ASP):

Altitude	Times – min/sec	Distance – nm	Fuel – lb/side	Rate of Climb
10,000ft	2.20	18	610	4300 fpm
20,000ft	3.54	30	700	6400 fpm
30,000ft	5.22	43	810	6800 fpm
40,000ft	7.52	62	960	4000 fpm
45,000ft	11.01	93	1160	1600 fpm
48,000ft	14.03	110	1200	1000 fpm

At low and medium IAS the controls were light and well balanced, but as speed increased above 450kt IAS a progressive stiffening was experienced until at the maximum permissible speed (535kt) the rudder was almost immovable and the elevators were extremely heavy. As the ailerons were fully powered, stick force did not increase with speed, instead movement was limited by restrictors at speeds above 410kt so that full stick travel did not produce full aileron movement. Below 250kt the elevator lost some sensitivity although it remained effective throughout. This factor, together with the impressively effective air brakes, made it necessary to pay very close attention to the ASI when in the circuit or on an instrument approach. This was not a very desirable feature in an all-weather fighter and some improvement in elevator feel was called for.

Manoeuvrability up to 40,000ft was adequate, but speed could not be maintained in turns at large angles of bank above this height. At 45,000ft, the maximum speed that could be achieved in a thirty-degree bank was 0.90 IMN. Even when a pilot was in a position to trade height for speed, turn radius was limited by the onset of buffet associated with 'g' stalling. During high-speed flight, trim changes were moderate up to 0.92 IMN, but at 0.925 a fairly strong nose-down trim change occurred which made it difficult to maintain height accurately or to track a target. Acceleration was good up to 35,000ft but became progressively worse as height was gained. At 48,000ft it was impossible to accelerate from 0.70 IMN in level flight. At high altitude the lightness of the ailerons and elevators made a high demand on the pilot's abilities with regard to instrument flying, a situation that was made even more difficult if speed was increased to 0.925 IMN with its associated trim change.

On the approach there was little alteration in trim when the flaps and undercarriage were lowered and on landing the aircraft tended to hold off just above the runway, usually needing a slight push force to put it on the ground. The average landing run was 1,600 yards although this could be reduced to less than 1,000 yards with full braking. Crosswind landings were successfully carried out in winds of up to 28kt at ninety degrees to the runway heading. In CFE's opinion the Javelin was capable of intercepting bomber targets flying at Mach 0.85 and 45,000ft, although its radius of action on internal fuel of only 131nm at 45,000ft (allowing a bad-weather procedure on return) was described as being 'quite inadequate'.

By now the Javelin was about to enter squadron service but it could only do so after the compilation of a long list of restrictions limiting various combinations of speed, height and g-loading to keep the average pilot out of trouble. Although spinning was prohibited, Pilot's Notes for the Javelin FAW.1 included comprehensive details of the aircraft's behaviour, as an inadvertent stall would almost inevitably result in a spin. If the following did not dissuade pilots from keeping well away from the stall/spin condition in a Javelin, then nothing would:

'The direction of spin is usually unpredictable, even from turn to turn. The rotation is very slow, and the nose pitches up and down fairly regularly, through as much as seventy degrees. The rates of yaw and roll will vary with the pitching. The stick forces are very light throughout, and there is no "kick back" on the stick. However, the rudder moves fiercely fully one way and the other, and the forces may be extremely heavy; it is recommended that the feet are merely kept lightly on it throughout the spin. The airspeed varies from "off the clock" to about ninety knots.

When the aircraft is clearly in a spin take the following action:

i) With the control column fully back apply full aileron in the same direction as the spin.
ii) With full aileron applied, move the control column fully forward into the corner.
iii) Keep the feet lightly on the rudder pedals.

It is unlikely that this action will have any effect for one or even two turns; certainly it seldom has any immediate result. The control column should be held fully in the corner; the direction of spin may reverse, and in this case the control column should be held right forward and moved sharply fully over into the new direction of spin. No force should be used to oppose any rudder movement.

Recovery generally follows one of two main patterns, type (i) being the more usual:

i) The rotation ceases, and the aircraft hangs in a nose-down attitude for a second or two. However the control column must still be held fully in its corner until the aircraft does a sharp nose-down pitch or "bunt". Minus $2\frac{1}{2}$g is about the usual figure for this and is quite unmistakable. Once the aircraft has done this, the spin has stopped. The speed rises rapidly, and only then should the controls be centralised, and the aircraft eased out of the dive. Attempts to centralise the controls and recover in the stage when the rotation has ceased, but before the aircraft has "bunted", will lead to a further spin with delayed recovery. The rudder should be left alone; when recovery is complete it will centralise itself.
ii) After taking recovery action, the aircraft enters a fast spiral in a steep diving attitude. The spiral may be in the same direction as the applied aileron, or against it, but this condition may usually be recognised because: a) the pitching ceases, b) the speed rises, c) the rate of rotation is steady and fast. Once the speed is over 200 knots, the controls may be centralised, and the aircraft eased out of the dive. The rudder will centralise itself when recovery is complete, and it should be left to its own devices.'

Javelin FAW.1s of No. 46 Squadron.

46 Squadron, under Wing Commander F.E.W. Birchfield DFC, became the first operational unit to receive the Javelin when XA570 was delivered by Flight Sergeants Bob Hillard and Gray Murrin of 187 Squadron on 24 February 1956. One of the first pilots to convert was Flight Lieutenant Howard Fitzer.

'As the first RAF fighter to be designed from the outset for all-weather operations, the prospect of greatly improved performance over the Meteor and the radical delta-wing design presented an eagerly awaited prospect for 46 Squadron. Despite the lack of a two-seat trainer, transition to the aircraft provided no major problems. The Javelin was roomy, comfortable and easy to fly, but I felt that it needed more power. The only vice appeared to be its characteristics at the stall. The experience of other pilots suggested that recovery from a stall (probably invoking a spin) would not be possible at lower altitude (below 15,000ft) or on instruments – a serious flaw in a night/all-weather interceptor. Handling was good except when power control "manual reversion" was experienced on the Mk.1. In that condition it was extremely heavy on the controls, particularly during turns exceeding thirty degrees. To sum up, the Javelin inspired affection rather than confidence, it was built like a tank and flew like one!'

At first, aircraft serviceability was extremely low and although three more Javelins arrived in March, flying for the month amounted to only twenty-six hours. The main items requiring attention were electrical systems and the Rotax starters. By the end of May, however, the situation had improved markedly and during the month fifteen aircraft flew a total of 226 hours, with night flying taking place four nights each week. The main emphasis in training was the navigation conversion programme with AI exercises taking priority.

Further problems were experienced during June, which saw the Javelins twice grounded for inspection by Dowty following irregularities with their hydraulic systems. In addition, numerous engine changes were carried out, modifications were made to electrical systems and reinforcing work had to be performed on engine air intakes. Apart from replacing the Sapphires, the work was undertaken by the appropriate firms. During the month two aircraft were involved in accidents. On the fifteenth Wing Commander Birchfield and Flying Officer R. Chambers became the RAF's first Javelin casualties when both were killed in XA570 during a night approach. They were returning to Odiham after carrying out practice interceptions with another Javelin and had requested a QGH/GCA. Instead of being picked up at the usual 12–15 miles at 3–4,000ft however, the aircraft appeared on radar screens at six miles and 2,000ft. This was too close for GCA to accept and the approach controller continued with QGH information, clearing the pilot to descend to 1,000ft. Birchfield acknowledged and advised that he was in visual contact with the airfield at one and three quarters miles range. Shortly after, all contact was lost.

The Javelin was found at dawn the next day, wreckage extending for about 400 yards downhill through tree-covered common land. From the trail of debris it appeared that it had struck the ground in a fairly flat attitude with the under-carriage up. The normal engine settings for a QGH/GCA were 6,750rpm at 250kt, but due to the Javelin's relatively high drag in the approach configuration it was possible to enter a state of pronounced sink almost approaching a state of 'mush', especially if its light elevators were mishandled. Even a slight nose-up control input applied inadvertently could result in rapid loss of speed. From the timings of R/T calls it appeared that the pilot had not slowed to the correct

XA627 of No. 46 Squadron flown by Flight Lieutenant Howard Fitzer.

approach speed and, despite being less than two miles from the threshold, was not in a position to land.

During the investigation into the crash Birchfield's regular navigator stated that he had been forced to prompt his pilot with regard to heights and speeds on several occasions giving further weight to speculation that the accident had been caused by faulty instrument flying or cockpit preoccupation. Indeed the choice of Birchfield as C.O. of the RAF's first Javelin squadron seems odd. His last operational posting had been on Spitfires in 1943 and he also had minimal night experience which on Javelins amounted to ten and a half hours, with just three and a half hours on instruments. The only other accident to occur in June involved Flying Officer Tony Warner in XA624 when the undercarriage retracted on landing, resulting in Cat 3 damage but no injury to the crew.

46 Squadron's new C.O. was Wing Commander H.E. White DFC AFC, a former night-fighter 'ace' with 141 Squadron, who presided over the Javelin's first major achievement when 1,000 hours were flown by eight aircraft in less then two months. Before these trials could be attempted however, fuel inlet pipes needed attention due to cracking, and a further mod had to be introduced when Flight Lieutenant J.W. Tritton and Flying Officer D. Roberts lost part of their canopy shortly after take off on 17 July. When the remains of the hood could not be found, an advertisement had to be placed in a local paper for its return!

The intensive flying programme commenced on 13 August and the figure of 1,000 hours was finally passed on 4 October, an achievement which owed a lot to the setting up of a night rectification team to prepare aircraft for the following days flying. Throughout the coming months 46 Squadron took part in various exercises commencing with *Beaverbrook* on 19 October when Javelin crews claimed six USAF B-36D bombers flying simulated attacks at heights up to 40,000ft. The following day they were up against a very different type of target, Hunter F.4s of 247 Squadron, which were engaged at 45,000ft at Mach 0.85. By December 46 Squadron had fourteen Javelins on strength but, due to lack of spares and problems following engine changes, average daily serviceability was only 4.5 aircraft over the month. Flight Lieutenant D.R. Young did not help matters on the sixth when he damaged the starboard wingtip and aileron of XA619 after demolishing the cab of a contractor's lorry which had been parked too close to a taxiway.

The first night exercises took place in January 1957, four Javelins departing for Church Fenton on the seventeenth to operate against Valiants flying at 40,000ft and above, with another five carrying out similar sorties from West Malling on the twenty-fourth. Results were highly encouraging with nine Valiant 'kills' being credited and a similar short detachment took place the following month from Duxford. Several problems were encountered early in the year including two incidents of air-brake failure at altitude due to control-run icing, affecting Flight Lieutenant Jock Fraser and Flying Officer Tony Warner in XA619 and XA623 respectively, and one case of engine failure (also XA623), a safe landing being made by Flying Officer E.J. Scott. Trouble was also being experienced with the undercarriage up-locks culminating in an accident to XA625 on 4 April when Squadron Leader H.G. James AFC DFM had to land with the port wheel retracted. Despite the Javelin's reputation for being unpredictable after departure, Flight Lieutenant P.A. Gifkins got away with an inadvertent spin when he lost control whilst carrying out a steep turn during practice cine attacks at 24,000ft. His aircraft (XA624) behaved itself on this occasion and the spin was recovered in text book fashion after losing 9,000ft.

During April, 46 Squadron began rehearsing for a starring role in a BBC TV production called 'This Is Your Air Force Now' which was to be broadcast live the following month. This involved low-level practice attacks being made on Valiants, an event which was to be filmed by a camera crew mounted in the cargo compartment of a Blackburn Beverley. Despite the differences in speed of the aircraft involved the flying sequences were eventually shot successfully and the programme was shown on 15 May. Before that, Wing Commander White and Flight Lieutenant R.H. Bateman, together with their respective navigators, took part in a trial on 9 April to ascertain the level to which the A.I.17 radar was affected by the dropping of Window. Flying line-astern and slightly to port and starboard of a Valiant at 40,000ft, it was found that the radar lock was only broken when the radar's strobe velocity switch was in the Off position, together with a high concentration of Window. When the switch was On and the delivery rate of Window was normal, navigators found that the equipment retained its lock with ease.

Around this time Flying Officer Colin Edwards joined 46 Squadron as a navigator and recalls his introduction to the Javelin:

'I joined 46 as part of a new young crew – in fact I think we were the first 'first tour' crew to go on to Javelins. My pilot at the time was very nervous of the aircraft as there had been several recent fatalities. He, and other timid pilots were particularly scared of stalling and so used to do long approaches more suited to Heathrow than Odiham. It was an amazing contrast to fly with the better pilots. I flew with Harry White soon after I joined the squadron and the difference was remarkable. His circuit seemed to be a continuous turn with the aircraft levelling its wings at the last moment. He flew much slower and like many of the experienced pilots would switch the stall warners off. These were new on the Mk. 2s and played a warning tune when the speed was low or when a high-speed stall was imminent. I had a lot of fun scaring my pilot to death by playing an identical tune on a mouth organ! Looking back I suppose this did little for his confidence.

It was actually possible to fly the Javelin from the back seat. If we undid a panel on the right-hand side of the cockpit we exposed the control rods. This could be used to give them a playful tug when the pilot was on approach – always valuable if he was wasting valuable drinking time by insisting on practising circuits. We could also do barrel rolls. These were made easier by jamming the crowbar in the controls thus having our own joystick.

I seem to recall Valiants as being particularly difficult to see and remember the luxury of being able to take my head out of the visor to look at the Vulcan we had just intercepted. Even though we were right underneath it I had to work out its shape from where the stars weren't. On exercise we flew very close to targets particularly during head-on interceptions (which were the norm) because we had to do a blind turn from eleven miles and often felt the bump as we went through the target's slipstream. How effective we would have been in anger is difficult to say. I can remember our boss saying that few of us would get in behind our target and even fewer would shoot it down. We could certainly have intercepted all the Russian bombers in service at the time – providing they played the game and came above 10,000ft and didn't evade too much. We believed that they would have to come fairly straight for the last 100 miles where we would be getting them.

We frequently practised operating without ground control – this would be either by "loiter" or "broadcast" systems. We also practised against jamming targets, usually B-66s. We had few problems with first generation V-Bombers but had to be very careful with the Vulcan and Victor 2s, both of which would be able to run away from us. It was essential that we rolled out very close behind if we were to use our guns. Canberras could embarrass us by flying too slow! They would weave at high altitude making it impossible for us to hang in the air within gun range. Low-level interceptions by night were very difficult as the ground returns obscured the target. It is interesting to note that our orders were to ram the enemy if we had used all our ammunition, and I also remember an intriguing order to surround the target!

One unusual experience with 46 was called "Lightstrike". As I understand it this was part of service politics when the RAF tried to prove that we could intercept fast moving MTB or E-Boat type vessels, thus forestalling moves to equip the Navy with more aircraft. The game was that the boats would be found by maritime aircraft (Shackletons or Dutch Neptunes) and we would then be called in. We usually picked up the boat at about six miles and the pilot started a dive at one mile with the target illuminated by flares dropped by the Neptune behind the boat. As soon as the pilot was visual I would transfer my attention to the altimeter shouting out the heights as they rapidly decreased. I think we were supposed to level out at about 400ft, although I do remember calling the heights right down to the deck during some daylight practices. I almost expected to have to continue to call the depths in fathoms!

We used to provide year-round standby in the cockpit, ready to go. This was usually at Waterbeach or Wattisham. Long hours, often freezing cold. One day our telebrief to the GCI station became crossed with the local butcher's telephone and we spent the day receiving orders for sausages etc. We were really the forgotten few. To keep warm I used to take my holdall full of clothing so that I could put my feet and legs in it to stay warm. We were only treated once. Fighter Command decided that we should have some entertainment and called on all squadrons to donate records so that we could have a kind of Forces Favourite requests whilst we waited. We were on the first night of this exciting new development. We were asked what we would like. My pilot asked for a Bach fugue. After about ten minutes they said that they didn't have that, what else would be like?

Flying Officer Colin Edwards later flew with No. 60 Squadron at Tengah.

He asked for anything by Ted Heath's band. Again ten minutes wait and an apology. Then I requested anything by Chris Barber. Again ten minutes and a sorry. My pilot, "Lefty" Wright, then suggested it would be more sensible if they told us what was on offer. After ten minutes they did. We could have either "At the Drop of a Hat" or "Carousel". Such was the luxury we lived in.'

Having performed for the cameras earlier in the year, 46 Squadron's Javelins had a live audience in early September when nine aircraft led a formation comprising twenty-seven Javelins and a similar number of Hunters at the SBAC Display at Farnborough. Flying from Tangmere, the flypasts took place on each day of the show, the only exception proving to be the final public display on 8 September when thirty-six Javelins flew in sections of twelve, an event that led to Glosters, the public, the commentator and those in authority, reacting with delight, enjoyment, confusion and displeasure in that order!

Such large-scale flypasts were not without their problems as the amount of sky that was 'contaminated' was enormous and despite the issue of NOTAMs, small club aircraft often got in the way. Take off could also be a hair-raising experience as the prolonged running of large numbers of aircraft could strip part of the top surface from tarmac runways, the debris in turn damaging airframes and being ingested into engines. In addition, the turbulence created by large numbers of aircraft taking off in quick succession was severe and similar participation for Farnborough in 1958 led to the fatal crash of a Hunter F.6 (XG133) of 19 Squadron shortly after take off from Duxford.

241

Before 46 Squadron's Farnborough involvement, XA618 suffered a mishap on 21 August when the port engine starter disintegrated, a situation that was not uncommon. On this occasion, however, the explosion punctured the No. 1 fuselage fuel tank and escaping fuel was ignited by hot gases and sprayed onto the ground beneath the port wing causing flames to spread along its length. The left-hand side of the aircraft was badly burned before the fire section managed to gain control. Flying Officer Colin Edwards later had a ringside seat for another spectacular blow-up which occurred in Germany, one that was watched with more concern than usual.

'I sat next to an aircraft at Sylt during an air-firing camp when the usual happened and flames immediately shot out from just behind the nav's cockpit. We waved all sorts of signals at the crew and they waved happily back, not realising they were on fire. Most of the aircraft on the line were armed and so there was some panic whilst the neighbouring aircraft were moved. In the end we watched the Javelin burn out with feelings of sorrow because it was loaded with several bottles of whisky ready for the trip back to the U.K. All was not lost however. When everything had cooled down we found a bottle of dimple Haig on the tarmac. It had fallen several feet without breaking.'

In August, 46 Squadron received the first of its Javelin FAW.2s which it was to fly until disbandment in June 1961. The FAW.2 incorporated the American A.I.22 radar instead of the British A.I.17 but initial experiences were not good, as recorded in the Squadron ORB:

'During the month [September] six more Javelin Mk.2s arrived bringing the total number on the squadron to twelve. This necessitated a lot of time being spent on acceptance checks on the new aircraft. A large amount of aircraft unserviceability was due to A.I.22. This radar equipment proved to be unserviceable after almost every sortie and caused a heavy load to be put on the radar section. The task of servicing A.I.22 was made more difficult by the shortage of spares and test equipment. The main radar section is still unable to set up a complete bench set for testing the AI owing to lack of spares, and no spares or test equipment for the track side of the AI are available. On the search side of the equipment a certain amount of spares are available but owing to the high unserviceability rate, the spares are not enough to cope with the demand. In a lot of cases components had to be removed from the aircraft and bench serviced before being replaced in the same aircraft. This sort of servicing causes an aircraft to be on the ground for an unnecessary length of time. On two new aircraft, XA776 and XA814, it took seven days to service the A.I.22 on acceptance and it was only when the equipment had been completely stripped down that it was found in both cases that the equipment had been wired up wrongly at MU'

Unfortunately the radar situation was not to get much better as Flying Officer Colin Edwards recalls:

'We had a lot of trouble with A.I.22 which, as I recall, was due to the failure of the lock-on system which never worked well. The maximum range of all these radars was very similar – somewhere around twenty miles at altitude but down to half that or less at low level. The A.I.21/22 systems had a PPI indication which was helpful if we ever wanted to map read (really only possible for coast lines), but this did not make much difference to our interception work where we were concerned with angle off and range. One potential difference in the systems concerned the 21/22's ability to restrict its "beam" to a very narrow width and height giving a much faster blip repetition rate. In theory this was very useful in following an evading target at close range. The most extreme example was "oriental sector scan" when the beam could be cut to five degrees. Thus the target was illuminated in a sharp torch-like beam. This was fine when you were straight and level but as soon as you banked it was necessary to move the scanner (this was supposed to be overcome by the lock-on of A.I.22).'

In keeping with the procurement policy of the time the Javelin was produced in a variety of marks, each with a short production run. By the end of 1957 the RAF was flying no less than five different versions of the Javelin, the FAW.1/4/5 with A.I.17 radar and the FAW.2/6 with A.I.22. The smaller scanner dish of A.I.22 resulted in a shortened nose-profile, the radome being hinged to allow servicing, unlike that of the A.I.17 variants which had to be removed before work could be carried out. Apart from the first few examples, the FAW.2 featured an all-flying tail developed to improve high-speed handling (a feature that was to be included on all subsequent marks) and the FAW.4 introduced the use of vortex generators to extend the buffet boundary, thereby increasing manoeuvrability at altitude. Despite its size, the Javelin's endurance was limited and an attempt to increase its range resulted in the FAW.5 which featured two additional fuel tanks, each of 125-gallon capacity in the wings. The FAW.6 was virtually the same as the FAW.5 except that it featured A.I.22 radar. Power for all Javelins up to the FAW.6 came courtesy of the Armstrong Siddeley Sapphire Sa.6 of 8000lb.s.t.

All the various marks of Javelin were tested at CFE commencing with the

FAW.2 XA808 of AWDS.

FAW.4 in October 1956. As it was over 1,000lb heavier than the FAW.1, its performance in some respects was inferior, a fact that was reflected in the climb when it took over two minutes longer to reach 48,000ft. The controls were well balanced although they were somewhat heavier and fatigue was noticeably greater during gunnery sorties and other training exercises involving high 'g'. Problems were also experienced with the tail trimmer which was slow in operation. Above 40,000ft this, together with the 'q' feel and artificial static stability built into the control system, combined to make the aircraft very difficult to trim accurately, requiring a high degree of concentration during high-altitude intercepts which became extremely tiring.

The FAW.4 also featured an audio stall-warner which greatly increased freedom of manoeuvre. Turns could be tightened well beyond the onset of buffet, so much so that pilots flying at high IAS were surprised at the amount of buffet that was encountered before the warning was heard. This allowed greater use of the aircraft's manoeuvre capability without the risk of an inadvertent stall or spin. There was also a definite improvement in the Javelin's characteristics above 0.92M due to the all-flying tail. However, the least satisfactory aspect of the Javelin remained, its rapid loss of speed in turns when the nose was well above the horizon. This was particularly noticeable above 40,000ft or when flying in the circuit at low power. In fact the FAW.4 had a slightly worse performance than the FAW.1 in this respect and during a 180-degree turn at 45,000ft using sixty degrees of bank, speed dropped from 0.90M to 0.815M.

During high-speed flight the nose-down trim change was less violent than in the FAW.1 and also occurred at a higher speed (0.95M compared with 0.925M). This was followed by a nose-up trim change at 0.98M necessitating a push on the stick to get the aircraft up to 1.04M, its limiting speed above 35,000ft. Maximum level speed at high altitude was lower than the FAW.1, reaching just 0.88–0.89M at 48,000ft. With ventral tanks fitted the limiting speed above 20,000ft was 0.95M, which was easily attainable in a dive. At speeds above 0.93M there was increased buffeting and the aircraft was also liable to yaw and roll sharply at about 0.94M. The limiting speed with ventrals was recognised by the onset of Dutch rolling.

The FAW.4 also had inferior acceleration, taking one minute twenty-two seconds to increase speed from 0.85M to 0.90M at 45,000ft, twenty-eight seconds longer than the FAW.1. To try to get round this a technique was evolved to utilise the aircraft's rapid increase of speed in the dive by descending up to 2,000ft below a target. The Javelin then continued to close at the lower height until the target was 1,000 yards away and 30–40 degrees above, a climb then being initiated to bring it to firing range at 500 yards.

The slightly reduced performance of the FAW.4 gave controllers severe problems in positioning the aircraft above 40,000ft, a factor that was exacerbated by the A.I.17 radar, the CFE report going so far as to say that interceptions of targets above 40,000ft were made in spite of, rather than because of the performance of A.I.17. The range of the equipment meant that a successful interception depended initially on the GCI controller being very precise in positioning the fighter and ordering it to turn. The implications in the face of ECM were obvious.

With its comparatively narrow azimuth, scan the errors that could be accepted in the initial positioning of the Javelin were reduced still further, while the roll stabilisation as tested was so ineffective that it could not be used in the trials except in the gentlest of turns. It was thus open to doubt as to whether the Javelin, equipped only with Aden guns and A.I.17, would be able to destroy high-performance bombers with rear armament.

The CFE assessment of the FAW.4 was that it was capable of intercepting a target flying at 0.85 TMN and 45,000ft when operated in the clean configuration. When ventral tanks were fitted however, the fastest target it could intercept was one flying at 0.77 TMN, although radius of action was more than doubled. This produced something of a dilemma in that the likely threat would dictate the way that the Javelin was operated. For intercepting high-speed targets above 40,000ft it was imperative to use the aircraft clean, whereas for intercepts at 35,000ft and below, the performance difference between the clean and tanked aircraft was extremely small and the increased range offered by the tanked aircraft was an advantage that became more important as target altitude decreased.

Over the next few months the other marks of Javelin passed through CFE beginning with the FAW.5, its increased internal fuel capacity making for even more permutations when it came to working out performance and range. Compared with the FAW.4, the extra 1,430lb of AVTAG made no significant difference to intercept capability, the climb to 45,000ft taking just over one minute longer and, until the extra fuel had been burnt off, acceleration and turn performance were slightly inferior. The main advantage was that radius of action was increased to 227nm (assuming a bad weather letdown on return) and sortie times raised to 65–75 minutes which, in certain situations, allowed more than one interception to be attempted per sortie. If climb performance was the prime factor it was possible to isolate the No.3 fuel tank in each wing during refuelling which reduced internal fuel by 1,800 lb. This reduced the time taken to climb to 45,000ft by one and a half minutes, and to 48,000ft by almost two and a half minutes, but had the effect of reducing radius of action to 115nm.

When ventral tanks were carried radius of action was increased to 383nm, but apart from this there was little real tactical advantage. During the trials a number of sorties were flown during Exercise *Vigilant* where it quickly became apparent that ventral tanks were an embarrassment if scrambled for specific targets at 30,000ft or above. Assuming a high-speed target at 45,000ft, the FAW.5 was likely to be ineffective until it had been airborne for 40–60 minutes, by which time weight had been reduced thereby allowing improved manoeuvrability and acceleration.

In terms of overall performance the FAW.2/6 proved to be inferior to the other marks of Javelin, taking respectively three and a half minutes and four minutes longer to reach 45,000ft than the FAW.1. Surprisingly, these times were even slower than the FAW.5 which had a higher take-off weight. There were no obvious reasons for this although the theory was put forward that the redesigned nose profile to accommodate A.I.22 radar may have increased drag. Maximum level speed was also 0.01 IMN lower, acceleration times were longer and radius of action at 45,000ft (bad-weather procedure) was reduced to 121nm. General handling characteristics were, however, similar to the Javelin FAW.1/4/5.

By early 1958 the Javelin was in service with six squadrons and, despite its size and complexity, the conversion process had been relatively straightforward. Squadron Leader Mike Miller AFC, of 23 Squadron, recalls some of its qualities:

'The Javelin was quite manoeuvrable and could hold its own with most contemporary aeroplanes, perhaps not quite a Hunter, but it wasn't far short. Like all aircraft, the higher you went the more readily you went into buffet and above 50,000ft in a Mk.9 you couldn't pull more than about 2g. The book said that once you were into the buffet, and certainly if you hit the stall warners, you had to recover. However, once you got used to the aeroplane it was perfectly reasonable to fly it in the buffet, but, of course, you were losing speed and you weren't getting anywhere. Even at height it was reasonably docile and there was quite a margin for you to play with.

The Javelin was only just a supersonic aeroplane, from the company's point of view it was always boosted as such but I think that the only comment to that must be the American who took one look at the Javelin's thick wing and said – "That thing is supersonic, gee it sure says a lot for thrust!" The best way to get a Javelin past the speed of sound was to roll it on its back and pull down into a vertical dive. You could do it with full throttle and push into a forty-five-degree dive, but it took longer. There were no adverse control aspects at all, you just watched the Mach meter – it tended to hang at around Mach 1.0 and then it would suddenly jump to 1.01 and you knew that you were through.

We regularly flew with one engine throttled back to conserve fuel but if we were in dire straits we thought nothing about shutting an engine down. The relight system was excellent and I never had any trouble in relighting. The Javelin certainly made life a lot easier when it came to carrying out practice interceptions. In the old days with A.I.10 the pilot flew entirely on instructions from the navigator until he got a visual which could be as close as 300ft on a really dark night. Part of the sophistication of the A.I.17 was a collimator which produced a little green dot on the gunsight which gave you the target once the navigator had locked on to it. It only had about a five-degree cone, but it would stay locked out to maybe 25–30 degrees. Until you got it back to within five degrees you weren't sure you were following it exactly, but at least you knew which way to go.'

Flight Lieutenant Don Headley of 64 Squadron recalls how the collimator was used in one particular night training exercise:

'Two or three of us used to do full tail-chases during which the navigators kept us at 1,000 yards. We had our lights out and the whole idea was to try and throw the chap behind you off your tail. We found that if the lead aeroplane pulled his nose up slightly and rolled on his back, the one behind didn't see this. If you then pulled through, the first reaction of the pilot behind was to push forward on the stick because the collimator dot was seen to be going down. However there was no way that he could follow such a manoeuvre. In the end we found a way round the problem. When an aeroplane rolled on its back the green dot did a little jiggle up and down and if this happened you turned on your back immediately so that you could then pull through and follow him down.'

Although the Javelin's sophisticated systems had taken some of the guesswork out of night interception, it was still possible to scare yourself as Don Headley discovered one dark night:

'We were extremely keen in those days and I decided to intercept someone who was on his way back home. I had a different navigator that night and thought that he was keeping us 1,000 yards behind, but instead he had decided to get a Gee fix without telling me. I was following a single tail light so it was impossible to appreciate the range. Suddenly this dirty great big shape loomed up ahead of me and I only just managed to haul back on the stick and go over the top of it. When I landed one of the other pilots, Colin Grindley, was signing the Form 700 and looked a bit shaken. He said, "Nearly had it tonight, an aeroplane nearly hit me and when I got back I had to do three circuits before I could land." I didn't say anything but then my navigator laughed in the background. Grindley said "It was you, you b . . . .. Headley!" After he had calmed down a bit he said "Oh well, it's not so bad now, as long as I know that it was intentional!"'

At Leeming, home of 228 OCU, it was standard practice for instructors to carry out 'staff trailers' where they flew 100–200 yards behind a student crew so that the staff navigator could get, as nearly as possible, the same radar picture as that in the student's aircraft. By such means an accurate assessment could be made of the student nav/rad's control of a practice interception. Despite such close proximity, no serious problems were experienced.

Whatever else might be said about the Javelin, one thing that it could always do was slow down quickly. The limiting speed for maximum deployment of the airbrakes was 430kt which produced a gut-wrenching 1g deceleration and a descent rate in excess of 15,000ft/min. This capability was found to be extremely useful in allowing the aircraft to stay at high level, where its engines worked more efficiently, for as long as possible. Flying Officer Hank Prosser of 89 Squadron remembers the technique and an occasion when the Javelin's powerful airbrakes caused a certain amount of embarrassment:

'The airbrakes on the Javelin were not a lot of use in the main operational task but were spectacularly successful at facilitating a rapid descent. One could be about twelve miles from base at 40,000ft and join the circuit at 1,000ft on a straight-in approach from a rather interesting descent angle. On one occasion however, we were providing an escort with eight Javelins to greet the arrival in the U.K. of the German President. We had to rendezvous with his Air Force plane at 18,000ft somewhere over the coast in two lines of four aircraft in close line-astern, either side of the dignitary.

Visibility was very poor and when the target finally came into visual contact we were obviously going very much faster than the President. Our gallant leader just put out his airbrakes without warning and those of us in line astern had to take very necessary immediate and dramatic avoiding action. Some welcome from the RAF!'

The Javelin's ability to decelerate rapidly could come as a shock to those who were not aware of its capabilities as Flight Lieutenant Noel Davies recalls:

'During my time at the All-Weather Development Squadron at West Raynham I gave a demo to a civilian (probably an MoD man). Coming back into the circuit under full power at about 400 knots I opened the brakes. It was like hitting a brick wall, the brakes were around 2 x 8 feet on top and below each wing, and they came out almost at right angles. Needless to say there was a grunt in the back as my guest lurched forward and hit his (helmeted) head on the coaming. I apologised and put them in again, at which point the full power took hold and he banged his head on the headrest. A most graphic demonstration, however uncomfortable!'

With three years experience on night fighters, Flying Officer Guy Woods first came across the Javelin with 151 Squadron when the unit swapped its Venom NF.3s for FAW.5s in May 1957.

'The squadron was on a long detachment to Turnhouse while they extended the runway at Leuchars, so we converted to the new type there. This was done by the Javelin Mobile Training Unit, an outfit which went round the squadrons with mobile classrooms and a couple of Valetta aircraft fitted out with the new A.I.17 radar for the navigators to get to grips with. The Javelin was a quantum leap as far as the all-weather force was concerned. It was big, powerful, had a good radar, four 30mm cannons and the ability to operate at high subsonic speeds well above 40,000ft. It could turn quite well at these higher levels and you could complete an interception at 50,000ft with a little care. And, of course, it had ejection seats which, coming from Venoms, I really appreciated!
    The radar still had a two-scope display but the Range/Azimuth picture was in a B Scope format which was different from the PPI of the A.I.21. This took a bit of getting used to, but of the two formats, I preferred the B Scope. It gives a very distorted view of the outside world but overall is a much better display for interception work. A rough and ready azimuth/elevation display was piped through to the pilot's gunsight so he could follow evading targets. This took a load off the navigator but we still practised the art of following evading targets from the back seat. The radar was supposed to be roll stabilised but the system was totally useless and was never used. However, we could lock the radar on to the target which took most of the heat out of evading Visual Ident runs. Whereas with the Venom we had our work cut out to get up to something like the Canberra's

Air-to-air view of two No. 23 Squadron Javelin FAW.7s.

operating height and had only a marginal overtake capability, with the Javelin we could now catch these quite easily.'

The next Javelin in the development sequence was the FAW.7 which was flown for the first time on 9 November 1956. Significant advances included the installation of two Sapphire Sa.7 engines each of 11,000lb.s.t. and a revised flying-control system offering pitch auto-stabilisation, fully-powered hydraulically operated rudder, yaw stabiliser and electro-hydraulic three-axis autopilot. It was also the first Javelin to carry the Firestreak air-to-air missile on under-wing pylons which were carefully waisted to avoid excessive drag rise due to the high local Mach numbers that were generated. In addition to the provision of vortex generators, the buffet boundary was further extended by thickening of the aileron trailing edges.

The Javelin FAW.7 was tested at CFE between March and June 1958 and involved three aircraft, XH747, XH749 and XH752, XH 748 having suffered Cat 3 damage on 2 April when it lost a wheel on take off. Carrying on the tradition of the early Javelins, problems were soon encountered on start-up. The BTH turbo-starter motor as fitted to the Sapphire 7 used isopropyl nitrate (IPN) ignited by a small cartridge. Each starter had a triple breach and an IPN tank holding two gallons which was sufficient for three starts. The starter motors and cartridges gave persistent trouble throughout the trial, which was sufficiently serious as to affect the operational capability of the aircraft. Of the other new features on the FAW.7, conditions during the trial did not allow the yaw damper to be tested to any great extent – although it appeared to be effective in damping out large yaw disturbances, it had little or no effect on the small amplitude, high frequency oscillations experienced during high-speed flight.

In still air the FAW.7 took off in 700 yards (900 yards when fitted with ventrals), a firm backward movement of the control column being needed to obtain the correct climb attitude, which was about nineteen degrees nose up. Acceleration was much more rapid than the early marks of Javelin and climb speed (450kt IAS) was reached seventy seconds after brake release. The constant IAS climb became a constant Mach climb at 0.85 (reached at about 12,000ft) at which point considerable attention was required to maintain trim, a fact that became especially important when passing through the tropopause. When taking off in turbulent conditions crews had to be prepared for severe buffeting as speed increased, and difficulty was also experienced after leaving the runway as the artificial horizon gave false pitch information due to acceleration errors. It was also of little use in the climb as the nose position was too high to be interpolated with sufficient accuracy and the best technique was to refer to speed, heading and rate of climb. Times to height for the FAW.7 are shown in the following table (times in min/sec):

| Height | Clean | | | Ventrals | | |
	Time	Distance	Fuel used	Time	Distance	Fuel used
2,000ft	1.10	4.5nm	500lb	1.15	5nm	500lb
10,000ft	1.50	10nm	630lb	2.05	12nm	710lb
20,000ft	2.45	19nm	910lb	3.15	25nm	1080lb
30,000ft	3.50	27nm	1160lb	4.30	36nm	1360lb
40,000ft	6.05	46nm	1510lb	7.10	59nm	1780lb
45,000ft	8.10	63nm	1720lb	10.05	83nm	2120lb
48,000ft	9.55	78nm	1810lb	13.05	108nm	2460lb
50,000ft	12.10	96nm	1980lb	—	—	—

In terms of general manoeuvrability the aircraft was classed as adequate for its role when flown to 45,000ft (clean) and 40,000ft (ventrals). Compared with earlier marks, buffet in turns was slightly more pronounced although there appeared to be a wider margin between buffet onset and the start of the audio stall warning. Maximum rate turns were best made inside the buffet boundary but outside the limit set by the warning which, when it sounded, was usually accompanied by a lightening of stick forces and rapid loss of speed. At high altitude, accurate control of height during anything other than gentle turns was difficult and close concentration was necessary to anticipate trim changes.

During simulated high quarter attacks a pitch oscillation of 1½–2 degrees at about two cycles per second set in between 0.91–0.94M, sufficient to prevent steady tracking and gun aiming. The lowest height that this characteristic could be induced was 37,000ft and it ceased when speed was reduced below 0.91M. On later Javelins a pitch damper was incorporated in the control system to try to eradicate this problem. As a result of excessive tailplane control forces at speeds above 0.95 IMN, 'bouncing' or other forms of attack at and above this speed were not recommended.

The FAW.7 had superior acceleration to previous marks, taking just thirty-seven seconds to increase speed from 0.85–0.90 IMN at 45,000ft (sixty-seven seconds faster than the FAW.6). This was not maintained to higher altitudes however, and at 48,000ft acceleration had once again deteriorated, placing the onus on the pilot not to lose more speed than necessary during turns. There was a small but useful increase in level speed, although this meant that the aircraft was flying more often at speeds where it was affected by the nose-down trim change due to compressibility. Various methods were tried in the descent, the most satisfactory for fuel economy and comfortable instrument flying being 0.85 IMN/350kt with throttles closed and full airbrakes. Descending from 40,000ft to 2,000ft in this configuration took two and three quarter minutes, covered 22nm and used 200lb of fuel. Experiments were also carried out to ascertain gliding range. In glides from 50,000ft to 2,000ft at 215kt IAS with both engines idling, the aircraft flew 250nm in forty-five minutes and used 1750lb of fuel (7lb/nm). This could be improved still further by stopping one engine and idling the other. In this condition 147nm were covered in twenty-seven minutes on 650lb of fuel (4½lb/nm).

Radius of action of the clean FAW.7 was 114nm at 40,000ft (bad-weather reserves) and 140nm at 48,000ft. Up to 45,000ft the performance penalty when carrying ventral tanks was small and the additional fuel gave a second attack capability and much more tactical flexibility where GCI had been degraded. Above this height the use of ventrals reduced performance so that the aircraft could only operate effectively after it had been airborne for at least forty-five minutes. At lower altitudes however, ventrals were essential, as there was no performance penalty and increased fuel demand dictated their use.

In conclusion it was considered that the Javelin FAW.7, when scrambled from the ORP on U.K.-based early warning, could intercept and close to gun range on the following targets at a distance of 70nm from the U.K. coast:

	Target height	*Target speed – TMN*
Javelin FAW.7 – int fuel	50,000ft	0.83
	48,000ft	0.85
	45,000ft	0.87
Javelin FAW.7 – ventrals	48,000ft	0.82
	45,000ft	0.84

The improved performance of the FAW.7 eased the task of the nav/rad and the GCI controller, as well as increasing the chances of success and decreasing target penetration distance. A limiting factor was the search range of A.I.17 which, on targets above 40,000ft, was around 14nm. Of this the navigator would use up 4nm in assessing the contact and, deciding on the type of interception required, so crews invariably had to resort to short range procedures, making blind turns to get behind the target at 1nm range.

The Javelin FAW.7 entered service with 33 Squadron at Middleton St George in July 1958 and was followed shortly after by 25 Squadron as recounted by Flying Officer Guy Woods:

'My pilot (F/L K.J. Bassett) and I completed our tour with 151 Squadron at the end of 1958 and were posted as a crew to 25 Squadron at Waterbeach to form part of a nucleus of experienced Javelin crews prior to the squadron converting to the FAW.7. When we arrived, 25 were still flying Meteor NF.12/14s so we had a couple of months on the old Meteor before getting into the new mark of Javelin. This one was heavily armed with four Firestreak missiles in addition to two 30mm cannon, and with the uprated Sapphire engines, was quite a performer, with a climb rate which compared favourably with the Hunter. The extra armament in particular gave us a much increased ability to take out higher performance targets.

The Mark 7 was thought by many to be the best of the Javelins in terms of overall performance and combat capabilities. The radar was much the same as the old A.I.21 in terms of pick-up range (i.e.15–25 miles or so) but our tactics were changing to meet the expected threat. We concentrated on interceptions of aircraft which were always assumed to be on a recip-rocal heading to ours, simulating the Javelin force going out to meet a mass raid. The radar performance left us with little chance of adjusting the inter-ception geometry at long range, so we always did a 210-degree turn when the target reached a range of 12–13 miles. This catered for the target which was dead head-on and would put us behind it at a good range with thirty degrees of convergence to complete the interception. Any displacement from the target's track was a bonus allowing us to maintain radar contact all the way round the final turn, whereas with little or no displacement, contact was lost for some of the time. Similarly, if the track-crossing angle was less than 180 degrees this was also in our favour.

The threat to the U.K. was still deemed to be at high level, but as time went on the targets became more interesting. All three V-Bombers were on line by now and they could cruise at a much higher level, and faster, than the Canberra, putting us back to square one again. However, Firestreak at least gave us a significant advantage over this type of target. Air-to-air gunnery practice continued and we also now had the chance to fire missiles at Jindivik pilotless drones. I didn't get to fire one of these in my remaining time with the squadron – I had to wait many years before having a crack at one with a Sidewinder from a Phantom!'

In the opinion of Squadron Leader Mike Miller, the Firestreak missile was the making of the Javelin:

'The Firestreak missile turned the Javelin into a really effective weapons system, rather than being just a pleasant aircraft to fly, and with it you could cope with any opposition of the time. It required quite a demand of services from the parent aircraft, particularly specially monitored electrics and ammonia to cool the infra-red eye. It had good performance and would give you an increment of Mach 1.7 over your own speed and would take out, theoretically, 10,000ft of height. Even if you were up against a light Vulcan at 55,000ft or more, you could still hack it with the Firestreak-armed Javelin.

The trick was to get acquisition and once this had been achieved you could be confident that the missile would take care of things. The range bracket was roughly three miles down to one mile and you had to come in on a curve of pursuit and get within a thirty-degree cone. There was an acquisition light up by the gunsight but you had to be careful as the ammonia bottle only lasted fifteen minutes and the missile itself took three minutes to arm. It didn't really matter if the aircraft was pointing upwards and losing speed, as long as you had launch speed, which was about Mach 0.70, you could fire the missile. As soon as you had launched you could turn away which saved you having to get close to Russian Bears with their 20mm radar-laid guns.'

The final production version of the Javelin was the FAW.8 which was powered by two Sapphire Sa.7R engines equipped with limited afterburning of 12,300lb.s.t. above 20,000ft. Already blessed with an excellent rate of climb, the FAW.8 could reach 40,000ft in four minutes, a significant improvement and could make 50,000ft in nine minutes. Other features were a Sperry autopilot, Gloster-produced pitch auto-stabiliser, and drooped wing leading edges. The FAW.9 was a modified 7 featuring the Sa.7R and aerodynamic improvements of the Mark 8. The use of reheat on the Javelin was a bit of a mixed blessing as Mike Miller explains:

'The reheat was a very simple system which was done towards the end of the Javelin's life. It was designed to compensate for the extra weight of the missile system in an attempt to give the aircraft back the performance of the Mark 7. Our guidance was that the reheat should not be used below 20,000ft. Below that height and especially at low level, you actually lost

Javelin FAW.7 XH779 of No. 23 Squadron.

power with reheat because the system was such that fuel diverted to the reheat actually robbed the main engine of fuel and you lost main engine rpm by about 2–3%. At height where there was excess fuel-pump capacity and with more fuel available, the reheat worked in the proper sense. It certainly improved your turn performance at altitude – if you had a Vulcan turning on you at 50,000ft or above, you needed the reheat to stay with it. But altogether it was rather a poor compensation for having hung missiles on the Javelin and in some ways it was a bit of a joke. In fact we used to refer to it as "Wee-heat"!'

The Javelin FAW.9 entered service with 25 Squadron at Waterbeach in late 1959. Guy Woods, by now a Flight Lieutenant, recalls its introduction and changes in tactics:

'Halfway through the tour we swapped our FAW.7s for FAW.9s which were re-worked 7s with afterburning engines. The afterburners were pretty ineffective below 20,000ft, in fact they reduced thrust at sea level, but they enhanced climb rate, ceiling and turn performance above that height. With the new mark we were able to complete interceptions at around 50,000ft and, indeed, a little above, although the aircraft's oxygen system supposedly limited us to 50,000ft. The squadron bosses didn't like us using reheat too much because it substantially reduced flying hours on an aircraft that didn't have much endurance in the first place.

We had a few incidents – in one, starter motor fuel (Avpin) had collected in the large equipment bay of one aircraft and caused a big explosion on start-up. This ripped the under-fuselage open from nose to tail and caused the hurried evacuation of the crew. Fortunately the ladder was still in place so at least they didn't have a ten-foot drop to the ground to contend with! In those days we had very few "career" officers on a squadron and those that we had were usually ex-Cranwell cadets. One of these had an unfortunate experience when starting up a Javelin for flight. He hadn't noticed that the undercarriage "up" button had been selected and when the hydraulics came on line, the gear started to retract. He managed to shut down before the main wheels started to move but this left an amusing sight of one Javelin in a line of about ten with its tail sitting high in the air. Needless to say, the pilot's career suffered a setback.

I did have one rather frightening experience at night. We were flying at about 45,000ft when the Javelin started pitching and yawing quite violently – all symptoms of a stalled situation. We started dropping like a stone and I kept a beady eye on the altimeter and airspeed indicator reassuring my pilot that we were actually still flying. While all this was going on the GCI station decided to pass a whole load of information to us, to which my pilot replied, "Shut up, I'm fighting to control my aircraft!" We lost a good 10,000ft before he realised that it was the yaw damper which was causing the rudder to travel violently from one end stop to the other. Normal flight resumed after the offending equipment was switched off. Other than that, I experienced the occasional engine or hydraulic failure, and sundry other malfunctions, but nothing that could be considered life threatening.

A year before I left the squadron I completed the All-Weather Fighter Combat Leader's course at West Raynham with my flight commander. A notable character on the day-fighter side of the course was one Flt Lt Paddy Hine who eventually retired as an Air Chief Marshal. We explored a whole new area of radar fighter tactics on this course. There was a lot of emphasis on air-to-air gunnery and all aspects of the Javelin's weapons system were studied. Interceptions at various levels were practised including those at very low level over the sea against targets flying at all speeds, something we didn't normally do on a squadron. We carried out these interceptions against low-level targets flying at moderate speeds on one engine to conserve fuel. Against higher speed targets we used both engines, but we were limited to a maximum speed of 535kt at low level because of tailplane flutter problems, although the Javelin could have gone a lot faster.

We were also taught and practised interceptions against jamming targets with both noise ECM and window/chaff. Specialist jamming Valiant bombers provided this service and we didn't normally get the chance to experience this during routine squadron training operations. The only time we would get to see both forms of jamming would be during major exercises. Interceptions could be successfully completed against noise jammers without too much trouble and you were only fooled by window the first time you saw it! Overall – the Javelin was well liked in service, it performed well, had a good radar and was very comfortable for both crew members. I certainly enjoyed my time on them.'

Although Javelins could easily cope with the Canberra, the RAF's V-Bombers were another matter as Mike Miller recalls:

'The most difficult target of all was the Vulcan, the Victor wasn't quite so bad, and the Valiant was that much easier again. The Vulcan, with its pure delta wing, flew very high and although it couldn't out-turn a four-gun Mark 7, if it was light (no bomb load and light on fuel) it could out-turn a Mark 9. You had to be very careful with them or you could end up in an extremely embarrassing situation. The C.O. of 617 Squadron used to take great delight in doing this out in Singapore when they came out on exercise. We would do practice interceptions and he would often finish up on the tail of a Javelin. In reality I don't think this would have happened with a fully operational aeroplane with full bomb load and fuel on board, but the Javelin and Vulcan were like types, both deltas and they must have cruised at about the same speed, in fact I wouldn't mind betting that a Vulcan has been supersonic in its time going downhill!'

Even though the ban on aerobatic manoeuvres in the vertical plane remained throughout the life of the Javelin, it was certainly possible to get into trouble at other times. During his time on Javelins Flying Officer Hank Prosser witnessed two fatal accidents.

'Most navigators would have had their crew loyalty strained to the utmost had their pilots looped a Javelin and may well have "shopped" them. I

Wg Cdr Mike 'Dusty' Miller
O.C. No. 60 Squadron
Tengah.

would have probably tried it had I been a year or so younger and been solo but I had learned a bit of sense by the time I got to the Javelin era. Despite this I did actually see one stall. This occurred on 19 September 1958 and involved Flight Lieutenant Derek Kenney (of 89 Sqn) at Stradishall. He overflew the runway in preparation for a practice display routine, pulled hard around to the right in a level turn at about 1,000ft but seemed to come to an immediate grinding halt. The Javelin (XA779) then spun into the ground just to the west of the airfield, killing the pilot and Randy Lewis, the navigator.

Later, when I served at 228 OCU, Leeming, one of the exercises that we had to do with the trainee operational pilots was to get them to demonstrate the stall-warning alert at high altitude. The "nettle grasping" approach was recommended. From a sensible speed of Mach 0.85, you went into a steep bank and pulled hard. This produced an immediate audio warning whereupon you released the pressure and normal flight resumed with 0.80 still on the clock. If one went into it timorously, the speed bled off very quickly so that one came perilously close to the real thing before the warning sounded, and with little speed margin in hand to recover.

My final posting was to 41 Squadron. Although based at Wattisham, the squadron was detached to Geilenkirchen while the runway was resurfaced. On 29 August 1961 I did one of my first trips there and was being led back in close formation for a run in and break by Laurie Hatch, and his navigator John Northall, in XH971. We joined the circuit at about 1,000ft doing perhaps 450kt when he pulled the break. It looked a dramatic manoeuvre and immediately the wings broke off and the aircraft disintegrated before my disbelieving eyes. I flew straight ahead for about ten miles in shock. He had pulled 11g – the Pilot's Notes limit was 5.5g. Mercifully the bulk of the fuselage, although landing near the marriage patch, caused no further casualties. The airfield was strewn with shredded aluminium, a completely unnecessary loss of two lives and an aircraft.'

The Javelin may have been designed as a relatively short-range bomber-destroyer but by the early 1960s its deterrent effect was needed far from the European theatre for which it had been conceived. Britain still had influence in the Mediterranean, Africa and in the Far East, but suitable staging posts were becoming increasingly difficult to find, and the use of those that remained often resulted in a trail of unserviceable aircraft along the route. In-flight refuelling had been pioneered in the 1950s by the Meteors of 245 Squadron and the technique proved to be the ideal way of rapidly reinforcing troublespots, wherever they might be. The first Javelin unit to take on an air-to-air refuelling capability was 23 Squadron at Coltishall. Mike Miller recalls some of the problems:

'In-flight refuelling involved some quite tricky manoeuvring. You only had about four knots to play with as the drogue from the trailing hose of the tanker had automatic jaws in it which gripped the nozzle and you had to hit it at more then three knots but less than seven knots overtake speed. Anything less than three knots and the jaws would not open to allow contact, but a hit at more than seven knots was liable to cause the hose to "whip" which could break the nozzle of the probe. You approached in a slight climb in-line with the trail of the hose, and in turbulence it could bounce about and you might have to get the tanker to change height. This was especially difficult at night as the tanker might not be able to see the best way to go. Even in clear conditions the drogue itself created turbulence and when you got close you had to work the throttle gently to maintain the correct closing speed.'

The problems of achieving a successful contact in turbulent conditions are recalled by Flight Lieutenant Howard Fitzer, also of 23 Squadron:

'Apart from the difficulty of achieving initial hook-up, any subsequent undue movement of the fighter in any plane relative to the drogue, particularly if the drogue itself was unstable, tended to induce a "snake"-like movement in the hose. What initially appeared to be a tenable oscillation could by a process of compounded fighter-pilot corrections and drogue instability, become a violent "nozzle-snapping waggle". If side loading thus induced exceeded 1,000lb then the probe nozzle was designed to snap off in order to avoid structural damage to the aircraft. Unfortunately a "snapped-off" nozzle would remain firmly locked in the drogue, thus preventing further use.

The problem of turbulence was highlighted during a trial in which I was required to attempt flight refuelling at low level (about 2,000ft) in the Welsh hills in mid-summer. In the presence of strong turbulence I finally succeeded (after eleven attempts) in hooking up to the tanker, only for a "snake" to develop in the drogue sufficiently severe as to induce nozzle failure and a lateral collision between the drogue and the nose of the aircraft, the latter being slightly damaged. The trial was abandoned and as far as I know was never again attempted. This general problem in the presence of turbulence was also aggravated by the extreme length of the Javelin probe (20ft) which in itself amplified (at the tip) any angular displacement of the aircraft.'

The second Javelin unit to become proficient in air-to-air refuelling was 64 Squadron. One of the unit's senior pilots was Flight Lieutenant Don Headley:

'As you came in to pick up the drogue for the first time it was a very unusual experience. All your life you had been trying not to hit anything in the air and then you had to intentionally try to fly into something – it was very odd. One of the problems was that the Javelin was quite temperamental in pitch control, the all-flying tailplane made it very sensitive and this was exaggerated by the great big refuelling pole sticking out in front of you. It took a lot of concentration to make yourself relax and fly it in.'

The first long-range deployment using air-to-air refuelling took place in October 1960 and involved six Javelin FAW.9s of 23 Squadron flying to Singapore, backed up by Valiant tankers of 214 Squadron. In June 1961 Exercise *Pounce* saw eight aircraft, four each from 23 and 64 Squadrons, fly to Karachi for ten days, again using in-flight refuelling, although on this occasion fuel was not the only precious liquid carried as Don Headley recalls:

'We refuelled over France and Malta, night-stopped in Cyprus, then re-fuelled over Turkey before flying across Iran to Bahrein. The next day we flew to Karachi, refuelling twice on the way. Before we went someone happened to mention that he had discovered how much a beer cost in Karachi and that we would never exist on our allowances. The day after, someone came up with a solution to the problem. It turned out that a can of Long Life was exactly the same length as a 30mm shell which meant that we could carry beer in the ammunition tanks. Another chap said that they would probably blow up at high level so we sent someone up the next day to 45,000ft with a can of "Long Life" in each wing. When he landed we had two of the most delicious cold beers we had ever tasted. We flew out with four cases, two for the pilots and two for the navigators, and also filled tea chests with cases of beer which were then nailed down and marked "Javelin spares". When we night-stopped in Cyprus we persuaded the doc to give us empty medicine bottles with a label on saying "to be taken as required with fruit juice" which we filled with Cypriot brandy. All in all our ten days passed just right!'

Shortly after returning to the U.K., Iraq began to make threatening moves towards Kuwait and the Javelins were rapidly prepared to fly back out to the Middle East. Don Headley was one of those tasked to go.

'We were told we had twelve hours to get home, pack our bags, and take four Javelins up to Coltishall to pick up four Firestreak missiles each. We stopped the night then flew out to Cyprus staging through Orange, Pisa, Malta and El Adem. The plan was then to in-flight refuel over Turkey and down past Iran to Bahrein. In the event, Turkey decided to stay neutral and we were stuck in Cyprus. I can remember one day doing my inspection, pulling the "noddy cap" off the missile and all the glass from the nose of the Firestreak was inside. The glue had melted in the sun. Some of the others were the same. That immediately grounded the missiles and they had to be taken off the aeroplanes. Ultimately, Iraq did not invade, which was, perhaps, just as well.'

Throughout the life of the Javelin one of the most serious problems encountered was a critical situation affecting the Sapphire engine known as 'centre-line closure'. Mike Miller experienced this phenomenon whilst serving as C.O. of 60 Squadron at Tengah in Singapore.

'Centre-line closure was the Javelin's Achilles heel in a way. A lot of aircraft were lost in the early days and the problem wasn't discovered. All that was known was that the aircraft blew up over the North Sea. It turned out that when aircraft were flying in cu-nims, large quantities of super-cooled water droplets were being ingested into the engine which caused the casing to shrink and touch the compressor blades. These then broke up and passed down through the engine, wrecking not only the compressor, but the turbine and very often bits flew off, quite spectacularly. In this respect the Javelin was at a disadvantage because it had two engines close together with hydraulic pumps and gearboxes in-between. In such a situation you could easily lose the aeroplane, if not the crew.

The eventual modification was a typical bodge – it was almost literally sticking very tough carborundum paper around the casing of the compressor so that when the blades touched, they rubbed themselves down, the engine kept going and at the end of the day you had a slightly less powerful engine. I did experience this in the Far East one evening flying from Butterworth to Tengah. Visibility was clear but we had to cross the Inter-Tropical Front which went right up to about 60,000ft. I couldn't get over the top of it so we went through at about 53,000ft and whilst we were going through both engines suddenly hiccupped and then sort of coughed (if a jet engine can cough), picked up and carried on. When we landed and looked at the jetpipes there was white metal in both. An

Javelin FAW.9s of
No. 60 Squadron.

investigation showed that both engines had suffered centre-line closure, but the mod worked and the aircraft went on flying.'

The Javelin finally bowed out of RAF service when 60 Squadron was disbanded at Tengah on 30 April 1968. It did so in spectacular fashion with a flypast that was devised by Mike Miller.

'Because of the infinitely variable control of the airbrakes on the Javelin it was perfectly possible to fly formation in reheat. The reheat itself was either in or out, you had no control over the power, but you could control the speed of the aircraft with the airbrakes. The trick was for the leader to select half airbrake then the box formation would formate using airbrakes rather than throttle. The disbandment parade was held at sunset and we did a flypast in diamond nine formation. After the inspection, we came back with a box four in complete darkness with nice long flames coming out of the back, something that I don't think had been done before. We only prac- tised it once because it was the end of the time for the aeroplane. We found that when the aircraft broke to go round the circuit downwind the pilots of the formating Javelins had destroyed their night vision and they couldn't see each other. To get round this we mounted Canberra downward ident lights between the engines on the back panel of the Javelin fuselage, and when we looked at them after the flypast, the lights of all four aircraft were on the point of meltdown!'

The disbandment of 60 Squadron was not quite the end as far as the Javelin was concerned. XH897, which had seen service with 25, 33 and 5 Squadrons, initially as an FAW.7 and later as an FAW.9, was delivered to A&AEE at Boscombe Down in 1968 where it was painted in a striking red-and-white colour scheme. Over a period of seven years it was used for investigations into position- error correction, photo-chase duties and for calibration work in connection with the test programmes for Concorde and the Multi-Role Combat Aircraft (MRCA). On completion of these tasks XH897 was flown to the Imperial War Museum collection at Duxford on 21 January 1975 where it is still preserved.

INDEX

261